GERALD FINZI

His Life and Music

Diana McVeagh

THE BOYDELL PRESS

First published 2005
The Boydell Press, Woodbridge
Reprinted 2006, 2007
Reprinted in paperback 2010

ISBN 978–1–84383–170–9 hardback
ISBN 978–1–84383–602–5 paperback

The Boydell Press is an imprint of Boydell & Brewer Ltd
PO Box 9, Woodbridge, Suffolk IP12 3DF, UK
and of Boydell & Brewer Inc.
668 Mt Hope Avenue, Rochester, NY 14620, USA
website: www.boydellandbrewer.com

A CIP catalogue record for this book is available
from the British Library

The publisher has no responsibility for the continued existence or accuracy
of URLs for external or third-party internet websites referred to
in this book, and does not guarantee that any content on
such websites is, or will remain, accurate or appropriate.

Papers used by Boydell & Brewer Ltd are natural, recyclable products
made from wood grown in sustainable forests

Printed in Great Britain by
CPI Antony Rowe, Chippenham and Eastbourne

Contents

List of Illustrations   vii

Preface, Editorial Conventions, and Acknowledgements   ix

Prologue   1

1. London and Yorkshire 1901–22   3

2. Gloucestershire 1922–26   22
Early songs 22; By Footpath and Stile 23; Motets 27; Severn Rhapsody, Requiem da Camera 28; Only the Wanderer 35

3. London 1926–28   37
Nocturne, Prelude, Drummond Elegies 38; A Young Man's Exhortation 39; Dies Natalis I 43; Violin Concerto 52

4. Midhurst and Marriage 1928–35   55
Milton Sonnets 57; Grand Fantasia 58

5. Beech Knoll 1935–38   74
Oboe Interlude, Bridges Partsongs 77; Earth and Air and Rain 78

6. The Munich Crisis 1938–39   94
Dies Natalis II 102

7. Ashmansworth 1939–41   106
Single songs 113

8. At the Ministry 1941–45   125
Prelude and Fugue, Elegy, Bagatelles 133; Let us Garlands Bring 134; Farewell to Arms 136

9. For St Cecilia 1945–47   141
Lo, the Full, Final Sacrifice 148; Love's Labour's Lost I 149; For St Cecilia 159

10. Consolidation 1947–48   164
Before and After Summer 169

11. Intimations of Immortality 1948–50   178
Clarinet Concerto 179; Intimations of Immortality 187

12. ... and of Mortality 1950–51   193

13. Speculation 1952–53   203
Magnificat, Anthems 209; White-flowering Days 213

14. Men of Goodwill 1953–54   214
Love's Labour's Lost II 216; Grand Fantasia and Toccata 220; Eclogue, Romance 221; In Terra Pax 227

15. Return to Chosen Hill 1955–56   233
Cello Concerto 238

16. Epilogue   251
Late Harvest 257

Appendices
1   Catalogue of Works   267
2   Bibliography   278
3   Newbury String Players' Repertory   282
4   Joy Finzi's Memoir of Gerald   289

General Index   291
Index of Finzi's Compositions   303

Illustrations

Between pages 118 and 119

Gerald and his mother
Gerald and his brothers and sister

Gerald at Harrogate

Arthur Bliss and R. O. Morris

Gerald Finzi
Joy Finzi

The Finzi family
Finzi with Kiffer

Church Farm, Ashmansworth

Finzi in wartime

A page from the autograph of *Dies Natalis*

Between pages 214 and 215

Fruit gatherers at Ashmansworth

After the first performance of Finzi's Clarinet Concerto
Newbury String Players

Between rehearsing *Intimations of Immortality*
The house-party at Gloucester, 1956

Joy Finzi

Gerald Finzi

Joy and Gerald Finzi
Finzi with his sons

Howard Ferguson
Barbirolli, Finzi, Robin Milford

Finzi with William Waterhouse
The church and cottage on Chosen Hill

'A song outlasts a dynasty'

Gerald Finzi

Preface, Editorial Conventions, and Acknowledgements

I met Gerald Finzi twice, briefly: during an interval of The Marriage of Figaro at Sadler's Wells in 1956, and later that year in the Festival Club of the Cheltenham Festival. By then he was mortally ill, and his wife Joy was the more vivid presence. So I know him as he knew Gurney, Parry, Hardy: through his work and his letters.

Joy Finzi invited me to write this book and put the material at my disposal. She and Howard Ferguson approved early drafts. My first thanks are to them. Howard was particularly illuminating about Finzi's music and composing methods. Joy occasionally corrected a fact; she never challenged an opinion. If anything I wrote surprised her, her invariable response was 'Oh really, how fascinating!'

It was Joy who drew my attention to Colette Clark's Home at Grasmere, in which selections from Dorothy Wordsworth's journal and William Wordsworth's poems are interleaved as a continuous text. That gave me the idea of using Joy's Journal as I have done. Excerpts from it are printed in italics. I have silently corrected a few spelling mistakes, but not her grammar, which is so characteristic of her.

The Finzis' friends generously shared their memories with me, gave me hospitality, and many in time became my friends. I thank particularly Gerald's sons Christopher (Kiffer) and Nigel for their unfailing help, and all the people who allowed me to interview them: Peggy Bendle, Mags Black, Lady Bliss, Edmund Blunden, Jim Brown, Alan Bush, John Carol Case, R. N. Carvalho, Ron Coomes, Jeremy Dale Roberts, Sybil Eaton, Audrey Evans, Dr Neville Finzi, Barbara Gomperts, George Gray, Peter Harland, Herbert Howells, Graham Hutton, Thea King, Jack Kirby, Richard Latham, Kenneth Leighton, Mrs Leverson, Mrs Mesquita, Kirstie Milford, Toty and Dorothy de Navarro, Mrs Dolly Neate, Ralph Nicholson, Edith Pike, Katharine Powell, S. W. Ranger, Lydia Riesenecker, John Russell, Tom Scott, Tony and Ruth Scott, Richard Shirley Smith, Anna Shuttleworth, Kitty Stein, Jean Stewart, Vera Strawson, John and Alice Sumsion, Olive Theyer, Cedric Thorpe Davie, Ralph and Ursula Vaughan Williams, William Waterhouse, Janet Watson, Laurence Whistler.

Quotations in direct speech are from my conversations with Joy and with people who knew Gerald. I jotted down her comment on page 80 – 'but they never seemed difficult to Gerald!' – within ten minutes of her saying it; the same applied to such remarks as Edith Pike's 'Many's the time I've wished Mr Ferguson to glory.' I recorded later interviews on cassette, and these tapes I have given to the Bodleian Museum.

I call Finzi's friends by the names he called them. So Antonio de Navarro is 'Toty' and Cedric Thorpe Davie is 'Ceddie'; Gerald's son Christopher was always Kiffer. The exception is Howard Ferguson, who was 'Fergie' to Gerald (see page 59). I asked him what he would like to be called in the book and he replied 'Oh Howard, please: I don't want to be confused with the Duchess.'

Finzi corresponded with over 250 people, and seemingly kept every letter he received; mostly they kept his. Quite often he also kept drafts of letters he sent. I am grateful for the following permissions: to quote the letters of Finzi by Nigel Finzi; of Howard Ferguson by Hugh Cobbe; Toty de Navarro by Michael de Navarro; Sir Arthur Bliss by Gertrude H. Bliss; Ralph Vaughan Williams by Ursula Vaughan Williams; William Busch by Julia C. Busch; Anthony Scott by Richard Scott; Cedric Thorpe Davie by the Keeper of Manuscripts, St Andrews University, and the estate of Cedric Thorpe Davie. For permission to quote from Edmund Blunden's letters and poems I thank the Harry Ransom Humanities Research Center at the University of Texas at Austin; the extracts are reproduced by permission also of PFD (www.pfd.co.uk/) on behalf of the Estate of Mrs Claire Blunden. I am grateful to Dr Sheila Callender for information about Finzi's illness.

Excerpts from Finzi's Requiem da Camera are reproduced by permission of Banks Music Publications; all other excerpts from his music are by permission of Boosey & Hawkes. The photograph of Finzi's MS. Mus.c. 381, fol. 28r is from the Bodleian Library, University of Oxford. The group photograph in the plate section was taken by Shirley Russell (Carson). I thank Jo Finzi, Nigel's wife, for her professional assistance in collating, scanning and retouching the photographs; and for designing the jacket. I am grateful to the BBC Written Archives Centre, Caversham Park, Reading, and to the Bodleian Library for their ready assistance.

I thank William Waterhouse and Jeremy Dale Roberts for reading drafts of the book and making helpful suggestions; and I am grateful to Stanley Sadie for checking the pages on Finzi's eighteenth-century research. Bruce Phillips and Andrew Porter both gave me expert advice and constant, unstinting encouragement.

The author and publishers are grateful to all the institutions and persons listed for permission to reproduce the materials in which they hold copyright. Every effort has been made to trace the copyright holders; apologies are offered for any omission, and the publishers will be pleased to add any necessary acknowledgement in subsequent editions.

Diana McVeagh, March 2005, August 2010

Prologue

Fork after forkful of good compost he slung round the base of the Pitmaston Pineapple Russet; then straightened up and looked lovingly round his young apple orchard. Over the hedge was the little church, where in a couple of days they would be giving a concert. Across the lane, behind the high flint wall, was the house they had built. Joy was drawing or sculpting in her studio over the old stables. Soon she would cross the yard, and there would be coffee round the big kitchen table by the Esse cooker. Then he would sprint up his own steep stairs to his music room. On his large sloping desk were the sketches of the song he was working at; two lines of music had flashed into his mind the night before, as he read the Hardy poem. When he composed, his gaze could wander westward through one window, and through the other could sweep down towards the south.

He bent to pick up the fork, and fondle the cat which rubbed against his leg. To the friend who found him at work here in his orchard, he said – with that characteristic jerk of the head and challenging flash of the eye – 'I shall never make a stir in the world: I live a happily married life and there is nothing to say about me.'[1]

[1] Unpublished obituary by Toty de Navarro.

CHAPTER ONE

London and Yorkshire

1901–22

Gerald Raphael Finzi was born when the twentieth century was one year old: the year that Parry composed his *Ode to Music*, Elgar his *Cockaigne*, and Vaughan Williams his 'Linden Lea'.

He was born in a substantial London house, which stood in a wide tree-lined road running across the slope up from Maida Vale. His parents had moved to 53 (now 93) Hamilton Terrace NW8 in 1897, and their fifth and last child was born at ten minutes to seven on the morning of Sunday, 14 July 1901. His doting mother, Eliza Emma – known as Lizzie – kept a little notebook, in which she recorded that at birth he weighed the good large size of 10lb 2oz. He was breast-fed for three months and was a 'sweet, placid babe'.

The name Finzi – now so much a part of English song – is common in Italy. There the Finzis can be traced back to the second half of the thirteenth century, the first recorded Sephardic family members being bankers in Padua; others were notable rabbis, physicians, and merchants. The most versatile and distinguished was Mordecai ben Abraham Finzi (d.1476), scientist, physician, and banker, who lived at Bologna and Mantua and was known for his mathematical and astronomical works. Giuseppe Finzi (1815–1886) was a confidant of Garibaldi, Mazzini, and Cavour.

The family tradition is that Judah (1763–1838) – (also known as Leon, following a Jewish custom) had qualified as a physician in Padua before settling in London. He married a widow, Simha Perez, née Carvalho, from Jamaica, and they had a son Samuel Leon (1811–95). He became a surgeon-dentist,[1] designing a drill for removing decay, which could be used at all angles of the mouth 'without inconvenience'; he showed it at the Great Exhibition of 1851. According to his grandson Gerald[2] he was an enthusiastic amateur violinist, and a member of the Beethoven Society. After his first wife died he married Harriette (Hadasa) Abraham, born on 29 August 1821, whose liveliness caused her to be known as the Belle of Bristol. She married her dentist from her optician father's house, 19 King's Square, Bristol, on 13 March 1850.

Their son was Gerald's father, John Abraham Finzi, known as Jack, born on 28 June 1860.[3] Of Jack's two brothers, Daniel went into music publishing. The

---

[1] At 6 Dalby Terrace, City Road, Islington.
[2] Gerald's memories in this chapter are taken from his Black Book, see p. 197.
[3] At York House, 357 City Road, Islington.

elder, Leon (Judah) Moses, studied at University College, London, and became a physician, setting up a practice in NW8 just round the corner from his brother Jack. Leon's son, Neville Samuel Finzi (1881–1968), became an international authority on radiotherapy. He was a familiar figure at St Bartholomew's Hospital, 'bounding up the stairs of the outpatient block, three at a time, or racing across the square. His energy seemed inexhaustible, but not his patience, for he did not suffer fools gladly nor trouble overmuch to express disapproval with tact.'[4] Nevertheless his charm was irresistible. He loved children and babies, and they loved him. He brought to his recreations as great an enthusiasm as he did to his work, and his achievements as an alpinist were reported in the press. He kept a large and elegant house in Harley Street, and gathered around his table 'some of the most interesting personalities of the time'. Change alpinist to pomologist, and Harley Street to Ashmansworth, and Neville and his younger cousin Gerald had much in common.

Gerald's father Jack was educated at University College, London, where he became friends with Frank Heatherly, the son of Thomas Heatherly, founder of a notable art school (which Clifford Bax, Arnold's brother, attended). Another friend was Raphael Meldola, an industrial chemist, who discovered oxazine dyes. Gerald was called after him, though as an adult he never used his second name or initial. *Raphael Meldola: his Worth and Work*[5] tells much, indirectly, of Jack Finzi. Meldola (1849–1915) was the grandson of a Chief Rabbi, and came of a Sephardic family of aristocratic, learned men. He was 'inordinately fond' of cats (as his godchild Gerald came to be). Of high principle, he held that every scientific man should justify his existence and add to the accumulation of knowledge. Natural history was his passion; he became President of the Entomological Society, and was proposed for fellowship of the Royal Society by Charles Darwin. His great joy was to spend his leisure in the country, and this he shared with Jack Finzi, whose 'real interest lay in natural history and scientific ideas'. Gerald's early recollections were of holidays in Norfolk, the Sussex Downs, and the Isle of Wight.

Jack Finzi began work as a clerk, licking stamps. He asked for a sixpenny rise; when it was refused, he walked out and founded his own business as a shipbroker, which flourished as Finzi, Layman, Clark & Co. In 1885 he made his first transaction on the Baltic Exchange. Two years later he married Eliza Emma Leverson; the ceremony, conducted by the Bevis Marks synagogue, was at her home, 4 Kensington Gardens Square, on 8 September 1887. He was twenty-seven, she twenty-two. To them were born Kate in 1890, Felix John in 1893, Douglas Lewis in 1897, Edgar in 1898; then in 1901 came Gerald Raphael.

No longer Judah, Samuel, Daniel – the Old Testament names; for Jack Finzi was not a practising Jew. 'His friends, his reading & speculation were all of a

---

4   *British Medical Journal* (20 April 1968), p. 181.
5   London, 1916.

rational scientific kind,' according to his son Gerald: 'Darwin and the neo-Darwinians were his bread and butter.' Despite a permanent injury to one leg, Jack Finzi was a good sportsman: he boxed, played tennis, and later golf. His portrait shows a direct, slightly challenging gaze. He was well-read, easy to get on with, and musical, singing lieder in a pleasant baritone voice. Prosperous in the City, he was, like so many businessmen of his time, extremely cultivated.

His wife Lizzie was born on 19 February 1865. Her grandfather, Montague Levyson, was a diamond merchant, one of whose descendants, Ernest, a gambler who worked in the City, married Ada Beddington; after they separated she wrote the Little Ottleys novels (as Ada Leverson) and became Oscar Wilde's 'Sphinx'. Lizzie's mother was Kate Hyam, a member of the Ashkenazi family, originally from Hamburg, which founded the Manchester clothing firm Hyam Brothers. Lizzie's parents were ill-matched. Lizzie's father, Montague Richard Leverson (1830–1925), was earthy, her mother fanciful. He left her and went to the United States, returning to acquire a doctorate at Göttingen in 1872. Gerald admired him enough to make notes on his life. At the age of eighteen 'he through [sic] off Judaism & celebrated the event by a dinner of all the forbidden foods'. His London home became a centre for 'lovers of freedom, revolutionaries, refugees'. Like Giuseppe Finzi he counted Mazzini and Garibaldi among his friends; and also Victor Hugo. He published first on copyrights (London, 1854), then on legal matters, then, after qualifying in medicine at Baltimore, on homoeopathy and against vaccination, being violently anti-Pasteur. He remarried at the age of seventy and lived in bliss and Bournemouth until his death at ninety-five.

Lizzie's mother, deserted by her roaming husband, kept an English girls' school in Hanover, in her ancestral country. A strong, independent figure, she was loved and respected by all the pupils, among them her own daughter. Lizzie was the school pet, and probably a little spoilt. But she was not the only child. Her sister Hettie married a Hanoverian banker called Schwabacher, and her two brothers, Louis Pianciani Leverson[6] and William Ellis Leverson, became tobacco merchants. All four were slightly deaf, but differently, so that one had to be shouted at, another whispered to – a disability Lizzie's son Gerald fortunately did not inherit.

As a successful businessman's wife, Lizzie had servants and a nanny for the children. But Nanny thought four children quite enough, and, besides, the fourth, Edgar, was delicate; even his mother thought his face 'weeny . . . almost puny at times'. So naturally Edgar became Nanny's favourite, and she refused to look after Gerald: a special nurse had to be engaged for him. In time Nanny took him on, but he was the least loved of the five. Not by his mother, though, whose notebook records her children's progress. The eldest, Kate,

---

[6] He married Emily Meyer, and their granddaughter is Esther Rantzen, the television personality.

became a weekly boarder at school the year Gerald was born. The next year, 1902, Lizzie summed up her situation:

> We were married fifteen years on Saturday last. A long time to look forward to, fifteen years, & so short to look back upon. Our Katie has much improved in every way, she is bright, intelligent & good-looking, full of fun and vivacity . . . Felix is intelligent, always wanting to invent; a dear, affectionate & thoughtful son. Douglas bright & handsome, a sweet, winsome nature. Edgar still with a small, pale face, quick-tempered, musical. He will be four years old soon, please God [the delicate child was the only one to need the supplication]. Baby Gerald is 'sunshiny', bonny, yet quick-tempered; very fond of music . . . chats away in his sweet Baby language.

The following year her stocktaking was equally happy. Kate and Felix were both at school in Brighton, Felix leader in the singing class. Douglas was learning the piano and Felix the violin (obviously it was a home where music mattered). 'Our bright little merry hasty-tempered Edgar' was 'as sharp as a needle with his wits'. Then came Baby Gerald Raphael, 'chatting away, loving music, bustling about; such an affectionate sweet little rosy-cheeked pet. God bless and protect them all.'

But in 1907 the shipbroker's wife was moved to write in bad but admirably defiant verse:

> Sons, daughter and parents, united, there can come no harm
> As the proud sailing vessel rides the storm-wave,
> So we Finzis united misfortune will brave.

For there had been hard times. Lizzie had been ill, and both Jack's brothers had died. Worst of all, in November 1906 Jack was operated on for cancer. He lost his right eye and part of his upper jaw. 'Oh God, what have we not suffered, what agony have we not passed through; but the dear life is safe!' wrote Lizzie. But his condition grew worse. His nephew, Neville, was studying medicine, and Jack paid for him to specialise in cancer research; but to no avail for him. Gerald remembered that his father 'once showed me his eye socket. It was a great shock to me. I was, I suppose about five [he must have been over six]. I remember finding a peach in the garden & being told to take it to him. He was in the dining room, standing up. I felt awkward & – blind man, feeling the fruit, & then stroking my head. After that he was mostly bedridden.' Gerald also recalled: 'my simple mother once pointed out to him the beneficence of God, to which he replied "He must be a very cruel God to make me suffer so." '

Jack's sufferings ended on 1 July 1909. In *The Times* 'an old shipowner' paid tribute to him: 'He never lost the refined courtesy of his Italian ancestors, and while he built up in twenty-three years the successful firm of shipbrokers which bears his name, he was probably more proud of having gathered together one of the finest private collections of entomological specimens in England. The personal charm of a lovable character completed the picture of an intellectual business man not easy to replace even in the City of

London.'[7] Six months after his death, Lizzie wrote in her little book: 'Oh, what has not happened since the last words were written! Jack, my Love, my adored Husband has been taken from me – Think of it if you can, the loss the loss the loss to me . . . Oh God, help me to stand up bravely & do my best for my children.'

Very little up to this point would have interested the adult Gerald Finzi. He came to hold the view that environment was so much more important than heredity that parents and ancestors were irrelevant: what mattered was to create for oneself the best conditions in which to develop one's gifts. That, however, he was not yet capable of doing.

His widowed mother turned for emotional support to her two Leverson brothers, the tobacco merchants, who were executors of the Will and trustees. She was comfortably off, for her husband had left over £22,000, a considerable sum in those days. But she had the responsibility of five children. At Jack's death her eldest, Kate, was nineteen, her youngest, Gerald, a few days short of his eighth birthday.

It would have been natural for her to seek the company of her married sister in Germany. Possibly on Edgar's account (as a child, he had two operations) the family was staying at Königstein about 1911, in a sanatorium directed by a Dr Kohnstamm. There was a boy there, Gregory Frumkin, of Polish origin, unhappy at a school in nearby Frankfurt. Mrs Finzi and Katie, who both spoke German, were kind to him, and he became devoted for life to Katie. Douglas impressed him by his daily boxing exercises, and Edgar with his daily hours of drawing. (Gerald was rather young to be noticed.) By now the older children knew exactly what each wished to do: Kate to write, Felix to be involved with electricity, Douglas to be a poet, Edgar an artist. For little Gregory it was 'a breath of fresh air . . . to meet foreign people who were so nice'.[8]

Then on 7 July 1912 Douglas died of pneumonia at Bradfield College. Mrs Finzi left Hamilton Terrace, and (probably on Raphael Meldola's advice) bequeathed her husband's moths and butterflies to University College, London; it was found to be an extensive reference collection, in perfect condition, and is still used. Mrs Finzi moved for a time into the Curzon Hotel. Gerald became a boarder at Kingswood Preparatory School at Camberley, very much an army town. The school had a bias towards the services; Gerald hated it, and used later to say he hadn't learnt a thing there. He was the only piano pupil, and was kept in the same form for four years; a boy who did brilliantly there ended up 'only as a director of Watneys'. He remembered it as the kind of insensitive school, in his opinion, where they cut down a little copse in which the boys enjoyed building 'pretend' houses.

It was here, however, that Gerald had a crucial experience. He developed some childhood infectious disease towards the end of the 1913 Spring term; all the other boys went home, and he was kept alone in the sanatorium. He

[7]   19 July 1909, early edition.
[8]   Letter to Joy Finzi, 14 December 1980.

found nothing to do, nothing to read but a Bible. Feverish, alone, possibly made a little heady by the superb prose – altogether in a condition of heightened sensibility – he noticed the floor of his room glowing in the dark every night after his coal fire went out. He told the nurse, who thought he was making it up. One night the floor burst into flame. In what kind of exalted or threatened state one can only imagine, he resolved there and then to become a composer. When the nurse eventually came, it was found that the fire had crept along the joists of the old house. So the child had been right, and the adults wrong.

He determined to get himself taken away from that school. He pretended to have fainting fits, one dramatically in the bath. His mother was alarmed, having recently lost a son as well as her husband. Edgar was still delicate, so Mrs Finzi engaged a tutor and took her two youngest children to Switzerland, for the good mountain air to strengthen them. On the way she pressed Gerald into giving his first and last public appearance as a pianist, playing a little piece of his own at a charity concert at St Valery-en-Caux.

Gerald looked back on his time in Switzerland as the best education he could have had. He was able to read, and to develop as he wished. The tutor, Walter Kaye, made little impression on him; neither did Switzerland, nor Königstein, nor 'abroad' in general, except in the contradictory sense that he became passionately English. The impending war in 1914 brought the family home. On the way, splendidly undeterred by German threats, Mrs Finzi bustled her children round Paris to show them the Louvre and other sights before the Germans got there.

By then she had lost a second son. Felix, after school at Repton, had taken a job with a tea company in India, and in 1913 he died in Assam. He had been warned of a weak heart, but persisted in smoking heavily and taking sleeping draughts. Years later Gerald by chance met his doctor, who confirmed his suspicion that Felix had died, whether deliberately or not, from an overdose. Poor Felix, what homesickness or adolescent confusion might have caused him to end his life a few days before his twenty-first birthday!

Back in England, Gerald and Edgar were sent briefly to Mount Arlington school at Hindhead, where Gerald scored a success as the slave-girl Morgiana in a musical, *Ali Baba*. Mrs Finzi then made a home for her grown-up daughter and two remaining sons in Harrogate. This may have been because Walter Kaye was a Harrogate man; or because the spa town on the edge of the Yorkshire moors had a healthy bracing reputation; or because in central north England it was as far as could be from possible Zeppelin raids. They moved first to Pateley Bridge, then in October 1915 into lodgings at 13 St Basils, South Drive, Harrogate.

Like any spa town of the period, Harrogate maintained its municipal orchestra. In 1903 Parry had opened the Royal Hall (designed by Frank Matcham), which then held weekly symphony concerts. The conductor in 1914 was Julian Clifford, a trifle flashy but Leipzig- and London-trained, and a friend of the enterprising Dan Godfrey of Bournemouth; Clifford's soloists were of international standard. Moreover, he had conducted the second performance of Vaughan Williams's *London Symphony*, in 1914, at Harrogate. Mrs Finzi asked him to suggest a music teacher for Gerald. By good fortune, Clifford recommended no middle-aged, run-of-the-mill teacher, but young Ernest Bristow Farrar. Farrar had studied composition with Stanford at the Royal College of Music, and then been organist at the English Church, Dresden, and at St Hilda's, South Shields, before coming to Christ Church, Harrogate, in 1912. More important for Gerald, he was a practising composer whose work was performed. Stanford had conducted Farrar's *The Blessed Damozel* at a Leeds Philharmonic concert in 1908, and Farrar himself conducted his new *Heroic Elegy* ('for Soldiers') at Harrogate in 1918 while on leave. In 1915 he was thirty, old enough to have had some experience, young enough to understand a thirteen-year-old. Photographs of him show a sensitive, rather dreamy face, and bear out Stanford's description of him as 'very shy, but full of poetry'.[9] Much of his music, however, has vitality and vigour.

1915, FARRAR'S PUPIL

Farrar took Gerald on after hearing him play, but advised him that there was little chance of making money by composition, so that unless he had private means he had better study with a view to teaching. Gerald naturally took no notice (and his mother did not object), so he set himself to gain all he could from Farrar. He turned up to lessons 'with a huge music case, full of music & books which almost weighed him down',[10] and a little notebook in which he entered all sorts of queries about composers. On non-lesson days he would sit hopefully on the fence outside the Farrars' house, 15 Hollins Road, just five minutes away from his own, waiting to be invited in, or to go for a walk on the moors. Teacher and pupil went together to the town concerts, and Farrar obtained Clifford's permission for Gerald to attend rehearsals. Farrar found his young pupil a little lacking in concentration but showing a bent for composition; and with so much energy and enthusiasm that he tried to learn two or three piano sonatas a week.

The Finzis, new to the north, had few friends. Gerald flatly refused to follow his brothers to public school, which, in his opinion, turned out men all of one pattern: and Mrs Finzi was loth to part with her 'ewe lamb'. Kate and Edgar were firm friends, but Gerald and Edgar had never got on. Gerald remembered Edgar as strange: he never grew properly: even his mother had described him as 'puny'. He couldn't bear to be touched, and he kept snakes and lizards as pets. He was jealous of Gerald from birth, and during the

9   Durham University Journal, New Series (Dec. 1918), vol. 22, no. 1, p. 30, obituary.
10   Olive Farrar to Joy Finzi, 13 January 1957.

Harrogate days they hardly spoke to each other (though it must be admitted that his older cousin Neville remembered Gerald as a horrid little boy who pinched people).

There was, however, one experience that Gerald and Edgar shared. One day they happened to be together looking at the grey landscape when the sun came out. They turned to each other and smiled. It was the only time there was any genuine communication between them – and Gerald always remembered it.

There is a familiar melodic figure in Finzi's music, immediately recognizable, crucial to his musical personality. It opens the piano prelude of his setting (probably composed 1947–48) of Hardy's 'Childhood among the ferns':

> I sat one sprinkling day upon the lea,
> Where tall-stemmed ferns spread out luxuriantly,
> And nothing but those tall ferns sheltered me.

It is then sung at the words 'the sun then burst . . .'. Finzi, like Hardy, had sat in a 'pretend' house of 'green rafters'; he, like Hardy, questioned the wisdom of those grown to 'man's estate'. The song may embody the boy's memory of the shared sunburst and the single moment of communication; and Example 1.1 may spring from that profound childhood experience.

Ex. 1.1

One single moment of communication was how Gerald remembered it – and memories have their own validity. But there was another side to the story. His sister Kate, twenty-four at the outbreak of war, trained as a probationer, joined the Red Cross, and went to the military base hospital at Boulogne in October 1914. (At the same time, in the same place, Almroth Wright and Alexander Fleming began the work on wound infection that led to penicillin.) Two years later Kate wrote of her experiences in *Eighteen Months in the War Zone: The Record of a Woman's Work on the Western Front* (Cassell, 1916). The *Times Literary Supplement* reviewer[11] called the book lively and unpretentious, but the adult Gerald

---

[11] *Times Literary Supplement*, 9 November 1916.

described it as 'a dreadfully poor "war diary" '. He was too severe. Indeed, it is full of such phrases as 'fine strapping fellows', the 'flower of English Man-hood', and the 'jaws of death'. Kate does rather trail her gentility, referring to her 'modicum of French and *savoir-faire*' as a traveller, speaking as 'one who has heard most of the great music in most of the great capitals', and remembering 'home' where there was a 'gong to announce "dressing time", and soft décolleté frocks donned before long mirrors, and well-appointed dining-tables'. But this sheltered young Englishwoman, in her first fortnight at Boulogne, ate horseflesh, was told that the Germans had murdered a girl and cut off her breasts and a foot, worked in a clearing station in conditions no better than at Scutari, receiving casualties covered in blood and vermin in the stench of gas gangrene, and, as the only German speaker at the camp, com-forted a young Saxon prisoner as he died from tetanus.

1915, THE SOCIETY WEEKLIES

In August 1915 Edgar posted out to his sister vol. 1 no. 1 of *The Society Weekly*, edited by E. & G. Finzi – the kind of family newspaper many people were sending around during the war. 'Society' was obviously meant in the sense of fashionable socialite, for the first issue is full of wicked take-offs of Kate, 'the Duchess of Vanity' (many of the jokes and references made sense if the *Weeklies* and Kate's book were read together). Edgar drew pictures of Kate with a nut-cracker nose and hairy chin and wearing specs; Gerald contributed a poem, a waltz for voice and piano, and Chapter 1 of 'The Proud Girl of Wimereux', all poking fun at her pretensions:

> It was a bright summer's day at Wimereux, as a stout pimpled lady with a conceited air marched through the muddy streets. . . . She passed an infant being mercilessly beaten by an older boy. The poor wee mite was writhing in agony and waving its arms about piteously. She carefully stepped aside that its arms might not touch her skirts. 'Huh,' she muttered, 'a case of the survival of the fittest'.[12]

Haughtily, she bought lorgnettes, two boxes of face powder, a box of rouge, and a packet of curling pins (to wear make-up in 1915 was considered very 'fast'). She is portrayed as vain, fault-finding, lazy, heartless, and bossy. Butlers and maids are particular targets of ridicule. Then she finds her dog dead 'with a knife in its heart':

> She was just tying her nightcap on when she perceived that the door was slowly but surely opening. What could it be? It was intolerable that death should come while she was yet so young. She thought of all her past life. How she might have saved her two small brothers, Edgar and Gerald, so much pain by not singing to them, – how happy she had been in the olden times when domineering was the order of the day.

The second issue adds to the family phrase-book 'Art! What a fine profession!

---

[12] Most of *The Society Weeklies* were destroyed in a fire after these extracts were copied.

But not a very lucrative one, I'm afraid. How do you expect to make a living out of it?' This applied to Edgar, whose increasingly acid and powerful caricatures of public figures and military types in the *Weeklies* exposed the degradation and brutality of war. (There is also a satirical drawing of Kate being presented at Court by Mrs Finzi.) Gerald disappears in the third issue 'on account of a tiff with the Editor', rejoining later with the occasional verse and drawing. In making up his stories Edgar drew on his own childhood. Poor Katie, now portrayed as a German spy, returns by Zeppelin to Königstein, where Doctor von Kohnstamm is described as a toad, and drawn with an enormous beer-belly, puffing clouds of pipe-smoke. There are references to their school as 'the Camberley concentration camp' and to their holidays from 'the torture house' ('shades of the prison house . . .').

Kate seemed to take the ragging in surprisingly good heart, and after she had been home on a week's leave in December 1915 Edgar's editorials become friendly letters to her. He tells her how he attends art school and begins to work in water colour, then ('a red-letter day') in oils; in his mother's words he 'is a genius'. Through his pages the atmosphere of the home comes out strongly. Each issue had a motto, among them 'une erreur est pire qu'un crime' [Boulay de la Meurthe], 'what fools men are!' and 'Light, more light' [Goethe's attributed dying words]. Family catchphrases – 'it's not an English thing to do', 'because it isn't done' – suggest some clash of values. There were difficulties over the unusual name: suggested variants of Finzi were 'Frizi, Fringi, Frige, Fringe'. Edgar drew two pages of differently shaped noses (Broken, Roman, Grecian, Nosey Parkery, Dickens, potato, Hebrew, and Finzi) with the comment 'you can always tell a Finzi by the retroussé nasal organ'. What problems did this family of Jewish and German-Italian descent run up against in wartime Yorkshire?

When they moved in February 1916 into their own house, Birkholt, 22 Duchy Road, the *Weeklies* gave a sad picture of their unpacking their dead brothers' belongings. Each remaining boy now had his own room – Edgar his 'beloved studio' – and they drew up a convention: 'We, the undersigned, do hereby agree . . .' to protect each other's privacy. Regular features called 'Days in the Life of the Finzi Family' and 'Geraldisms' show Gerald as the older Edgar saw him:

> Suddenly an extraordinary noise is heard upstairs, which gradually grows louder and resolves itself into a weird, unearthly sort of singing. Gerald, who is responsible for the appalling row, suddenly shoots in at the door like a thunderbolt, singing.

A series of riddles includes: 'What is Gerald for? To "jabber" ' (one of the uncles in his Will left Edgar what Gerald remembered as a fortune, but to Gerald he left only a gold watch, because he talked too much). Two of Gerald's sayings are astonishingly revealing: 'Yes!! I'll teach you who Gerald R. Finzi is!!!!' ('an offer of education', explains Edgar dryly, 'used only when feeling choleric'). And ' "O, child of my dreams!!!" ' (an expression of intense rapture)'. The emotions prompting both sayings were to come together in time to create *Dies Natalis*.

There is a hilarious scene, recorded by the *Weeklies*, in a Harrogate café between Katie and her two brothers, and some officers at another table. The officers wink at Katie:

Ge: Are you going to be introduced, Ka?
Ka: No!!!!!!
Ge: (in a loud sonata): Why?
(no answer)
Ge: (in a louder sonata): Why?
(no answer)
Ge: (in a loudest sonata): WHY?
Ka: (sharply) Because it isn't done!!!!!!!!!!!
(Silence while Gerald digests this interesting piece of information, then:)
Ge: Why isn't it done?

Curiosity, persistence, and absorption in music are admirable traits; but not traits always appreciated in a younger brother. So, having no-one congenial of his own age, Gerald drew close to his mother. Lizzie Finzi was genuinely fond of music, played the piano to him in the evenings – 'things like Liebesträume'[13] – and even published a couple of studies.[14] Emily Ellis, their maid, recalled that 'Mr Gerald looked up to his mother, & worked hard all day & then played over what he had done' to her. Mrs Finzi declared to Emily: 'he is a Genius'. (So both her sons were geniuses.) He used to put the work away then start again, saying 'I don't know if I will finish it, but if I do I hope it will be great.'[15]

Emily, only ten years older than Gerald, went with him to concerts and on walks when Edgar was occupied and Mrs Finzi too weary. She had by now lost much of her money, which her brothers had invested before the war in Germany. 'Poor Mrs Finzi' in Emily's opinion 'had a hard time standing alone to cope with everything.' Emily would sometimes read to Gerald as he lay on the rug in front of the fire with his two cats, Harold and Whisky: 'he loved his cats very dearly & found a bit of peace with them'. Already cats; and already apples. Their next-door neighbours had a wonderful selection of apple trees, and when the fruit was gathered Gerald, who 'was very keen on apples', made Emily climb with him through a trapdoor to their loft to see what sort of harvest it was. They heard a sound and in their hurry to get back stuck their feet through the ceiling. Mrs Finzi was out, and the fair-minded Gerald rushed out of the house and down the road to meet her and confess before anyone else could tell the story.

Gerald's room was at the top of the house, lined with white book-shelves. Emily was not allowed to dust it: work, he would say, was more important.

13 Finzi to Thorpe Davie, 20 September 1956.
14 L. Finzi, *Deux études pour le pianoforte* (Novello, 1906).
15 Emily Ellis letters to Joy Finzi, undated, after Finzi's death.

Once he even locked her in the cellar when she disturbed him by cleaning the stairs! She remembered he never wanted to go out anywhere, unless it was to hear music; and that he was always reading. Apart from the Farrars, he was close only to a photographer, Nita Taylor, and her friend Olive Ismay. They loved his frequent visits, the talk and the laughter. Their studio was rather austere, but what furniture they had was antique and beautiful. The effect on Gerald was dramatic. When his mother was away on a visit he sold everything in her rather 'pernickety' drawing room except the grand piano! She adored him so much there was apparently no trouble.

In February 1916 Kate, who had worked hard in foul conditions in France, was sent home owing to failing health. She began preparing her diary for publication. Edgar helped her. Gerald felt left out, the more so when the book was published later that year. Then in August 1916 Ernest Farrar joined up. Gerald was deeply upset at the thought of studying with someone else. Farrar recommended Edward C. Bairstow, the organist of York Minster, as the best teacher in the area, but Gerald was horrified by the tales of Bairstow's strictness. So for a time he went for lessons to another Harrogate organist, Frederick Hemsley. This was disastrous: he was the sort, in Gerald's scornful words, who 'uses a wicker table & thin nib'.[16] He still felt himself to be Farrar's pupil and sent work to him by post. Also went questions, among them one on Haydn's domestic affairs, another on how to notate cymbals sounded with drumsticks, a third requesting his teacher's photograph. Farrar wrote back encouragingly, advising him to 'stick in hard' at work, to 'devour' all the music he could lay his hands on, and to think himself lucky he had the opportunity and the time to practise.

Gerald went to London to see Farrar, who took him to the Royal College of Music where the great Sir Charles Stanford tested him, noted his lack of facility, and advised him against a musical career. He was not the only student to suffer such a crushing judgment. Whatever the underlying effect, Gerald took no notice. When Farrar moved to Cambridge, Mrs Finzi and Gerald again turned up to visit him. But it was plain that the boy needed regular supervision, so in December 1917 Bairstow agreed to interview him, guarding himself by saying he could accept only a really promising pupil. The next month Gerald began work.

He travelled the twenty miles from Harrogate to York twice a week for piano and composition lessons, and often sat with Bairstow in the organ loft during services. At first he used to be seen walking about York with his mother: he clung to her, as she to him. Soon he was the only one left in the nest. Katie had married a 'bounder with charm', as Gerald's cousin Neville described him. In August, Edgar joined the RAF, becoming a lieutenant. But for all Gerald's youth he held his own with Bairstow. A letter from Bairstow to Mrs Finzi on 3 April 1918 tells its own tale: 'your son and I are beginning to understand one another better now'.

---

16 Kate's papers.

Before long a double blow fell. Farrar, commissioned in the Devonshires, was sent to France. While Mrs Finzi was away from home, news came that Edgar was missing in the Aegean. After ten days at the front Farrar was killed, on 18 September 1918. Then it was confirmed that Edgar too had been killed, on 5 September.[17] Both young men died only weeks before the Armistice, and the end of the war, on 11 November.

One's thoughts go first to Lizzie Finzi, bereft of her husband and now of her third son. Indeed, it seems possible that shock on shock was more than she could sustain. Her earlier fanciful nature turned in later years quite eccentric, to the amusement of outsiders but to Gerald's exasperation. He at the time was devastated, though more by Farrar's death than by Edgar's. The bond between a teacher and an eager pupil is close, and Farrar was young enough to be his first real friend, a man whose ideals became his own.

J. B. Priestley had gone out to the front with Farrar, and wrote to Olive, his widow (Gerald kept a copy of the letter), that he considered him 'a representative of one of the finest types of humanity, a creative artist, freed from all little meannesses and jealousies'. In addition, Olive wrote to the grieving boy that Ernest would live 'in the lovely music he has written'. On Gerald, at seventeen, committed to becoming a composer, that thought laid a heavy obligation. He was the 'lucky' survivor; and his mother's emotional investment in him, the only son left of four, cannot have eased his burden; there must have been some feeling of guilt. When he consciously became a pacifist is not known, whether in reaction to Camberley, or to the Great War, or later; but with what sympathy it can be understood.

Understandable too is his grasp of how short is life, how precious is youth. In 1953 he wrote to the poet Edmund Blunden describing his first meeting with Farrar: 'then I was about fourteen and he just over thirty. Now I am over fifty and he is still just over thirty.'[18]

It was fortunate that work with Bairstow had already begun. Besides being a fine organist, and since 1913 running the York Minster choir and the city's musical society, Bairstow conducted those crack choirs of the north, Leeds and Bradford. The first choral concert Gerald heard was in Leeds Town Hall, conducted by the 'beloved tyrant', as he came to call ECB. After that, he went over regularly to attend the Leeds rehearsals.

Bairstow was a formidable organizer, and into his house came many of the leading performers of the day. His Bach Passions on Palm Sunday were renowned. Often Harry Plunket Greene was a soloist, and Gerald would have admired how vividly he brought words to life, and studied his Interpretation in Song (1914), particularly its pages on prosody and metre. Another friend often

---

[17] His body was recovered and he was buried at Stavros, and mentioned in despatches.
[18] 23 August 1953.

in Bairstow's home was the violinist Sybil Eaton, already the dedicatee of Herbert Howells's First Sonata. Four years older than Gerald, she was beautiful enough to be – at a worshipful distance – his first love.

Bairstow followed the continental tradition of giving lessons with others present, so Gerald 'sat in' on organ and solo singing lessons: Bairstow was an exceptionally good singing teacher, Elsie Suddaby being among his pupils at that time. He was himself a composer, and in every way the best, if conservative, kind of Kapellmeister. Sybil Eaton remembered that at the time Stanford and Parry were his gods; he had little use for Elgar, still less for Debussy and Ravel.

In 1919 George Gray (later the organist of Leicester Cathedral) became Bairstow's articled pupil. He was older than Gerald, having served in the war, but the two students were present at each others' lessons. Gray was struck by Gerald's independent views. He resisted working the usual academic harmony and counterpoint exercises, and astounded Gray by his strong-mindedness and frankness with Bairstow. What he undoubtedly learnt was the importance of setting words well. 'Week after week points arose in this connection,' Gray remembered, and Gerald heard the practical value of these principles when attending singing lessons. His routine was regular. Twice a week he arrived by train from Harrogate at about ten and went straight to the organ loft (Matins was sung most days). Bairstow often used to leave after the anthem, his assistant 'playing out' the congregation. Finzi went to his house for his own lesson, and stayed for others till his twelve o'clock train. 'I can see him now,' remembered Gray, 'rushing for his train with his shock of black, rather curly hair, and his rather ungainly gait.' He seemed very healthy, sturdy and 'well covered'; neatly dressed in good clothes, with no extravagance or 'artiness' about him. 'He had a striking look: one would notice him in the street and remember him, perhaps because of his rather foreign (a little dark-skinned, I think) appearance. I would say he had an Italian look in those days.' Gray found him, in spite of his forthright opinions, rather reserved and shy, but 'a charming and friendly soul'.[19]

AFTER THE WAR

As soon as the war ended, Gerald began to explore England. In 1919 Rutland Boughton revived his festival at Glastonbury, and during August Gerald spent a packed and happy week there. Boughton was an idealist, a rural romanticist, who would have been happiest in a colony of self-supporting farmer-musicians. An energetic advocate of English music, he disliked what he thought of as the stale routine of London music-making, finding compensation for the lower technical standards of amateurs in the freshness of their attitudes. He was a vegetarian, and if Gerald was not one already, he became one then (writing to ask Bernard Shaw where to get sandals made without leather). He was eighteen and impressionable. The Somerset countryside was

[19] Letters of 10 and 23 January 1958.

rich and warm after Yorkshire, and the people were friendly. The festival programmes were adventurous: as well as Boughton's own music drama *The Round Table*, Gerald heard E. J. Dent revive Locke's *Cupid and Death*, Edmund Fellowes lecture on Elizabethan music and direct madrigals. He heard Ireland's Phantasy Trio, Elgar's Quartet (then only one year old), and Vaughan Williams's *On Wenlock Edge* sung by Steuart Wilson. He heard pieces from the Fitzwilliam Virginal book, including Peerson's *The Fall of the Leaf*. He also heard a setting by Clive Carey of James Elroy Flecker's 'To a poet', a poem that tellingly reinforced what Farrar's widow had said, that Ernest would live on 'in the lovely music he has written'; by then Flecker too was dead, at only thirty-one, of tuberculosis:

> I who am dead a thousand years,
> And wrote this sweet archaic song,
> Send you my words for messengers
> The way I shall not pass along. . . .
>
> Since I can never see your face,
> And never shake you by the hand
> I send my soul through time and space
> To greet you. You will understand.

From about 1919 one of Katie's Jewish friends, Vera Somerfield, became a friend of his. She was ten years older than he, and painted and sketched. After a disastrous first marriage, in 1923 she married Frank Strawson (born Strauss), a director of the publishers Gollancz. Gerald and Vera developed a curious, bantering friendship, the earnest student writing letters to her that were part aphorisms, part reading-lists, part reproofs for what he considered to be her worldly, frivolous way of life. His cocky, know-all tone would have been irritating were it not that in one of his first letters he asked encouragingly about her painting, 'done *any* work?' and then said 'I'm v. tired & have had a heavy, heavy day. I always mean to say so much but when it comes to writing I say nothing.'[20] His usual opening to her was 'Thank you, Madam, for your letter'. But often he does not sign his name, except by a tiny initial g, right at the foot of the page, or in a corner, or even on the back: it is almost as if he did not have much confidence in his identity.

He tested his principles against hers, in deadly seriousness, but feeling secure enough in her affection to tease her. He tossed out, raw and fierce, the ideas that were beginning to shape his life. On classical education: 'it takes off the tip of the imagination. Blake, Schubert, Dickens, Shaw, Cobbett, Clare. A few of the uneducated people! Of course, when you make yr own education its splendid. But disciplined education is foul & wicked.'[21] He refers to his 'violent socialistic tendencies and aversion to uncles'[22] (which puts the Leverson tobacco merchants in their place). He has no time for ceremonies,

[20] 22 December 1919.
[21] 22 December 1919.
[22] 24 February 1920.

vanity, or show. Mention of a wedding causes him to quote from Hardy's *Inter-lopers at the Knap*: 'why should a woman dress up like a rope-dancer because she's going to do the most solemn deed of her life except dying?' The consecration of a bishop brought to his mind 'Ceremony was but devis'd at first /To set a gloss on faint deeds, hollow welcomes' from *Timon of Athens*. Race-crowds in York drove him to 'song': 'Never have I been to races; /Well I know them from the faces/ Of the swine who haunt such places.'[23]

The pair recommended books to each other. It was natural for him, after coming under Boughton's influence, to suggest Morley's *Cobden* and Hudson's *A Shepherd's Life*. He enjoyed Benvenuto Cellini's autobiography, while poking fun at the rather biblical Everyman translation. He deplored Arnold Bennett's lack of ideals in *The Old Wives' Tale*, but wanted to know of any connection with George Peele's comedy (1595) of the same name. Romain Rolland's *Jean-Christophe*, a novel about a composer, roused him to laugh and blush alternately as he read of 'the tremblings, intoxications, profound emotions . . . Oh! the lack of humour & the eternal parallels & similes; the heavy moralising. Thank God for Thomas Hardy & a little dignity.'[24] A performance of J. M. Barrie's rather fey *Mary Rose* he found 'amazingly beautiful'. He was 'bitterly disappointed in 'the new Masefield' [*Reynard the Fox?*]: 'he used to deal with great problems of human nature. Now it's only steeple chasing.' [25]

Vera's travels abroad earned only his scorn. 'Your effusions about Vence are most dull,' he told her. [26] His reading of Yeats's *Ideas of Good and Evil* must have confirmed his low opinion of cities. He spent his own holidays in pastoral England and Wales. 'Great Somerford is a tiny little English village. Pigs, fields, thatched cottages, lanes, an Inn, a parson, squire, & about two hundred inhabitants – no cinemas, theatres or barrel organs. Perfect quiet – heavenly.'[27] Another holiday meant he could see 'all the places of interest. Malvern, Bredon, Gloster, Worcester, Tewkesbury etc etc.'[28] He spoke of folk dancing from experience of having seen 'the real thing'. Going again to Glastonbury in 1920 he impressed on Vera that Boughton's music-making was not an attempt to compete with professionalism: its importance was that the people made music themselves. 'How wonderful it wd be if every village were a Glastonbury.'[29]

He dismissed as of no interest a programme without a 'single native work'. He wondered if she knew of 'any intelligent persons in London at present' who would go to the English Singers concert of Morley, Weelkes, Wilbye, Bateson, Gibbons, and Purcell. He heard Elgar's *The Dream of Gerontius*, which he was 'old-fashioned enough to think fine'[30] (Elgar's music was out of favour in

[23] 24 May 1921.
[24] 10 March 1921.
[25] 24 November 1920.
[26] 24 February 1920.
[27] 6 April 1920.
[28] 29 July 1920.
[29] 19 June 1920.
[30] 24 November 1920.

the 1920s). He danced 'incessantly' for several days on account of the success of Holst's 'great work' [The Planets]. Butterworth's music he considered summed up 'our countryside as very little else has ever done'. But, surprisingly, he had his Berlioz period (he found his Faust 'grander than ever'), telling Vera that 'all' he wanted her to bring him from Paris was full scores of the operas Benvenuto Cellini and Les Troyens; The Childhood of Christ and the Te Deum!

Holst's name (as un-English-sounding as Finzi) led him to a thought that was to become a lifetime preoccupation. He quoted from Vaughan Williams's article (July 1920) in the newly founded Music & Letters that Holst was English since the family had been in England more than a hundred years. 'There is a good deal of unclear thinking prevalent on the subject of race and nationality,' Vaughan Williams had written. 'Everyone is to a certain extent of mixed race.' 'You may as well learn it by heart,'[31] Gerald commanded Vera, pointing out that Holst was no more German than Grieg was Scottish.

As for the Russian ballet, which he teased her for liking, 'the movement is spent', he declared in 1922. (He had seen it in June 1921.) He put both Vera and Charpentier in their places: 'You are a fool about Louise [just revived at Covent Garden]. Louise is the property of arty, sentimental women . . . La Bohème, that Bull's body for every matador critic, is superior in nearly every way. . . . If you imagine Louise is musically progressive you'll have a great many shocks yet.' Then he produces his own shock, for not everyone in 1920 would have considered Delius progressive: 'Wait until you hear Delius' opera A Village Romeo and Juliet in London this season. That'll wake you up.'[32]

On the back of a small, black-bordered sheet of Birkholt paper Gerald wrote three times the initials RVW and the name Holst, and added Butterworth, Parry, Elgar, Gurney – and 'Hurrah!' On the front he pasted a cutting: 'If the British people have a defect it is that they are wanting in industry – Lord Robert Cecil,' and in his own hand 'Like the British workman, it is thoroughly efficient – it does its job well – advertisement for Sunlight soap.' The paper is from a collection he was gathering of comments on the English character, some cut out, some copied from books, periodicals, newspapers. They show Gerald's wide, serious reading, his curiosity, his observation of contradictions, his instinct to hoard and preserve, and his conscious investigation of what it means to be English. He also began a collection of poems.

Bairstow was encouraging, assuring Mrs Finzi he would do what he could for her boy 'if I never received a cent for it. . . . One can help the real thing when there is a chance to do.'[33] He was as good as his word. Gerald's setting of Christina Rossetti's poem 'Before the paling of the stars' was the anonymous 'carol' sung at York Minster evensong during the week 26 December 1920. It was also sung there, named, on 30 December 1922 and several times after. On

---

[31] 24 November 1920.
[32] 24 February 1920.
[33] 8 August 1920.

14 February 1922 Parry's 'Jerusalem' in Gerald's scoring was given at a Leeds Philharmonic Society concert, 'effectively orchestrated by an anonymous hand'.[34] Bairstow's later pupils sometimes heard him say about Gerald: 'if only we could combine that boy's ideas with my technique!'[35]

Gerald had a week of solid concert-going in London to the British Music Society's inaugural Congress in June 1921. Three names he came across that week were to be part of his life. He heard Adrian Boult conduct and Harold Samuel play, he read programme notes by R. O. Morris.

There was no doubt where his musical heart lay. When he and his mother were on holiday in Gloucestershire in Spring 1921, they 'paid a visit to Vaughan Williams's birthplace – a little village called "Down Ampney". His father had the living about 40 years ago. So we rang the vicarage bell & delighted the vicar by telling him that the house was the birthplace of a celebrity. (He hadn't even heard of RVW!) . . . I was shown over the house from top to bottom so that there cd be no chance of missing the room where our hero was born! Many will make the pilgrimage but we are the first!!'[36]

Finzi's devotion to Vaughan Williams is apparent all through his life and work. The older man was not at the time the towering figure that the great middle symphonies were to make him. But the first performance of the *Tallis Fantasia* in 1910 had sent Ivor Gurney and Herbert Howells pacing the streets of Gloucester, unable to sleep. Vera remembered that at Glastonbury Vaughan Williams handed Gerald an unsealed note (which Gerald naturally peeped at) to give to Boughton 'to introduce Mr Finzi. He is one of us.' Heady moment for an aspiring composer! Certainly, after hearing *On Wenlock Edge* there, Gerald took himself to every Vaughan Williams first performance he could.

1920, GURNEY'S 'SLEEP'

For all that, Gerald's moment on the road to Damascus was his discovery of Ivor Gurney's song 'Sleep'. Gurney's *Five Elizabethan Songs* were published in 1920, and Gerald took them along to Bairstow, as he did any new publications of interest; Elsie Suddaby sang them in her lesson. 'I remember saying of "Sleep",' Gerald recorded, 'one has the feeling that the man who wrote that can't live long – there was such intensity contained in lyric form.'

Perhaps there was more to it, so strong was Finzi's identification with this song. 'O let my joys have some abiding' runs Fletcher's passionate last line. What does abide, this bereaved young man might well ask – who had lost father, three brothers, teacher, and who had already had to move from London to Camberley to Switzerland to Harrogate. The song posed and answered his question: it was at once the search and the haven: music abides. Again he learnt that the creative artist has the chance of immortality.

Discovering that the songwriter was also a poet, he got hold of Gurney's

34 *Yorkshire Post*, 15 February 1922.
35 Letter from H. Watkins Shaw, 29 August 1980.
36 4 April 1921.

two war-volumes, *Severn and Somme* and *War's Embers*, and read those loving evocations of the West Country, written mostly in the trenches from, in Gurney's own words, 'the central fires of secret memory'.[37] He too, like Gurney, would 'go climb my little hills to see Severn, and Malverns, May Hill's tiny grove'.[38]

So in August 1921 he took the road from Gloucester to Ross, turned off into the lanes and climbed up May Hill. He saw Wales to the west and before him the Severn winding down to the sea with Gloucester Cathedral backed by the Cotswolds and Gurney's Cranham Woods. He looked east over to Chosen Hill and Bredon Hill. He stood by the 'tiny grove' of pines planted for Queen Victoria's golden jubilee 'that Gloster dwellers/'Gainst every sunset see', and took snapshots of Vera Strawson and a friendly donkey. He got to know Mrs Brace, a cottager who lived on the slope, and in approved fashion expected her to sing him folksongs. In that rich country, fruit lay ripe on the ground for the taking, and with his keen vegetarian's palate he savoured the apples in the villages round about.

He resolved to make his home in the countryside that had nurtured Parry, Elgar, Vaughan Williams, and Ivor Gurney.

[37] 'That county'.
[38] 'The fire kindled'.

CHAPTER TWO

Gloucestershire

1922–26

Gerald and his mother moved south in spring 1922. In his luggage he took with him some sketches and songs.

The earliest song lasts just eight bars, a simple hymn-like setting of Herrick's elegy 'Upon a child', poignantly dedicated to Mrs Finzi, the mother of three dead children. There is a pert touch to Herrick's 'The fairies', de la Mare's 'O dear me', and Stevenson's 'Time to rise' that thankfully did not reappear, though the beefy setting of Herrick's 'Ceremonies' foreshadows the later rumbustious but catchy 'Rollicum-rorum'. Finzi had his brief Celtic period, from which come two nondescript settings of Padraic Colum. More adventurous are two of Fiona Macleod: 'The twilit waters' has an independent atmospheric accompaniment, low vocal tessitura, and sensitive declamation; in 'The reed player', ambitiously set for voice with strings, wind, and brass, the contours look forward to A Severn Rhapsody. Settings of Chaucer's 'Rondel' and W. H. Davies's 'The battle' (between a lily and a rose) are both exercises in archaism. 'The cupboard' (R. Graves) is a ballad whose dramatic style and dialogue Finzi would not attempt again until 'Channel firing'.

Raleigh's 'Even such is time' ('Epitaph') holds the seeds of later Finzi. Time's progression stimulates marching beats within changing metres, parallel chords in contrary motion, and a climax clearing from D minor to a triumphant D major, ending on a chord of A minor. The song is earnest, elevated, but directionless, though it foreshadows the second Milton Sonnet. It also shows how theoretical Finzi's writing was at this time; he intended it for unison male voices, but the compass is such that Bairstow pencilled in 'bass' and 'tenor' alternately. (Finzi's tiny crabbed manuscript must have given Bairstow many a headache.) In the same style is Herrick's 'Time was upon the wing'; it is for baritone with a central unaccompanied female chorus, and ends with a pause sign and 'attacca' – was it at one time intended for the Requiem da camera?

Christina Rossetti was the poet who most engaged Finzi at this time. The carol, 'Before the paling of the stars', performed in 1920 at York Minster, was charming enough for the organist of Vassar College in the USA (had Bairstow recommended it to him?) to write in November 1923 asking for an alto part at the climax; Finzi provided a couple of bars, but thought it 'not worth while bothering over'. In his Op. 1, Ten Children's Songs, he set poems from Rossetti's Sing-Song: A Nursery Rhyme-Book. Finzi said he composed them about 1921, but they were variously revised, one was rewritten, and some were altered from unison to two-part songs (see Appendix 1). They are slight, attractive, and neater than the unpublished songs; in the hypnotic 'Lullaby' lies the germ of the great 'Fear no more the heat o' the sun'. There are two instrumental pieces, a 'Bird' Allegro in the 'Toy' style, and 'A passer-by', Finzi's only tone-poem (perhaps a piano draft for orchestra) based on Bridges' 'Whither, O splendid ship'; this opens in Lisztian, modernistic style but subsides into trudging chords and a bland apotheosis. It is perhaps chance that the poets of Finzi's best early songs are his contemporaries. The setting of de la Mare's 'Some one' is genuinely spooky, and Edward Thomas's 'Tall nettles' and John Freeman's 'English hills', both evocative pastoral poems, prompt ruminative songs in a style Finzi was later to make more positively his own. He set lines and phrases of many other poems, but left only fragments.

One mature feature is present in embryo in several of these songs: the mood and figuration change for the last lines, such as 'O steadfast onward tide' ('The twilit waters') into a plainer, simpler, more measured statement. This has the summing-up, clinching effect of the final rhyming lines of a sonnet, and was to become a Finzi characteristic.

By Footpath and Stile, Op. 2

The main work, a song-cycle for baritone and string quartet, Finzi called By Footpath and Stile (1921–22). He may have had Vaughan Williams's On Wenlock Edge and Butterworth's Love blows as the Wind blows as models for chamber music song-cycles, but he marks out his own poetic territory: not Housman or Henley for him. Instead he chose six poems (see Appendix 1) by Thomas Hardy: 'Paying calls', 'Where the picnic was', 'The oxen', 'The master and the leaves', 'Voices from things growing in a churchyard', and 'Exeunt omnes', all published in or after 1914, when Hardy was in his seventies (a setting of 'My spirit will not haunt the mound' remained unpublished). The poems, which deal with death, loss, doubt, the past, withdrawal, and separation, are from three collections; so the sequence of thought was Finzi's own. In the fifth, 'Voices from things growing in a churchyard', it is the dead, now living on in daisies, ivy, woodbine, who are content, and speak 'in a radiant hum'; but still the music begins bleakly and ends inconclusively. Many an adolescent indulges in black feelings but Finzi had personal experience, and his choice of the final song, 'Exeunt omnes', makes this explicit: 'And I still left where the fair was?' He was young and Hardy was old, but he too had cause to feel himself a sole survivor.

The voices of composer and poet are quiet, almost domestic. Their dead are 'at home'. There is a long instrumental introduction. Finzi's word-setting, though not yet strictly syllabic, is too respectful to sound free. His care for meaning, however, is shown in his stress on 'in these years' (that is, during the 1914–18 war) in 'The oxen'; but other felicities in this and in the first song date from his part revision in the 1940s. He does not shirk the unpleasant realism of 'kennels dribble dankness' any more than in later songs he was to shirk 'the glebe cow drooled' or 'thy worm is my worm'. His modal harmony is limited, and often oscillates across two chords, as if locked in time, to and fro, never forwards. He generates excitement by working up a figure rather than by chord-changes, and much of the texture is formed by imitation. The vigour in 'The master and the leaves', though over-busy, is welcome. There is a poetic nightjar, and a rustic fiddler tuning his open strings at the Dorchester fair – more obvious word-painting than Finzi allowed himself in later songs.

The final verse brings an image to be found right through Finzi's output. Any words that suggest the inexorable passing of time – as here 'I mark your early going And that you'll soon be clay' – bring the hint, almost the threat, of a march: common time, regular beats, the bass moving by scale or in ostinato. Finzi may have inherited this from Holst, possibly from the 'sad procession' in Holst's *Dirge for Two Veterans* (1914). Another striking image in *By Footpath and Stile* comes from the opening of 'Voices': a dark sustained stubborn sound for viola – a melancholy undertow – beneath the broken figures of 'all day cheerily, all night eerily'. The work is a true song-cycle, in that the last song recapitulates three earlier ones, as if to review the dead. In sum, the greyness of the gentle music seems due more to inhibition than to reticence. Finzi had found his poet, but not yet his own voice.

It is a relief to discover a happy little single song dated 1921, Shanks's 'As I lay in the early sun', its euphoric accompaniment suggesting swings and cuckoos. Finzi revised this, possibly during his last year. A problem for anyone studying his output is the gap – sometimes of years – between his first and last thoughts about even the shortest piece. So where to place it in his chronology, at its inception or when it takes its final form? In this case, exceptionally, both early and late versions survive, showing how in the second verse he lightened the piano part, adding imitation, and extended the vocal phrase 'and all laughter . . .'.

1922, PAINSWICK

While looking for a house, Gerald and his mother stayed as paying guests with a Mrs Champion at Chosen Hill Farm, a handsome house on the slopes at Churchdown (known locally as Chosen) midway between Gloucester and Cheltenham. The name was already part of English music, for Herbert Howells had inscribed his A minor Piano Quartet (1916) to 'the hill at Chosen and Ivor Gurney who knows it'. Soon Gerald found King's Mill, one of the oldest, most beautiful houses in Painswick, and moved in during July 1922. At the time it was dilapidated, and so not expensive – 'a rambling ruin with a stream running through it' Vera Strawson called it. But Gerald saw its potential, furnished it sparsely and simply, planted a hedge for privacy and a herb garden to provide flavouring. He worked in a big room with the long windows through which the weavers had passed the cloth in the days when Painswick was a flourishing centre of the wool trade. At first he put his 'socialist' principles into practice, and declared that he and his mother would do all their own cooking, housework, and gardening. But his theories often ran ahead of his experience, and he soon discarded that idea: it would give him too little time to compose. Bairstow chose a Broadwood baby grand for the new house. He now sought Gerald's advice, asking him to make suggestions for a historical programme of early British choral music. 'I do miss you,' he added. Gerald hopefully sent him an anthem of his own, which Bairstow promised to perform.

That year, 1922, the Three Choirs Festival was at Gloucester, under Herbert Brewer. Gerald, having scored 'Jerusalem', must have felt a link with Parry, and at the festival he heard *Blest Pair of Sirens*, the *Ode to Music*, and the Symphonic Variations. A tablet, unveiled that year in the Cathedral to Parry's memory, called him simply 'Hubert Parry – Musician': all, Gerald felt, that was needed. There were first performances of works by young men who were to become his friends: *Sine Nomine* by Herbert Howells and the *Colour Symphony* by Arthur Bliss. London was now accessible, and Gerald began to go up to concerts. He would catch the train from Stroud, often walking back the same night to King's Mill over the hills under the stars.

1923 began, he told Vera, with 'the most terrible news I have had for five years' [that is, since Farrar's death]. 'Ivor Gurney has gone mad'.[1] Gurney's health and mind had finally given way, and just before Christmas 1922 he was taken from Gloucester to the City of London mental hospital at Dartford, Kent. In fifty years, Gerald declared enthusiastically if wildly, his songs would have replaced Schubert's. 'In his line, Gurney is *supreme*. I always said he wdn't live long – his work was such a consummation.' He goes on 'Butterworth, Ed Thomas . . .', perhaps to link their short lives, but the last page is missing. He had begun the letter 'My poor V, As usual, yr generalizations about Art are wide of the mark.' He hotly disputed that musicians were 'weedy' compared with athletes, instancing the long lives of Verdi and Byrd (and predicting that 'RVW will get to eighty'). 'Art,' he insisted, 'is ordinary conversation & like speech is to bring affinities into spiritual contact.' Affinities were closest between those who shared custom and climate, 'in other words *environment* (Heredity, in this case, is only "rooted" environment)'. And so, he concluded grandly, creative artists represent their civilization.

In April 1923 he attended the Stinchcombe Festival, at Dursley, near Stroud. Diana Awdrey (later Oldridge) organized it on the pattern of Vaughan Williams's Leith Hill festivals, where local amateur choral societies competed and then joined in a final concert. Vaughan Williams was judging, and Adrian Boult was on the committee. A couple of weeks previously Gerald had heard Vaughan Williams's Mass in G minor and written on his programme simply 'What a man!' He had heard the *London Symphony* during 1920, and been to the first performance of the *Pastoral* at the Queen's Hall in 1922, and then gone to Bournemouth to hear the composer conduct it himself.

At the 1923 Three Choirs Festival he found the new things (Bax, Alexander Brent Smith, Malcolm Davidson) disappointing, he told Vera, but 'no, never

fear: I'm not jealous. The better they are, the more I love them.'[2] He and his
mother overstepped their budget of five pounds by ten shillings, 'but it was
worthwhile doing things in the grand manner & having nice meals & two
coffees. On the Thursday morning there was rather a crush so we waited until
nearly everyone had left the Cathedral. Lo & behold! Elgar walked down the
aisle & started talking a few yards in front of us. Need I say that he wears
stays?'

He began going to local festivals of folk-dancing, and later he joined a
sword-dance team called Greensleeves. A fellow dancer, S. W. Ranger, recalled
that he was always alone, was very quiet, and that no-one knew he was a
composer. Remarkably, Ranger remembered what a *bad* dancer Gerald was,
with no co-ordination, no memory for pattern. But he was a delightful
companion. On one occasion they went for a long walk together, Gerald
singing folksongs all day.

Curwen had accepted some of Finzi's songs, and 'The cupboard' gained
brief but favourable reviews in *The Sackbut* and *The Musical Times*. He had obviously had things turned down, and must have written indignantly to Bairstow,
who wrote back 'Your experiences are the experiences of all other musicians,'
and told him to ask Vaughan Williams how many times he had had his
compositions returned! He explained that with a first composition a young
composer had no reputation to back him − 'there is nothing more to say
except that I did mention you to RVW'.[3]

On 24 October 1923 the British Music Society put on *By Footpath and Stile* at 6
Queen Square, Bloomsbury, performed by Sumner Austin and the Charles
Woodhouse String Quartet. It received five reviews, all favourable and encouraging. *The Times* [Fox Strangways] thought that with a 'good deal more grip
[it] would stand as a not unworthy parallel to *Wenlock Edge*'. The *Daily Mail* said
it needed to be sung 'with more variety and lightness,' which, together with a
remark by Bairstow − 'you will learn the ways of the London pro. before
long'[4] − suggests that Gerald was not happy with the performance. His uncle
William read *The Times* and wrote him a pleased but stuffy letter that provoked
Gerald into fulminating to Vera 'in future, *none* of the family will be told about
my doings'.[5] The BMS thought well enough of the work to perform it again in
Liverpool on 18 February 1927.

Towards the end of 1923 Gerald plucked up courage to write to Vaughan
Williams, asking his permission to use 'The truth sent from above', a folksong
Vaughan Williams had collected through Mrs Ella Leather in Weobly (not far
from May Hill). Gerald had already composed his own piece so it was fortu-
nate that Vaughan Williams replied: 'As far as I am concerned, with pleasure.
But please ask Mrs Leather as well.'[6] He added that Mr Finzi ought to know

2   7 September 1923.
3   2 June 1923.
4   4 November 1923.
5   3 November 1923.
6   17 November 1923.

that he himself had used the tune in his Fantasia on Christmas Carols. Gerald noted his reply at the foot of Vaughan Williams's letter (a habit of his). 'Of course' he knew VW's work, 'but my thing is so slight that I did not think it worth while apologising for doing the same.' The word 'slight' was a change from 'insignificant'. The alteration reveals much: Finzi would never consider himself a major, or a great, composer. Equally, he would never feel himself – or any other artist – to be insignificant.

VAUGHAN AND TRAHERNE

Once settled in Painswick, he turned to the seventeenth-century poets Henry Vaughan (already set by Elgar and Parry) and Thomas Traherne, and composed two motets for chorus and orchestra, planned as two of six anthems. His setting of Vaughan's 'Up to those bright and gladsome hills' (Psalm 121) is conventional for all its seven-four signature, but sensitively composed for a cathedral acoustic – he dedicated both motets to Bairstow. (The quotation from Byrd's 'Attollite portas' between the last two verses is probably a private tribute to Bairstow, who was researching the period.) The second motet is more ambitious. Finzi chose Traherne's poem 'The recovery' (the one that begins 'Sin! wilt thou vanquish me!'). It is strenuous music, with Hymn of Jesus clashing triads and a con fuoco trumpet solo. He sends the sopranos up to B on the syllables 'thee' and '[di]-vine', one of several examples of impracticality that drew from Bairstow the rebuke that 'voices, like feet, come in different sizes'. His ambitious orchestra included three flutes, three trombones, tuba, and organ, though he allowed that instruments might be omitted, and he published the motets in 1925 with organ accompaniment.

In 'The brightness of this day' (the last half of Vaughan's 'The true Christmas') there is much that Finzi, with his dislike of ceremony, might identify with. Christ's life was a 'check to pomp and mirth' and the true Christmas is not owed to 'music, masque nor showe' but to quiet humility. He sets these words in free declamation for baritone over a pedal, and then for the rest of the poem uses Mrs Leather's tune antiphonally for double choir. All three pieces have marching basses moving by step, familiar ('I mark your early going') from 'The master and the leaves' (see p. 24) and probably again influenced by Holst, whose psalm 'To my humble supplication', in similar idiom, Finzi heard at the 1922 Three Choirs Festival.

The conjunction of Finzi with Vaughan and Traherne had a larger significance than is to be found in just these settings. In the preface to his Vaughan collection he found the Latin verse 'Ad Posteros', a warning to consider posterity: time soon forgets (see p. 122). As for Traherne (1637–74), Finzi had come across his poem in Bertram Dobell's collection, published in 1903. He would have been drawn to the romantic story of the obscure clergyman of Hereford who died at the age of thirty-seven. For over two hundred years Traherne had been lost: little was published during his life: 'centuries had drawn their curtains round him'. His poems were discovered in a notebook picked up for a few pence on a bookstall in the winter of 1896–97. Dobell identified and published them two years after Finzi's birth, so that when Finzi was twenty-two, Traherne was, so to speak, only nineteen, and had never been set to music. (Finzi in a programme note to *Dies Natalis* later described Traherne's disappearance in what became a favourite quotation of his from Arthur Quiller-Couch: 'there are springs and streams which suddenly dive into chasms and are lost – to emerge into daylight at long distances, having pierced their own way through subterranean channels'.)

Dobell in his introduction says that Traherne's parents failed to appreciate that their child was an uncommon type,

> and that the ordinary methods of dealing with children were inapplicable in his case. His early and innocent thoughts, he says, were quite obliterated by the influence of a bad education. He found that those around him were immersed in the trivial cares and vanities of common life; that they were wholly wrapped up in the outward show of things.

How eagerly, after Camberley and Kate, Gerald would have responded to that!

Dobell quotes the passage where Traherne debates with himself whether he should pursue worldly prosperity, at the cost of his higher aspirations:

> I was so resolute that I chose rather to live upon ten pounds a year, and to go in leather clothes and to feed upon bread and water, so that I might have all my time clearly to myself, than to keep many thousands per annum in an estate of life where my time would be devoured in care and labour.

Finzi's private income was more than ten pounds a year; but here was support for his resolution only to compose, not to teach or to do any other money-making task.

Dobell remarks Blake's and Wordsworth's affinities with Traherne and advises his reader to peruse the *Immortality Ode*. He quotes the first three paragraphs from the *Centuries* (not published until 1908), beginning 'Will you see the infancy of this sublime and celestial greatness?' It was in 1923 that Finzi set Traherne's 'Recovery'; and in September that year he begged Vera Strawson 'please make every effort' to get him a copy of *Centuries*. By 15 November 1923 he had it. So came the first stirrings of *Dies Natalis*.

A Severn Rhapsody, Op. 3; Requiem da Camera

That year, 1923, he composed *A Severn Rhapsody*, dedicated to Vera, and prefaced by Rupert Brooke's: '. . . Oh! yet Stands the Church clock at ten to three? And is there honey still for tea?' That quotation would fit awkwardly into Finzi's later ethos, except for Brooke's love of England and the fact that he, like Farrar, died in the war. The *Rhapsody* is Finzi's first instrumental composition of any length, modestly scored for chamber orchestra, and in the tradition of Delius, Butterworth, and early Vaughan Williams.

Was the reference in the opening bars to Butterworth's 'cherry-tree' motif (see the second bar of Ex. 4.3d) a conscious tribute? Probably, since Finzi used it again in his 1925 song 'Only the wanderer' (see p. 35). But in Butterworth's song 'Loveliest of trees' the phrase is initially a single, graphic line, and in his *Shropshire Lad Rhapsody* it is a chain of consonant thirds, though the themes are developed to strong, intense climaxes. In *A Severn Rhapsody*, a D minor phrase tugs against a bass E flat; Finzi, however, makes little of the dramatic potential of that, and not until his final bars – too late – is the implicit conflict resolved. The *Rhapsody* suggests a probing but tentative personality. The often-changing metre makes for pliant rhythm; and there is melancholy in the opening wind sound. The music's wistful character derives, too, from discords resolving onto open fourths and fifths, and from the frequent use of triads in first or second inversion. The texture is freely polyphonic, and the melodies are seamlessly extended. At the climax, the second 'theme' briefly becomes bass to the first (four bars before F), and a wrench from G minor to A major, gawky but full of character, opens onto two confident, fully scored, diatonic bars. Towards the end comes another echo of Butterworth, or perhaps of Vaughan Williams's 'Clun': oscillating chords rock to and fro, flute and cor anglais float 'with great peace' over them.

Much in the *Rhapsody*, as in all Finzi's early music, is influenced by Vaughan Williams, particularly by the *Pastoral Symphony*: the rounded shape of his melodies, often pentatonic, often running between duplets and triplets; the way the melodies interweave, grow different tails, change intervals and time values, flexibly evolving while keeping their basic shape. The *Rhapsody* demonstrates Finzi's affinity with the older composer, and how impressionable, how receptive, he was. What it lacks is the massive power behind such works as the *Tallis Fantasia* and the *Pastoral Symphony*, the grasp of form, the firm underlying planes of tonality and modality. But however warmly Finzi admired Vaughan Williams, he was his own man in vocal music. For Vaughan Williams, heightened emotion finds expression in melisma; Finzi was to adhere to the one-note-to-one-syllable system.

In 1923 Finzi set what was probably to him Hardy's most significant poem, which gathers round it a nexus of allusions and emotions. Hardy called it 'In time of "The Breaking of Nations"' (taking his title from Jeremiah 51.20), and wrote it at the turn of 1915–16, when the *Saturday Review* asked him for a few encouraging lines in the black days of the war. He recalled an incident of 1870 during the Franco-Prussian war, when he had watched a man and his old horse harrowing a field, then discovered that the battle of Gravelotte had been fought that same day. In the Great War Hardy reflected on the contrast between devastation and the lasting country things – the cultivation of the land, the bonfire of couchgrass, the young lovers – and sent off the three verses that begin 'Only a man harrowing clods'. Now in pastoral Gloucestershire Finzi set them for baritone and piano. (He must have shown the song to Vaughan Williams, for at the end of the 1923 autograph he wrote 'RVW suggests' over an alternative ending.)

In his later revision, Finzi kept the images of the distant bugles and the plodding horse, but rewrote the second and third verses. To characterize the couple in their timeless love comes a hint of what may be called Finzi's 'dance of delight', instrumental voices duetting in thirds and sixths (Ex. 2.1) as the poem reaches the triumphant conclusion: 'War's annals will cloud into night Ere their story die.' The song is more earnest than inspired, but central to an understanding of Finzi's mind.

Ex. 2.1

He completed the *Requiem da Camera* for baritone solo, chorus, and chamber orchestra in 1924, making four movements (though by 1928 he had discarded the first version of the Hardy). The Prelude is scored for the same orchestra as *A Severn Rhapsody*, with shapes and rhythms now becoming familiar: overlapping imitations, inversions, the 'cherry tree' phrase, treading bass scales, oscillating harmonies, all to be used in the following movements. Towards the end of the Prelude a long cantilena for oboe, *senza nuances*, over deep tolling bells is Finzi's most overt tribute to Vaughan Williams, to the *senza misura* solo that opens the last movement of the *Pastoral Symphony*. Next come verses from Masefield's 'August, 1914', of which, when it was published in the *English Review* in the autumn of 1914, Elgar declared 'that is the best thing written yet. . . . We are fighting for the *country*' (though for his own war 're-quiem' he later turned to Binyon). Finzi's chorus enters unaccompanied with 'How still the quiet cornfield is tonight'. Such a magical passage as Example 2.2 might come from his *Intimations* of 1950.

Ex. 2.2

A crescendo of bitonal chords over a five-four ostinato ('century after century') brings together Finzi's 'march of time' and his horror of war, in a strong controlled climax: the sudden entry of 'Death like a miser' is shocking. Then follows the Hardy song 'Only a man harrowing clods', already discussed. To close his Requiem, Finzi chose W. W. Gibson's 'Lament' from *Whin*. Through Gibson, Finzi asks the same question as at the end of *By Footpath and Stile*: 'we who are left', how shall we go on living? and tenderly broods over the 'little things': the sun, the rain, a singing bird. The movement ends with the *senza nuances* cantilena now in duet for clarinet and horn, and an evocation of the Last Post.

This non-religious Requiem is a restrained, even monotonous, work, personal and quiet. Finzi dedicated it to Farrar's memory, but surely also had in mind other artists – Butterworth, Edward Thomas, Gurney, Brooke – killed or maimed in the war. It is more than a tribute: the mainspring of Finzi's devotion to his art was his recognition of his own escape from war's carnage. All his life he was touched by the pathos of artists who died young. It seems astonishing that later he wanted to withdraw his Requiem (it bears no opus number), though in his early days he did everything he could to publish it, among other things submitting it to the Carnegie Trust, who turned it down.

DETMAR BLOW

No doubt memories of the view from May Hill had gone into the making of *A Severn Rhapsody*. But there was another view of the river, from the terrace of a great house, which was by now part of Gerald's experience. He had come to know the Blows. Detmar Blow at the age of twenty-one had happened to meet the old John Ruskin in Abbeville Cathedral, and together they crossed France and journeyed to Italy, reading Gibbon, sketching, and gathering gentians. Home again, Detmar found himself admitted to the circle that included William Morris and Edward Burne-Jones. He became an architect, specializing in building private houses in the Arts and Crafts style, valuing traditional building methods, fitness for purpose, and the sensitive use of simple materials. In 1910 he married Winifred Tollemache, of Helmingham Hall, Suffolk, a descendant of the Keeper of the Privy Purse in the time of Henry I. In 1914 Detmar began building his own house, 'Hilles', on a ridge at Edge above the Severn. Gerald loved the story of how the site was chosen. Detmar's shepherd showed him where a vixen used to bring her cubs to play in the last light of the setting sun; there, on that sheltered spot, Detmar built his house. 'Hilles' was a bountiful, easy-going household of a scale and quality beyond anything Gerald had known; and exactly what he needed to unfurl his tight character.

He would walk the mile or two up from Painswick, lift the iron latch of the great fourteen-foot door into the stone-flagged hall, which welcomed clean or muddy boots, and at once be absorbed into the family activities. There might be a weeding party in the garden, or country dancing, or a game of highwaymen with the four children (the little boy Purcell among them, for Detmar claimed to be descended from Dr John Blow, who was 'succeeded' by Purcell). Winifred nursed and tended her children herself and regarded them, however young, as people, not to be banished to a nursery but to be brought up, Traherne-like, by example and persuasion. Above all, the parents fostered each child's individuality. At the time Gerald knew them, everyone – family, children, visitors, and domestics – ate together as part of Detmar's ideal of re-creating the feudal life. On Christmas Eve there was a huge tree, and (since Detmar was Lord of the Manor of Painswick) up to a hundred neighbours and tenants would come to receive presents, and to feast, and dance to his fiddle-playing or listen to the little organ. No-one who shared the lamplight and firelight of 'Hilles' ever forgot it. Winifred – secure in position, grand but casual in manner, her maternity absorbed in her own young children – was an altogether easier mother-figure for Gerald than anxious little Lizzie.

Gradually Gerald's circle grew to include Sydney Shimmin, who taught music at Cheltenham Ladies College; the Gloucester solicitor Jack Haines, friend of the Dymock poets Edward Thomas and Robert Frost, and himself a poet; and Jack Villiers, friend of the Blows. Though Gerald was neither the chairman nor the secretary, he was the driving force in the formation of a Painswick Music Club. The programme of the first concert, on 4 October 1924, casts back to Glastonbury: Elgar's Quartet, and On Wenlock Edge ('Vaughan Williams is now regarded as one of the greatest living composers,' the programme note rather belligerently stated). Mollie Hull, the wife of the Hereford Cathedral organist Percy Hull, played the piano with the Snow Quartet. Steuart Wilson sang, and in his solo group included Vaughan Williams's 'Evening Hymn' (Bridges) and Dowland's 'His golden locks' (Peele). At the next concert there was a Boyce Sonata, Howells's 'Chosen Hill' Quartet, and Gurney's 'I will go with my father a-ploughing'.

Gerald was now twenty-three. The shape of his future life can be discerned in the names he was drawing around him. To celebrate his birthday in July he went to the first public performance of Vaughan Williams's *Hugh the Drover*, given by the British National Opera Company. When that autumn he saw Vaughan Williams's *Shepherds of the Delectable Mountains* at the Victoria Rooms, Clifton, part of a festival organized by Napier Miles, he wrote on the programme: 'One of the greatest moments of my life'.

His songs 'The fairies' and 'Ceremonies' were performed by John Booth and Harold Craxton at the Wigmore Hall on 25 January 1924, when two songs by Rupert Erlebach were also given. Erlebach, who became secretary of the (Royal) Musical Association, was working in the Royal College of Music Union office, and was a link with Marion Scott. The young men became friendly and Erlebach's home provided a useful overnight bed for Gerald in London. Ursula Greville sang 'The cupboard' at the Albert Hall on 9 May 1925. Then on June 4 Dan Godfrey at Bournemouth gave the first performance of *A Severn Rhapsody*, which had won a Carnegie Award, ensuring publication, so following *A London Symphony* and *The Hymn of Jesus*. (Godfrey, Vaughan Williams, and Hugh Allen were the Carnegie examiners.) Stainer & Bell also accepted Finzi's motets.

Another Carnegie Award that year went to Ivor Gurney's chamber song-cycle *The Western Playland*. Marion Scott, Gurney's friend and confidante, had became the guardian of his manuscripts after his committal to the Dartford asylum. Gerald had heard of her from Ernest Farrar, whose violin pieces she had played. She had studied at the Royal College of Music, then led the Morley College orchestra under Holst, and formed her own string quartet, which specialized in contemporary English music. She was also a busy journalist. She co-founded the RCM Union, and through this befriended young students, giving many a chance to perform at her London home. She may well have been the moving force behind the première of By Footpath and Stile. Gerald sent her his motets and Severn Rhapsody, which she accepted with warm, shrewd praise. He enquired about Gurney's unpublished work; sensing his interest, she enlisted his help in copying string parts for The Western Playland. Nothing more came of his further suggestions at that time.

He also sent A Severn Rhapsody to Herbert Howells, and they met when Howells was spending a weekend at a hotel in Painswick early in 1925. The two young composers (Howells was nine years the elder) had much in common. Both loved Gloucestershire: Howells had been articled to Brewer of Gloucester Cathedral, and had known Gurney. Both were Carnegie prize-winners. Both venerated Vaughan Williams. Both were short men, sensitive, with a fierce, almost possessive love for English lyric poetry. In spite of all this – or perhaps even because of it – they were always a little uneasy in their relationship: each had his share of truculence. Gerald had lived so secluded a life that he was unusually intense, his views having been formed by his solitary reading. He was convinced that pastoral beauty was necessary for his inspiration, and felt he could compose only in sight of a ploughed field. The violinist Sybil Eaton, visiting Painswick to play for the music club, found him full of theories, and so keen to propagate them that he used to take an armful of leaflets on his walks and leave one on each gate and stile, spreading the gospel: they were, she remembered, not religious, but in some way ethical, maybe vegetarian – definitely 'on the side of the angels'. (Then, of course, he had to retrace his footsteps, to see if any had been taken.)

To a young man like Howells, without private means but with a wife and child to support, Gerald's life seemed enviable. To others he seemed poor, oppressed by his mother, and inclined to stick too closely to his self-imposed routine. Some found his dedication even absurd, thought he took himself too seriously – 'Gerald's world was Gerald's self', recalled Howells – and were shocked at the way he expected his mother to be subservient to his needs. She however was willing and eager, still speaking in awe of him as a genius. And she was happy: it was a time, she wrote later, which 'now seems to me like a dream – a happy peaceful dream . . . the dignity of the old Mill-House and the peace therein will never be forgotten'.[7]

For all that, it was an idyll that could not last. Two years earlier, when they had been at King's Mill only eighteen months, Gerald had written despairingly to Vera: 'I don't know what we're going to do or what is going to happen.

---

[7] Kate's papers.

Only quiet, peace & some freedom, O Lord. At present I feel like John Clare who wrote "Dear Sir, I am in a madhouse. I quite forget your name or who you are. You must excuse me, for I have nothing to communicate or tell of, and why I am shut up I don't know." Nor do I.'[8] He could not live with his mother for ever. Torn between loyalty to her and irritation at her fussy ways, he found himself locked in conflict, and nearing a breakdown. One of the first books he had recommended to Vera was Edmund Gosse's *Father and Son* (1907). He had already acted on the closing line: 'he took a human being's privilege to fashion his inner life for himself.' Now he must so fashion his outer life. As 1925 opened he put King's Mill on the market and arranged to make weekly visits to London for counterpoint lessons with R. O. Morris.

1925, R. O. MORRIS

Morris, then nearing forty, had a reputation as the country's best teacher, on the stricter side. In his *Contrapuntal Technique in the Sixteenth Century* (1922) he insisted that counterpoint should be studied in composers' works; and he set out his principles in his witty first chapter. There were, Morris pointed out, fifty-seven exceptions to Rule LX1 in a single Mass by Palestrina, 'and [quoting Luke 23. 31] if these things are done in the green tree, what shall be done in the dry?' Music written to meet text-book rules was 'a purely academic by-product'. So what to do? 'Follow Byrd and Palestrina, or follow Mr Rockstro and Professor Prout?' Gerald owned the book (Bairstow had told him in 1923 that 'it was just the thing'), and from it he would have learnt not to patronize earlier centuries, to distinguish between rhythm and metre, and to consider the effect of modes on the tonality of his own day. All the music examples were from genuine composers (except for the famous two from Bugsworthy's *Conceits and Vapours* Nos 10001 and 10002, which even honest Morris was forced to write himself – that alone would have endeared him to Gerald). There was, too, the added attraction that the Morrises were sharing the Vaughan Williamses' house in London at 13 Cheyne Walk, the two wives being sisters. So during the summer of 1925 Gerald went up to Morris for 'a short sharp course of 16th-Century Counterpoint'.

On 10 March 1925 Bairstow had kept his promise, and at the York Musical Society conducted Gerald's Two Motets. They were not altogether appreciated; so the splendid Bairstow repeated them at the end of the concert, and again at Leeds on 18 March. By then Gerald had left Painswick and moved back to Mrs Champion on Chosen Hill. He seemed undecided where to live, looking for a little house on his own. He sought advice from friends, and asked for an interview with Adrian Boult, then conducting the Birmingham Orchestra and fast becoming a champion of British music. Thinking the young man too hidden away in a backwater, Boult advised a move to London, and a life lived more among musicians. Gerald, who despised towns and celebrities, wrote on the back of a programme of a 1925 London concert: 'Oh the bloody fools &

---

8   3 November 1923.

humbugs in this concert hall! To think I'm probably going to have to live amongst them.'

In the meantime the Howells family came to Mrs Champion for five weeks holiday over August 1925. Herbert needed the balm: he was smarting from the reception given to his Second Piano Concerto, played by Harold Samuel, which a single violent objector in the audience turned into a sensation. His four-year-old daughter fell in love with Gerald and asked him to marry her. He couldn't do that, but he composed 'a little carol for Ursula Mary Howells' to Gurney's words 'Winter now has bared the trees' and dated it 16. xii. 25 (see p. 176). Writing to thank him, Howells reported 'and on Christmas Eve I told Gurney about it and it seemed to please him!'[9] It was the nearest Gurney and Finzi came to meeting.

In November 1925 By Footpath and Stile was published by Curwen, at Finzi's expense. With no practical experience he had not thought to provide a piano arrangement under the strings, for which Bairstow chided him. On 1 December A Severn Rhapsody and the Requiem Prelude were performed at the London Contemporary Music Centre, by the London Chamber Orchestra under Anthony Bernard. R. O. Morris wrote to tell Gerald that Vaughan Williams thought it the best music he heard that evening (the programme included van Dieren and Hindemith). 'Rather a shock to find (in the Sunday Times) that E[rnest] N[ewman] also liked it – but you'll live that down in time.'[10] Not only Newman: there were five other reviews, all encouraging, though they noted some influence of Vaughan Williams and Brahms. It was an achievement for this young outsider, without the backing of a school, a university, or a music college; without a father's guidance, or an inherited home or library. He was making his own way.

'Only the Wanderer'

There are several undated songs that Finzi may have composed in Gloucestershire; one dated 1925 is of Ivor Gurney's poem that begins 'Only the wanderer'. (Gurney's own setting was published in 1928.) Gurney, from the Somme, looked back longingly to his Severn meadows; Finzi, having decided to leave them, said goodbye in the finest song he had yet written, basing the piano part on the 'cherry-tree' theme of his Severn Rhapsody. Three of the four vocal phrases begin with a sustained note and a tied triplet (x); three contain rising fourths (y), each a third higher than the last; the last bars of the second and fourth phrases 'rhyme' (z), and the opening of the fourth line inverts in retrograde that of the second (w). Such internal reflections give poise to the flowing lyricism (Ex. 2.3). Under the first phrase, the bass rises in warmth; under the last, it sinks in farewell. The song, his only Gurney setting apart from the carol for Ursula Howells, is subtle and touching.

[9]   28 December 1925.
[10]   6 December 1925.

Ex. 2.3

&

So 1925 had been a good year. The next would contain his move to the London he disliked. On the last night he climbed to the church on the top of Chosen Hill as the villagers rang in the New Year. Had it been day he could have seen his own May Hill, Elgar's Malverns, Gurney's Gloucester. As it was midwinter, he looked at the frosty stars and heard the bells rising from the valleys and the plain below. He stood on his beloved Chosen Hill, ready for the next step in his 'chosen' life. Then with the ringers he went into the sexton's small stone cottage to enjoy the cider and the singing; but it was the moment of solitude – the bells, the stars, the quiet – that lodged in his imagination.

CHAPTER THREE

London

1926–28

Detmar Blow, as agent to the Duke of Westminster, found Gerald a house on Westminster land, 21 Caroline Street (now Terrace), near Sloane Square, a charming row of Georgian houses, two rooms to a floor. He moved early in February 1926, with Winifred Blow among his first visitors. In the basement he installed Edith and Wilf Pike. Edith had been working for Neville Finzi's family in Harley Street, but she had just married and was looking for a flat. Gerald and his mother went to see her; Mrs Finzi discussed the domestic details; Gerald asked only 'do you like cats?' She did, so she got the basement flat free and in exchange battled with cooking nut roasts and chestnut stew. Faced with macaroni, she tried to steam it, so Gerald sent her for a meal to Shearns, a famous vegetarian restaurant, to get ideas. Even the poor cats had to become vegetarian – they survived by catching mice. He had the house distempered white and put up blue curtains. A deal chest of drawers and wardrobe came from Painswick, and he bought chairs that Edith considered comfortable 'in theory'. On his mantelpiece, flanked by a collection of wine bottles of all shapes and sizes, were two Victorian photographs of the moon, fascinating brownish prints (while living here he drafted his setting of Hardy's 'At a lunar eclipse'). He worked during the mornings, in carpet slippers and open-necked shirt. In the afternoons he usually walked in Battersea Park – *always* on Thursdays, when the barrel organ played in Caroline Street.

Moving house from Painswick to London had entailed financial rearrangements. His mother made over to him some money left by *her* mother; and to make sure she could legally do this, she consulted her brother. His mind ran along lines other than Gerald's and – suspecting a less than studious motive for the move – he asked 'who is the woman?' Gerald was deeply affronted, and tried not to see or speak to him again. But the query, though grossly expressed, was not an unnatural thought: Gerald was twenty-five, and it seems there *was* as yet no 'woman'. His mother (after several years' searching) found herself a house at Hundon near Clare in Suffolk but used Caroline Street as her London *pied à terre*, as indeed Gerald used Hundon as his country home. Naturally she enjoyed her brothers' company (they all spoke with slight German accents) and liked dressing up in her pastel best when they called in a chauffeur-driven car to take her to the theatre, Gerald thunderously absent.

To his mother's sister, Aunt Hettie Schwabacher, the only member of his family Gerald respected, he wrote reasonably enough when she mooted the claims of family feelings, that 'the relatives are not much more than names to

me now. You know how environment changes us & in the last ten or twelve
years my way has so diverged from that of the family that I can't see the good
of "renewing acquaintanceship". . . . One of the Uncles once said (quite
rightly from his point of view) "If Gerald were not a lazy boy he would be
earning a pound a week." This is several years ago & yet now I don't earn £10
a year! This doesn't worry me in the least – the maximum work for a business
man is probably a minimum for one doing my sort of job.' It was, he thought,
only the 'print and publicity' of his recent December concert they liked, and
'the usual turn of bad criticism – if I even get as far – will make them quite
glad not to have known me!!!'[1]

'SW1 looks very nice,' he told her, 'but it's a stuffy, smoky place'; and no
sooner was he established there than he got out of it whenever he could. He
sent postcards to his mother from Leith Hill in March and from Winchester in
April 1926. Also in April he heard Boult give a concert in Andover. On Whit
Monday he was watching the Morris dancers at Bampton, Oxfordshire (the
last traditional group), and marked the tune 'Rufty-Tufty' on his programme.
In June he was on Bredon Hill. In July and August he went walking in East
Anglia (and again the following year, when he saw March Church). He
became so sunburnt that a little girl greeted him with 'Hullo, black man!'
Then he attended the second Dolmetsch Haslemere Festival: he found the
atmosphere there a trifle precious, so as he left he mischievously turned all the
signposts at the road junctions the wrong way round!

Nocturne (New Year Music), Op. 7; Prelude, Op. 25; Elegies, Op. 5

That year, 1926, he composed his Nocturne (New Year Music), for full orchestra
(he revised and cut it before its publication in 1950). Already in the motet
'The brightness of this day' he had chosen words decrying noisy celebration
of Christmas. Now, in an introduction to his Nocturne, he talks of 'sober sadness'. 'Here, then, are no merry-makings and such-like, but something of the
mood which is well suggested by the words of Robert Bridges – "when the
stars were shining, Fared I forth alone." ' Bridges' poem is 'Noel: Christmas
Eve, 1913', and 'sober sadness' are Charles Lamb's words, from 'New Year's
Eve' (Essays of Elia). Lamb ponders on the lapse of time as it affects man's mortal
duration, speaks of the First of January as 'the nativity of our common Adam',
and of the peal of bells ringing out the Old Year: 'I never hear it without a
gathering-up of my mind to a concentration of all the images that have been
diffused over the past twelvemonth.' Finzi loved New Year's Eve, even though
he found it the saddest time of the year; he brought his own recent Chosen
Hill experience together with Lamb's and Bridges', and created a desolate
introspective soulscape. The double-basses set up a deep brooding from
which emerge tentative gropings towards the light, in imitative phrases that

[1]   5 February 1926.

hardly ever repeat exactly. (In 1950 he deprecatingly referred to the texture as 'linear' and 'constipated'.[2]) A Brahmsian woodwind 'organ' chorus leads to warmer sounds. An all-embracing six-four tune, made solemn by timpani rolls, reaches a climax roughened by augmented triads, from which overlapping imitations descend. Humanity departs, and in the immensity of the dark night the observer listens and speculates, alone. Vaughan Williams, writing to Finzi in 1935, praised 'the true Hardy spirit'; and generously described the big central tune as 'just the sort of melody I have wanted to do all my life & have never brought off'[3] (he who had composed the 'Where the great vessel sailing' tune in the *Sea Symphony?*).

Between 1926 and 1929 Finzi drafted *The Fall of the Leaf*, though he repeatedly revised it and the scoring was incomplete at his death (see p. 253). In the 1920s he intended it as the third movement of a symphonic suite, *The Bud, the Blossom, and the Berry* and had quoted that phrase with its refrain 'Hey, down-a down derry' to Vera Strawson in 1922. The first movement was published after Finzi's death as Prelude. If as 'Bud' it was intended to represent Spring, it must be deemed a gloomy piece, unless it suggests the first dark stirrings of growth. The solos and more open texture of the middle section, and possibly the expansive flourish of the final bars, may date from Finzi's rescoring of the work for strings. Nocturne, Prelude and *The Fall of the Leaf* might be Finzi's version of Haydn's Seasons, his reaction to the cycles of the year. But *The Fall*, even in its final version, is a top-heavy piece, its powerful climaxes melodramatic rather than thematically motivated, though its opening – the leaf caught on its spin to earth – and the close of Saturn-like chords, are striking.

In 1926 Finzi set (but perhaps later revised) three poems by William Drummond of Hawthornden (1585–1649), a poet then little-known. He, not Drummond, called them Elegies. As in *By Footpath and Stile*, the subjects are sombre: 'so near our cradles to our coffins are'. Drummond used the poems to diversify sonnet sequences and called them madrigals, which gives a clue to Finzi's treatment. He set them for unaccompanied mixed voices, briefly and deftly, packing them with ingenious conceits. They need an expert choir and are more inventive than successful, but their nervous energy, fragmentary style, and inconclusive tonality show an unusual side of Finzi. The poems led him to a line he often quoted: in Drummond's *Flowers of Sion*, following 'Life a right shadow is' (which he set), comes the sonnet 'No trust in time' (of which he sketched a setting); it ends 'And twice it is not given thee to be born'. The urgency of that thought motivated Finzi's life.

A Young Man's Exhortation, Op. 14

After so much introspection, it is a relief to turn to a song that begins 'Call off your eyes from care/ By some determined deftness'. Hardy, like Finzi newly arrived in London to spread his wings, wrote the poem at about the age Finzi

---

[2]   To Thorpe Davie, December 1950.
[3]   5 July 1935.

was now. It was the first song Finzi composed (the erased date 1926 on the autograph can just be deciphered) for his second Hardy cycle, *A Young Man's Exhortation*. During the next three years he gathered fifteen songs for tenor and piano, finally selecting ten (see Appendix 1). Still the subject is ageing and death. There is no narrative, unlike in *Die schöne Müllerin* or *Winterreise*: the thread is an emotional one, linking the young idealist as he matures to his gentle end under the yellowing trees. Finzi headed the two parts with Latin quotations – in English, from Psalm 90, they read: 'In the morning it flourisheth, and groweth up', and (before 'Shortening Days') 'In the evening it is cut down, and withereth'.

The opening title song shows a new vigour and freedom of declamation. Finzi spreads the first stanza over six bars, but crunches the second into four. In the phrase 'Put forth joys dear as excess' the syncopated stress on 'dear' gives the word value, just as tossing 'blind' onto the song's highest note gives recklessness to 'blind glee'. The song begins in strict imitation, as if for a closed form; but Finzi breaks his pattern for the fourth stanza and slackens into quasi-recitative for Hardy's speculative 'what do we know best?'; suggests by his march-rhythm that time is inexorable; then by setting voice and piano in unbarred unison – 'if I have seen *one* thing' – affirms that the artist must seek within his dreams for vision. Through the five verses the song settles in or touches the keys of A flat, F, A, F sharp minor, and D. The effect is not restless, but responsive to the poem's changing thought; and the final E major chord (enharmonically related through the G sharp to the opening A flat) suggests a future unfolding.

In 'Ditty' the simple vernacular tune and word-setting sound natural but are in fact artful: perfect for the contented but not complacent rural lover. Not every composer could find the flexible melody to make audible the parenthesis '(Such will not be, but because Some forget Let me feign it)'. The song has a strophic-variation form that Finzi was often to use. All five stanzas sound alike in their diatonic folksong style, but far from being exact copies they are reassembled from a collection of melodic figures. Example 3.1 shows one such tag – a few scale-notes and a drop of a fifth, found at different points in each eight–line stanza: almost identical in stanzas 1 (line 6), 2 (line 5), and 5 (line 5); the scale inverted, but the drop of a fifth kept, in stanzas 3 and 5 (both line 1); rhythmically expanded to stress 'kissed' and 'loved' in 4 (line 1). Each is trimmed and stressed by the words. If the tune were for an instrument, it would be fiendish to memorize; for the singer of words, it is impossible to forget. Finzi clinches each verse, as did Hardy, with the same refrain: 'where she dwells'.

The flirtatious hussar in 'Budmouth dears' has a rousing shanty-like tune. It is the only strophic song in the set, though the piano's witty changing textures and registers disguise this. Shadows touch the next song: the poet imagines his own past obscurity. So that future generations shall honour his love, he builds 'Her temple': Finzi writes warm, round phrases in E flat, reaching expansively toward D flat. But what of the poet himself? Hardy changes his

Ex. 3.1

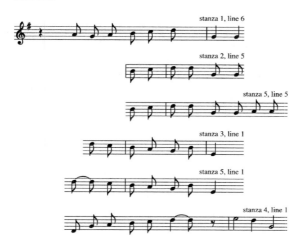

dactylic metre to spondees to give weight to 'None now knows his name', and Finzi communicates acceptance of this anonymity by even crotchets that close in distant F minor. Though lyrical and sounding spontaneous, the song is a dense web woven from the three motifs in the piano introduction, itself repeated under the poem's fourth line. At the climax – 'splendour upon her' – the three melodic motifs seem to fuse. In the fifth song comes withdrawal to detachment. Finzi chose Hardy's poem 'The comet at Yell'ham' but, ignoring the heat and speed implicit in 'fiery train', composed a trance-like song that places the loved one against infinity. The piano begins and ends icily at the top of the keyboard, its bitonal lines remote from each other and from humanity, descending to enclose the singer only briefly.

The opening *senza misura* of 'Shortening days' is declamation at its finest, with bare three-part writing (imitations starting not on the expected beat), thin as autumn sunshine, and with fluttering spurts for the sparrows. Perhaps (as Rubbra thought) Holst's 'who are these coming to the sacrifice' from his *Choral Symphony* lies behind Finzi's 'coming with pondering pace' as his cider-maker progresses from F major to an A major climax in ever- thickening chords. By 'The sigh' love is in the past: after four descriptive verses, reflections lift the song from G major to a 'transfigured' Schubertian E major. In 'Former beauties' the Budmouth dears are sourly described as now aged and withered. The ghostly dream-like dance is in the watcher's memory only, and as it vanishes into the high register the return of the opening dissonance makes it sadly clear that 'they cannot know what once they were'. The singer's final phrase (Ex. 3.2) seems to carry the central compassionate message of the whole cycle.

'Transformations', like 'Voices from things growing in a churchyard' from *By Footpath and Stile*, celebrates regeneration. The vigour is welcome, but the

Ex. 3.2

figuration is too busy, and the sly references to 'Her temple' and to 'they cannot know what once they were' hardly make their point. In the tenth and last song, 'The dance continued', the watcher himself is absent and sleeps beneath the trees. 'Regret not me' says Hardy; but Finzi's music speaks of regret as well as resignation: the piano postlude echoes the forlorn phrase 'I did not know . . .'. It is a moving song, a forerunner of the magnificent late 'Harvest' (see p. 260).

Finzi set three other poems by Hardy in 1928–29, which he may have considered for the cycle. 'Two lips' (1928) is one of his simplest songs, two stanzas separated by an imperfect cadence; but the lips first kissed 'in fancy' were finally kissed 'in a shroud', so Finzi gradually moves from a brisk, folk-like idiom to a sustained phrase that sadly outlines the compass of the first verse. 'I say, "I'll seek her side" ' (1929) is a dramatic vignette of a man wracked with indecision, a woman tormented by waiting. From the headlong passionate opening the music gradually loses impetus to mirror the man's procrastination. This control of pace and the variety of piano figuration make it one of Finzi's more striking songs, and may partly date from his revision in 1955. In 1860 Hardy watched the eclipse of the moon, and the contrast between the stellar universe and infinitesimal human lives had a powerful hold on him. Finzi's setting of 'At a lunar eclipse' (1929) is austere and, though obviously influenced by Holst's *Egdon Heath*, audacious. The unbarred but regular piano chords move 'in even monochrome', the soaring voice in 'curving line'; voice and piano are linked by fugato and imitation. There is awe in the sudden thinning into three-octaves unison at 'and can immense mortality . . .' (Ex. 11.5c). As the uniform bass threatens to become monotonous Finzi breaks the rhythm with the perplexed cry 'nation at war with nation', and finally the singer reaches a triumphant top A.

'Oh fair to see' (1929), to words by Christina Rossetti, contains what was to become a melodic fingerprint (Ex. 3.3). The song is in C minor. The singer's third phrase rises through pairs of thirds to the fifth of the scale. In this case, the fingerprint also shows Finzi's way of illuminating a special word harmonically. It begins with a second inversion of an E flat triad on a strong beat, then the bass descends by step, the 'tenor' is suspended over the barline, and resolves by a momentary flash of C major for 'de-light', like an unexpected shaft of sunlight.

Ex. 3.3

Dies Natalis, Op. 8 (I)

For his next work Finzi turned to Thomas Traherne, discovered during his Painswick years. Traherne's account of his childhood intuitions is among the most rapturous in English literature. Finzi's response was almost certainly instantaneous: he never set any text unless at least one line clothed itself in music at his first reading. Surely some lines must have so composed themselves in 1923 (see p. 28), when he first read Traherne's poems and extracts from the prose Centuries of Meditation; and his discovery of prose and poetry in one and the same volume may explain why, unusually, he set both in the cantata. This was to become Dies Natalis, for solo high voice and strings. The history of its composition is confusing, but in its final form (1939) it comprised 1 Intrada for strings alone, 2 'Rhapsody', 3 'The rapture', 4 'Wonder', 5 'The salutation'. In 1926 Finzi composed what at the time he called Intrata [1], Recitative [2] and Aria 'Dies Natalis' [5] (the opening of this last occurs in a sketchbook dated 1925). To complicate matters, he also composed another 'Intrada' to different words by Traherne.

Traherne's Centuries are numbered paragraphs, in groups of one hundred, of reflections on religious and moral subjects, written for a friend, Susanna Hopton, and called a Handbook to Felicity. The text of Finzi's complete Dies Natalis consists of one prose passage from the third Century, and three poems among those considered by the 1906 editor Dobell as Traherne's finest. Dobell suggests that the poems he singles out 'gain considerably' as parts 'of a continuous poem'. Possibly that idea suggested Dies Natalis – the title was Finzi's own. He was composer enough to be ruthless with Traherne's words. For the 'Rhapsody' he plucked just what he wanted from the first three prose paragraphs of the third Century. Far from the lines running as they do in Traherne, only the opening sentences of Traherne's and Finzi's texts coincide. After that Finzi chose sentences from paragraphs 2, 1, 2, 3, 2, in that order. He omitted any specifically religious references. He even dropped words from sentences: 'I was a little stranger' wrote Traherne; but the phrase has a different nuance after Victorianism, and becomes 'I was a stranger'. In 'The salutation' and 'Wonder' he set only selected stanzas.

Dies Natalis opens with Intrada for strings alone, musing on themes to come in the 'Rhapsody'. Then the voice enters. Nothing could be more intimate and confiding: 'Will you see the infancy . . .?' By now Finzi was at home in his one-note to one-syllable style; and his word-setting is a personal amalgam of naturalistic speech-rhythms and heightened eloquence. The rhythms of the Intrada are regular and even: a lilting six-eight, and an instrumental semi-quaver turn derived from the coming 'venerable CREATURES DID THE AGed seem'. Once the voice enters, its dotted speech-rhythms give the same melodies a quite different vitality. There are problems for a composer in setting prose, since it has no regular line-lengths or rhymes to suggest a structure. Finzi uses a four-note figure in the manner of a rhyme, though – skilfully – not always at the phrase-ends (Ex. 3.4)

Ex. 3.4

He matches some phrase-endings, but expands the second of the pair with rhythmic augmentation (Ex 3.5).

He 'rhymes' two full lines of melody, too, though he underlays 'the green trees . . .' with a bland chord, and 'their sweetness . . .' with a stinging chord, and then expands 'almost mad with ecstasy' just as he did 'splendour and glory'. Three times he repeats an identical melodic phrase: 'I knew not . . . I knew not . . . I dream'd not . . .', but the differing harmony makes each sound fresh. Into his six-eight metre he introduces many duplets, so that the line runs easily between twos and threes, making all fluid, volatile, and questioning. When the movement was published he marked it *recitativo stromentato* (accompanied recitative).

Ex. 3.5

The harmony sounds inevitable but is cunning. In the opening lines there are only two root position major triads, to highlight the words 'greatness' and 'divine'; then under the word 'angel' there is a lift from G major-B minor to E major. The central 'O what venerable . . .' is a more formal melody, warm and cantabile, to give a structural core to the recitative. This theme was developed and brought to a big passionate *poco stringendo* climax in the Intrada, so in the 'Rhapsody' it carries greater emotional force than its brief statement there might suggest. At the vision of the young men and maids the strings dance in Finzi's delicate 'figure of delight' (see Ex. 2.1), upper lines duetting this time over a thrummed bass; but otherwise the accompaniment tends to echo the voice's cadence figures. The last line – 'Everything was at rest' – is set limpidly in G major; but Finzi does not sustain that through 'free and immortal', which slips into gentle modal discords. There perhaps lies the remarkable hold this music has on so many people. It sings of human ecstasy, sharp and glorious, but knows that the chance of immortality is fragile.

A weakness in much of Finzi's music is the limited variety of his harmonic pace, of the possible play between harmony and metre. His chord-changes are usually regular, and rhythmically predictable. In 'The salutation' he turns this feature to positive effect. The bass is mostly four even beats, but the strongly patterned upper instrumental part runs almost the length of the accompaniment. Another aria of 1926, 'His golden locks' (later part of *Farewell to Arms*) is similar. The sense of advancing technique, of new-found identity, is strong. What had happened?

This, maybe. On his move to London in 1926 Finzi naturally began going to more concerts, to the point where he was hearing other men's music at least every other night. Hubert Foss and Charles Kennedy Scott founded the Bach Cantata Club that year, giving their concerts at St Margaret's, Westminster. Finzi went to the first meeting on 15 February, and heard three cantatas. He went to another in March. That month, too, he was at the B Minor Mass ('the finest performance I ever heard', he noted on the programme); his name, and that of his cousin Neville Finzi, are listed as honorary members of the club. He also heard all-Bach instrumental concerts conducted by Henry Wood and then Barbirolli, and Harold Samuel's keyboard 'Bach Weeks'. Bairstow's pupil would be no stranger to Bach, but the immersion Finzi had in 1926 was exceptional. It was the Bach Choir's jubilee in June, and – Vaughan Williams

was the conductor – Finzi heard three all-Bach concerts. He went to the
Oxford Heather Festival, probably for the first performance of Vaughan
Williams's *Sancta Civitas* and R. O. Morris's *Toccata and Fugue*, and there heard
another all-Bach concert. There were two more at the Haslemere Festival.

Probably consciously, for he used the term 'aria', Finzi took from Bach a
technique to strengthen his own in 'The salutation'. The instrumental
ritornello offered him a formal framework over which he could project his
chosen words. It is the technique of the chorale prelude, but here the singing
line, instead of being a plain hymn-tune, is inflected to the stress of the words.
Finzi was no longer chained to speaking-rate. He could sustain a long line,
even through the second syllable of a word like 'begins'; and contract and
expand his melody as much for formal balance as for verbal inflection. Any
tendency towards meandering recitative was checked. The voice is independent of the string accompaniment, soaring to an exultant climax of
possession as in Example 3.6.

Ex. 3.6

On the page 'The salutation' looks simple: the first accidental does not occur
until the nineteenth bar. But the play of rhythm and interval between voice
and ritornello is intricate, and not only justifies but depends on the steady
unyielding bass. Although the discords are low-powered, they work with the
syncopations and suspensions to propel the music ever-forward.

Possibly Bach's influence was refracted through Parry. The instrumental
lines of 'The Salutation' and Parry's 'To everything there is a season' (*Beyond
these Voices*, 1908) are strikingly similar, though Parry's supports a contrapuntal
chorus, not an expressive solo line, and it is precisely there that Finzi's individuality lies. He might well have known Parry's cantata through Bairstow; he
certainly admired it in the 1950s. Stephen Banfield hears the influence of
Bliss, of his *Pastoral* (1929), and the *Serenade* (1929), possibly of the Clarinet
Quintet (which Finzi heard in 1933) on Finzi's instrumental 'Intrata' (1926),
and conjectured plausibly that what Rubbra in his article of 1929 (see p. 58)
called the 'Intrata' might have been the separate song, and that what Rubbra
called 'Recitative' might have been 'Wonder' in original guise. However, by
January 1933 the 'Intrata' was certainly an instrumental piece, as William
Busch was able to suggest that a friend of his with a string orchestra might
perform it[4] (Busch did not start keeping Finzi's letters till 1936). A recently
found autograph of the song 'Intrada', undated, has a pencil superscription in

---

[4]   12 and 17 January 1933.

Finzi's hand: 'This was intended as the introduction to a set of short Traherne songs for sop & piano (not a second *Dies Natalis*). Not enough time left to complete so it can be included in a set of "various" songs' – which suggests a date after Finzi knew of his fatal illness. In his catalogue Finzi gives no dates for *Dies Natalis*, though in his programme note for the first performance he says three movements (he doesn't say which!) were composed in 1926. Even if it is never known how *Dies Natalis* was put together, what was written first, what revised, what substituted, nothing can detract from the published work's integrity.

The song 'Intrada' ('An empty book is like an infant's soul') certainly shares the thought of *Dies Natalis*. Finzi sets the words, from Traherne's First *Century*, in characteristic flexible recitative. '. . . in which anything may be written' opens up to a half-close in G minor; the resolute 'I have a mind to fill this with profitable wonders' is on-the-beat C major; for 'things strange and common' the voice keeps to bare octaves and fifths over transforming chords; 'truths you love, but know not' reaches warmly but mysteriously into the new region of E major. Brief, packed, with just one flowering bar for piano, the little arioso shows perfectly how Finzi interprets the modulations of the poet's thought through his own.

At R. O. Morris's home Gerald met a fellow-student, Howard Ferguson. Howard was seven years the younger, and still at the Royal College of Music where he was Morris's student for composition. He had been born in Belfast of not particularly musical parents, but Harold Samuel, the outstanding Bach pianist of the day, heard him play as a boy at the Belfast Musical Competition, and was so impressed that he offered to take over his musical education; so, when he and Gerald met, Howard was studying privately under Samuel and living in his Clarendon Road house in West London, looked after by Pu (May Cunningham), Howard's ex-nanny. Their first meeting was unmemorable (though Gerald at once wrote to ask if he might see Howard's recent violin sonata). A few weeks later they made a considerable impact on each other – literally – when, like all musical London, they went on 9 November 1926 to hear Richard Strauss conduct his Alpine Symphony: 'The presence of the master' (Howard recalled) 'should have guaranteed the solemnity of the occasion; but the high-light of the evening was undoubtedly one of the noisier climaxes . . . in which the thunder machine (or was it the wind machine?) toppled over and crashed unheard into the middle of the startled orchestra. As the audience left the hall, Finzi and I cannoned into one another by chance, both of us helpless with laughter; and from that moment our friendship was sealed.'[5]

5   *Music & Letters*, April 1959.

Almost at once Howard went off to the United States, to continue studying with Samuel during one of his concert tours, also visiting R. O. Morris for lessons at Philadelphia, where Morris had gone as director of the theory department at the recently founded Curtis Institute.[6] Gerald asked Howard to buy him a full score of Bloch's Concerto Grosso in New York; Howard asked Gerald to get him a catalogue of the Flemish Art exhibition at Burlington House, in case it closed before his return. It was the first of many such exchanges. Once Howard was home in May 1927 they went together to the William Blake exhibition - Gerald owned the three-volume Nonesuch edition of Blake. There soon began the weekly sessions much like the Vaughan Williams–Holst 'field days', when the two went through each other's compositions, got to know music by playing it as piano duets, and generally set the world to rights. For one such meeting Howard offered 'as bait' *Der Rosenkavalier*; before long it was *The Bartered Bride*, then *Fennimore and Gerda*; and Gerald was asking for Scarlatti and Rameau operas, which Howard had to tell him could not be borrowed from the Royal College of Music library. Howard had never met anyone so utterly absorbed in music, his curiosity insatiable and his energy boundless. After reading through one opera, Gerald was ready to tackle another couple. 'Being the less fluent pianist of the two, he generally stationed himself at the extreme top of the keyboard and there played whatever vocal or instrumental part came his way, several octaves too high, rather loudly, and with a distinctly capricious sense of time values.'[7] Edith despaired of ever serving meals punctually: 'Many's the time I've sat waiting on the stairs wishing Mr Ferguson to glory – more than my job was worth to knock. Whenever there was a pause, I coughed.'

Howard, sharing the home of an international artist, going through the student mill at College, and already taking engagements as a pianist himself, was both more practical and more worldly than the older Gerald. Soon he was copying scores for him, reducing them to piano-duet versions, and practising his fast music to play to others. He also – and this does seem strange – added dynamic and phrase marks, since Gerald composed without a thought for his performers. By Christmas 1927 the pattern was established enough for Howard to add to his letter a wicked sketch of 'the seer of Caroline Street under the influence of inspiration': Gerald, crowned on a canopied dais, composing at the piano; and at his feet the 'willing workers' – Howard and the cats, busy copying.

It was probably through R. O. Morris too that Gerald came to know Arthur Bliss. Bliss was at one of Gerald's early performances. 'I like that work very much,' he told him, and was struck by the directness of Gerald's reply: 'Well, tell me what you didn't like about it.' Bliss had been up at Cambridge, suffered a year under Stanford at the RCM, and fought through the war. His *Madame Noy*

---

[6]   Finzi's impression of Ferguson's arrival may be seen in *Letters of Gerald Finzi and Howard Ferguson* (Woodbridge, 2001), p. 5.
[7]   *Music & Letters*, April 1959.

Newmayers, almost next door, or one of the
~~other~~ many shops in that road.

I think that is all.
All best wishes for '28 and kindest
regards to the concerto!

A.

The user of Caroline
St under the influence of
inspiration.

(Willing workers)

and *Rout* quickly won him a reputation as an advanced composer. In 1922 he conducted the first performance of Vaughan Williams's *The Shepherds of the Delectable Mountains* at the RCM, and then worked on his *Colour Symphony* at Vaughan Williams's house, loving the 'wonderful atmosphere of quiet sustained work'. He got to know ROM well, 'or as well as he allowed anyone to penetrate his reserve', and described their playing chess together, a cat curled up purring on RO's lap, a glass of claret at hand, and 'his elegant fingers moving the pieces with sure logic to my final defeat'.[8] By the time Gerald met him, Bliss had married his American wife Trudy in Santa Barbara, had worked in the theatre and travelled a good deal. Within months of their first exchange of letters in 1927 he was off to Venice, he and Leon Goossens taking a gondola to rehearsals of his Oboe Quintet. It was not Gerald's world, but he was pleased to visit Arthur and Trudy first in their flat, then at their eighteenth-century house on the edge of Hampstead Heath. Arthur's letters to Gerald, though kind and supportive, were short and to the point, and he did not keep Gerald's replies, so that what remains does not altogether indicate the warm regard the two men came to hold for each other. In the early days a note such as 'Dear Gerald, When are we going to see you? I hope all is well. Let us know. Yours AB' would be followed by an invitation to lunch.

Edmund Rubbra, Gerald's exact contemporary, moved in less sophisticated circles after an early background rather like Elgar's. Then, winning an open scholarship to the RCM, he worked under Holst and Morris. He studied the piano with Evlyn Howard-Jones, who lived near Gerald and introduced them to each other. Wholly absorbed in music – when he visited Caroline Street he never 'saw' Edith, to her amusement – Rubbra found in Gerald a warm, sympathetic listener whose judgment he trusted, and whose opinion he sought, from every meeting carrying away something 'of vital importance'.[9] From his first postcard to Gerald in 1926 they saw a great deal of each other, playing over works in progress; and he dedicated his Phantasy Op. 16 of 1927 to Gerald. Edmund's frequent letters are almost always about his own music, ending with queries about Gerald's, but he too did not keep Gerald's replies.

Gerald's second letter from the Vaughan Williamses, this time from Adeline, was to thank him for taking snapshots to send to Philadelphia of the Morrises' cat Henry, whose 'lovely eyes & whiskers' had come out so well (though Howard remembered Henry with loathing as a gross orange animal). Gerald had called his cat after the folk song, Rufty-Tufty. He was now establishing his 'field days' with Vaughan Williams, inviting himself to Cheyne Walk, enclosing a self-addressed postcard with 'no – yes – day – time –' on the back, like an army field card, for Vaughan Williams to fill in. In the same way he invited himself to R. O. Morris, Holst, and Herbert Howells. His insistence did not put the older composers off; they recognised his need and his single-mindedness.

8   A. Bliss, *As I Remember* (London, 1970), p. 74.
9   *The Times*, 12 October 1956.

During 1925 Finzi had begun to compose a Violin Concerto for Sybil Eaton, calling it a concerto for small orchestra and violin solo, so stressing that it was not a display piece. At Chosen Hill he had finished the slow movement. He now worked on the outer movements. Sybil, who had moved to London from York, was the only performer he knew well; she was flattered to accept the dedication. He sought her out for help, often arriving at mealtimes, as oblivious to the hour as he was to her room-mate to whom he never bothered to speak, his mind being wholly on his work. He did not know much about the fiddle, and if she asked him to recast a passage to make it lie better under the hand, he was taken aback and quite unable to do it. He surprised her too by playing the orchestral part each time at a different speed. When she asked him what tempo he wanted, he replied politely 'that's for you to say'. She subsidized and gave the first performance with the British Women's Symphony Orchestra under Malcolm Sargent at the Queen's Hall on 4 May 1927, but of only the second and third movements – Gerald had been unable to complete the first in time.

The Daily Mail critic called him 'a clever young composer, who takes himself too seriously and keeps his eyes too close to the music-paper'. Sargent didn't think much of the Concerto, called it amateurish, and he and the hardened orchestral players rather pooh-poohed it (Gerald's suspicion of the profes-sional, nurtured by Boughton, must have been reinforced). To recover, he took himself off to a cottage address near Faringdon, climbed the White Horse Hill daily, and, he wrote to Vera Strawson, 'conversed at night with Agricola & St Augustine on the Ridgeway'.[10]

Vaughan Williams, however, asked to see the score, made suggestions, and wrote to Gerald in December 'We've fixed up the concerto now. It only remains for you to write it.'[11] Vaughan Williams had since 1920 been the conductor of the Bach Choir, whose concerts in those days included instru-mental as well as choral works. He decided to perform the Concerto and prac-tised conducting it with Constant Lambert as the pianist (of all the unlikely personalities to have been, even fleetingly, involved with Finzi). Holst came to the final rehearsal, and spent that night helping Gerald revise the orchestral parts. The full work, with a new first movement, was given by the London Symphony Orchestra at a Bach Choir concert, in the Queen's Hall, on 1 February 1928.

This time the criticisms included speculation as to Gerald's nationality (a Signor Finzi was prominent in Italian politics at the time), which drew from R. O. Morris in Philadelphia an angry letter decrying the 'insolent personal comment in The Times'.[12] (As late as the 1950s Times critics were forbidden to comment on personal appearance.) Holst, in the month of the first perfor-mance of his Egdon Heath, took the trouble to write that he agreed with Vaughan

[10] 27 May 1927.
[11] 2 December 1927.
[12] 20 February 1928.

Williams that the first movement should be scrapped, but that the other two 'are the best things I know of yours'.[13]

Violin Concerto

That makes an interesting point, for Finzi's replacement first movement – his whole Concerto, in fact – is modelled on the baroque style of Holst's Fugal Concerto (1923) and Vaughan Williams's *Concerto accademico* (1925). Both were part of the decade's neo-Classical trend (Stravinsky's *Pulcinello* was performed in London by the Diaghilev Company in 1920), which Finzi, a regular concert-goer, was well aware of. Finzi's first movement is athletic and ingenious, but the counterpoint is anonymous, unremitting, and the movement lacks defining tonal structure; Holst's is much airier, with far more light and shade. Finzi's third movement, a hornpipe, is breezier than his first, and he introduces his folk-like tune, distantly related to 'The dark-eyed sailor', more naturally than Holst does his, 'If all the world were paper'. Finzi, however, seemed determined to prove his modernity, for he immediately subjects his sailor to bitonal severities. Indeed, it might be that for the only time in his life he was attempting to be up to date. The Concerto's outer movements reveal an extrovert Finzi with a lively energy, lacking only a clear direction. The work is significant, for it was his first three-movement instrumental composition, and it was given an important London debut. Its comparative failure must have left a scar, and he chose to publish only the slow movement, as Introit Op. 6.

In that, however, he achieves a mood of rapt contemplation. The diatonicism of the opening is tempered by the number of secondary minor triads (five G minor and A minor chords in the first two bars of F major) so that the feeling is one of supplication as much as security. There is no 'sonata' contrast, but a tissue of imitation. The steady footfall is counter-balanced by suspensions and by the entries crossing the beat or pulling against each other is augmentation. Towards the end there are glimpses of desolation: the bass sinks down four consecutive fifths and the violin falters. After a brief cadenza, flute and solo double bass in unison but three octaves apart move in chilly canon with the violin, and off-key Mahlerian horns sound distantly. The Introit has a rare sweetness; but its generating melody and placid rhythm are too featureless to avoid monotony. Finzi shortened it before the score was published in 1943. Edward Lockspeiser, in *Music & Letters*, October 1944, considered it derived from Vaughan Williams's Fifth Symphony; this drew a letter from Vaughan Williams, pointing out that his symphony was composed eleven years after Finzi's Introit!

[13] 7 February 1938.

In the same concert as Finzi's Violin Concerto had been Robin Milford's Double Fugue, Op. 10. Milford wrote to congratulate Finzi; and in the course of the letter commented that he found it hard to expand his ideas. Gerald, admitting that was his second try at a first movement, acknowledged the same problem (incidentally revealing why his appreciation of Mozart was limited). 'Don't you think the cause is plain enough? It's much easier to build big structures if you can write a chord & hold it over fifty bars by means of tremolos, Alberti basses, arpeggios and the like. In that way a lot of people seem to find it quite easy to expand no ideas at all! But with a close and concentrated texture it's a much more difficult job.'[14] It was probably the experience of performance that led him to take some lessons in orchestration from Gordon Jacob during 1928.

Vaughan Williams, having conducted Gerald's Concerto, invited him to a run-through of two works of his own; so in early spring 1928 Gerald went to Morley College to hear Norah Day and Vally Lasker play extracts on two pianos from *The Fat Knight* (later *Sir John in Love*) and a new ballet. *Sir John in Love* was not performed until 1929, and *Job* (concert version) not until October 1930, so Gerald's comments to Howard must be among the earliest made. They are certainly perceptive:

> What I heard of *The Fat Knight* contained the worst music VW has ever written, though it goes with great pace and has certain new rhythmical developments (as far as he is concerned). *Job* is quite another matter. It lasts fifty minutes and embraces all things. The beginning and the end are as lovely as the loveliest parts of *Flos Campi*, the violent parts are equally satisfactory. There is a curious grave and ceremonial quality about it.[15]

(When the ballet was staged in July 1931 the Vaughan Williamses invited Gerald to their box for the matinée.)

At the end of February 1928 Gerald developed suspected tuberculosis, before antibiotics a serious, often fatal, illness. He was advised to go to the King Edward VII sanatorium at Midhurst for six months. Vera Strawson sensitively lent him money, knowing that funds were low for private treatment. Howard hoped he would take things easy while waiting, but supposed that was 'about as much use as telling an avalanche to stop avalanching!'[16] At the loving insistence of Winifred Blow, Gerald went down to 'Hilles' in Gloucestershire to be looked after, ' "Till my time comes" ' as he wrote to Howard. 'I curse almost as vehemently as Job'.[17]

[14] 22 March 1938.
[15] 10 April 1928.
[16] 6 April 1928.
[17] 10 April 1928.

Vaughan Williams's *Job* was ringing in his ears. Thomas Hardy had died a few months earlier, and *The Daily Telegraph* was publishing some of his last poems; Howard cut them out and posted them to Gerald, so Hardy too was in his mind. The following year he set Hardy's 'Waiting both', which includes the lines 'For all I know, Wait, and let Time go by, Till my change come' – a para- phrase of Job's 'All the days of my appointed time will I wait, till my change come'. Finzi's verbal memory was never exact, but it seems possible that he was applying the words to his own situation. The immense and strange chords, which seem almost over-powerful for the song after 'till my change come' (Ex 3.7), might have had their genesis in this anxious waiting.

Ex. 3.7

At the time, he reported to Howard, he found it impossible to work in the Blows' 'happy open household', but played with the children, 'painting three savage looking red-Indians and being killed (and eaten) by them as a bear'. There was too the view that had inspired his *Severn Rhapsody*, twenty or thirty miles of country 'and the shining Severn winding below'. He was amused to meet a fellow guest, Ethel Smyth, and though he enjoyed her 'brilliant conver- sation', he noted her self-absorption; when he turned on the radio to hear Walton's *Sinfonia concertante* (Gerald had recently been at the first performance) she said that 'all wireless sounded out of tune to her, but that we must be sure to listen-in to a concert of her own works on such and such a date!'[18] He was cheered that Herbert Sumsion was to follow Herbert Brewer as organist of Gloucester Cathedral. He had already met John (as Herbert Sumsion was known to his friends) and his wife Alice, and liked them both. For his thank-you to 'Hilles' he composed a Grace, which Winifred delightedly praised for its 'precision and rightness'.

A reading of Maurois' *Disraeli* prompted him to the expression, in a letter to Howard, of a thought that came to permeate all his philosophy: 'how posterity lays the lion and the lamb together; that there is no ultimate truth about anything (except as we see it) and that everything we hate most in the world, even to baseness of motive, may triumph equally with what we admire most – and bring equally good results!'[19]

[18] 22 April 1928.
[19] 22 April 1928.

CHAPTER FOUR

Midhurst and Marriage

1928–35

At the end of April 1928, having made a Will leaving his books to Vera Strawson and feeling like Shakespeare's whining schoolboy in his first term, Gerald went to the sanatorium at Midhurst. He found the Sussex countryside wonderful, praised the medical care, and was soon given the encouraging diagnosis: pleurisy rather than tuberculosis. However, he dismissed his fellow patients, despite their general goodwill, as bank clerks and people you meet behind a counter. It was not snobbery, nor 'imagined superiority', but there was no-one he could talk to, not a single intellect; and no work was possible. 'I feel like Samson in bondage'[1] he told Howard Ferguson (he was never shy of borrowing a Biblical phrase for his own use). He was struck by the differing views on treatment: 'rest & more damned rest', but the last medical superintendent had been all for exercise, he told Vera. 'So one decade of fools contradicts the next.'[2]

'Don't despair,' Arthur Bliss wrote to him, 'you will come out after an enforced slack with much fresher ideas,'[3] and assured him that Vaughan Williams talked a lot about him. R. O. Morris wrote from Philadelphia, advising him 'Think. Meditate. Improve the Soul. Excogitate the Concerto.'[4] As soon as Morris was back in England, he and Arthur visited Gerald at Midhurst. Gerald asked Howard, who stayed nearby for two weekends, to send him some miniature scores, and made a piano reduction from Howard's own performing version of Schütz's *Sinfonia sacra* 'Fili mi, Absalon', which Keith Falkner had recently sung. At the RCM Howard heard the fourth symphony of Mahler, who roused Gerald's sympathy for the underdog (though like most Londoners in the late 1920s he knew little of Mahler's music). 'Hearsay holds him in contempt, but I never feel like that as I know he went through Hell in his lifetime and I've a sympathy for the metaphysicians.' That took him on to develop his 'lion and lamb' theory, for 'all thoughts have been thought (the rest is splitting of hairs)' and 'the mind's range is as a stone tied to a string and whirled round – now this side, now that side, but never beyond a limited radius, unless [remembering the exhibition they'd seen together] it flies off altogether and becomes a Will Blake. So the best thing, in theory, is to get back to musical patterns & designs which *appear* to have (but probably have not)

[1] 30 April 1928.
[2] 1 May 1928.
[3] 30 April 1928.
[4] 7 May 1928.

more variety than when guided by external ideas. But as for practice — that's best explained by Drummond in "I know that all beneath the moon decays".[5]

Howard, less introspective than his friend but sensitive to his fundamental pessimism, pointed out that if all thoughts had been thought then all music must have been written, and they would cease to try to compose. 'Thank God we are incapable of this. Cheer up, old lump, it is bloody, but things are only aggravated by worrying over them.'[6] There had been an earlier occasion when he and Gerald had dined with Vera Strawson's brother-in-law, the psychoanalyst Eric Strauss, and the talk had turned serious. Howard, then still in his teens, was a natural optimist. 'You really believe that everything in the world is for the best?' Gerald demanded, and dissolved into peals of disillusioned laughter when Howard answered Yes.

Gerald came out of Midhurst in July with a clean bill of health. The report described him as 'well-built and healthy, height five foot six-and-a-half inches. An arrested lesion, chiefly pleural, with probably slight returning dry pleurisy.' Into a couple of London days before going to his mother at Hundon he crowded a performance of Stravinsky's *Les Noces*, which he liked — 'not as European art, but rather in the same way as we should like some curious oriental or asiatic music' — and of *Così fan tutte* — 'as charming as ever'. Rubbra, he reported to Howard, who was at home in Belfast, had now abandoned socks, 'so it's sandals and five toes: — But, he has written a magnificent fugue for piano.' Arthur Bliss was livening up the Philharmonic committee. Herbert Howells had visited Caroline Street, and 'alas, I played him a Hardy song & he said "a lovely poem", which of course is quite right. Anyhow, I'll forgive him.'[7] At Hundon Gerald read and enjoyed Trollope.

At that time, 1928–29, he was fairly open in his tastes. He recommended to Howard a German choir singing Walther, Schütz, Praetorius, and Bach — 'I'm sorry when foreigners can teach us anything, but they certainly can.'[8] He found Ravel's Violin Sonata 'a bit bloodless and dull' but wouldn't back his opinion against Ravel 'who knows perfectly well what he is about & is a brave little composer, courageous and looking forward, & in his way as manysided as VW — only with the Devil's technique.'[9] On the other hand, he dismissed Debussy's Cello Sonata as 'not possessing a single idea'.[10] He found Kodály's *Háry János* suite 'a first rate piece of work', and thought some of *Oedipus Rex* 'v. fine'. He liked Bloch's *Israel* except that 'once he came to a climax he never seemed to come off!' Though Howard said to him about some broadcast 'you can turn off for the Mozart', Gerald was not totally agin Mozart and Haydn, singling out as delightful Haydn's E flat Piano Sonata (Hob. xvi/49) and the slow movement of Mozart's A major Concerto (K. 488). What really surprised

5   15 June 1928.
6   17 June 1928.
7   To Ferguson, 14 July 1928.
8   To Ferguson, 20 October 1928.
9   To Ferguson, 20 October 1928.
10   To Ferguson, 2–15 August 1929.

him was a performance of Verdi's *Falstaff*, which he found 'deadly'. Apart from 'Sir, your servant,' 'When I was young' and the final fugue, 'there was not a note worth hearing twice. Compared with *The Fat Knight* [he'd seen the first performance of Vaughan Williams's opera at the RCM in March] 'Verdi only got the better in one way: the libretto was much more lucid.'[11]

He also heard Keith Falkner sing Bach's cantata *Ich habe genug*, No. 82: 'was there ever a longer aria than the second?' ['Schlummert ein'] he asked Howard. 'In one mood throughout & *perfectly justified*.'[12] It sounds like a defence of his own arias 'His golden locks' (*Farewell to Arms*) and 'The salutation' (*Dies Natalis*). During 1928 he had turned from their serenity to two works that greatly extended his reach.

Milton Sonnets, Op. 12

In the first of these he set, for tenor and small orchestra (though the orchestration came later), the two Milton sonnets, 'When I consider' and 'How soon hath time'. It would not occur to him to be daunted by the fact that they are among the world's best-known poems; and it is impossible not to relate their substance to his own trauma that year. Milton at the age of twenty-three lamented that 'his late spring no bud or blossom' showed, and then, on facing his blindness, grieved for his 'one talent which is death to hide'. Finzi was twenty-seven, almost unknown, a slow worker, and facing possible death. Ten years later he admitted to Robin Milford that he had been in a 'queer state' at the time, and called his settings 'rather gnarled & uncompromising'.[13]

However, one could wish them still more uncompromising. Finzi's norm of dissonance is low, at its extreme in simultaneous semitonal clashes – minor seconds or major ninths – used mostly for instant colour (as in 'with lips thin-drawn, And tissues sere' in 'Former beauties', see p. 41). In the introductions to both Sonnets such clashes occur so frequently that they tend to cancel each other out – stab after equal stab of pain lacks cumulative force. There is a straining for effect, as if Finzi were searching (as perhaps in his Violin Concerto) to 'modernize' his conservative idiom. The first Sonnet has no key signature but many accidentals, emphasising the self-conscious discordancy. That said, the Sonnets are still powerful and sombre. The first rises to an exultant climax, then fines down to make the famous last words, magically touched by the horn, into a quizzical, undogmatic ending. For this Finzi uses a characteristic deflected cadence, the voice rising surprisingly to the fourth, not the expected third, degree of the scale, the harmony not on the tonic D, before the clarinet resolves the phrase (Ex. 4.1).

---

[11] 23 April 1929.
[12] 28 December 1928.
[13] 29 September 1938.

Ex. 4.1

He had used a similar device in 'Ditty', for the shock at 'In the thought that she is *nought*' (see p. 40): his handling of cadences is often extremely subtle. In 'How soon hath time' he interprets the resolve – to use time effectively – by passing from claustrophobic imitation to processional block chords, and by clearing the ambiguous four flats of the start into F major, then into A major. The effect is exhilarating and resolute. Awkwardly expressed though they may be, Finzi's Sonnets deal with big emotions. He dedicated them to Edmund Rubbra.

In 1929 Rubbra contributed an article on Finzi, at the editor Richard Capell's request, to a series on Younger English Composers in *Monthly Musical Record*[14] (the others included Rubbra himself, Warlock, Lambert, Bliss, and Berkeley). This was Finzi's first, and for many years his only, assessment in print, so the information it gives is valuable, particularly as it is clear from the letters that Finzi collaborated freely. Rubbra discussed *A Severn Rhapsody* and *By Footpath and Stile* (both now published). Of the unpublished music, he described the Milton Sonnets, the Requiem, what was composed of *Dies Natalis* and of *Farewell to Arms*. He dealt with the recently performed Violin Concerto, and reported that Finzi was then engaged on a Piano Concerto. Rubbra concluded that the circumstances of Finzi's training had 'tended to make his work curiously introspective; and what it has gained in concentration it has lost somewhat in expansiveness'. He praised its economy and severity. Finzi was 'an uncommon musician, one gifted with a mind refreshingly free from cliquishness and preciosity'.

Grand Fantasia, Op. 38

The second work in which Finzi stretched himself was the Grand Fantasia. In 1928–29 he intended it as part of a concerto for piano and strings, and composed a slow movement (published posthumously as Eclogue, see p. 221); but Morris advised him to follow the Fantasia with a fugue. As so often with Finzi, the work remained incomplete. When in 1953 he added a Toccata with full orchestra (see p. 220), he revised the Fantasia. But it existed by 1929, when

---

14 Vol. lix, no. 703.

Rubbra described it as 'free, decorative and improvisational'. It is a work of surprising rhetoric and virtuosity.

Again, circumstances may explain this. Like the Violin Concerto, and the arias 'The salutation' and 'His golden locks', the Fantasia is influenced by Bach. It so happened that during 1927–28 Finzi heard several performances of Bach's Chromatic Fantasia, one by Harold Samuel; and he must often have heard Bairstow play the 'great' G minor Fantasia and Fugue. There is, too, a combative element in Finzi's Fantasia. In 1928 he was privately calling the projected concerto 'Dave', from the Old Testament story (1 Samuel 17) of David and Goliath. (Howard Ferguson, in letters, used to ask 'How's Dave?', and gradually the name became transferred to Gerald himself, so that Finzi and Ferguson were Dave and Fergie to each other.) The symbolism of David, who fought the tall Philistine Goliath, meant a good deal to Finzi, who had fought his way out of bourgeois family life only to become threatened by tuberculosis. It might have been this inner turmoil that enabled him to dig deeply into his Romantic heritage as well as into Bach, for the Fantasia is his richest, widest harmonic exploration to that date, even perhaps in his whole output.

The Fantasia is his sole big work for one performer, and extraordinary that it was composed by a mediocre pianist who never as an adult performed in public. After the first bar the orchestra is silent, rejoining only after some seven minutes. There are no words to direct the music; it sounds improvisatory and is unbarred. It is abstract and eccentric, and unusual for Finzi in that the elements of rhythm, figuration, and harmony dominate, with little melody and no imitative part-writing. It is 'about' the conflict between plain, dotted, and triplet rhythm; between brilliant single-line runs and fist-fuls of chords; between crunched dissonances and innocent concords. The arresting start is an on-the-beat knocking fourth; the bass descends in whole tones; the 'knock' is halved in speed and thickened into sixths. From this rhythm, from bravura runs, a couple of broken-chord figures, and a series of massive chords, Finzi builds the opening rhetorical paragraphs. When the even rhythms change to a dotted baroque-style, the chromatic tensions of the harmonic minor tighten, then find release in mini-cadenzas. After a climax of false relations (F natural and F sharp) the dotted rhythms subside into triplets, the piano writing thickens to a more Brahmsian texture; and the first cantabile leads to a dolce 'white-note' passage, the quiet heart of this dramatic work (Ex 4.2). There is a sense of relief, of tragedy accepted.

Ex. 4.2

This settles into C major, the furthest possible retreat from the opening B flat and the eventual close in D. From there a finely controlled build-up begins. A long quickening *crescendo*, with the initial 'knock' now fully absorbed into the texture, leads, as Rubbra described in 1929, to the climax when the orchestra enters 'most dramatically with the initial figure of the whole movement'.

The Fantasia is not really a display piece: the bravura element is there, but the title 'grand' is unfortunate and misleading. The music is not grandiose, showy, or dazzling, any more than basically a Bach fantasia is. It is too inward-looking, too claustrophobic even, for that. In essence it is profoundly sad.

It is, however, the most complete absorption of Bach into Finzi's style, since the motoric elements in the Violin Concerto are nearer to pastiche. In his earlier work the influence of Tudor music, revived particularly by Terry at Westminster Cathedral (1901–24), is strong. The closely imitative textures within a limited compass, often even when instrumental, suggest the Byrd fantasias, and their modern re-working in Vaughan Williams. Cobbett's prize for a 'phantasy' string quartet was part of the movement. Finzi's early quotation from Byrd's *Attollite portas*, his recommending to Vera Strawson a concert of Weelkes, Wilbye, Gibbons, Bairstow's request for help in forming an early historical programme, all prove his interest in the period. Many of Finzi's early themes are rhythmically smooth, upward-reaching, bounded by a 'yearning' seventh, as in Example 4.3a, b, c, d, from the Requiem, *Footpath and Style*, and *New Year Music*, and all stylistically comparable with Butterworth's 'cherry tree' ('about the woodlands I will go').

Ex. 4.3

However, in the later 1920s other patterns and features become common, as in Example 4.4a, b, c from the Introit, and the ritornellos to 'His golden locks' and 'The salutation'.

Ex. 4.4

Such figures are essentially instrumental, not vocal; they suggest major–minor tonality, not modes; they have strong angular shapes and regular metric divisions, not the curving folksong-like contours of earlier Finzi. The invention-style passing notes were of course present to a degree even in the early unpublished songs; but they now begin to infiltrate less structured pieces than the arias, even lyrical song accompaniments, as in Example 3.2. Passages in the Fantasia suggest Brahms's piano writing. It is this integration of baroque and the more pianistic figuration into Finzi's generally romantic idiom that gives his mature music its individuality.

Gerald had very much the characteristic English suspicion of brilliance and facility. He saw Noel Coward's *Bittersweet* and vastly underrated its particular skill: 'the music that "everyone does", only perhaps a little more derivative. Yet how I wish I cd do these ordinary things that everyone else seems to be able to do.'[15] One can't help feeling he had no such wish at all! He also went to hear 'the Duke of Ellington' whose playing he found 'slightly aphrodisiacal, & all far too dazzling for my slow mind'.[16]

The Morrises, though genuinely fond of him, found him a trifle pompous and unworldly, and teased him by nicknaming him Burlington, after the 'most vulgar thing in the house' – their lavatory system – which Gerald did not find at all funny. Edith recalled that he never laughed, being 'so wrapped up in himself'. But Gerald and RO shared a nice sense of bathos, and saved newspaper cuttings for each other, the more fatuous the better. In their way RO and Jane were a curious pair. RO's pupil, Howard Ferguson, remembered as his greatest moment the time when RO during a lesson said in his very tired

---

[15] To Ferguson, 12 August 1929.
[16] To Ferguson, 21 June 1933.

voice: 'yes, Howard, I like that'. RO had a marvellously clear mind, but gave the impression of being totally unenthusiastic. Jane was a witchlike creature, who looked older than he, but was childish in the violence of her reactions; indeed RO always called her 'my child'. Cats – their charms, accouchements, snaps of, illnesses of, and burials – loom large in her letters to Gerald. His lessons had by now turned into friendly visits to show RO his work; in return he did jobs that ranged from making fair copies and piano duet versions of RO's compositions to letting in furniture-removers when the Morrises moved to Glebe Place after the Vaughan Williamses went to Dorking.

Gerald was developing a gentle, courteous way of disagreeing, when need be, with his friends. Howard was full of enthusiasm for Mary Webb, whose *Precious Bane* had just been praised by the prime minister, Stanley Baldwin. Gerald, with the tougher Hardy as part of his mind, replied that he'd only glanced over her poems and 'so probably got quite a wrong idea when I thought them a bit wishy-washy', but added 'I shall certainly get them'.[17]

Both Gerald and Howard were making headway. Howard had formed a piano trio, which broadcast in 1929, and Keith Falkner and Boult performed his *Lyke Wake Dirge* at Birmingham in January 1930. On 20 November 1929 the Oxford University Press gave Gerald an invitation concert at Amen House (then in Warwick Square). Howard with Kathleen Long played the Grand Fantasia and a movement from a chamber symphony on two pianos, and John Armstrong sang the new Hardy song-cycle of ten songs (*A Young Man's Exhortation*). Rubbra found the Grand Fantasia 'by far the best work'. Bliss wrote to tell Gerald that he was aware of a 'gifted sensibility' and 'an original beauty'. However he noted a sameness of emotion in each song – 'you are at present harping on one string, however deliciously. The last work played [the Fantasia] gave promise of something more, something different to the somewhat nostalgic country dreaming that permeates a good deal of the rest. I was honestly much impressed by passages that had promise of a very deep and original outlook. What you want for the full consummation of it is not more writing, but more living. You must have your full nature exploited by fate (and luckless man you will!) before we shall get the real you.'[18] Gerald's reply was not kept, but might be guessed by referring to Vaughan Williams's 1920 essay on Holst (which Gerald had previously recommended to Vera Strawson): 'To "live" is an expression which has had much harm done it by second-rate writers who seem to think that "life" is limited to pretending you like absinthe and keeping a mistress in Montmartre.'[19] Arthur's next postcard ran: 'I do mean the mistresses'. He was no doubt teasing; but his motive was concerned and kind. He meant 'more living' as Henry James did in the famous passage in *The Ambassadors*, through Strether's impassioned warning to little Bilham in Gloriani's garden: 'Live all you can . . . Live!'; and he was frank

17 2 January 1929.
18 20 November 1929.
19 *Beethoven's Choral Symphony* (London, 1953), p. 68.

enough to write what many people at that time might have thought. Vera was one who noted Gerald's scorn for ordinary mortals.

Another friend who warned Gerald (in a letter strikingly like Auden's to Britten of 31 January 1942) against going 'through life only meeting the people you choose which is all very pleasant and comfortable but has I feel some definite disadvantages'[20] was Herbert Lambert, the photographer and instrument maker. Herbert Howells introduced them. Lambert's double interest meant that his photographs of Elgar and Vaughan Williams are among the most penetrating ever taken; and in his workshop at Combe Down near Bath he was making harpsichords and clavichords very early in the revival. Howells composed 'Lambert's Fireside', the first of his clavichord pieces, in 1927, and Lambert sent his first letter to Gerald soon after. He gave him the address of Morley the clavichord maker, and tactfully offered him a fee to arrange a Purcell Saraband and 'Heartsease' for chamber ensemble for a local play. Lambert spent his working week in London; he came to Gerald's Amen House concert, and put him in touch with Maurice Jacobson, Curwen's reader, who however turned down his songs.

It was at that point he wrote his friendly warning. Besides cutting the well-known silhouette of Gerald,[21] he had taken some photographs of him and found the 'prunes & prisms' expression of some of them quite unfamiliar: when they were together they were always talking so Gerald had no chance to look 'proper'. As was his habit, Gerald wrote a footnote (unseen by Lambert) on the letter, refuting the charge – 'the composer is within himself & externals are of no consequence. Life cd never be pleasant or comfortable or even worthwhile for this composer, but for composition . . . why waste time in a grocery or haberdashery establishment, which is all that outworn theoretical teaching amounts to. Others can do it so much better.'[22]

1930, ROYAL ACADEMY OF MUSIC

He had just begun teaching one day a week at the Royal Academy of Music. To Howard he mocked 'the Royal Crematorium . . . the theory of music, harmony, the first species and such things about which I know nothing and care less. What a lot of tarradiddle & bunkum it all is.'[23] But characteristically he worked hard. Bairstow was glad he was to teach: 'you take a lot of settling down into a steady rhythm', he wrote, but 'eventually you will'.[24] Finzi was a composer outside the RAM's usual terms of reference, as at that time Vaughan Williams's music was not well known there; but 'the magic letters "VW" were always on his tongue', William Alwyn recalled. 'He was a gentle little man, Italianate and dapper, and very kind in his judgment of other composers – a

[20] Undated, early 1930.
[21] Letter from his widow to Joy Finzi, 7 December 1956.
[22] Undated, early 1930.
[23] 7 January 1930.
[24] 22 December 1929.

rare quality.'[25] He impressed his colleagues by the high quality of his work and by his probity.

In the holidays he joined the Lambert family camping at Rhossili on the Gower Peninsular in South Wales. 'How gay he was,' remembered Lambert's wife Georgie. She made him a zip-up boiler suit to keep him warm while working. She sent it to Mr Gentle Frenzi, and he repaid her with a suitably academic fugue, its subject beginning G[rand] C[omposing] C[ostume]. There were weekends at Bath, and walks along the towpath, the Roman roads, and over the Mendips, 'Gerald always with a well-thumbed & heavily pencilled book of verse in his pocket from which he & Herbert would read aloud during our picnic lunch & discuss the relative merit of this or that poem from the musician's point of view.'[26] Gerald, accepted by the parents and children alike, was in fact nearer their son John's age, and together he and John went canoeing from Salter's Yard on the Thames up the Kennet and Avon canal to Bath, Gerald's interest having been caught by some articles in The Observer on canals by a William Bliss.

It was Lambert who introduced him to the oboist Sylvia Spencer, and in August 1930 commissioned him to write a concerto or suite for her. He was not sure of the right price ('white mice I know are threepence halfpenny each') but offered him twelve pounds. Probably Lambert also prompted the Bridges part songs. He wrote Gerald a humdinger of a letter on the need for part songs of quality − Gerald having apparently refused to consider them 'proper work'.

1930, GRAHAM HUTTON

At Easter 1930 Gerald walked a wonderful thirty miles over Dartmoor, then to Polperro, Falmouth, and Penzance, and continued by boat across to the Scillies. There he put up at a small hotel, and at breakfast found a cheerful party of northerners breaking the more usual British calm. Into a lull came the comment 'personally, I likes me 'errings soused'. Gerald glanced up, met the amused eye of an equally solitary young man, and a friendship was born.

Graham Hutton, on his way to becoming a distinguished economist, had a highly trained mind and a string of degrees. He had never met anyone quite like Gerald, who had great penetration into what he knew and loved, and simply dismissed everything else. Gerald was anti-authoritarian, scorning convention, formality, and bourgeois standards. He was anti-public school, anti-doctors, -military and -businessmen. He was suspicious of education, which blunted natural perceptions, and he held that intelligence was inborn, that the village man was as good as the educated. There might have been a touch of sour grapes in his attitude, thought Hutton, had his nature not been so sweet and his loves always stronger than his hates. He was a last-ditcher, who would go to the stake for his ideals. Composing was of course more valu-

[25] Letter of 1 August 1982.
[26] 7 December 1956.

able than anything else, but he worked for the capital gain of the arts, with little thought of personal renown.

On the Scillies they took a boat and Gerald sang to the seals, who sang back. Then and on later occasions they walked miles together, Gerald thrusting forward with a long stride, often reciting Hardy poems or singing folksongs. They walked the Ridgeway, Gerald barefoot; and dropped into a village at tea-time to ask at the Post Office if there was a cottage, preferably with feather beds, where they could put up. There was a mystical element in Gerald's feeling for the land, in his passion over the dignity of working the earth; and he would quote Blake, Samuel Butler's Notebooks, and reams from Hardy's *The Dynasts*. Walking up to thirty miles a day and arguing all the way, Gerald would yet keep alert, sharp eyes – 'he never missed a mousehole' – and once, hardly daring to breathe, they watched dragonflies mating. He struck Hutton as of mountain stock, possibly north Italian or Greek, and sleek as a seal or an otter. Any crassness, cant, or platitude would make him laugh till the tears came, chortling and shaking all over. They took a punt on the Thames, called at Kelmscott to see William Morris's house, read Webster's *The Duchess of Malfi* together in the evenings. Hutton found Gerald extremely well-read in English literature, but insular in his taste: for him, 'the blacks began at Calais'.

1930, FLANDERS AND GERMANY

A holiday in August, his only trip as an adult to Europe, was fairly disastrous. Vera and Frank Strawson took him to Belgium and Germany. He found her 'the most fussy traveller I have ever known . . . Travels entirely in terms of hotels . . . always too hot or too cold . . . wishing to leave museums or art galleries almost as soon as she is in them.' Her dislikes irritated him so much that he made a list of them and confronted her with it; 'hates turnips, parsnips, Kia-ora; railway journeys, sea-journeys . . . cannot walk on cobbles, or climb towers . . .'.[27] As she remembered it, however, a nasty traffic accident near Dunkirk, which left him with a scar for life, quite put him off the rest of the trip.

From his jottings in a notebook diary it seems he liked Belgian and French café life. He noted the balsam and Lombardy poplars above the cobbled roads in Flanders; and the great courtesy but poor physique of the Belgians. He saw the Menin gate at Ypres, where the signs of battle had already almost vanished. To some extent the journey must have been a pilgrimage: here Farrar had died, Blunden and Bliss had fought; earlier, Hardy had explored the field of Waterloo. He noted a religious procession in Belgium on the way to Ypres; 'firework procession in Bruges – dance – torchlights'; and in Germany 'little student bands singing hi hi ho'. (Joy Finzi recalled his mentioning some influence from this on one of his Shakespeare songs: possibly, she thought, the strumming postlude to 'Who is Sylvia?', composed two years later.)

In his notebook there is the word 'anti-semiticism' and the swastika sign.

---

27 Gerald's notebook.

'German seriousness still rampant . . . absence of Daily Mirror type of vulgarity.' In Weimar he found the war memorial ugly, noted the reek of German cigars, and that museums closed too early, but also the respect for art and culture. He noted the unsatisfactory milk system in Germany; also 'Latrine system good in Belgium, so open & unashamed. Too much spitting. Adverts for ven. disease in Belgian lav. & for aphrodisiacs in German lavs.' and the 'naked bodies everywhere down the Rhine, boating, basking, bathing'. 'Is it instinct of Puritan sterness or Catholic joy,' he asked himself, 'behind German activity & energy. For instance. Revival of Puritanism wld bring in England a revival of work & intensity. But it wd also lead to a revival of formal dress & a horror of the bare body. How do Germans manage both.'

His mother occasionally visited her sister Hettie Schwabacher in Hanover; Gerald thought her the only fairly intelligent member of the family. But he was adamant about seeing as little as possible of his English, let alone his German relations (none of his friends realized he was of Jewish descent). His sister Kate's marriage was breaking up. In distress she landed on him at Caroline Street: 'terribly glad to see any of my own people. Thanks for having me & helping me clear away cobwebs in my own mind.'[28] He sent a further cobweb-clearing letter after her: 'Don't you know by this time that work is long & life is short and that no philosophy in the world can alter the fact that this particular rearrangement of matter, which we call work, can only be done under another given set of conditions-within-conditions. . . . It can be done but once & therefore shd be put before everything else.'

He made his position even clearer to her after he began work at the Royal Academy of Music: 'even if I had nothing to do, I shd not accept the invitation. This is not to say that I don't appreciate it, but that I shd hate the party with all the "interesting people". The fact that you can't grasp this without imagining some would-be-superiority makes me despair of ever being able to explain. What you say about the shades of Strawson superiority or Jews (or even that agonising superscription of Professor – do you *really* imagine I like that sort of thing) is so completely & utterly off the mark that it makes me feel like an Englishman who knows no Japanese trying to explain to a Japanese who knows no English.'[29] (As Butler wrote of his Ernest Pontifex: 'His father and grandfather could probably no more understand his state of mind than they could understand Chinese'.) It might, however, be inferred from letters to Gerald from his mother that he was prepared to pay off Katie's debts in 1931, the year of her divorce – 'to me it seems a mistake; it would be a precedent', Mrs Finzi advised him. His cousin Wilhelm Schwabacher called on him on a London visit in 1931, and gave him a book of his poems. In it Gerald wrote 'I remember him as a typical German student, with the usual duel slash across his face & with military leanings . . . I told him that I thought the Nazis would soon be in power. (He ridiculed the idea) . . . I only hope his German verse is

28 25 March 1930.
29 21 March 1932.

better than his English . . . With the advent of the Nazis he committed suicide.'

Gerald must have been encouraged that on 20 January 1930 the BBC, with a view to finding new works, included his *New Year Music* in a 'try-over' without an audience. Then five of his already known Hardy songs were given at a Music Clubs concert at the Grotrian Hall on 15 January 1931. They were praised: Richard Capell, Frank Howes, and Eric Blom recognized their quality, but OUP, Curwen, and Boosey & Hawkes turned them down – there was little market for songs.

By now Gerald was getting restive at the Academy. Vaughan Williams had organized a Wigmore Hall concert of R. O. Morris's works on 14 November 1930, for which Gerald had guaranteed five pounds. Perhaps that gave him an idea. Early in 1932 he approached his fellow-professor Alan Bush with the suggestion of promoting recitals of works 'not more than thirty (or twenty) years old'. They drew in William Alwyn and Norman Demuth. Finzi wanted proper Academy backing, so that they would not be seen as a small group fighting authority. Bush arranged the first concert, then a committee was formed, which Gerald hoped would have young people continually brought in. From the start he was against their doing their own works – 'it gives a handle to any possible grousers'.[30] His initial suggestions were Bartók's First Quartet and Piano Sonatina, Vaughan Williams's Four Hymns, Hindemith's Third Quartet, and Falla's harpsichord Concerto. Leon Goossens had promised Bush to play Bax's Oboe Quintet with the Griller Quartet, but was proving hard to pin down. Gerald – never one to rate a performer above a composer – suggested making a definite date 'whether it suits prima-donna Goossens' or not. He also proposed Ireland's Cello Sonata, but Bush reminded him that the Academy wanted fifty percent RAM/RCM composers, and suggested asking one Jervis-Read to play his own piano compositions. Gerald pointed out that Jervis-Read was not 'a representative European composer & therefore has no business in this programme. If we start tampering with the standard . . . in the second concert, what will the twentieth be like.'[31] Gerald was in charge of the concert on 16 June 1932, held in the Academy theatre, when 'anything from thirty to sixty had to be turned away'.

CEDRIC THORPE DAVIE

A friend made through Howard in the early 1930s was Cedric Thorpe Davie. Ceddie was just leaving the Scottish National Academy of Music as a student and coming to the RCM. He and Gerald crossed swords amiably on how music should be analysed and form taught, in particular comparing Elgar's Violin Concerto with Brahms's. Gerald gently teased the younger man about his 'system': 'But it failed to distinguish, when it got cut & dried / Form that's

[30] 21 March 1932.
[31] 17 May 1932.

organic from form that's applied.' He continued the discussion: 'I love Brahms through & through (no: not *Rinaldo*) but it's no good being blind to the fact that form & content were nearly always two separate things with him . . . Formality,' he went on irrefutably, 'has about as much to do with form as bugs with buggery.'[32] Ceddie often joined Gerald and Howard for concerts, making a beeline for the unreserved seats in the balcony of Queen's Hall. Gerald's shock of gypsy-black hair and intense hazel-green eyes, which darted all over the place, always attracted attention. The moment he came in, he was a personality. Short but not little, he appeared, even to someone who didn't know him, deeply committed to whatever he was doing. Usually, waiting for the concert to start, he talked earnestly with his companions. But there were gleeful moments. On one occasion he went to the lavatory and came back in stitches, having opened a cubicle and found Dame Ethel Smyth sitting there!

1930–33, MEETING JOY

His friendship with Vaughan Williams prospered and he was present at the private play-overs of the older composer's Piano Concerto and – with Holst – Fourth Symphony (three years before its first performance). Knowing that he felt cooped-up in London, Mrs Vaughan Williams often invited him for 'mild tennis' at their Dorking house, The White Gates, and occasionally asked him to 'care-take' when they were away. He also took long walks, in Shropshire, in Devon, and in Cornwall. But though country holidays were all very well, he needed something more permanent. Through a casual friend he rented a cottage, 'The House above the Trees', for six months from March 1930, at Lye Green, near Crowborough in Sussex. It was on the estate of 'Bingles', where lived Mrs Black and her two beautiful tall daughters. They had been warned by the friend 'on no account to disturb the Beethoven'. But the first time Gerald lit the cottage fire it smoked. Unwillingly the elder daughter, acting as landlord, went to deal with his complaint. Gerald opened the door to her, and fell in love.

For Joy it happened more slowly. She was at a dreamy, self-absorbed stage (though she dealt promptly enough with the chimney). Music had always been part of her life. She had learnt the violin and composition and conducted her suite for strings at Moira House School in Eastbourne. An obscure new girl (who became the novelist Rumer Godden) was awe-struck at her many gifts, her wide and serious eyes, and her demonstration of Jaques Dalcroze eurhythmics. After leaving school she played in amateur orchestras, attended the Three Choirs festivals, and developed her interest in sculpture. She had outstanding natural co-ordination; she and her sister Mags played tennis to county standard; and everything she did was done with ease and grace. Her father died when she was eighteen and – thinking it might be useful – she learnt to type.

Joy was born on 3 March 1907. Her father Ernest Black had in 1889

32 July 1933.

married Amy Whitehorne, a resourceful person who at the age of seven rescued her younger sister from drowning. Ernest's mother, Rosalinda Blow, was a Scots Presbyterian; Joy had an uncle who was Moderator of the Church of Scotland. The Whitehornes were precious-stone merchants, and the Blacks were in East India trade; there was wealth and comfort in the family. Bingles, on the edge of Ashdown Forest, was a house of sufficient quality to have been described in the *Country Life* series in 1914: 'A Lesser Country House of the 16th century'.[33] Life there was unhurried and happy. Gerald found himself playing cricket in long grass, missing very easy catches. He struck a fellow-cricketer, the violinist Ralph Nicholson, as a chap who didn't have to worry about things too much; there was surprise that he could devote his time just to composing. Though at Bingles he was always on the fringe of the party, friendly but not effusive, it was clear that he and Joy liked each other's company.

He knew that she was the only woman for him, but he did wonder whether he should marry at all. He had some insight into his demanding character. Compared with his composition, nothing mattered. His dedication was absolute, but he could work only slowly, and within his own conditions. He had just enough money to support himself. He feared the intrusion of marriage, feared Joy's livelier, easier way of life, feared even that her money might be an unacknowledged attraction. He knew too that her friends and family, in particular one cousin Florence, were doubtful about him. He won Joy's sister Mags over by his love of the countryside, but Mrs Black teasingly called him Mr Fizzi.

Gerald and Joy went to concerts together. She was involved with an amateur choir at nearby Withyham, and persuaded him to conduct it through the 1931–32 winter season. It won at the local Spring Festival. This was practical experience to reinforce Lambert's request for partsongs. Joy first heard Gerald's music at a concert promoted by OUP on 17 February 1932, and understood it completely: 'It simply *was* Gerald.' *The Morning Post* picked out three songs as especially good – 'Proud songsters', 'Fear no more', and 'To Joy' (not Gerald's Joy, but Edmund Blunden's lament for his dead baby aged forty days). The *News Chronicle* found Finzi's talent 'already mature . . . he has written much music of a recognizably high order.'

To get right away and think about it, he took passage on a cargo boat that happened to be going to Cairo over Christmas 1932 (Joy organized and booked it for him). Mrs Vaughan Williams wrote saying she was glad Gerald was going 'prepared for every sort of life'. When he boarded the ship at Dover he decided it was all going to be splendid: 'the Captain's a nice quiet chap, who produced a yo-yo this evening!' he wrote to Howard.[34] He had a wonderful voyage, and found that being on the bridge of a small ship in a high sea was exactly like the last movement of the Second Brahms Sextet. He

33 5 December 1914.
34 4 December 1932.

saw much of Cairo outside the usual tourist itinerary, and, putting into Lisbon on the way back, bought a dozen bottles of port for R. O. Morris. Once home, he visited Holst to tell him about it.

Two further events probably helped Gerald to make up his mind to propose. One was the death of Joy's mother that winter, leaving her vulnerable but released. The second was that he found himself being zealously courted by another woman. Ruth Harrison, whose translations of French writers caused Howard to call her the Lady of the French Letters, had fallen in love with him, and suggested an affair. Acutely embarrassed, Gerald turned to Howard to help him draft a gentle, tactful letter, which throws light on how he recalled his childhood, and contains his first quotation from Wordsworth's *Intimations*:

> In writing, you did the most sensible thing in the world . . . For me, on the contrary, and for the first time in my life, or since my infancy (for I *suppose* that there was a time when 'every human sight to me did seem apparelled in celestial light' – though I can't remember it) things have appeared rather more happy & clearly . . . But there was never any remedy but work.

At the foot of her letter he pencilled the note: 'Poor girl, I was always afraid of this & that is why I kept the correspondence as much as possible to postcards & philosophy! [But he bought her book.] The day I received her letter March 25th 1933 I had become engaged to my darling Joy.' Perhaps knowing that another woman found him desirable had given him courage. Coming back one night from a Queen's Hall concert – Joy driving – he asked: 'I suppose you wouldn't shock cousin Florence and marry me?'

ENGAGEMENT

It shocked Joy to the extent that next day she found herself at the mercy of one of the bad asthma attacks she had suffered since she was a baby. She knew that she was totally involved with Gerald, but had never thought about marrying anyone, and felt herself 'quite removed from the world'. Gerald simply stormed into her bedroom next morning, took it for granted she'd said yes, and very efficiently started telling her all the disadvantages of marriage with him, how little money he had, his shyness, his need for privacy and quiet. Joy, scarcely able to breathe, found herself engaged to a torrent.

For some weeks they kept the news private. In April Gerald borrowed a cottage in Cornwall, on the Helford river, with 'a tree to dive off, boating & no visitors' as he wrote to Howard. He included the – for him – astonishing statement: 'I've no wish to do any work!'[35] Back in London, he confessed apologetically to Sybil Eaton that he hadn't worked quite so hard recently, 'this sort of thing's very upsetting'. Sybil was naturally curious about Joy. 'She says she doesn't mind what clothes I wear, so that's all right.' 'Yes, but what is she like?' Long pause. 'Well, I'll tell you who she's *not* like, and that's Harriet Cohen' –

[35] 13 April 1933.

which spoke volumes to anyone who knew that socially minded, sophisticated pianist.

He wanted everyone to meet her, and to show her everything. He sent a telegram to Detmar and Winifred Blow at 'Hilles', saying 'coming with joy' and arrived with Joy. He took her to see Holst, then near the end of his life, in an Ealing nursing home lying on an iron bedstead. Holst looked at her, thinking perhaps of his own marriage, and asked: 'what are you going to do with Gerald?' Joy, who hadn't thought of doing anything with him, was at a loss and said tentatively perhaps she'd encourage him to sit down for meals. That evening, most inappropriately, they and Howard went to see *Otello* (Melchior singing in German), Howard having to tell him 'the best way & the full time it takes . . .' to get from Ealing to Covent Garden.

Howard found that Joy took his part in Gerald's life for granted: it simply meant 'three tickets, of course,' for everything. 'It's a great and glorious thing to Gerald and me,' Joy wrote to him. He was struck that from the word go her idea was to match her life to Gerald's, and that she seemed to know exactly what he wanted. To Gerald, Howard wrote (after threatening them with an avalanche of silver salvers if they wouldn't suggest a present): 'you have been a damned good friend to me, you have never changed one whit, and you have always been there.'[36] Vaughan Williams wrote 'My Dear Gerald, How glad I am for you both. You are both lucky ones & are going to be very happy. Yrs RVW.'[37] Not all Gerald's friends took their marriage so much for granted: a funny little thing like Gerald, thought Sybil Eaton, and she so tall and radiant! It was, thought Graham Hutton, as if he was confirming his love of England by marrying Britannia.

The two composers were busily occupied, Howard with an Octet, Gerald with an Oboe Interlude. Dan Godfrey broadcast Gerald's *New Year Music* on 11 March 1932, then performed it at Bournemouth on 16 March. Introit, the salvaged movement of the Violin Concerto, was played by Anne Macnaghten and conducted by Iris Lemare on 31 January 1933 at one of their notable concerts promoting contemporary British music (when Britten's Sinfonietta had its first public performance). At last Hubert Foss at OUP accepted Finzi's Hardy songs, *A Young Man's Exhortation*. Marriage to Joy meant that Gerald would give up his teaching at the Academy, and he greeted his last day there in July with 'Allylewya! Allylewya! Allylewya!'[38]

1933, MARRIAGE

They found a house in Hampstead, 30 Downshire Hill, round the corner from Keats Grove where Joy's Aunt Lily lived. A 'carroty-headed devil' who'd been a suffragette, Aunt Lily was full of good works and was musical too, and Gerald quickly fell for her. Hampstead was high and quiet, with few cars in those

36 19 August 1933.
37 Undated.
38 To Thorpe Davie, undated.

days. They built out a bathroom and planted a fig tree. They were married on 16 September 1933. Gerald didn't want his fussy mother or his interfering sister present, so they asked the Vaughan Williamses if they could be married from their house in Dorking. Ralph hoped he could play the harmonium, but it was a simple registry office wedding, and Joy, when handed their marriage certificate, said matter-of-factly that she would put it away with her dog licence.

They drove up to Hampstead for lunch with Aunt Lily, and on to East Anglia, calling on Gerald's mother, then rambling through Suffolk and Norfolk. Romantically, in Norwich they struck a good production of *Romeo and Juliet*. Less romantically, they set out at five in the morning for the Blakeney bird sanctuary, quite forgetting it was the wrong season of the year, with no birds. Then up to Scotland – till the end of his life Gerald kept some white heather they picked together – and back to Downshire Hill. Within seconds of coming through the door, Gerald was dealing with the post and answering letters. Joy's typing came in useful after all.

On 8 November Dan Godfrey broadcast the Introit, and on 5 December *A Young Man's Exhortation* had its first full public performance, at the Grotrian Hall, sung by Frank Drew. John Coates was to have sung it, and when Gerald took the music to him he found that Coates had tactfully laid out some Italian songs on the piano to make him feel at home! In the event Coates had to withdraw because of ill health.

Joy and her sister Mags had sold their Sussex house, and with it went Gerald's country retreat. The newly-weds scanned the advertisements, and saw a house they liked called Beech Knoll at Aldbourne in Wiltshire. They bought it at auction for £1,800. For a time they moved between their town and country homes. Gerald's Edith was installed at Hampstead, where she found life more regular than at Caroline Street – 'three courses and coffee'. Mags was a frequent visitor. Joy learnt the use of sculpting tools at the Central School of Art and Design under John Skeaping, and began modelling a head of Howard. She also took violin lessons from Sybil Eaton. Gerald's partsong 'Nightingales' was published; he sent a copy to Holst in his clinic, who wrote back that the nightingales 'are a joy'. By the time Kennedy Scott performed the partsong with the Oriana Choir on 5 June 1934, Holst was dead. Gerald still went to every concert of British music he could, and also that year heard Boult conduct the first English (concert) performance of *Wozzeck* and Stravinsky conduct his *Perséphone*. The Finzis went to the first Glyndebourne season.

Gerald persuaded Curwen to withdraw his early publications, including *By Footpath and Stile*, which now seemed to him 'really bad works'. He wanted a clean slate. His cousin Neville, whose article on radium had just been printed in *The Times*, noted that he was becoming 'less inhuman, less self-engrossed'. Friends too remarked a softening in him, and more humour, since Joy loved to tease him. The change is noticeable in his handwriting: formerly so cramped and small, it relaxes and expands. He had never felt so well in his life.

Their son Christopher was born at Downshire Hill in July 1934, Gerald steadily reading the *New Statesman* upside down in the next room. Soon they realized there was more trouble than pleasure involved in keeping up two homes. Besides, Joy was discovering how awkward and uncomfortable Gerald could be at social gatherings. Now that he was married, more invitations came his way; and there was some feeling among Londoners that performances were the result of meeting the right people. Such a farce, thought Joy; the thing was, to write the music. She herself felt shy in this new world, but was wise enough to see that Gerald's gaucheness would be no help to him at all. So early in 1935 they sold their London house and settled into Beech Knoll.

CHAPTER FIVE

Beech Knoll

1935–38

Beech Knoll lay on what was then the edge of Aldbourne village, six miles from Hungerford in Berkshire. The house was large and old, with lawns and the copper beech that gave it its name, and a big walled fruit and vegetable garden. There were two outbuildings. One became Joy's studio where, masked to protect her asthmatic chest from the dust, she sculpted and carved. They turned the other building into a badminton court, and also used it for country dancing, which Joy organized for their village friends. They built a cottage for a gardener and his wife, and enlarged the kitchen wing to take day and night nurseries. It was characteristic of Joy to engage two girls who had been daunted by life to look after her babies. Audrey Evans, the Norland nurse, had been with a difficult family for her first job. Peggy Bendle, the nursery maid, was a raw fourteen-year-old, unhappy with adopted parents. Joy took Audrey to country-dancing days in Devizes, and Peggy to sing in Bach's B minor Mass with the Marlborough Choral Society. Both Audrey and Peggy were struck that there was no class distinction. They all lunched together in the nursery, including Gerald. He was no longer a fanatical vegetarian (though he astonished people by biting into a grapefruit like an apple); now he ate eggs and fish, and enjoyed smoked salmon, sometimes chicken or bacon. He reckoned he was better than anyone at scrambling eggs and always cooked them himself. There were delicious nut dishes, and cheeses were sent down once a fortnight from a specialist shop in London.

Howard Ferguson was now leaping ahead as a composer. His Octet was broadcast and published, and his Two Ballads were given at the 1934 Gloucester Three Choirs Festival. Gerald went to hear them, bravely driving himself alone, at thirty miles an hour or under all the way, and stayed a night or two, having refused the first offer of accommodation because his prospective hostess had a butler – 'so unnerving'. (He gave up driving after he turned the car over, trying to avoid a duck.)

In 1935 Frank Howes, then the editor of the English Folk Dance and Song Society Journal, asked Gerald to review *Folksongs from Newfoundland*, edited by Maud Karpeles (a selection from her 1929–30 collection). The accompaniments, commented Gerald, were 'serviceable, impersonal' – anonymity being usually regarded as a cardinal point in setting folksongs 'perfect and complete in themselves' and no more in need of amplification 'than is a Purcell Fantasia, or the Enigma Variations'. Gerald however thought there was the attitude of the arranger to consider. 'A tune, or even a verse, lights up an excitement within him. Here is something with which he wishes to be identified, and which he also wishes to share.' The result might be 'a new work'. One essential quality was tradition – 'a communal thing, and not to be confused with maypoles, varsity ties and blood. It is like a cable along which one can speak to infinity, and like a cable it must be charged and alive, for once the life ceases, tradition becomes convention.' In his letter to Howes, Finzi declared that folksong 'has been like food, grammar or counterpoint, it helped to build me up'.[1]

The same year, 1935, Cedric Thorpe Davie, to celebrate leaving the Royal College of Music to study in Budapest, composed with a fellow-student a spoof oratorio called Lot, and gave it at a Hampstead party. Telegrams from R. Strauss ('Heilichiste Gruss'), Walford Davies ('Blessings on beautiful music') and Lot himself ('What about my daughters?') could possibly have been traced to Harold Samuel, Howard, and Gerald. Gerald sent Ceddie off with mock regrets that it was too late to warn him against drink and women ('I don't warn you . . . I'm all for it' added Joy) but was quite serious that study abroad would be a 'complete waste of time musically'.[2] He kept him posted about what he was hearing in England: Bax no. 6, 'which I'm certain will be exactly the same as Bax no 5, 4, [3], 2 & 1 – buzz, buzz, buzz'[3] (but he went to the Three Choirs that year to hear Bax's The Morning Watch – 'the better Bax, I think'[4]). Walton's Symphony, now complete with last movement, was 'terrific, as far as technique, nervous tension & cerebration'[5] went, but he still felt 'the Jovian thunderbolts of VW 4 are more significant'.[6] To Budapest he sent high praise of Bartók's First Quartet; and a request for Ceddie to get him Beethoven's Opp. 130 and 131 in the Peters piano duet version, since that volume was no longer being issued; then, in an ominous parenthesis: '(I expect they've discovered that Beethoven had some Jewish blood in him & that they'll gradually ban him in Germany.)'[7]

John and Alice Sumsion, not far away in Gloucester, were frequent visitors to Beech Knoll. John and Gerald would go off on two- or three-day walks, no longer covering the vast distances that Gerald did as a younger man, but a more comfortable ten to twelve miles a day; Gerald loved the ancient feel of the Ridgeway and the Vale of the White Horse, the wild flowers, and the country lore. They went up Snowdon together 'but alas, found that we were not the first',[8] as Gerald reported to Howard. For George V's Jubilee in 1935 the Finzis stayed with the Sumsions, and that night climbed up May Hill to the bonfire, helping a heavily pregnant Alice. Gerald rejoiced to see the hilltop being used for a beacon, as it had been for the Armada.

[1]   24 October 1935.
[2]   12 August 1935.
[3]   5 November 1935.
[4]   30 August 1935.
[5]   14 August 1935.
[6]   9 February 1936.
[7]   5 November 1935.
[8]   2 May 1935.

Life was pleasant and leisurely. Ticked off by the orderly Howard for dating a letter just 'Wednesday', Gerald replied that 'one day more or less never seems to matter'.[9] If he felt he wanted a night in London, there was always a room with Joy's Aunt Lily or with Howard: 'we might go on the razzle together – wine, women & song, or failing all three – a concert & theatre or two'.[10] There were walks of 'five or six hours on the downs & not a soul seen the whole time. The sort of day in October that closes with a frosty mist & you come home to a fire & an egg for tea.'[11] In 1935 Gerald and Joy took a three-day summer break at Abbotsbury in Dorset, then a winter holiday at Helford in Cornwall: 'a grand time', he wrote to Howard, 'walking, sketching (Joy, not me) typing (Joy, not me) reading – one of the objects of the holiday was to get the "Seven Pillars" [T. E. Lawrence] digested, as it deserves. Joy is proving a wonderful cook, & even I have made a magnificent sardine-dish.'[12] Though Howard was often holidaying and touring on the continent, Gerald never went abroad again: 'Chartres is one of the few places abroad to which I have always wanted to go, but doubt if I'll ever get there. I feel so un-at-home out of England.'[13] He used to say 'I've had abroad, like Chopin,' and got as much excitement out of going from one county to another as most people derive from foreign travel.

1936, PERFORMANCES

On 2 July 1935 Finzi conducted for the first time, his New Year Music, in a broadcast with a section of the BBC Orchestra. The Drummond Elegies, the Milton Sonnets, and the early Rossetti children's songs were published during 1936 by OUP (though Gerald was none too pleased with the terms he obtained, grumbling to Howard that 'the effrontery of the OUP is positively Italian or German'[14]). Early that year there were three concerts of first performances. In London at a Lemare concert at the Mercury Theatre on 6 February, Steuart Wilson sang the Two Sonnets, the aria 'His golden locks', and the song 'When I set out for Lyonesse' (with orchestral accompaniment). On 23 March 1936 the Elegies were broadcast; and the next day Leon Goossens and the Menges quartet gave the Oboe Interlude at the Wigmore Hall. Boosey & Hawkes sent a representative to hear the Interlude and to Finzi's surprised delight offered to publish it, and also the new set of Hardy songs for baritone and piano, Earth and Air and Rain. All this was music composed before Gerald's marriage, but the recognition now was welcome.

9   17 May 1936.
10   6–14 October 1936.
11   To Ferguson, 21 October 1935.
12   17 February 1936.
13   To Ferguson, 23 September 1935.
14   19 October 1935.

Oboe Interlude, Op. 21; Bridges Partsongs, Op. 17

The oboe concerto or suite commissioned by Herbert Lambert in 1930 had turned into one movement for oboe and string quartet. In 1932 Holst suggested Finzi should enter a *Daily Telegraph* competition for chamber music, but he completed the Interlude only just before his wedding in 1933. 'There's some decent music in it & a certain amount of rant, which I had to stick in to fill things up when I got rather rushed towards the end,'[15] he told Howard Ferguson, who replied perceptively that the 'rant' might well turn out to be the best music. Finzi sent the score to the Macnaghten Quartet hoping for a performance, but to his chagrin it was turned down; it was then run through by the Jessie Snow quartet and an oboist called Butterworth. At that stage Finzi hoped to make it part of a complete quintet, and reserved the opus number 22 for it. Possibly he revised the Interlude; early in 1936 he sent it to Leon Goossens, who asked for the dedication.

It covers a surprising range: the modest title and ambling gait are deceptive, for it is a big impassioned piece. The sonority for string quartet is in turn delicate and vigorous, and the oboe arabesques almost suggest a concerto. The themes have an affinity with the 'Rhapsody' in *Dies Natalis*; the central *sostenuto* theme in particular with 'O what venerable creatures . . .'; but whereas that is fresh and sparkling, this is more troubled, more sensuous, as the melodies twist and twine over dissolving harmonies. It is, for Finzi, slightly exotic; his *Flos Campi*, as it were (though Vaughan Williams was rather taken aback by it). In the recapitulation the scoring for strings is first etiolated, then full and urgent; and – as in *A Severn Rhapsody* – the climax is marked by a brief new variant of the theme, striding in bold block chords (but the second fff climax is one too many). The strings close around the tolling oboe internal pedal to form an hieratic end. Later Finzi scored the Interlude for oboe and string orchestra.

Another work Lambert encouraged was the set of seven unaccompanied partsongs to words by Robert Bridges, composed between 1931 and 1937 (with others sketched and discarded). Finzi had been unable to find a publisher for the early ones. Holst suggested the difficulty lay in the treble and tenor parts going above G natural; Finzi kept his occasional A naturals and contributed towards OUP's publishing costs. He did, however, feel that he lacked experience with choirs at this time; and later, comparing his partsongs with those of other composers, he called them old-maidish and finicky. He was too critical; his are a pleasure to sing, refined rather than finicky, but they are conservative, more like his early Requiem than his Drummond Elegies. Each voice is of equal worth and sings (almost) the complete text with no repeated words. The group is slighter in content than, say, Holst's seven Bridges partsongs (Holst's are for different forces) and in one only, the five-part 'Nightingales', is there the throb of passion that sounds in the Inter-

15 17 August 1933.

lude. But how Finzi, just married to his Joy, must have enjoyed setting 'My spirit sang all day' with its chime of 'joy', and concluding 'thou art my Joy'!

Earth and Air and Rain, Op. 15

Finzi did not call *Earth and Air and Rain*, his next set of Hardy poems, a cycle as he had *A Young Man's Exhortation*; but more appears in the plan of these ten songs for baritone and piano than simply a care for balance. The point of the first, 'Summer schemes', is the contrast between the resolve – 'we'll go – we two' – and the doubt in the last lines of the verse – '. . . but who shall say What may not chance before that day!' Finzi goes to the heart of this. He contradicts the metrical stress, which, mechanically, would read 'We'll *go, we two,* to *that* arched *fane,*' and throws the couple's purpose into relief, setting the crucial words to long, even notes and 'rhyming' the melodic drop of a fourth (Ex. 5.1).

Ex. 5.1

Charmingly, the birdsong 'shakes' and 'trills' are sung to long plain notes while the piano carols around them. Finzi's piano writing has become more idiomatic; the springs and cascades in the second verse inspire delicate figuration. But both verses end speculatively, and the C naturals in the final bars of a D major song bring foreboding.

Next, a journey is made – Hardy's to Cornwall and his Emma. Finzi catches the traveller's impatience by the accentuation 'When I set OUT for Lyonnesse', and carries the snap of 'Lyonesse' into the spare, obsessive accompaniment. He keeps up the pace of his swinging tune throughout, even notating, Brahms-like, the *rallentando* at the end. The tonic major for the trio, as unobtrusive and tender as Schubert's in the first *Winterreise* song, signals the romance at the journey's end; and the magical change in the traveller is triumphantly symbolized by the progression through E flat into G major ('. . . marked with mute *surmise* My radiance . . .') before he arrives home to E minor. 'Lyonnesse' is deservedly one of Finzi's best-known songs, a splendid tune and an example of how reflexively he uses an A, B, modified A form to carry a developing situation.

In 'Waiting both' Hardy sets a human against the universe: star and poet speak to each other, and patiently wait for eternity to reveal the purpose of creation. Blunden described the poem as confronting us like 'the eye of a bird on a nest'.[16] As in the earlier song 'The comet' (p. 41), Finzi uses the extreme registers of the keyboard with the human voice isolated in the middle. The

---

16 E. Blunden, *Thomas Hardy* (London, 1942) [1958 edn], p. 258.

bass creeps in semitones to suggest timelessness; but plunges down consecutive fifths to mirror man's capacity for change, and the cadence fans out to immensity (see Ex. 3.7).

'The phantom' was, in Hardy's life, the outcome of 'Lyonnesse'. Both concern his first wife Emma, 'Lyonesse' his dazzling meeting with her, 'The phantom' his sad guilty return to Cornwall after her death. Both songs are enhanced ballads, with the beat of movement throughout, but with their form modified to indicate change. In 'The phantom' time acts on the lovers: he ages, she is held, young as once she was, in his memory. Hardy's title was 'The phantom horsewoman', and Finzi binds the sections of his long song together by the dotted six-eight cantering motif in the piano, developing it linearly, not in the imitative tissue of his earlier songs; and he uses discords to propel movement, not just as points of colour. In the first stanza the spare accompaniment places the watching man at some distance. In the second, urgent syncopation closes in as he sees the phantom; in the third, feverish chromatics insinuate the vision into his brain, day and night. When finally the 'ghost-girl-rider' breaks free, the cantering motif is given for the first time joyously to the singer. The piano's bare coda leaves only her haunted memory.

The fifth and seventh songs are conversational, as was the earlier 'Ditty'; but have a new quality of whimsicality. 'So I have fared', Hardy's macaronic verse quoting Latin tags from the Psalms, with twisted syntax and double rhymes ('tryst, I; fecisti!'), is all rather learned; and Finzi wittily parodies this in his reciting-note style. But the last two verses darken, and their strict summing-up of a life – 'through many suns' – brings Finzi's familiar march of time (see Ex. 8.1). The teasing and tender 'To Lizbie Browne' mirrors the opening song in looking at lost chances. Stanzas 1, 3, 5, 7, and 9 almost match melodically, as do stanzas 2 and 6, 4 and 8; but Finzi's 'matches' are seldom exact. To enjoy his relish for sound and meaning, compare 'So swift your life, And mine so slow, You were a wife ere I could show Love', from stanza 5 (see Ex. 16.1b) with its equivalent melody in stanzas 1 and 3. The girl's name chimes eighteen times, giving Finzi a constant against which to play rhythmic variations (to emphasise the 'flexible and wayward' beat he uses the direction *Ravvivando al Tempo* for the first time). This is not a song for a singer to indulge in: not heavy with nostalgia, but a rueful backward smiling glance; and is the bar after 'you disappeared' a sly reference to Elgar's 'angel' motif? Between these songs comes 'Rollicum-rorum', a good hearty tune, not quite obvious because of its three-beat bars in duple rhythm and the side-slip at the end of each verse out of and back into the tonic key. (Keith Falkner suggested the high octave ending.)

'The clock of the years', like 'The phantom', is about time. In the former, the man grew older, the woman stayed young. In this the dead woman – unnaturally, frighteningly – grows younger and younger in the Faustian pact between Spirit and man, 'till she was nought at all'. It is a big dramatic scena, part recitative, part lyric. Finzi combines his resources powerfully. Not only does the melody climb an octave and a half to the grand command 'Cease! . . .

it is *e-nough*' (the song's highest note) but the tonality brightens from D minor to B major. The rhythmic motif for 'Agreed to that' is diminished as the woman wanes to babyhood, then is thundered out for piano alone, as the change is found to be irreversible. The compassion in the phrases 'to my great sorrow' and 'the memory of her' gains sympathy for the arrogant man who dares to meddle with time; and the ending is worthy of Hardy's superscription from *Job: 'the hair of my flesh stood up'.* 'In a churchyard', the ninth song, finds the dead more at ease than the living. If there is cynicism in the poem, Finzi ignores it, with lilting rhythms and an ennobling moment as the dead speak at 'Now set among the wise'. That phrase is transformed and transposed a semitone up as the hearer absorbs 'the strange tale' and himself becomes wiser.

In 'Proud songsters' life's cycle restarts. Britten (*Winter Words*, 1953), in the only poem both he and Finzi set, pounces on the *proud* 'brand-new birds', sets up a joyous piano device, and with no change of texture but with a two-bar modulation in and out of a 'bright' key points up the irony of such vitality for such brief lives. Hardy's poem, published the year after his death at 87, blends stoicism, tenderness, and wonder: an old man's recognition that songsters come and go. Finzi writes no birdsong. but in a long piano introduction a syncopated pattern of appoggiaturas full of longing gives place to Example 5.2, which seems to hold all contradictions within it.

Ex. 5.2

When the voice enters the piano settles down, but between the verses it again strains towards a climax, till the D major diatonic benediction of the last stanza. The quiet ending (Elgar again?) weighs up the particles of 'grain, And earth, and air, and rain . . .' but then gently comes down into the minor. The hint of rebirth is Finzi's answer to the doubt of the first poem in his set. 'Proud songsters' is one of his finest, most individual songs.

The dated songs in *Earth and Air and Rain* cover the years 1928–32, and the set is richer than *A Young Man's Exhortation*. Adeline Vaughan Williams, after a broadcast, wrote to Finzi of the 'exquisite cunning that makes the words shine out so clearly. I only failed over "So mean I" . . . – a pity Hardy had to twist his words thus.'[17] When Joy Finzi was asked why Finzi so often set difficult words she replied in amazement: 'But they never seemed difficult to Gerald!' It was she who selected the phrase *Earth and Air and Rain* for the title.

[17] 21 February 1937.

During 1931 Finzi set 'To Joy' by Edmund Blunden. This Joy was Blunden's baby – 'thrust out alone Upon death's wilderness'. At the time Blunden was living in East Anglia, and some see in the arch of this song, and in the sullen heavy chords between the verses, the wide landscape and brooding clouds of a Suffolk storm. As in Finzi's setting of 'Fear no more the heat o' the sun', the emotion is the stronger for being contained in a slow dance measure. Happier is 'On parent knees', attributed (with a learned footnote from Finzi) to Sir William Jones (1746–94) as a translation from the Persian. The poem presents an antithesis: at birth, the baby weeps, while those around him smile; at death, he smiles, and those around him weep. Brief, in a single stanza, Finzi's song is perfectly balanced. Most of the song is sustained, with quaver movement, and Finzi points the moral at the song's half-way point by a silence, then by setting the admonitory injunction 'So live' to equal crotchets.

Four further Hardy settings belong to the 1930s. 'Let me enjoy the earth' has delightfully idiomatic piano writing; it is fresh, diatonic, and relaxed, until exclusion from Paradise prompts a surprising out-of-key fifth at the end. 'I need not go' also begins fluently. Not until 'by cypress sough' is it hinted that the over-patient lover is in her grave. The melody runs so naturally that it is easy to overlook how Finzi broadens the rhythm for 'the world somewhat' and 'if some day', and contracts it for 'I am come again' to make the sense clear; and how dramatically he inverts a rising fifth, prominent in the lyrical tune, for the negative 'Ah, no!'

'I look into my glass' has a Wolfian intensity, as an ageing man scans his reflection, bitterly aware of the contrast between his old body and still ardent heart. In the piano part Finzi's repeated notes – A's and D's – suggest numbness; but they develop into pulsing chords, increasingly chromatic as passion 'shakes this fragile frame', before subsiding once more. The tenor cries out 'would God it came to pass' on the highest notes; and, having begun on a high D, ends on a low D. The song is packed, compressed, and powerful.

Even finer, but more discursive because the poem tells a story, is 'In years defaced' (1936). Hardy once again treats of time and human love. Verse 1 describes the secret lovers of long ago; Finzi's doleful introduction picks up the past sadness, his upward rush of semi-quavers the couple's sudden emotion, a stabbing appoggiatura the world's indifference, the bass disturbance the lovers' fears. By verse 2 that is in the past, and an exquisite couple of *cantabile* piano bars lead to the relative major and Finzi's most serene manner, though the 'gale' figure reflects the couple's 'fears'. In verse 3 Hardy revives the old folk-belief that shepherds have the power to catch echoes of long-ago emotions, which Finzi's limpid piano descant to the 'lonely shepherds' affirms. In a magical phrase, placed high so as to sound ethereal, the singer whispers that such love will for ever linger in that place. The intervals of 'till earth outwears' at the end are the same as 'two sat here' at the beginning, an identification both musical and poetic. The whole song is permeated by that three-note figure — two conjunct notes down and a leap up of a fifth — transformed, inverted, placed at differing points in a phrase.

On 12 May 1936 Joy made the first entry in a Journal she was to keep, with significant gaps, until Gerald's death. It was his idea that she should write it. He felt that the past was easy to forget; and he had occasionally (as on his foreign holiday) kept notes himself. The Finzis had been married two-and-a-half years. Her conviction of his stature was growing, and was endorsed by the recent performances, publications, and broadcasts. Perhaps the premature deaths of Herbert Howells's little son in 1935 and of Herbert Lambert early in 1936 had increased their sense of precariousness.

They were staying with Gerald's mother in Suffolk when Joy began to write, and possibly the presence of the two women in the one house provoked him into defining his thoughts on relationships: there was a tearing away from the old irritating maternal bond, and a feeling of gratitude towards the wife who had set him free. Joy and Gerald had begun to consider building their own house, which would embody their chosen way of life. It was a moment of crux. It is significant, too, that the first sentence in the Journal is about Vaughan Williams. Joy used to write in bed at night, in pencil in a brown-covered exercise book, making entries only when something struck her as worth noting. In the earlier years, though the intentions of the pair were identical and the writing is all in Joy's hand, there is a clear difference in the strands of their personalities: Joy's eye for colour, shape, and detail in vivid, allusive prose and phonetic spelling, and Gerald's pronouncements recorded, it seems, verbatim (extracts from the Journal are printed in *italics*). The first entry runs, complete:

> *Saw VW's first performance of the Poisoned Kiss at the Arts Theatre, Cambridge. We stayed at Hundon with Gerald's Mother.* 'I feel toward my Mother what Beecham must feel towards the world, — snip, snap, snoram! I feel towards her, as I feel to no-one else, as a result of an enforced relationship based on kin-ship — not akin-ship. Akin-ship is more than a kin-ship — why else should we marry.' [Then from Keats's letter[18] to Benjamin Bailey:] 'I am certain of nothing but of [sic] the holiness of the Heart's affection[s] and the truth of Imagination.'

That was the sole entry for 1936. The birth that August of their second son, Nigel, went unrecorded. The buyers of the Downshire Hill house allowed them to go back for the event, for Joy to have the same doctor. Gerald, greeting mother and new baby, said 'Good. Now no more babies. Let's get back to work' — the astringency delighted Joy, but might shock over-sentimental

[18] 22 November 1817.

admirers of *Dies Natalis*. So, babies put in their place, it is understandable that the second and third Journal entries should begin, like the first, with 'first performance of . . .' In June 1937 they heard the broadcast of *Don Juan de Manara*, Eugene Goossens's opera: '*A work of Goosens* [sic] *can't live, it hasn't the bones of life in it*,' was Gerald's verdict as Joy recorded in her Journal. '*There is no selection anywhere – style is selection or selection is style . . . Goossens is second hand Strauss in opera.*' They went to London for the first performance by Boult and the BBC Symphony Orchestra of Howard Ferguson's Partita: '*a fine work*'.

To Howard, Gerald went on writing in the same old relaxed manner. The week before the first Journal entry (and perhaps it explains its reference to Beecham's attitude to the world), he wrote: 'Beecham's "Sit down, you bitch" (I'm told to Lady Cunard, who rustled in late) *did* come over the wireless.'[19] Then 'Have you been to the Surrealists exhibition yet? I hear that Walton went to the private view & bought a kipper on the way. It was surreptitiously hung on to some convenient nail or projection, & for quite a time was admired by the particular artist's admirers as a point of balance!'[20] That August (1936) Gerald heard the Prom devoted to the thirty-four-year-old Walton and thought he 'stood the test of a one-man show v. well, & showed a greater range than I had realised before – with P[ortsmouth] P[oint] & Façade at one end and the sym, via the vla con, at the other. One may like or dislike the cold, glittering detachment about it all, but one can't help feeling that, technically – for sheer mastery & management – there has never been anything quite to equal it. If he were not so incalculable I shd say that he wd burn out between thirty-eight & forty-two [i.e. 1940–44] & that such nervous tension cd not last a lifetime.'[21]

Howard suffered a grievous loss when Harold Samuel died on 15 January 1937, aged only 57, some weeks after a coronary thrombosis. Gerald wrote to Howard offering help: 'a wire or phone call will send me North, South, East or West for you.'[22] It was the loss of his contribution to the commonweal of the arts that struck the Finzis most: 'terrible to think of all [his] knowledge choked'.[23] Joy wished a death mask had been taken. Once the funeral was over, Howard went to Beech Knoll for companionship and rest. Cedric Thorpe Davie, getting married, asked the Finzis to find a pub near them for their honeymoon, and brought his bride over to Beech Knoll almost every day.

In early June the Finzis went on holiday to the Aran Islands, off Galway, where Joy, but not Gerald, had been before. It had not changed much since Synge wrote his *Riders to the Sea*. They had seen Robert Flaherty's recent documentary film, *Man of Aran*, scripted by Pat Mullen, an island man; also in the party were Mullen's daughter Barbara (to be known for her television role as Dr Finlay's housekeeper) and Maud Karpeles, whom Gerald had come to

19   1 or 8 May 1936.
20   17 June 1936.
21   14 August 1936.
22   7 November 1936.
23   To Thorpe Davie, 18 January 1937.

know after reviewing her edition of folksongs. As a vegetarian, Gerald delighted in the islanders' superb physique, 'all done on bread, potatoes, tea & occasional fish', and marvelled at their laughter, humour, and dancing. It was quite usual for a young cottager couple to stand up spontaneously and dance a jig, reel, or hornpipe; and on Sunday nights, when everyone danced on the quay, the nailed boots made a wonderful 'swish' which put the clip and the clop of the Tarantella into the shade. 'As usual, the priest is the villain of the piece,' Gerald wrote to Howard, though even the priest hadn't succeeded in stamping out this 'wonderfully innocent pastime'.[24] Seeing Hindemith's *Nobilissima visione* performed by the Ballet Russe the following year, he concluded: 'Now I know that the only sort of dancing that moves me is when something speaks through the dance, rather than when the dance speaks for itself, which is only another word for ritual, I suppose. Anyhow, "Job", those Hindu dances from Serakaila, this Hindemith ballet, a morris jig like "I'll go & enlist for a sailor" or the dance of the kings of the Isle of Man (as danced by Billy Cain) – anything of this sort makes the flimsy-flamsy-on-the-toes, pas-de-deux, corps-de-Ballet stuff too ridiculous for words.'[25]

APPLES

During these years Gerald began taking an interest in apple trees. Then he heard a broadcast by Morton Shand, 'The Disappearing Apple', lamenting the loss to cultivation of many English varieties. Fired by enthusiasm, he wrote to Shand; and so began his involvement in a life-long crusade. Shand had produced a book on French wines in the 1930s, and was interested, not only in things of the table, but simply in the quality of life. He read Dr Robert Hogg's celebrated *Fruit Manual* (1860–84) in which were listed over seven hundred varieties of apple; but by the 1930s, when the great private estates were dwindling, Shand could find only forty or fifty in nurserymen's catalogues. How many of the lost ones, he wondered, were excellent; and how many might still be found in small orchards, their value unregarded?

As a result of the broadcast, people from all over the country sent in apples to be identified. Shand was then living at Bath, and a friend at nearby Long Ashton Pomological Research Station helped him. Gerald, with Leslie Martin, later the architect of the Royal Festival Hall, and a Miss Holliday in Yorkshire, began searching for rare trees. They secured scions, exchanged grafts, and began to plant their own orchards. Shand kept the records and arranged for an extra scion of every rare tree to be grown in the National Fruit Trials Collection. They were all amateurs, none of them interested in the commercial market. Shand's point – it was in accord with the philosophy of Gerald's whole life – was that it was a pity any good thing should disappear. Most English counties had their own good apples; if local market gardeners stocked them, they could be saved from extinction. Gerald joined in with the enthu-

---

[24] 30 May 1937.
[25] To Ferguson, 3 August 1938.

siasm of a Vaughan Williams collecting folksongs. Good apple country and good folksong country were often the same, and some of the best was in Gloucestershire around May Hill. It was all as English as could be, for apples grow better in England than anywhere in the world. As a vegetarian, Gerald was particularly fitted to enjoy them. 'The shades of flavour which the Apple can offer are, *sui generis*, almost inexhaustible,' wrote Shand. 'It is in no sense an exaggeration to say that, except for the world's few really great wines, nothing we eat or drink presents such fascinating diversity of savour within the compass of a single generic type, or affords such a rare delight to the epicure.'[26]

Gerald now began to work on behalf of Ivor Gurney, in an asylum in Dartford, Kent. Plunket Greene's *Charles Villiers Stanford* (1935) mentioned Gurney, and Fox Strangways in his *Observer* review of the book also referred to him. Gerald wrote to Marion Scott with the idea of publishing some articles about Gurney in *Music & Letters*, which Fox Strangways edited. He suggested asking Vaughan Williams and de la Mare to contribute. She welcomed the idea, but the project hung fire. She had collected Gurney's manuscripts, preserved every scrap he wrote in the asylum, and arranged some publications. Her own *Beethoven* had come out in 1934; she was now working on her little *Mendelssohn*, and her major Haydn studies were engaging her time. She visited Gurney often, and interviewed his doctors. She was also looking after her old parents, and was fifty-seven herself.

Gerald wished to visit Gurney, as Vaughan Williams had recently done. Marion suggested his first visit should be in the company of Herbert Howells, who had known Gurney well; but only days after she wrote, Howells's son developed meningitis and died. So it happened that Gerald never met the composer whose works he was to do so much to promote.

Early in 1937 Gerald persuaded Marion to lend him some of Gurney's autographs to copy. When Howard Ferguson was staying at Beech Knoll after Samuel's death, he and Gerald played through more than a hundred songs, compared versions, and began sorting good from less good. Gerald saw the problems: 'I think the eventual difficulty in "editing" the later Gurney may be great: a neat mind could smooth away the queernesses – like Rimsky-Korsakov with Mussorgsky – yet time and familiarity will probably show something not so mistaken, after all, about the queer and odd things.'[27] An index was needed, and further opinions; so in March Gerald and Howard spent a 'field-day' with Vaughan Williams. Herbert Howells was brought in, and Marion was to catalogue the autographs. Vaughan Williams wrote to Hubert Foss of OUP, who in August accepted twenty songs for publication. By now Eric Blom was the editor of *Music & Letters*, and asked Gerald to gather contributions for the

---

[26] Morton Shand, 'Older Kinds of Apples', *Journal of the Royal Horticultural Society*, vol. 74 1949.
[27] 30 January 1937.

January 1938 number, to be devoted to Gurney's poetry and music. Gerald wrote to de la Mare and – aided by Jack Haines in Gloucester – searched periodicals for Gurney's poems.

It became imperative to gain access to Marion Scott's autographs, for the final selection and checking. Gerald and Joy spent three days in London, cataloguing; and Gerald described the visit to Howard:

> She had not even managed to get copies of the published work to put with the complete works . . . I suggested looking into that large wooden packing case in her room, which she always assured me had nothing of importance in. I bundled everything out on to the floor & found about thirty complete songs of G's best period, dozens of notebooks, some with complete songs in, and a few thousand pages of various mss including 'lost' vln sonata mvts & so on. Joy & I worked till about 9.30 that night – the temperature of Maid Marion's room was 90 . . . It is rather incredible when you realize that everything was supposed to be ready for the cataloguing, sorted & in order, two months ago . . . I'm so polite to this fragile fool that I've not got the heart to remind her that I made time to copy out twenty-four of his songs in a month.[28]

'Maid Marion', he went on, had sent de la Mare the whole collection of Gurney's poems, 'sane, incoherent, unsorted.' He, Howells, and Vaughan Williams wondered if she had an unconscious resentment against anything being done for Gurney unless she did it, but beyond 'guarding the pile', like the little beetle in The Insect Play, she was incapable of doing anything. 'It's terrible to think that all this might have been done a dozen years ago, if his work had not been left in the hands of that possessive, incompetent, mulish, old maid, Marion Scott.'

Gerald wrote to Edmund Blunden, who, he believed, 'knew Gurney or had some liking for his work'. He told him Gurney had taken a turn for the worse and 'it wd be a good thing for some recognition to come to him, whilst he is still able, however slightly, to appreciate it . . . He is completely unknown to a new generation, & almost forgotten by his own.' He described the Music & Letters symposium: 'Wd you be willing to lend your name to the scheme, by way of a short appreciation?'[29]

At that time Finzi's name was unknown to Blunden, but he replied he would gladly contribute; he could only remember Gurney 'playing and singing his settings of his own poems, and one of John Clare's, with great enjoyment & cheerfulness'.[30] Delighted, Gerald reported this to Howard, adding that Blunden's handwriting was quite the loveliest he had ever seen. To Blunden he explained the legal complications, which 'boil down to the fact that no receiver has been appointed (an expensive job) & that his next of kin are not his best of friends'. The John Clare setting must be 'Ploughman sing-

28 15 August 1937.
29 28 July 1937.
30 22 September 1937.

ing', he guessed, a poem Blunden had included in his 1920 edition of Clare. Gerald added that Vaughan Williams had suggested that Gurney's mental trouble should not be mentioned, lest people 'begin to find disintegration in the work where nothing of the sort exists'.[31]

In November Marion Scott visited Gurney again: 'He seemed as if he could hardly believe all this recognition is coming to him.'[32] That Christmas he died. Gerald sent Marion £10 towards the funeral expenses and wrote to Howard: 'I went to his funeral, a sad little affair at Twigworth, and H[erbert] H[owells] played "Sleep" and "Severn meadows" on a wheezy little organ.'[33] He allowed himself a touch of cynicism, predicting that now the *Music & Letters* issue was out, many people would pretend to have been better friends to Gurney than in fact they had. 'But, Lord, I'm glad those articles came out before he died . . . It's been worth all the trouble & irritation & obstruction (which reminds me, – have you got the two vln pieces yet?!) & something, however much in the background, I'm honestly proud to have done, since his own "friends" hadn't the spirit to do it!' The symposium,[34] coinciding with Gurney's death, attracted press notice, including two appreciative articles by Richard Capell in the *Telegraph*, and the OUP publications were followed by a recital at Amen House on 13 April and broadcasts on 21 and 23 July by Isobel Baillie and Sinclair Logan.

WORDS AND MUSIC

During 1936 Finzi settled the songs of *Earth and Air and Rain* in their final order, discarding 'I need not go' and 'Let me enjoy the earth', and wishing he could have consulted Plunket Greene (who had just died). Keith Falkner sang them to Leslie Boosey, and then on 11 January 1937 performed five of them at an Iris Lemare Concert at the Mercury Theatre. Beforehand, Gerald was wishing Iris had put the title of the cycle on the handbill, and wishing he knew who the accompanist would be (in the event it was Howard). 'And yet I don't care sniggle-snaggle about either. No more songs now for a long time. Three cheers.'[35] But he did care, very much, about the principles behind song-writing. In *The Musical Times* of December 1936 Arthur Hutchings reviewed the publication of Finzi's Milton Sonnets (see p. 57). Hutchings considered music's ability to express abstract thought: 'one asks a composer who "adds" to Milton's sonnets: "what is to keep your hands off Hamlet's soliloquies?" . . .'. He made the sound point that an 'abstract poem shifts its local habitation from thought to thought, unlike a simple lyric which maintains the same atmosphere through a whole string of images'. So the composer must either follow the abstract thought, changing his texture 'incoherently', or write 'an indefinite background . . . a sort of highest common factor of all the

[31] 23 September 1937.
[32] 19 November 1937.
[33] 1 January 1938.
[34] *Music & Letters*, vol. xix, no. 1 (January 1938).
[35] 26 November 1936.

sentiments in the poem'. Finzi complied well with the latter demand,
Hutchings concluded ironically: 'his accompaniment never obtrudes on a
single word, but is, in the first place, one long obtrusion'. Finzi had attempted
a task that he should not have set himself.

Finzi rose in wrath in defence of what was becoming a cherished principle.
He wrote to Howard (and an almost identical paragraph to William Busch in
1938):

> And what a slating the Two Milton Sonnets get! I don't mind the adverse crit-
> icism at all – its quite impersonal & without animosity – but I do hate the
> bilge & bunkum about composers trying to 'add' to a poem; that a fine poem
> is complete in itself, & to set it is only to gild the lily . . . I rather expected it &
> expect it still more when the 'Intimations' is finished.[36]

Obviously, he went on, a poem might be unsatisfactory in that it had no archi-
tectural possibilities; no broad vowels where climaxes should be. 'But the first
& last thing is that a composer is (presumably) moved by a poem and wishes
to identify himself with it & to share it.' John Sumsion had hit the nail on the
head when he summed up a Kapellmeisterish cantata by saying 'He chose his
text, it didn't choose him.' Gerald went on: 'I don't think everyone realizes the
difference between choosing a text & being chosen by one. (They shd see
Pirandello's *Six Characters in search of an author*.)' But, he ended his letter to
Howard, 'much more exciting is Sibelius No. 4 . . . It grows & grows & grows.'
And '1937 will be Partita year!'

1937, TOTY AND NORFOLK

Through Howard, the Finzis came to know Alma José (Toty) Maria de
Navarro. Toty was a University Lecturer in Archaeology at Cambridge; then
unmarried, he lived in a beautiful and well-ordered house and garden in the
Worcestershire village of Broadway with his widowed mother. She had been
Mary Anderson, an American actress, who retired on her marriage to Antonio
de Navarro but welcomed to her home artists, writers, and musicians, Henry
James and Elgar among them. Harold Samuel was one who delighted to give
recitals in her music room. Toty adored music, for which he showed a fine
amateur's instinct. He also privately wrote poetry. Howard knew this and persuaded Toty to let Gerald into the secret.

A keen sailor, Toty invited the Finzis, his friend Ann Bowes-Lyon, and
Howard to Blakeney Point in Norfolk for a weekend's sailing in July 1937
(though Gerald warned him that the 'strenuous life' he was best at was A. H.
Sidgwick's: 'On the cabin roof I lie/ Gazing into vacancy'). On the drive up
Howard and the Finzis stopped in Suffolk to see Gerald's mother, who proudly
produced lunch she had cooked herself. Faced with a revolting dun-coloured
mess, Gerald wickedly asked her how she had made it. 'Well, first I boiled

---

[36] 19 December 1936 and 14 February 1938.

twelve oranges for half an hour . . .' she began, but was unable to finish for the gales of laughter.

They sailed a little in the estuary; but the real point of the holiday was the 'verse junketings'. Ann Bowes-Lyon's first book of verse had been published that year by Faber, and she had more poems in draft. The Finzis began another of their midwifery jobs, persuading both Toty and Ann to complete their work, patiently considering alternative versions, and then taking Toty's hand-written poems back to Aldbourne for Joy to type, add his third or fourth thoughts, and eventually gather into loose-leaf indexed books. Gerald so wished, he told Toty, that for Ann, a lone poet in a socially demanding family, he could be 'an up to date Perseus & slay a few of the snakes entangling her!'[37] He showed her poems to Sir William Rothenstein, whom he had got to know through Gloucestershire neighbours in his early Painswick days (Rothenstein drew Elgar and Vaughan Williams for the early *Music & Letters* numbers). He liked the poems, which pleased Gerald, who considered he had 'first rate judgement & has kept abreast with verse ever since his young days when he was mixed up with all the poets & painters of the nineties'.[38]

Early in September, the Finzis visited Toty at Broadway and were shown, so Joy wrote in her Journal, *a cherished giant white lily and rare gentians while unnoticed gardeners tended yew hedges and lawns.* They spent the afternoon in *a Shakespeare grotto with blue linoleum on the floor,* when Toty produced *the inevitable bulging suitcase of* 'immortal works'. Gerald pronounced: '*it is unusual to find the lyrical impulse increasing after thirty & the passing of adolescent urge — but in Toty his work goes from strength to strength*'. They made the visit from Gloucester, where they were staying for the Three Choirs — 'so much music', he told Toty, 'so many people to see, so much rushing about'.[39] There they heard Vaughan Williams's *Dona Nobis Pacem* — peace in our time.

For all his easy, carefree, holidaying life Gerald had his eye on troubled Europe. As well as collecting newspaper cuttings about English traits and characteristics (see p. 19), he now began obsessively to add to the mass of cuttings and hand-written comments (the earliest is from 1928) on what makes a Jew, on race, and on Jewish persecution in Germany. He made a list of Jewish composers: Mendelssohn, Mahler, Schoenberg, Cowen, Ravel, Bloch, Offenbach, Milhaud. In January 1937, hearing that a young friend of Howard's was off on holiday to Germany, he remarked: 'I hope he doesn't swallow the Nazi bull-shit.' To the letter he attached a newspaper cutting that read: 'From January 1 no "non-Aryan" German is allowed to play golf on a German course.' Gerald went on: 'If things appeared all rosy there, let him tell his first German acquaintance that he is a liberal — no need to go as far as communist! — or that his grandfather was a jew!'[40] Had some unpleasant experience lain behind that one-word 'anti-Semiticism' in his diary account

---

[37] 21 July 1937.
[38] 12 September 1937.
[39] 12 September 1937.
[40] 4 January 1937.

(p. 65) in 1930 of his own German holiday? The 1935 Nuremberg Laws only confirmed views that were already prevalent. In the Journal Gerald began speculating on the nature of tolerance, and what it meant to be civilized: 'to be civilized you have to be tolerant – to be tolerant you have to be cynical . . . those who move mountains are always little people . . . a hundred pages of printed matter is more important than the Napoleonic wars. Keats's contribution greater than the burning of Moscow.'

1935–37, STARTING THE HOUSE

The Finzis had never thought of Beech Knoll as their permanent home. The children were growing, and Gerald needed a workroom shielded from their noise. (When they were babies, sometimes a pram mysteriously shifted – Gerald had pushed it out of ear-shot.) Also, there was only one walk, up the lane on to the downs, that didn't involve passing through the village. Acutely self-conscious, he thought of himself as ugly, and hated to be watched.

They began searching; but houses are usually square and compact. After rejecting about a hundred up for sale, they thought they might have to build. Arthur Bliss had built a modern white house of 'light, air and space' in Somerset, and the Finzis visited him there during 1934. In June 1935 the Bliss's architect, Peter Harland, came to Beech Knoll to consider the possibilities. In early 1937 they at last found their sixteen-acre site. The first time we came to Ashmansworth, wrote Joy in her Journal, up the narrow climbing lane from a warm green valley, blue shadows lay with an intensity on snow that I have only seen in Switzerland. The ash trees made strong pattern against dark sunny sky. The village was eight miles south of Newbury, high on the edge of the Hampshire Downs, and the horizon stretched away to Winchester and beyond, on a clear day even to the hill on the Isle of Wight. Gerald needed a wide sky, for a childhood punishment of being shut up in a cupboard had given him a touch of claustrophobia. On the site was a group of Scots pines, said to have been planted to commemorate the accession of James I. Quietness sounds there, it seemed to Joy, and the earth has hospitality. Sadly, the neglected farmhouse was past being converted; outbuildings were retained, but a tractor pulled down the old Church Farm. Then Peter Harland began work.

1938, TONY SCOTT, ROBIN MILFORD

While they were still at Aldbourne they came to know Tony and Ruth Scott, who were living at Thatcham. Tony, ten years younger than Gerald, had what Gerald described to Toty de Navarro as 'a strange past of organ building & horsebreeding'. He had studied composition with Herbert Howells at the RCM, and his Fantasia for strings had its first London performance in October 1938. He began coming over to Beech Knoll for weekly lessons – he was (apart from those at the RAM) Gerald's only pupil. Gerald would not accept any fee, and provided only what he called 'a handrail to steady you'. Not long after they met, Tony reported on a contemporary music concert he had heard and had found little good in, mentioning the patron Mrs Behrend in connection with Britten. 'Bartók is the only one in that programme who excites me,' replied Gerald, '& where I don't understand him I wish I cd, whereas with the others there's very little behind the notes. It's curious about Mrs Behrend & Britten & reminds me very much of HH in his young days & "Lady Olga" [Lady Olga Montagu, Herbert Howells's admirer and benefactor]. Still, we may be wrong & I hope we are; but I've a strong suspicion that not many people can see behind the notes, without a considerable time-lag.'[41]

Another Aldbourne friend was Robin Milford. They had corresponded when his Double Fugue was performed by the RCM's Patron Fund's in 1926, and then in the same concert as Gerald's Violin Concerto in 1928. Robin was the son of Sir Humphrey Milford, the head of OUP when its Music Department was founded under Hubert Foss in 1923. He had studied with Holst, Vaughan Williams, and Morris. He and his wife had moved near Newbury in 1932, and in 1938 settled in the village of Hermitage, as Robin was teaching at nearby Downe House School. Two years younger than Gerald, he was then more established: his choral work A Prophet in the Land had been performed at the 1931 Three Choirs Festival. Prolific as a composer, indecisive as a man, Robin suffered from poor health and depression. Hardly had he and Gerald met again than he was put to bed for a month on glucose and milk. The two had been discussing Gerald's theories about environment and heredity, and Gerald, sympathising with his diet, wrote: 'Although I don't think much more is inherited than fatness, thinness & haemophilia, such a way of living is hardly a fair test.'[42] Robin was tortured with a sense of his worthlessness, and feared that his friends liked his music only because they liked him. Gerald wrote him four pages of thoughtful, compassionate sense, pointing out that he had been attracted to his work long before he met him, that Vaughan Williams had scores of pupils 'but I dont think there are many about whom he feels so positively. Of course, this doesn't mean that everything you write is sacrosanct! Like everyone else, you've got your dull pages, movements & works. (Are there more than a dozen works out of Mozart's six hundred, or the masses of Schubert, that are really worth dying for?) But it's work which "stands for something" & for which no apology is needed.'[43]

From October 1937 to March 1938 there is nothing in the Journal. Then on 12 March: the day of Germany's entry into Austria. Joy recorded Gerald's words: 'You must know what I feel like. It's like watching a man done to death, only this is a civilization and the last stand of central European culture.' Too distressed to sleep or work, he foresaw the persecution of those individuals who did not fit into a regime of physical force. 'I feel much more than ever can be said – look at the beauty of those violets.' (Was that moment perhaps the source of music for 'To me the meanest flower that blows can give Thoughts that do often lie too deep for tears'? He was, in spite of all the distractions, immersed in his setting of Wordsworth's Intimations of Immortality.) The next Journal entry, after his reading of Meredith's Love in a

---

[41] 25 June 1938.
[42] 19 May 1938.
[43] 22 June 1938.

Valley, runs '*Feeling is greater than experience . . . one cannot shout it out enough.*' The poem opens with what might have been a description of Joy in the garden at Beech Knoll:

> Under yonder beech-tree single on the green-sward,
> Couched with her arms behind her golden head,
> Knees and tresses folded to slip and ripple idly,
> Lies my young love sleeping in the shade . . .

It is no surprise to find an unfinished pencil setting of the verse among his sketches.

Toty de Navarro enticed them to Cambridge to see Vaughan Williams's *Riders to the Sea*, set in the Aran they had recently visited. Gerald, always quick to support his friends, went to London to hear Alan Bush's new Piano Concerto, and Rubbra came over to Beech Knoll from his Chiltern cottage to play them his Second Symphony. Gerald heard Mahler's Eighth, which his earlier warmth towards the composer did not survive; he had never been 'so bored in all my life', he told Toty. That August the Finzis and the Sumsions with their children spent a seaside holiday at Lulworth in Dorset. Back for a day or two in the middle to deal with house-building affairs, Gerald played his early Traherne work *Dies Natalis* (see p. 43) to Robin Milford, who encouraged him to send it to Percy Hull, the conductor of the next year's Three Choirs Festival. Gerald had now composed a fourth movement, 'Wonder', but 'I must get the other movt done [the quick one]'[44] he replied to Robin.

Then the building started. Gerald, mindful of Toty's profession as an archaeologist, told him: 'I did my duty to future holders of your Cambridge office'[45] and buried under the foundations a large sealed glass bottle with a few coins, and – copied out on the toughest paper he could buy – his own setting of Flecker's 'To a poet' ('I send my song through time and space to greet you') and poems by Housman, Blunden, Bridges, and Hardy.

In May 1938 the remains of Hardy's library was sold. Gerald looked in at the sale, but found even the cheapest book was beyond his means, though he bought Hardy's walking-stick (now in the Dorchester Museum). He did not collect souvenirs or autographs in the conventional way, but hated to think of the books being divided among 'dealers, bibliophiles & bibliomaniacs'. In the catalogue, he saw a first edition of the *Selected Poems*, inscribed '*To Florence Emily, this first copy is given by her husband T.H., Oct 4th 1916.*' Writing to Toty, he thought either one of them would cherish it more 'than some bloody dealer'.[46] He couldn't help thinking of 'She at his funeral': 'But they stand round with griefless eye/ Whilst my regret consumes like fire!' 'His kindred they, his sweetheart I', runs the key-line in the poem. He did not cite it in his letter, but the theme runs right through his life ('akin-ship is more than kin-ship – why else should we marry').

44 24 August 1938.
45 30 August 1938.
46 10 May 1938.

The background to Gerald's theories of heredity and environment was the nature–nurture debate, at its height in the 1920s. At its simplest, the controversy was over the relative importance of biological and cultural factors in determining human behaviour. The leader of the doctrine of hereditary influence was Francis Galton; Franz Boas held that social and cultural pressures were more important than genes in shaping individuals. At the time, there was little room for the modern idea that behaviour results from the interaction of genetics and environment. Pressed to its hideous extreme, Galton's theories led to eugenics and the Nazi concept of a master race and their treatment of the Jews. Gerald's rigorous self-formation meant that he was bound to favour cultural over biological determinism. He was impressed by *Coming of Age in Samoa* (1928), by Boas's pupil Margaret Mead, not knowing that the soundness of her early fieldwork would later be questioned. The debate continues in the twenty-first century.

1938, MUNICH

Finzi's spring and summer compositions that year were a Prelude and Fugue for string trio; what he called a 'nice setting' (but Rubbra confessed himself 'haunted by') of 'Come away, Death'; and 'He abjures love', a great song on Hardy's poem about the illusions of romantic love. The Journal begins again in September (paraphrasing Ben Jonson on Shakespeare): '*I love two people this side idolatry – Thomas Hardy and my Joy.*' It took an exceptional woman not to resent the order of that; even more so, to record it for posterity.

They had a week away in September, staying first with Gerald's mother in Suffolk, where they found she had painted her white conservatory brown and sold her white chickens so that they would not show up to enemy aircraft! Joy developed mild flu and retired to her bed. Gerald used the time by throwing out his mother's hoarded papers, possibly – as Banfield suggests – destroying evidence of the family's Jewishness. Gerald and Joy went on to spend three happy days by the sea at Walberswick; but their *apprehension of war was equalled by the apprehension that we might not stand by Czechoslovakia.* Back at Aldbourne, they drove over to Ashmansworth and found the new house up to the roof. Howard Ferguson, temporarily homeless after Harold Samuel's death, was living in the gardener's cottage on their Ashmansworth land to see whether he liked country life. They *talked of war and our abilities in relation to it.* Neville Chamberlain flew to Munich, where it was agreed to transfer the Sudetenland to Germany. *Peace without honour,* Joy recorded, *and no feeling of relief or satisfaction anywhere with us* . . . '*I can feel nothing but the suffering of humanity and the fear for the future of civilization.*'

CHAPTER SIX

The Munich Crisis

1938–39

In the early 1930s Gerald made the acquaintance of the composer William
Busch. They met from time to time in their bachelor days for a good
'tête-a-tête', as Busch recalled in a letter of 1936. Busch much admired
Gerald's songs and Gerald in turn admired Busch's Theme, Variations and
Fugue in F minor for piano (1929). In April 1938 Busch and his wife spent a
day at Beech Knoll to play over his new Piano Concerto to the Finzis, and
Gerald suggested that Busch should ask Howard to give a private play-through
with him. 'Be sure to ask Bliss and Rubbra,' advised Gerald, agreeing that
Edwin Evans ('alias God's cousin') should be asked, and also Richard Capell
and Eric Blom – 'about the most understanding critic in the whole country'.[1]

Busch was born in London in 1901, his German parents (who were not
Jewish) having become naturalized British subjects. He had studied in
Germany from 1921 to 1924 and was staunchly hoping for the best from the
Munich agreement. Gerald wrote of his lack of conviction that a firm basis for
peace had been established. (Joy copied this and Gerald's subsequent letters to
Busch into the Journal.) 'I'm sorry, my dear William,' he went on, 'but I feel
more than ever that the Nazi octopus is one of the most evil & retrograde
things in the world – quite as bad as the communism it pretends to counter.'
His thoughts were with 'the new batch of civilized people, social democrats,
Jews, liberals and pacifists etc. receding before the Nazi tide'.

> You will not, I know, take this for an attack on the fundamentally fine
> Teuton, but I can't understand how a very civilized person like yourself can
> stomach a party which, to suit an ignorant ideology, has scattered everything
> that a civilized person values, from religious tolerance to scholarship,
> reduced a one-time tradition of culture to a farce, denigrated & exiled some
> of the finest minds, & set new values on truth which, at their mildest, can
> only be called lies. I think something pretty low has been reached when a
> Niemöller has to suffer as he is now doing; when a Dr Schuschnigg (who, I
> think you will admit was a patriot, even if not exactly the particular patriot
> that Hitler wd have wished him to be) – is played with cat and mouse
> fashion, till his nerve & spirit are broken & is then faced with a trial, which if
> it comes off, will be about as preposterous as our own trial of Sir Walter
> Raleigh, some three hundred years ago . . . When 'the Lorelei' has to become
> 'anonymous', & Mendelssohn's memory is obliterated from the conservato-
> rium which he founded; when every profession is closed to the Jews & even

[1] 29 February 1938.

their names removed from the war memorials (can you beat this for caddishness and pettiness), when . . .

But he could have gone on indefinitely, he said, and could only hope that William's gentle spirit was right in hoping that all would be better when things had settled down in Germany. Gerald hoped so too:

> I shd really feel suicidal if I didn't know that a song outlasts a dynasty & that,
> seen in perspective, Walton's Viola concerto, VW's F Symphony, Howard's
> Octet, Sibelius No. 4, Gurney's songs, perhaps your new Piano Concerto
> [writing almost the identical letter to Robin Milford he tactfully substituted
> 'your fugue'], will make present day Germany look very small indeed, just as
> Napoleon and his ravages are now a dream, whilst Beethoven & obscure
> Schubert are the realities.[2]

No, he replied to Busch's next letter (which does not survive), he couldn't dislike the Germans on account of their regime, 'otherwise one wd soon have nobody in the world to like, if one thinks of Mussolini in Italy, the St Bartholomew massacre in France, the persecution of the Puritans in England'. He wondered whether the Nazi movement was symptomatic of something much larger, 'a genuine receding tide. The world has seen dark ages before.' As to William's point about a decadent Jewish element in post-war Germany, 'one must remember that there was a general post-war laxity & decadence all over Europe – by no means the prerogative of the Jews'. In his sane defence of the Jews, he saw no cause to declare a personal interest.

> I think a great deal is due to the fact that one notices if Gluckstein has been had
> up for keeping a disorderly house, but one doesn't notice it if John Smith is
> had up for the same reason . . . One sees quite a lot of it in England, where an
> anti-Jewish movement has been deliberately & artificially stimulated. You
> hear quite reasonable people say that the Jews have taken all the cottages in
> the country to escape air-raids & that there's nothing left for the others. It
> then turns out that there is indeed a Jew in a cottage, but nobody remarks on
> the forty others who are not Jews! . . . When I see that five thousand doctors
> in Germany are to have their degrees revoked, not because they are bad
> doctors, but because they are Jews or half Jews, I feel that something has
> been done that not a hundred years can put right.

All this, he concluded, 'on account of a racial theory which no responsible ethnologist apparently recognizes'.[3]

At the end of October the Finzis visited London to hear Busch and Howard give the run-through of Busch's Piano Concerto. Gerald had persuaded Vaughan Williams to attend, and his recommendation prompted a broadcast the following January by Raybould and the BBC Symphony Orchestra. It was a demonstration of Gerald's values, this promoting of a man's music while vigorously disagreeing with his political views. The next week, shocked to his

---

[2]   8 October 1938.
[3]   12 October 1938.

core, he replied to a letter from Busch in which he said that his cousin, living in Germany, reported that the Jews in her town were being 'well treated, except for the ban on social intercourse'. 'Just think what that means,' Gerald wrote back, appalled:

> Once a caste system is started it is practically inescapable. Children born into such an environment can never hold up their heads, or feel, or be, self respecting citizens, nor can they function intellectually, morally or physically as they wd otherwise do. That is why no Mendelssohn, Heine, or Einstein were born into the ghetto.

He used to think that Eurasians had all the vices and none of the virtues of white and black. It took him some time to realize that, banned by both groups, they 'must of necessity, *though not for any inherent reasons*, become outcasts. The caste system, such as in India, produces the same results.' Always when deeply moved he turned to verse, and Joy quotes in her Journal a poem by the little-known Richard Verstegen [Rowlands] (fl. 1565–1620), in which a holly tree 'set in a princely garden' thrives until the gardener thought it out of place, whereupon the tree 'now of grief grew dead'.

> If it were possible to bring up an 'untouchable' as a prince's son, he'd likely as not take on all the attributes of a prince's son . . . If your cousin really believes in such Nazi theories as that Jewish and non-Jewish races do not mix, she ought to smuggle back a few books by world authorities on this subject, people like Huxley, Haldane & Carr-Saunders and see what they have to say on the matter. After all, their opinions are worth more than the Rosenbergs, and incidentally they have no axes to grind. Of course the Jewish question is complicated enough by the religious question . . . I absolutely agree that in times of emergency it is necessary to remove disintegrating elements, whether Jewish or non-Jewish (though even here there are difficulties; to distinguish between opposition that is constructive & opposition that is destructive – Shelley & Beethoven wd never have survived an English or German Fascist revolution) . . . Personally, I do not think that Jewish artists will be able to practise in Germany, for Germany, for generations & perhaps centuries.[4]

Busch's reply set him off on absolute values and the nature of good and evil. He rather felt they were like knowledge and non-knowledge, two sides of the same coin. Consider, he suggested, manslaughter as conceived by English law or by Australian aborigines:

> Moral & Ethical ideas are in such a perpetual state of flux that it is impossible to draw a fixed line between the two ('to thine own self be true' is about the nearest approach to such a thing) . . . Custom & morality are so inseparable as to be almost husband & wife! To be a pacifist in England in 1914–1918 meant humiliation & suffering, but today it is almost a hallmark. It gave one a halo in Germany after the war, but now it leads to the concentration camp.

4   3 November 1938.

The virtues of one age are the vices of another, he went on, though he acknowledged Busch's concept of 'fundamental goodness' as wider than right or wrong. He found the idea of all races mixing together ideal, but not practicable, and hoped neither of his sons would marry aborigines! He also could not agree that art is 'above national boundaries . . . Nationality is not a matter of race & blood. It is a matter of culture, custom & environment . . . If anything, the trouble with the Jews seems that they are less assimilative & adaptable than many other people – probably owing to the strength of their culture & environment.' The crime in Germany was in preventing assimilation of the enlightened Jews – the Nazi concept of race was 'what you were you are, what you are you shall always be'. Should the English make scapegoats of the Huguenot descendants?

> Or shall we send Vaughan Williams back to Wales, where some century or other, an ancestor must have come from? Or Elgar to Denmark, or Grieg to Scotland. Holst's grandfather was a political refugee. Sibelius has hardly any Finnish blood in him. Wd you not say that all these, if not in themselves, then at some point in their ancestry, showed that they were 'adept at the adoption of extra-racial characteristics where this adaptability is needed?' The charge might be levelled at nearly everyone – at van Dieren's son, at you, at Rubbra etc.

Or, he might have added, at an English composer called Finzi. 'Meanwhile,' he went on, writing in the week of Kristallnacht, when thirty synagogues were set ablaze and seven thousand Jewish shops had their windows smashed, 'what is a typical Jew & has he any existence outside prejudice & imagination?'

> Is it that loathesome Whitechapel type, or is it the abstruse saint-like philosopher like Professor Alexander [who had just died]? Is it the proverbial miser or that most generous of men Harold Samuel? Is it the slick, superficial artist or the Myra Hess type? Is it the music hall vulgarian or Sarah Bernhardt? Karl Marx or Joachim? (both had beards). Is it the stock exchange parasite or is it Einstein? Is it the man of feeling like Mahler, or the man of intellect like Schönberg?

Surely the answer, he concluded, was that all these types existed among civilized people. And then he came to the nub of it: 'There is no Jewish race & no Jewish type, except where environment has made it.'[5]

1938, ALDBOURNE

He had asked Percy Hull if he would like to see *Dies Natalis*; to the early movements he had now added the slow 'Wonder'. He found it hard to work at such a time and was relieved to know that even Keats 'cd not write while his spirit was "fevered in a contrary direction" '.[6] The OUP edition of Keats's letters was one of the half-dozen volumes (another was the complete Hardy poems) he

---

5   11 November 1938.
6   To Milford, 29 September 1938.

would take with him to a desert island, he wrote to Robin Milford at the time of Munich. He begged him to look at Robert Bridges' poem 'On a dead child', which begins 'Perfect little body, without fault or stain on thee, / With promise of strength and manhood full and fair!' and directed him particularly to the last line:

Ah! little at best can all our hopes avail us
  To lift this sorrow, or cheer us, when in the dark,
  Unwilling, alone we embark,
And the things we have seen and have known and have heard of, fail us.

Things had not completely failed, he thought, while 'there's still the chance of keeping freshened "this soiled world". And that is what our job as artists amounts to. It's difficult enough to keep this in front of us in appalling times like these, but I'm certain its true.'[7]

Early in November, the Finzis and the Milfords went to a concert in Newbury, where Gerald and Robin each had compositions performed. It was a dismal affair, and Gerald wondered whether they ought not to retire from Newbury musical life and leave the field to the local man. He was there first, 'and', Gerald wrote to Robin the next day, with a rare flash of sarcasm, 'the length of his piano piece made me feel that he wd be there last'.[8] Joy had remarked that no-one over thirty should sing Finzi's 'Proud songsters', which set Gerald and Robin off into a discussion. 'If you have heard Henschel's records (made when he was eighty),' Gerald wrote to Robin,

you've heard something that wd convert you to the idea that old-age can retain freshness (see also 'An ancient to ancients' & [see p. 81] 'I look into my glass'. But, of course, there's no doubt that something usually does disappear, round about the late twenties, & young men, who have published a slim volume of verse, or made a few songs, soon pass their moment of ecstasy, & once the adolescent urge is spent they settle down to be critics, doctors, economists, biologists, solicitors, politicians & so on.[9]

Among his books, he said, he owned The Macmillan Report & the International Gold Standard by D. Graham Hutton, published in 1931, the year after he and Hutton had met in the Scillies; also Twilit Corners by D. Graham Hutton, 1925. (It didn't seem to occur to him that Hutton might have been a better economist than poet.) He went on to quote Maurice Baring, from 'C': 'remember that verse is the blossom of many minds, the fruit of few', and Hardy, who in Desperate Remedies echoes Milton's Lycidas and ironically talks about 'the age at which the clear spirit bids goodbye to the last infirmity of noble mind, and takes to house-hunting and investments'.

For Christmas 1938, Robin Milford sent Gerald his recently published Four Hardy Songs, and Gerald found that 'The colour' was dedicated to him,

7 29 September 1938.
8 9 November 1938.
9 9 or 10 November 1938.

'whose own settings of Hardy are at once my delight and my despair'. Gerald told him that the dedication 'really rather moved me (which is a thing I'd rather write than say) & I think its a lot to come from a pretty well known composer to one who is not'. He was writing on Christmas Eve, and would have to be up next morning at 4.30 when the local band came round after playing carols in *Greenwood Tree* fashion through the village: the Finzis traditionally gave them coffee or beer. 'It's lovely to hear Christmas carols, coming nearer & nearer, in the early hours.' He would miss that at Ashmansworth. Toty de Navarro sent them books as a present, and, thanking him, Gerald wrote: 'in these days, when one is feeling that mankind was Nature's greatest mistake, it's good to have a reminder, by way of Rodin & Michelangelo, of mankind's possibilities . . . Do you remember Wm Blake's sensible old Devil who said "The worship of God is Honouring his gifts in other men, and loving the greatest men best." ' [10]

Dies Natalis was accepted for the Three Choirs. Gerald sent what are now Nos 1, 2, 4 and 5 to Howard Ferguson for him to mark the phrasing and dynamics. This Howard did, except for 'Wonder' (4) in which he couldn't 'for the life of me find the "breathing places" which condition phrasing'. Gerald complained to Toty de Navarro that at Hereford he would be in dull company, with Dyson, Brent Smith, and W. H. Reed. 'All splendid people, but dreadful composers. Can it be that 1) I'm not a splendid person, but a better composer or 2) I'm a splendid person but they're the better composers.'[11] Over the New Year, his Bridges partsongs and Drummond Elegies were broadcast. Then Steuart Wilson broadcast 'The sigh' and 'Ditty', about which Vaughan Williams wrote to him: 'You *have* hit the nail on the head.' [12] His good fortune led him to think of Robin Milford and Tony Scott. Would Robin like to compose something for brass band, he suggested; and could Robin ask Tony to arrange something for Downe House School so that he might feel he was doing work that was wanted, that he would hear, and that had *got* to be done within a certain time – 'three very stimulating points'.[13]

By January 1939 Gerald was involved, he told Toty, in 'this business of packing up books, packing up books, packing up books, packing up books, packing up music, packing up music, packing up music'.[14] In the background to the building of the new house, which had taken up so much of their time and thought, was always the *haunting despair* of events in Europe, Joy recorded in her Journal, and *no feeling of assurance in the future*. Working one evening before the fire he said: '*Whatever comes, we must never forget how happy we have been together.*' He gave the new address, Church Farm, Ashmansworth, near Newbury, Berkshire, to friends, 'for the rest of our lives, I hope,' as he told Robin. He knew they were wished every happiness, 'or rather – since happiness as an end in itself is

[10] 17 December 1938.
[11] 17 December 1938.
[12] January 1939.
[13] 27 November 1938.
[14] 25 January 1939.

rather a contemptible pursuit – a life of much work, which amounts to the same thing'.[15] Though the house would have 'its usual measure of deaths, births, burglaries, frozen pipes & broken windows', he told Howard, 'it's got a very happy feeling'.[16]

1939, THE NEW HOUSE

While the building was pegged out on the site, the Finzis visited it one evening and – seeing how the sun's rays slanted – quietly shifted all the pegs round a few degrees so that the last light would shine into Gerald's work-rooms. Maybe he was remembering how Detmar Blow had built 'Hilles' on the spot where the vixen played with her cubs in the evening light. Early in February 1939 Detmar died, and Joy and Gerald went to the service in Gloucester Cathedral. It was at 'Hilles' that Gerald had learnt to love a house with a spreading view, a sturdy welcoming house open to the land. Now he was moving into such a home of his own.

They had chosen to use bricks, which grow more beautiful with age, and found what they wanted, handmade and sand-faced, in a kiln near Newbury. The builder's father had put down some oak, from which the floor, the window seats, and the great front door were made. Peter Harland designed for them a long low house, the entrance to the north, a long façade to the south, with Gerald's book-room and music-room one above the other with their own small staircase at the west end cross-wing, and children and domestics at the east far end, well separated by a big sitting-room. It had to have a steeply pitched roof to afford attics, and to allow the snow they could expect at six hundred feet to slide off. The huge underground rain-water tank from the old farm was incorporated beneath the building, pumped into the scullery. They wanted the upstairs windows low enough to see out of when lying in bed, high enough for tall Joy to look through when standing up. They had only two disagreements. She disliked the design of the porch – like a bank, she thought it – but, being Joy, made the best of it by planting jasmine to cover it. When he wanted the little room off the bedroom for yet more books, however, she was adamant: it became their bathroom. They sold their Beech Knoll furniture; friends observed there was nothing inherited in the new house: the break with the past was complete. Chairs and tables were made for them by Harry Davoll, a disciple of Ernest Gimson and the Barnsley brothers, who figures in William Rothenstein's painting 'Cotswold craftsmen'. True to the Finzis' concern for dying rural crafts, they employed local men for the joinery and internal fittings. There was no unnecessary ornament; textiles and walls were plain and neutral. It was a strong and serviceable house, a home to work in. The hall was tiled, the yard paved with Sarsen stones. Along the south façade a terrace was later laid by German prisoners of war. The eight-foot-high brick and flint garden wall upset some of the villagers who, Gerald

[15] 5 March 1939.
[16] Before 23 March 1939.

enjoyed telling his friends, decided they were nudists! It was, of course, to give privacy to them and shelter to their crops; against it they trained fruit trees. There was little decorative garden.

Wherever he went, Gerald planted. Digging a hole for a chestnut tree in the meadow, he found the shards of an Iron Age pot. Having just read William Rutland's new *Thomas Hardy*, he would have remembered that when the foundations were dug for Max Gate, Hardy's house near Dorchester, 'the spade came upon traces of the race that had ruled there so long before . . . there lay a skeleton, with Roman ornaments upon it, as it had lain for fifteen hundred years'.[17] Holding his own even earlier relic, and with his mind running too on his recent letters to William Busch, he speculated that '*when this pot was made, two or three thousand years ago, there was not a single person in the whole of the country who could consider any presentday inhabitant otherwise than an alien.*' '*We should not have one word in common and hardly any so called racial characteristics.*'

The next two Journal entries read: *March 9 G & I slept for the first time in the new house. March 16 German invasion of Czechoslovakia. G slept badly and woke at 4 am. Very miserable all day.* Joy added her own poetic comment:

> *Close mine eyes, and fold my dreams:*
> *The river flows.*
> *The patient earth and stella span*
> *Outwear the little print of man.*

We have nearly settled in now — and have worked very hard to achieve this end. 'This is what I have always longed for and now that it is ours we must work hard to justify it.'

Boosey & Hawkes had more or less agreed to publish *Dies Natalis*, provided Gerald would produce one more movement, a fast one for contrast. During May he finished it — No. 3, 'The Rapture' — *an angelic roundabout,* noted Joy. On 1 June the Finzis went with Tony and Ruth Scott and all the children for a fortnight's holiday to the Windmill at Overy Staithe, Norfolk. Joy, under East Anglian skies, found time for painting. While there, Gerald was horrified to hear that Booseys did not after all want to publish his work. Should he ask Elsie Suddaby, who was to sing it, to write a stinker to Boosey? He consulted Howard Ferguson: he couldn't believe that *Dies* had fewer probabilities of performance and sale than Britten's *Our Hunting Fathers* (which Boosey had recently brought out, and which Gerald had heard in 1937). Howard replied that *Dies* was at least attractive, and for strings only, whereas the Britten was most unattractive and 'requires Xylophones, Bedpans and lord knows what'.[18] Gerald refused to share the cost with Boosey, but — after OUP and Novello turned it down — eventually agreed to stand a guarantee.

During June, Cedric Thorpe Davie and his wife Bruno, Toty de Navarro, Howard, and Ann Bowes-Lyon all came to Ashmansworth, the first such gathering there (though the Vaughan Williamses had already called). 'You'll never

---

[17] William R. Rutland, *Thomas Hardy* (London, 1938), p. 76.
[18] 12 June 1939.

believe that we only have one spare room, when you first see the new house,'
Gerald had warned Ceddie, a Scot. 'It looks enormous, rather like Abbotsford,
but it's only one room thick, which wouldn't have suited Sir Walter at all!'[19]

Joy's Aunt Lily died that summer; Joy drew her on her death bed, and
Gerald went with her to the funeral. She had loved her 'not because she was
an aunt',[20] he was careful to point out to Toty, but because she was splendid.
'Somehow or other it was easier after having seen her,' he told Howard.
'Although I don't know anything about the future & have pretty few hopes, it
was something of a comfort to know what an empty shell was being buried.'[21]

Dies Natalis, Op. 8 (II)

The form *Dies Natalis* finally took was Intrada, 'Rhapsody', 'The rapture', 'Wonder', and 'The salutation'. Its chronology is uncertain (see p. 46). In his
programme note meant for Hereford in 1939 Finzi gave no dates – he wrote
about Traherne. He did, however, say that the music of the 'Rhapsody' was
based on the two main themes of the Intrada, implying that the Intrada was
completed first. But about 'Wonder' his letters are contradictory. He told Tony
Scott that the *last* two movements (did he mean to write the first two and the
last?) were written in 1926 and 'turned down by every publisher under the
sun'.[22] Howard Ferguson implied, when Finzi asked him to mark the phrasing
and dynamics, that he knew the movement well: 'I have never liked ['Wonder'] as much as the rest.'[23] He would hardly have said that had it been greatly
changed. Yet Finzi admitted to him it had been 'partially re-written'[24] and told
Howells in May 1940 that it had been 'entirely re-written'. Whatever its
history, the completed cantata is compact and coherent.

Dies Natalis is a celebration of childhood's joy and innocence. From his youth
Finzi rated imagination higher than experience (but how did he square that
with Hardy's turning to poetry at nearly sixty, and that most of Vaughan
Williams's symphonies came after he too was sixty?). Above all Finzi prized
intuition, loving Gurney for his 'intensity contained in lyric form'. It was not
real old age he deprecated – *that* he could venerate – but the dulling that often
came with middle-age. He responded most keenly to lyrical art, spontaneous
and unforced, and placed less value on the grand, the epic, or the monu-
mental. In his opinion experience blunted the edge of delight, and he found
little compensation in the discipline and wisdom that age might accumulate.
He prized sensibility over organization, naturalness not only above sophistica-
tion but above conceptual thought. He looked askance at Wagner, for instance;

[19] 23 March 1939.
[20] 27 June 1939.
[21] 23 June 1939.
[22] 22 September 1946.
[23] 4 January 1939.
[24] 16 January 1939.

at the end of his life he could admire his 'sheer intellectual force, combined with emotional force' but disliked the 'qualities of his mind which exude through every bar';[25] he would not involve himself in such dark and powerful passions of the human psyche. He left others to appreciate artists greatest in their mature 'third periods' – Sophocles, Rembrandt, Beethoven, Verdi, Titian.

Finzi's view of childhood derives first from Traherne, then from Blake and Wordsworth (and they in turn from Rousseau, though it is more an English than a European view). For them, each child is unique: important for its own way of perceiving, thinking, and feeling, not simply as a diminutive adult. This prelapsarian, asexual innocence contrasts with the Christian tradition of original sin. It has its dangers, if it ignores Lolita, The Lord of the Flies, the boy-murderers of the Bulger child in 1993; and if it diminishes adult achievement. But at its purest it represents the Romantic Child without being sanitised or sentimentalised, as in some turn-of-the-century Victorian and Edwardian literature. The singularity of Dies Natalis is that its burning intensity is neither sensual nor coy.

Finzi shared Blake's (and Hardy's) protest against hypocrisy and orthodox restraint, and revolt against creeds, systems, and codes. Both Finzi and Blake seemed to regard experience as corruption by the impediments of society – Traherne's 'Dirty Devices of this World' – rather than positively, as an accumulation of wisdom, standards, and skills, and the power to connect and synthesise. What gives Finzi's thought its own flavour is that he did not, like Blake, equate experience with the baneful influence of reason. Blake saw danger in enlightenment and rationalism. Finzi, on the other hand, aligned himself – at least consciously – with reason and tolerance.

But never to the extent that reason blighted his sense of wonder. In 'The rapture' – the 'angelic roundabout' – two of Finzi's early experiences fused and blazed. During a walking tour of East Anglia in 1927 he had stood entranced looking up at the early sixteenth-century roof in a Cambridgeshire church, three tiers of angels with outspread wings, alive with colour and movement in honour of the creator: 'good for March church roof', Howard Ferguson wrote to him on 4 September 1927, 'I am so glad it has revealed the Botticelli.' The Botticelli was the Mystic Nativity, and Finzi was so carried away by its circle of dancing angels above the oxen-stall that in 1931 he asked Howard to get him a print from the National Gallery. In 1939, when he was under pressure to compose a quick movement to complete Dies Natalis, his mind made a connecting leap, and on 2 February Joy recorded his thoughts: 'There is a great resemblance between the static and ecstatic . . . . I discovered this one day when I was standing in March church and looking up at the double hammerbeam roof and the hundreds (rows?) of carved angels – which gave the feeling of a Botticelli Nativity and were static from very ecstasy.'

'The rapture' is the epitome of Finzi's 'dance of delight'. In the swirling Allegro the accompaniment and the voice go their separate ways: trills, violins twining in thirds over a *pizzicato* bass, and syncopations give a springy airy bounce over which the voice's long-held notes sound like trumpet calls. The strings move mostly scalewise, the voice in great leaps: the phrase 'whom the whole world magnifies' is itself magnified, covering an octave and a fourth up to high B flat. The voice-part has (like the 'Rhapsody', see p. 44) its own internal structure. It is braced by perfect intervals − octaves, fifths, fourths − which repeat, echo, and rhyme. The vocal phrase for 'The stars do move The Sun doth shine to shew his love' matches the earlier 'O Sacred Light How Fair and bright'. For the swinging tune 'O heavenly Joy', *piu tranquillo*, strings and voice move in canon. Before the climax a string passage screws up the harmonic tension to an expectant pause before 'O how divine am I', and the singer, dramatically unaccompanied, demands 'Who mine Did make the same! What hand divine!'. The whole piece − the athletic voice, the dancing strings, the pregnant pauses − brims with energy.

After the vigorous, wide-intervalled 'Rapture', 'Wonder' (Arioso) is slow, almost painfully introspective. The phrases curl inwards; the closest possible imitations and semitone clashes make for dense texture and harmony. There is a sense of over-hearing a private devotion. But the words 'are all things here', 'did with me talk', 'how great, how fair', 'but twas divine', are set to rhyming musical figures, giving shape to what sounds a spontaneous meditation. Though deeply devotional, 'Wonder', like 'The rapture', ends with a blazing triumphant affirmation. 'The rapture' begins in G minor and ends in C major; 'Wonder' begins with two flats and ends on a D major chord; so tonally it opens the door to 'The salutation', much of which is securely in G major.

When Finzi sent the work to Arthur Bliss in 1940 Bliss wrote back: 'It is a beautiful work and very characteristic with its composer standing firmly in the middle giving a courteous bow to VW on the one side and JSB on the other.'[26] Possibly Bliss's own music was also a beneficial influence. The string textures − intimate or resounding − owe much too to Elgar's Introduction and Allegro, though the simpler Serenade shadows the themes, particularly of the Intrada. The great discord that introduces the Angel of the Agony in *The Dream of Gerontius* here introduces the new-born child; who then gazes on the 'orient and immortal wheat' wrapped in the *divisi* parallel strings of Gerontius's 'strange innermost abandonment'. Philosophically, *Dies Natalis* might complement *Gerontius*: in the one there is a soul on the point of death, in the other a soul at the point of birth. Finzi's vision of eternity − 'I thought it had stood from everlasting to everlasting' − was also Holst's in *The Hymn of Jesus* − 'to you who *gaze* a lamp am I' and Vaughan Williams's in the *Tallis Fantasia*. Finzi's false relations as the climax of so many phrases (bar 3, for instance, of the Intrada) were also the common English currency of his time. *The Lark Ascending* hovers over the music. More generally, Vaughan Williams's Four Hymns for tenor seem a potent influence: the free declamation of the first hymn; the actual themes of the second; the inwardness of the third; and in the last, the ground bass in Vaughan Williams, the Bach-like ritornello in Finzi, giving in each case a closed structure. At a deeper level Vaughan Williams's Five Mystical Songs, a work Finzi loved all his life, and – like *Dies* – drawn from the words of a single poet, may be an influence. Though Finzi disliked Mahler, his 'child's vision' has a good deal in common with the soprano's in Mahler's Fourth Symphony. Closer still is Tippett's *Boyhood's End* (1943), a single person's recapturing of intense early delights. Hudson's prose is less visionary than Traherne's, and Tippett looks further back than to the Romantics, formally maybe to Purcell's 'The Blessed Virgin's expostulation', but the music's bony counterpoint and winging coloratura is, like *Dies*, exultant.

The words of *Dies Natalis* are Traherne's but the sequence of thought is Finzi's. In the 'Rhapsody' (see p. 44) he celebrates natural beauty. 'The rapture' is all praise of the divine in man. In 'Wonder' the child ponders on his own relationship to the glories around him. In 'The salutation' the child asks how he came to be made, speculates on his rich inheritance and is humbled. He measures himself against eternity. The unending melody in the strings tells of the 'thousand, thousand years' against which his short life is set. He learns that beauty must be cherished: 'the Sun and Stars are mine; if these I prize'. It is significant that Finzi sketched but never completed a setting of Lamb's poem about childhood playmates – 'all, all are gone, the old familiar faces'. There is nothing of this nostalgia, nothing sentimental, diminishing, or indulgent, about *Dies Natalis*. No-one but Finzi could have composed this radiant and tender masterpiece.

CHAPTER SEVEN

Ashmansworth

1939–41

There had been a six-month gap in Joy's Journal. Then came *September 1 Declaration of war*. In fact, that was the day Germany invaded Poland. The Finzis were at the Royal College of Music in London, for the final Three Choirs rehearsals. As *Dies Natalis* was being sung, it was announced that the festival was cancelled: Gerald noted it on his programme of the abandoned festival. It was to have been his first performance at a major occasion. There is no mention of this setback in the Journal, but Gerald wrote to Toty de Navarro:

> A more unfortunate day for publication than Sept 1st cd not have been chosen & I must resign myself to the work being a complete flop for the time being. However, it's there for the future, whatever that may be, & I was lucky enough to get as far as the 2nd rehearsal (when it sounded quite all right).

His loss seemed to him 'a very small thing in a very big upheaval'. He could only wait until he was conscripted. He was afraid he wouldn't make a very good soldier as he'd 'never fired anything since bow & arrow days, but however pacific I am, I cdn't honestly have any conscientious objections about an affair of this sort'.[1] Writing almost the same letter to Robin Milford, he went on to worry about the effect of the ban on public gatherings, which meant there could be no concerts: 'can orchestras be got going again after a break, say, of five years?'[2] Robin, on Guernsey where he had been on holiday, took refuge in nostalgia, but Gerald would have none of that: 'I don't believe in your good old days! . . . children being hung for stealing 6d, or "witches" being burned alive.'

To William Busch he wrote at length, glad that William had reached a point where he was able to work. 'But how can I feel the same,' he cried, 'when I don't believe the same as you do, though I have all your loathing of war and of killing (and fear, too, of being killed, with so little of my life's work completed).' He could not believe the fault belonged to both sides. War might have been avoided had there been no Versailles, or no 1914–18 or Franco-Prussian or Napoleonic wars (he saw no real need to go further back than the League of Nations failure over Manchukuo). 'All events are completely inter-locked and there's not a thought or movement that does not have incalculable effect on existence. You, your forbears and your child may yet be the ancestors

---

[1]   11 September 1939.
[2]   4 September 1939.

of a Hitler at one end and a St Francis at the other.' He agreed with the diplomat and columnist Harold Nicolson, who believed the system established by Hitler to be the 'most evil form of human governance which has existed on the earth since the days of Genghis Khan'.

> How then, can I get an inner peace to work, whilst others are combating this partly for me, and when I know that if Nazidom does prevail – as it possibly may do – it will be the end of our culture for centuries; and that includes your music as well as mine . . . Still, as I've always believed, a song outlasts a dynasty, and I agree with every word you say about the real values in life. E. M. Forster, in a very good pamphlet called 'What I believe' says that some people call the absence of force and violence 'decadence' but he calls it 'civilization' and finds in such interludes the chief justification for the human experiment. Later on . . . I may be able to get down to music but it's difficult . . . with the foreknowledge of the useless and pitiful slaughter that will soon be beginning.[3]

1939, EVACUEES

The Finzis and their new house caused a little head-shaking in the village, which was an old-style community of working farmers and gentry. Quite apart from the high wall, the house seemed so big, Joy's alabaster fishes in the hall so surprising; and a composer, who didn't go out to work, a very exotic creature. But quickly Gerald was found to be natural, straightforward, and with no side. Possibly influenced by Vaughan Williams's membership of the Dorking Committee for Refugees, the Finzis had already taken in a political refugee. 'This house fairly swarms with Jews & Jewesses now,' Robin had written innocently to him in May. 'I'm dreading ours,' replied Gerald, but went on reasonably: 'there's always the chance that she may turn out everything that one hopes . . . After all, if you collected a score of people at random from Durham or York & they came to live amongst us, I wonder how many wd fit in.'[4] In fact they loved Becky, a wealthy Bavarian of Jewish stock whose family were nearly all exterminated; she came out on the last train bringing only her sewing machine with which she hoped to earn her living – but the Germans smashed it before her eyes at the frontier.

Joy, new to the village and able to be impartial, was made billeting officer – every house in a 'reception area' had to prepare to take one evacuee to every living room. Soon came refugees, Gisa Dietz (later Cartwright) and Mimi. Joy found Mimi a job in a hat shop in London, but young Gisa stayed with them to help cook, and remembered those two years as the among the happiest of her life. Frank and Vera Strawson, then living in London, arrived before their letter announcing they were coming, and stayed for the duration. With them came Frank's cousin, Lydia Riesenecker, a cultivated Czech Jewess who had played *skat* with Richard Strauss and been courted by Ysaÿe; she introduced

[3] 17 September 1939.
[4] 11 May 1939.

middle-European recipes to Ashmansworth. Before long Iris Lemare joined them.

There were eleven sleeping in the house (for a time Iris even slept on the loggia). They seldom sat down less than eight to a meal, and the house itself was still unfinished inside. Extra people, Gerald wrote to Toty de Navarro, explaining why he could not compose: painters in, putting books in order, manual work in the garden, taking children to school, Joy with bronchitis. With no garden made, just a piece of soil, which looked 'like a devastated Flanders village',[5] there were no fresh green vegetables, so the household took it in turns to gather young nettles to cook as spinach. Gerald, in real Hardy form, picked his from the edge of the churchyard, where others were too squeamish to go; and in October he went nutting. He planted Toty's moving-in present, the shrub *ceanothus burkwoodii*, in the place of honour against the bookroom window on the south wall.

Over Christmas, as no bombs had yet fallen, the evacuees went home, and Howard Ferguson came with his housekeeper. He had been in Belfast when war broke out, and stayed there to finish his Piano Sonata; but was now involved with Myra Hess in running the National Gallery lunchtime concerts. Edward Selwyn and the Stratton Quartet played Gerald's Oboe Interlude at the Gallery concert on 22 January, and on the 26th Elsie Suddaby (who long ago had sung Gurney's 'Sleep' to him) gave at Wigmore Hall the postponed first performance of *Dies Natalis*. It was a far cry from a great cathedral, that bleak Wigmore Hall at a January lunchtime, but friends came, and Gerald reported to Howard that it was 'a good enough performance'. It had come about because the conductor Maurice Miles had decided to get together a string orchestra, and — looking around for a new work — was introduced to *Dies* through Ernest Chapman of Boosey & Hawkes. (A substantial review in the *Musical Times* the previous October must have helped.) Miles had not met Finzi before and was struck by his charm and the 'otherworld atmosphere about him'. Vaughan Williams wrote 'Your tune is *beautiful* and Elsie sang it divinely.'[6] *The Times* called it 'a glowing and a strong work', noting its 'vein of spontaneous melody and a sense of verbal accentuation': it was 'Finzi's Week'.

Gerald and Joy drove home during the Great Frost to find no power, light, or telephone: 'not a big tree left which has not had fifty to eighty years of growth destroyed',[7] he told Robin; only their old pines held on. Sleet had frozen as it fell and turned every bough, branch, and twig into gigantic icicles. They weighed a twig, and found it was 28oz with ice, 1oz without. 'A St Bartholomew's night of slaughter,'[8] Gerald told Howard.

5   To de Navarro, 3 April 1939.
6   27 January 1940.
7   27 January 1940.
8   5 February 1940.

Life went on, those months of the phoney war. Their home was still new and visitors came to see it. Joy and Gerald biked over to Burghclere to show a friend the Stanley Spencer memorial chapel, and *stopped for gin, beer and ginger wine before tackling the hill home,* Joy recorded in her Journal. On 3 March, *the first day of Spring,* they walked from Marlborough along the Wansdyke till it dropped down towards Devizes, *in hot sunshine though snow was still lying in drifts in the shadows. G very happy . . . The day lingers on and on even when Venus is high above the beeches.* The Rubbras stayed, for Edmund – 'a ruthless spirit in an ageless body' – to play through his new Third Symphony. Gerald found it 'the most properly realised work that he has done so far . . . characteristic Rubbra in its hardness, its grinding, ruthless quality and superb technique'. They noted slight differences of opinion between the Rubbras. *ER says 'Antoinette is psychologically difficult at the moment'. But knowing ER's self-absorption one can guess its not only on one side.* Adeline and Evelyn Fox, Aldbourne friends, visited them, and Joy sadly noted their increasing age, remembering how Evelyn, when they had first met her, was *like the rising sun and as emphatic* – since then (Joy went on, with one of her startling inconsequences that leave one unsure whether they are intentional or owing to shaky grammar) – *the CBE and sudden serious heart attack leaving a bewildered shadow.*

Justin and Edith Brooke called on their way to Bedales school: *'Justin more like Cobbett than ever, but with his background of culture which Cobbett lacked.'* Justin Brooke had himself been at Bedales, then went up to Cambridge, where he founded the Marlowe Dramatic Society and played Faustus to Rupert Brooke's Mephistopheles (confusingly, the two Brookes were not related). Justin had worked for some time in the family tea business, then turned to fruit-growing in Suffolk, so providing employment for the rural community. In May the Finzis spent a week with them at Clopton Hall, their house near Newmarket, learning more about orchards, which Gerald was now planting in earnest: *sun and cuckoos and much interesting work to see.*

To avoid the 'damnable spring cleaning', Gerald paid his 'almost annual respects to the old man's ghost at Max Gate,' he wrote to Toty de Navarro. He went by bus to Dorchester, and walked from Milton Abbas over Bulbarrow and Woolland and Bell hills to Sturminster Newton, where Hardy spent the two happiest years of his early married life. 'A much nicer little house, externally at any rate, than Max Gate, standing right above the river Stour (& all very much like "Overlooking the river") (see p. 169). Then on to Shaftesbury & then a marvellous walk on the top of the downs from Shaftesbury to Salisbury & then on to Andover & home.'[9] He was particularly pleased to see the new Hardy room in the Dorchester Museum; and told Robin Milford that the manuscript of *Satires of Circumstance* was open at 'Tolerance' (Robin's setting of which was dedicated to him).

Early in May 1940 Germany invaded Holland and Belgium, and able-

9   To de Navarro, 21 April 1940.

bodied men between nineteen and forty-one became liable for national service. It was a time when all were called to account, to assess themselves, their value and their work. Robin Milford's father, Sir Humphrey, perhaps to cover his own despondency, remarked jocularly that the maids cleaning his study 'were far more efficient & useful than us so-called intellectuals'. 'The cobbler to his last,' replied Gerald when Robin recounted this, 'just ask yourself who has more profoundly moved civilization, Schubert and Shakespeare or the domestics who cooked for them.' It was an echo of what Parry had written to Vaughan Williams in 1915. 'Anyhow, I'm sure that whoever cleaned Bach's boots was not of more use than Bach.'[10] Howard sent him a *Daily Telegraph* letter[11] signed by leading figures in the arts who believed that artists 'are of more value to their country in their trained capacity, often in key positions, than serving generally with the fighting forces . . . Our art is a measure of our civilization, and our artists its guardians.' They recommended the setting up of a council of representatives from the professions to advise the Ministry of Labour 'to reserve some measure of our talent', and how best to use it in the emergency.

'Of course that's the solution, the only solution, if anything comes of it,' replied Gerald to Howard. 'I feel that our work, if not ourselves, is about the only justification for mankind's existence! And as for being the ultimate representatives of our countries & civilization, well, the point's not worth discussing, for there never have been any others . So you know that my feelings are the same as yours about the absurdity of Milford's "pioneering", you "nursing" or me "fighting". All I feel is that no self-respecting person (unless he's an out and out pacifist) can claim exemption on account of his own importance. His country must make that claim for him.'[12] (Later that year, with the backing of Vaughan Williams, a White Paper was published reserving outstanding contributors to Art, Science, learning or Letters.)

The German occupation of Boulogne on 24 May prompted Finzi to try to finish off some things, the Journal recorded, until he was called up. The Local Defence Volunteers (later the Home Guard) was formed, and he went to the first meeting dreading the firearm practice, but found it 'just like a Hardy scene of England during the Napoleonic wars'.[13] Robin Milford noticed the incongruity of a rifle standing in Gerald's music-room, and the disturbance to 'the peace of his excellently ordered composer's life'. In spite of the anguishing news, there was an evening's relaxation when with friends and Joy's sister Mags they played 'duets' for eight hands: Smetana and Haydn, which sounded mostly like Hindemith (the Finzis had just bought another piano, a second-hand Ebach, for £25).

As the Allied forces were beaten back to the Dunkirk beaches, Gerald sent

10   11 January 1940.
11   4 March 1940.
12   13 March 1940.
13   To Milford, 29 May 1940.

Robin the two volumes of Gurney's songs published in 1938, the result of his and Howard's badgering and cajoling Marion Scott and the Oxford Press:

> As you know, I've loved him & his work – though I never knew him personally – since I first got hold of 'Sleep' in 1920, & it still seems one of the great songs of the world. It's curious how the work of certain composers, often those not gifted with worldly wisdom, manages to survive through the intensity of the love a few people feel for it. I'm quite certain that if a few people hadn't felt like that about Schubert's work we shd probably never have heard of him.[14]

Alfred Chenhalls, an accountant who had studied music, and was the dedicatee of Ireland's piano piece *Cypress*, stayed a weekend at Ashmansworth. He was, Gerald reported to Robin, very much in the swim. He had brought the manuscript of Walton's just-composed children's duets with him. He had met Stravinsky, Alexander Korda, Greta Garbo, Winston Churchill – 'you know the sort of thing'. To him Poulenc was a force and Vaughan Williams a bore. '(I fancy that my own work is a joke, if it's worth thinking of at all!)' For all that, Gerald found him lovable and generous, and not a snob. 'But what I kept wondering all the time was whether he had ever really loved *any* music at all & whether those dull, unsparkling creatures like Gurney or Schubert were not better served by what I mentioned before, the intensity of love which their work was able to create in a few people.'

He agreed with Robin that Gurney's 'Nine of the clock' was not much of a song; there were poor songs in the second volume, too, put in for contrast, but also supreme things like 'Last hours' and 'The folly of being comforted'. What Gurney needed now, he thought, was a couple more volumes of the songs published separately in his life, with a few of those still in manuscript. Then there were 'quantities of most remarkable verse, some of it quite terrific, & all of it intensely individual . . . The "Music & Letters" number . . . only tells half the story.' The Journal continues what the letter was too discreet to say: *who will ever know . . . that Gurney had the greatest contempt for Howells.* According to Gerald's Gloucestershire friend, the poet Jack Haines, *Gurney used to say 'Oh, Howells will just get married, and that will be the end of him, and a Dr of Music, which is what he is best fitted for.' Both of these tragic prophecies,* wrote Joy in her Journal, *seem to have come true.* (Gurney and the Finzis were mistaken: *Hymnus Paradisi*, though not performed, had been composed, and when John Sumsion brought the score to Ashmansworth in September 1949 Gerald immediately agreed with him that it should be produced at the next Three Choirs Festival.)

1940, DUNKIRK

The day after the evacuation from Dunkirk began, and the country prepared to repel invasion, Joy recorded Gerald's saying: *Do keep my home going. I've got the thing I've always longed for, the right atmosphere and conditions to work in. Don't you see how I'm just*

---

[14] 29 May 1940.

beginning to flower, just starting to do my real work. Don't let it go. He picked up the same point writing to Justin Brooke's wife, Edith, discussing a book they had both read, C. Dover's *Half Caste* (1937), about the Eurasian question. He thought Dover had overstated his case, but 'if a man, say, of Justin's genius found himself thwarted and baulked on all sides owing to social pressure, something would have to explode somewhere'. He had no doubt that 'the possession or loss of self-respect is liable to make a "king from a coward or a coward from a king"... One can't flower without sunshine.'[15]

Howard Ferguson, in London, judged the situation bad enough to send the manuscript of his Sonata to the safety of Ashmansworth. But Gerald, for all his ignoring of his Jewishness, had no illusions about what might happen to him if the Nazis occupied England. In his book-room was a capacious cupboard under the stairs. He drilled a couple of unobtrusive breathing holes into the door, so that he could hide there should the house be searched; and had a sliding bookcase built to conceal it.

On 10 June Italy declared war on the Allies; Joy noted his saying (and the past tense makes it full of trepidation): *I love you so much. We have had a lovely life together. I don't mean going down Central Africa in a canoe, but making beautiful things, which is all that counts.* On 17 June she recorded *French have capitulated,* and copied into the Journal another letter to William Busch. At that moment, with his whole world crashing down, not even Gerald could claim there was a place for the arts. It was difficult for him, he admitted, to adjust to the fact that the agricultural labourer was in a reserved occupation while the poet, painter, composer, or philosopher was regarded as useless. 'And, in fact, when the barbarian is at the gate, I suppose he is.' He hoped that gentle Busch would not let his German ancestry make him bitter. And now, facing up to the implications of his surname in the week Italy declared war, for the first time Finzi took his own case openly into account: 'at that rate, I should be feeling the same over my Italian ancestry'. He quoted de la Mare:

> Oh, no man knows
> Through what wild centuries
> Roves back the rose.

Echoing E. M. Forster's current question, 'can you give the names of your eight great-grandparents?', what shocks people would get, he told Busch, if they knew the thirty-two strands of only five generations back, which went to their making! He found that at such a time, when 'all the horrible instincts of witch-hunters, papist persecutors, jew baiters, come to the surface', he could understand some of the outbreaks in the past. He recalled an article in the *Times Literary Supplement* in 1934 which told of a Frenchman to whom the writings of Seneca, when he read them before the French Revolution, had seemed 'over-strained and theatrical', but when he reread them during the Terror,

---

[15] 30 May 1940 (Journal only).

when 'the possibility of being whirled off to execution was continually impending, as in the days of Nero, they seemed exactly right'. In 1940 Gerald similarly found it easier to understand how the whole Huguenot, Catholic, and Jewish populations had had to suffer every inconceivable misfortune on account of the sins, real or imaginary, of one or two. 'However, you'd be the first to admit the deadly efficiency of the fifth column activities abroad and how, as a consequence, the innocent have to suffer with the guilty.' Sometimes he consoled himself with the fact that in 1807 no-one could possibly have imagined a Waterloo in 1815. At other times he remembered with dread how many civilizations had been overthrown.

Five days later France signed an armistice with Germany. Gerald passed a sleepless night. Day after day that summer of 1940 the sky was cloudless, but *never was it more impossible to sit in the sun*. Six-year-old Kiffer (as Christopher called himself) sensed the anxiety, one reason perhaps why Gerald took out and revised his Rossetti children's songs. Then he quickly set F. L. Lucas's 'June on Castle Hill', himself experiencing the contrast between the waving wild parsley and the threat of the guns.

Single songs

Lucas presents a flowery old fort, now warless. Finzi begins the second verse, 'earth sleeps in peace', ironically in the major, then – exactly as Lucas transforms his image of a 'honey-laden bee' into a plane 'laden' with bombs – transforms the initial 'on its grassy brow' motif into a threat. The controlled repeated chords are darkened chromatically, and the singer's notes get longer and lower, ominously whispering 'of wars to come'. In 1940 also Finzi revised his 1927 setting of Hardy's 'The market-girl', rewriting the middle. The song shows Finzi's parlando, conversational style at its best: the introduction so plaintive and bare; the piano bass octaves adding seriousness to 'sell . . . herself . . . too'; the ripple of movement at 'as I passed nigh'; the confiding tone at 'and so it began': here are tenderness, a humorous chuckle, and – unusually for Hardy and Finzi – a triumphant ending.

'To a poet a thousand years hence' betrays its early origin in its wide compass – it really needs two voices, tenor and baritone, even though Finzi revised it in April 1941. It is not absolutely coherent – too many keys, too many idioms for its length – but it remains one of his most poignant, personal songs. He knew Flecker's poem as early as 1919 (see p. 17), and it carries the creed of his composing life, confirmed when he buried the song under the foundations of Ashmansworth. The singer, dead a thousand years, addresses his friend 'unborn, unknown', then sends his 'soul' through time and space in a lyrical, soaring phrase that releases a confident, passionate Finzi. Old Homer, together with the supposed poet of the verse, with Flecker, Finzi, and the yet unborn listener – all linked by song, that all 'will understand'.

⊷

The circle of friends was beginning to break up. '*War is a great changer of addresses,*' the Journal notes, truly if a trifle sententiously. Tony Scott was joining the RAF, and the Finzis lunched with him and his wife Ruth — *drank coffee in the orchard, laying against haystack in the sun* — then brought them back to Ashmansworth. On the way Tony played his new fugue on a Newbury church organ, and at Ashmansworth Joy and Gerald played a new slow movement for violin and piano by Gerald (published posthumously as Elegy, Op. 22). They opened a precious last bottle of port and toasted an emotional Tony. Gerald privately summed up his pupil and friend: '*He has a curious stubborn mind, which works only in his own way . . . A Harrow education as well as the fact that he was a completely square peg in a round hole in his own home, were not the best things to help in his development . . . given a slightly greater facility, this might have turned him into a real creative artist.*' Gerald worried what enlisting might do to Tony's work. 'It pricks my conscience that you shd be having to break into your way of life whilst I am still able to carry on with mine.' He agreed that for Tony learning mechanics might be valuable as an after-the-war trade. 'In this way you are one of the wise virgins & I one of the foolish (with no reflections on either of us),' since Tony could certainly look to a more secure living in the future than he could; 'for I'm too old [at thirty-nine] & disinclined & incompetent to tackle any occupation outside composition & conceiving fruit cages!' He hoped for the time when Tony could 'get back to a room of your own, a piano & the work you want to do'. In the meantime, perhaps remembering how he had sent exercises to Private Farrar, he begged Tony to send him work and to 'keep the cogs oiled. I'm ready for anything, so long as I'm still free.'[16]

Next came John Sumsion in July, *needing a holiday and sympathetic company*, for Alice, his American-born wife, had taken their sons for safety to the States. Arthur and Trudy Bliss too were in the States, having been there for the New York première of his Piano Concerto when war was declared. Robin Milford, driven out of Guernsey by the fall of France, and now sharing Tony Scott's home, was distressed by 'all this parting & dissolution, & the horrid clouds of the future'. During August the Battle of Britain brought the Finzis' evacuees back. Howard Ferguson had joined the RAF with the Griller Quartet, as 'entertainers'. 'Do have your photo taken in uniform,' Gerald begged him, 'with a palm on one side and the hand resting on the chair.'[17] He sent a dreadful snapshot of himself in Home Guard uniform, which he called 'Father's home from the front'. Howard's *Three Diversions* was due for its first performance at the Prom on 13 September, and the Finzis of course planned to be there. At the end of August some bombs were dropped even at peaceful Ashmansworth. The next week the Home Guard was put on national emergency call, for inva-

16 23 July 1940.
17 2 August 1940.

sion was expected daily. Gerald, a platoon sergeant, was now on duty three evenings a week and kept one dusk-to-dawn watch.

In this tense atmosphere he set 'Channel firing', the poem by Hardy that begins 'That night your great guns, unaware, / Shook all our coffins as we lay'. He had begun it in April 1939, when Toty de Navarro suggested it to him. He'd read it a dozen times, he told Toty, but it had 'never made much impression on me till you drew attention to it. My setting's not finished but' (an echo of the boy at Harrogate talking to his mother) 'it shd be good when it is.'[18] Perhaps the Battle of Britain provided the stimulus. By 15 September he could tell Toty 'in spite of many Home-guard distractions' (or even because of them?) 'Channel Firing is finished'.

Toty begged him to publish it separately, at once: 'It should catch on now, even more than in normal times', with a special public. Gerald answered: 'You're wrong about publishing "Channel Firing" — it's quite the wrong time. One has to choose between recognition of the absolute insanity of all war & recognition of the necessity of this particular one. Anything that preaches the former vitiates against the practice of the latter. So you can count the withholding of "Channel Firing" as part of my war effort! But, seriously, I put a lot of store on the value of the artist to the community — even if the community doesn't want him — & however insignificant, even a small thing like this counts.'[19] (He eventually published it in 1949 in *Before and after Summer*.)

The Proms, after a fortnight of 'alerts' and air-raids, were forced to stop on 7 September when Queen's Hall was bombed. 'Poor everyone who was looking forward to their first performance,'[20] wrote Gerald to Robin. But, as with the cancellation of his own *Dies Natalis* the previous year, his thoughts turned quickly away from personalities. It was a compensation to think of any work of art 'from ancient China or Egypt onwards, & to realise exactly how much it has survived by way of wars, devastations, pestilence & the rise & fall of civilizations'.[21] The work of art, he said, turning again to Hardy, was rather like 'Only thin smoke without flame From the heaps of couch-grass.' The lines were from Hardy's poem 'In Time of "the Breaking of Nations" ', which Finzi had set in his early Requiem for the Great War (see p. 29). The small, homely country things would endure 'though Dynasties pass'; 'war's annals will cloud into night Ere their story die'. Finzi took the metaphor further, to make the poem and its maker that which will last: 'a song outlasts a dynasty'.

To William Busch he confided his concern for non-combatants: 'it's the thousands and thousands of homeless people without a penny that are the problem'; and he foresaw the horror of such things as the bombing of Dresden: 'it may turn into a war of retaliation on the civil population of

[18] 26 April 1939.
[19] 15 November 1940.
[20] 8/9 September 1940.
[21] 8/9 September 1940.

Germany'. The only gleam of hope he could see in the blitz on London was that it would give us 'a chance to rebuild courageously and decently'. Churchill, he considered, had 'all the imaginative grasp of an artist (for he is a great artist, as I think his work on Marlborough alone wd convince you)'. He might even bring about the federation of Europe or join the USA into the Commonwealth (a few months previously Churchill had offered France union with the UK). 'You can always expect great and imaginative strokes from him, just as you can always expect a pious sermon from Halifax or a business deal from Chamberlain.' Above all, 'the collapse of all that was built up over the last forty years in so many hours is, to a musician at any rate, one of the tragic things of this war, and now mediocrity, cheapness, playing-for-safety and keeping up the spirits are in the saddle. Still, the best will come through, and VW will still be speaking for us in a hundred years time.'[22] (In fact, Vaughan Williams spoke for The Composer in Wartime in a 1940 broadcast.)

One happy day that September they met Balfour Gardiner at the Milfords. They found him enchanting: to them it was like meeting a mythical person. They remembered the concerts he had promoted for young British composers before the 1914–18 war, and his financial generosity ranging from giving the first private performance of Holst's *Planets* to guaranteeing the education of the Milford's son Barnaby, or giving cottages to people like the conductor Richard Austin. *Some curious psychological peculiarity turned him from music to forestry and pigs at the height of his reputation,* observed Joy in her Journal; but they reckoned that among the composers born between 1870 and 1880 some would have backed him before Vaughan Williams or Holst as far as early promise was concerned. *He is a ruddy faced old bachelor, adoring children and with an individual wit and delightfully perverse ideas.*

Robin confided to Gerald that he was thinking of becoming a Catholic. Gerald spoke out; but then quickly wrote:

> Perhaps I oughtn't to have said all that I did about dogma. After all, those of my friends with fixed beliefs are certainly none the worse for it (outside the orbit of their beliefs!). If one believes in freedom of thought one shd be prepared to allow freedom to believe in dogma . . . though no rationalist cd ever be a fanatic, fanatics are not necessarily Hitlers & co . . . But you cd not believe that as an artist I cd be a rationalist, and yet you mention Hardy! His outlook, from my point of view, seems all that an artist needs. He had *ideas & feelings,* but no beliefs.

He reminded Robin of the story that the Wright brothers had only learnt to fly because no-one had taught them it was impossible. The limitations of so-called knowledge (which was what dogma pretended to be) were as dangerous as admitted ignorance (which was rationalism):

> I think the spirit shd be like a weather-cock, blown by the winds of feelings & ideas, & I hate the idea of fixing the weather-cock to N. S. E. or W . . . If

---

[22] 20 September 1940 (Journal only).

you accept the authority of the C of E you can hardly write a liturgical mass. If you accept the authority of the R.C. church you can hardly write an Anglican service. But if you accept neither & in their place put the duties of man & artist, you can, like VW write both.[23]

He admitted, however, that a dogma might be the right solution for Robin, who a month later became an Anglo-Catholic. It was not the first such confrontation Gerald had had that summer. Toty de Navarro had become engaged, but his fiancée had second thoughts because of his religion, before finally marrying him in October. 'As a rationalist,' Gerald wrote to their mutual friend Howard, 'I can understand her jibbing at all this (to me & you) Catholic twaddle . . . What crimes dogmatic religions are responsible for.'[24]

Another visit from Alfred Chenhalls, the man of the world, deeply disturbed him. Their values were so different that he made '*of me – of us – of our way of life – a gross caricature*'. There was discussion about which composers were important figures, and it led Gerald to ask '*who do you consider a great man?*' Chenny (was he possibly pulling Gerald's leg?) replied '*Hitler*'. To Gerald, Joy recorded grandly, *Hitler is a powerful person, a dangerous person, and a disease, but a completely unimportant person, who will leave nothing behind except a chapter in a history book. His whole world pales into insignificance next to the at present unknown work of some obscure poet, sculptor or composer.* (Ironically, Chenhalls looked remarkably like Churchill, and was killed when a plane carrying him was shot down by the Germans.)

Writing to Arthur Bliss (Joy copied the letter into her Journal), Gerald pushed to the extreme a view he had previously expressed to Robin Milford. 'Of course Trudy is right in thinking that the illness should be treated by the surgeon . . . We must develop a system of social biology which recognises rampant cells when it sees them – [Napoleon or Hitler] – and cuts them out in the early stages'; mercifully he added 'but doctors proverbially disagree'. He believed in the possibility of national states within a league of Europe 'which can be made impervious to disease'.[25] He considered Tolstoy's analysis of Napoleon in *War and Peace* pretty near the truth; and recommended reading Morley Roberts' *Bio-Politics* or Herbert Spencer's *The Social Organism*.

Joy, with never a long enough stretch of free time for sculpture, took a pad and pencil on her lap in the living-room and drew Gerald. At the time she was pleased; although the portrait is rough compared with the refinement of her later work, no photograph has better caught his sad reflective gaze. Gerald thought he looked a bit too heroic but told Howard 'she says its stubbornness'. On call as an emergency ambulance driver, Joy decided to simplify her life, and cut short the beautiful long hair that Gerald so loved. The household waited for the explosion. Gerald noticed nothing for about a week, then one night as they were preparing for bed, he asked 'I say, have you done something to your hair?'

[23] September 1940 (Journal only).
[24] 19/29 July 1940.
[25] 4 November. 1940

He felt increasingly isolated from music and friends, useless and depressed. Across the lane from their house was St James's church that gave it its name, Church Farm, a typical Hampshire Downs building, twelfth-century, with a small white weatherboard bell tower. Its wall-paintings had just been reconditioned, and Joy, who was helping, noticed the excellent acoustics. Being a reliable fiddler, she had always been involved in local music-making, coming over even from Aldbourne to the Newbury Amateur Orchestral Society. She suggested getting some players together in the church, thinking of chamber music. Gerald pointed out realistically that unless they were very good it would be a pleasure only to them and not to their audience, and, to her surprise, offered to conduct a group if she would find them.

'We've got a little body of twelve strings together,' he wrote to Tony Scott, 'people like Mrs Neate, Mrs Turner, Mrs Finzi etc & are doing Boyce Sym[phony] No. 4 (a delightful work, which Robin put me on to, rather like a procession of fat aldermen), Pastorale from the Corelli Christmas concerto, Bach Concerto in E, played by Rosie Roth [their leader] & Holst St Paul's Suite.'[26] They added the Sinfonia from Bach's cantata No. 156. The concert, on 28 December at 3.15, went off quite well, he reckoned. It pleased him that the chapel people came too, so that the church was crowded, in spite of petrol rationing and the early blackout in mid-winter. He would never make much of a conductor, he told Howard, but was glad that the players wanted to carry on 'as it's something to fill the terrible hollow feeling that the absence of music & music-making gives me'[27]; and it would be useful practice if he ever needed to conduct his own music. They called the group Newbury String Players.

They did nothing else about Christmas that year beyond the usual celebrations within the household. For him, he wrote to Robin Milford, Christmas would 'always be a time of silence & quiet, like Bridges'

> A frosty Christmas Eve
>> When the stars were shining
> Fared I forth alone
>> Where westward falls the hill

'Whether the bells sound or no [church bells were reserved to indicate invasion] I shall always hear them & it will always be frosty & starlit for me. For this reason I loathe Christmas crowds & only like the jollifications in theory (or in [Nathaniel] Hawthorne).'[28]

He asked Robin (who was in a 'boils-cum-suicide state') to write a review of the concert for the local newspaper. When Robin at first refused, Gerald admitted that he would 'rather run a mile than write half a column. I cd do

---

[26] 14 December 1940.
[27] 1 January 1941.
[28] 15 December 1940.

Sulky Gerald and proud Mum. She became eccentric, and during the war went to the police to report some locals as German spies (they owned a dachshund) carrying her umbrella upside down 'to disguise myself'.

The 'organ pipes' – Gerald, Edgar, Douglas, Felix, Katie. By 1918 Gerald and Katie were the only two left alive (see p. 197).

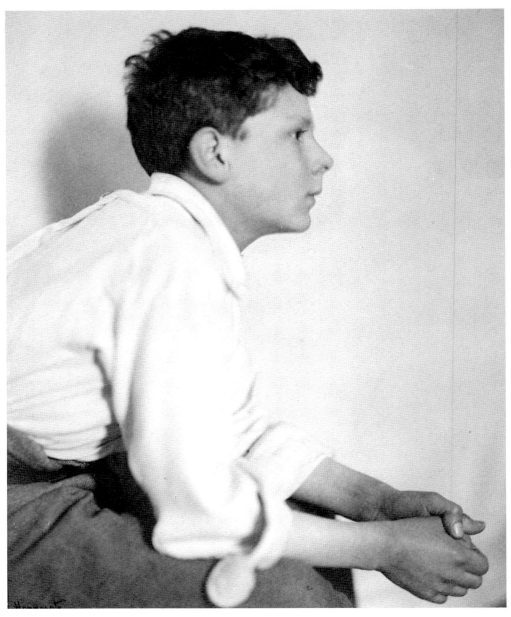

Gerald at Harrogate, taken by Nita Taylor and Olive Ismay, professional photographers and among his few friends at the time (see p. 14).

'Father's home from the front' (see p. 114). Gerald in Home Guard uniform in the loggia at Church Farm, 1940

'Sweetest hope that lookest smiling O'er the wilderness defiling' (see p. 178).

A page from Finzi's autograph of 'Wonder' from *Dies Natalis*. He wrote fast, holding his pen almost at right-angles to his forearm: a short sideways stroke produced a thickish note-head, a downward or upward stroke added the thin stem, all without raising the pen from the paper. He used a nib called 'time is money'.

the mile in ten minutes, but the half column wd take me ten hours. But then nothing comes easily to me.'[29] He picked up a point of Robin's about the paganism of the St Paul's Suite, making it unsuitable for church, and quoted from Herbert Read's *Annals of Innocence and Experience* : 'the highest manifestation of the immanent will of the universe is the work of art.' Gerald thought

> the idea that the arts shd act as handmaidens to worship, & that they are graven images if considered sufficient in themselves, is a great fallacy, a dangerous one &, in some cases, an evil one. Rutland Boughton & Alan Bush believe that the arts shd act as handmaidens to social reform & revolution, & how intensely they believe it, too. Hitler & Stalin hold similar opinions. Here we are, once again, at the roots of this *intolerance* . . . Thus Mrs S— of our village, was horrified that Mrs W—, a confessed unbeliever, shd come into the church to hear the music . . . Mrs W—, on the other hand, was appalled at the vicar's prayers, which she thought quite out of place. Mr A— the churchwarden, thought the collection of £11. 1. 6. [for the Southampton air-raid casualties] very remarkable. Oh, how much *bigger* music is than all this & why shd it be tied down to earth by a Communist rope, or a Fascist rope, or a Church rope or a Chapel rope, or a pagan rope or any bloody rope.

Incidentally, he went on, which religion? Why was the Bach concerto more religious than the Holst? and was the Sinfonia suitable just because it came from a church cantata (it was also the slow movement of a secular cantata)? He rejoiced to think that perhaps for the first time 'agnostics, R.C.'s, Anglo-C's, Jews, Chapel and C of E were all gathered together, seeing a beautiful sight, listening to decent music & with all their ridiculous differences dropped for at least an hour'.[30] (He might have had in mind an early mentor, Samuel Butler: 'the Church of Rome, the Church of England, and the freethinker have the same ideal standard . . . it is in the uncompromisingness with which dogma is held . . . that the danger lies.' Gerald did not have his baby sons christened, but as they grew encouraged them to explore all the religions, with a preference for the Quakers.)

His continuing correspondence with William Busch was also about tolerance. He was horrified that William thought he might be 'impatient & annoyed with *you* on account of your *ideas*'. They could surely disagree without personal feeling. He hastened to reassure William that he did not regard Germans as 'incorrigible criminals' and the British as perfect. The Nazi mentality existed everywhere and needed but a turn of the screw to bring it to the top. He thought such a regime possible even in England, given 'conditions which allow un-reason its full play, with all the prejudice, hysteria & scapegoatism that goes with it'.

> I don't believe in absolute free-will, but only free-will *within* determinism. That does not imply a Calvinistic idea of predestination – though there's a lot more in the idea of predestination than one realizes, if one thinks of it, not as

[29] 15 December 1940.
[30] 30 December 1940.

a limited religious idea, but as a complete interlocking of all events in time –
but the only analogy I can think of is a stone tied by a length of string to a
stick. The play within the length of the string is the free-will, the fixed
circumference is the determinism.

The differences in social structure meant that our airmen treated bombing as a
game, and Nazi airmen treated it as a creed. 'All madness, but not such
madness as appeasing an obviously mad tiger with lumps of (other people's)
raw meat & stepping backwards with each appeasement . . . The mad tiger shd
have been shot before. However, let us comfort ourselves with Plato's "For
such cities as no Angel, but only a mortal, governs, there is no possible avoid-
ance of evil & pain." '[31]

In March the Rubbras came to Ashmansworth for a week, and they all went
to hear Boult give Edmund's recent Third Symphony in Bristol, where the BBC
Symphony Orchestra had been evacuated in the mistaken belief that it would
be safe from air-raids. *A hilarious journey to Bath (where they slept) in the evening*
where changing trains, during an air raid in the dark, was like a hectic game of sardines; your
fellow travellers only voices in an unlighted carriage. Bath was a dimly lit aquarium –
searchlights criss-crossing overhead, and the streets full of dark shadows and laughter and the
stamp of service boots. Gerald thought *Boult too old to appreciate contemporary music and*
strange idioms – an extreme projection of his own cult of youth onto a man of
fifty-two who was still giving premières up to thirty years later, and who in
1947 introduced Finzi's own *For St Cecilia*. Bax's 1927 Overture was in the
programme: Gerald was interested that Boult agreed with him that he could
never remember one Bax symphony from the other (even though the Sixth had been
dedicated to him in 1934?).

1941, NSP

During April Gerald conducted Newbury String Players in three more con-
certs. On 5 April in the church at nearby Burghclere, NSP, increased to sixteen
players, repeated Bach's Sinfonia and Holst's St Paul's Suite and added a Purcell
Set of Tunes and Elgar's Serenade. Sophie Wyss, the Swiss-born soprano who
had given notable first performances of Britten and who lived nearby, sang the
Aria from *Dies Natalis*, Purcell's 'When I am laid in earth', Vaughan Williams's
'Evening Hymn' and a Byrd Lullaby. Then came a concert at East Woodhay
Church with works from their repertory. Before the war Newbury had held an
annual festival; on 30 April NSP joined the educationalist, Geoffrey Shaw, just
retired to Newbury, who conducted the massed village choirs in one Newbury
Festival concert, all that could be managed in wartime; the strings contributed
the Holst Suite and Robin Milford's Oboe Suite (Peggy Shiffer the soloist), and
Sophie Wyss sang, besides the Purcell and the Byrd, a song by Rameau and
two by Grétry, which Gerald scored for strings. It was the first of many such
scorings, and the first of the many occasions when soloists brought their own
repertory. Praising some performance of Howard Ferguson's in a letter, Gerald

[31] 19 November 1940.

added 'But, as Mrs Disraeli said "you shd see my Dizzy in his bath". And you shd hear my orchestra in their happy splashings!!'[32]

Tony and Ruth Scott spent a weekend leave at Ashmansworth, and were refreshed by the 'happiness and "sweet reasonableness"' surrounding the Finzis. Robin visited them too that weekend to hear his oboe work and sensed the same atmosphere: 'an oasis in a time of spiritual famine & pestilence'.[33] At the foot of Robin's letter Gerald's hand added a tragic footnote: 'Poor, poor Robin & Kirstie. The next day, on May 3, their beloved little Barnaby was killed by a van.' He was one week under six years old. Joy found it impossible to forget the *grey shattered pair going off alone after the funeral*; she offered them the Keats quotation 'For ever wilt thou grieve and [s]he be fair', and undertook responsibility for a memorial on his grave. Robin, at first calm and dignified, then broke down, writing during the summer to Gerald: 'We both seem to have our *particular* worries, yours that you wont live to write the work that is in you, mine that I *shall* live to be a burden to those that I love.'[34]

That Spring Joy noted the *big guns are firing on the coast, and machine guns in the bright air*. Gerald's call-up would be in August, when, for him, he thought, *the billows go over my head*. Believing that the artist is a *practical orderly person*, he began tidying his affairs. He still felt that in his case war service was 'an utter waste of time' but, agreeing with F. L. Lucas that at Munich 'we sold the Czechs for a few months grace, but the disgrace will last as long as history,' he had to live up to his beliefs. He was wholly in favour of selection boards in each profession, to advise the war office. 'Even so,' writing to Iris Lemare, 'it wd result in many injustices (can't you see the Dyson of the day saying "this man Schubert is obscure and of no professional importance, whilst Herr Kappelmeister Snopplegrober is a most capable conductor of the opera and must be reserved")'.[35] He found himself unable to compose any extended work 'with the sword of Damocles' hanging over his head. Words he himself had set best expressed, he said, what ceasing to work meant to him: 'That one talent which is death to hide / Lodg'd with me useless . . .'. So, fortified by the Psalms, classical Greece, and Milton, in July he had his medical examination.

1941, ABSALOM'S PLACE

That month he drew up a catalogue of his compositions. The supplementary volume of *Grove IV* had come out the year before with an entry for him, and he had been annoyed to find works listed that he had disowned (but in his own catalogue he allotted numbers to unfinished and planned works, as well as those completed). More important, the upheaval of his world since Munich had forced him to formulate his ideas, and as an introduction to his list of works he set out his creed as a composer. He headed it:

[32]　24 February 1941.
[33]　2 May 1941.
[34]　August 1941.
[35]　June 1941.

ABSALOM'S PLACE

It was Thomas Hardy who wrote

'Why do I go on doing these things?'[36]

and, indeed, if appreciation were a measure of merit and cause for self-esteem, it wd long ago have been time for me to shut up shop, class myself as a failure, and turn to something of what the world is pleased to call a more 'useful' nature.

Yet some curious force compels us to preserve and project into the future the essence of our individuality, and, in doing so, to project something of our age and civilization. The artist is like the coral insect, building his reef out of the transitory world around him and making a solid structure to last long after his own fragile and uncertain life. It is one of the many proud points of his occupation, that, great or small, there is, ultimately, little else but his work through which his country and civilization may be known and judged by posterity. (As to stature, it is of no matter. The coral reef, like the mountain peaks, has its ups and downs. 'If he cannot bring a Cedar, let him bring a Shrubbe.')[37]

It was, then, in no mood of vanity that Henry Vaughan wrote

Ad Posteros
Diminuat ne sera dies praesentis honorem,
Quis, qualisque; fui, percipe Posteritas[38]

(Englished by Blunden thus:

To After Ages
Time soon forgets; and yet I would not have
The present wholly mouldering in the grave.
Hear then, posterity.)

Nor was Absalom guilty of mere self-aggrandisement when we read in the second book of Samuel:

Now Absalom in his lifetime had taken and reared up for himself a pillar, which is in the King's dale: For he said, I have no son to keep my name in remembrance: And he called the pillar after his own name, and it is called unto this day, Absalom's place.[39]

And what of the main-spring of this curious force, this strange necessity?

There is no need here to go into the labyrinths of aesthetics and to discuss whether art is based on the need for communication or the need for orga-

---

[36] Hardy's last poem in *Human Shows*.
[37] Francis Quarles.
[38] Preface to *Olor Iscanus* (*The Swan of Usk*), known to Finzi since 1922 (see p. 27). He had asked Walter Kaye about it in a letter of 27 September 1931.
[39] Was this passage among those he read as a small boy, alone in the school sanatorium, with a Bible and the fear of fire, when he made his commitment to music; remembered, perhaps in the Midhurst Sanatorium, when he studied Schütz's 'Fili mi, Absalon' – now, at a moment of equal crisis, coming up in his mind? Hardy considered 2 Samuel 'the finest example of [narrative prose] that I know, showing beyond its pathos and power the highest artistic cunning'.

nized expression. For me, at any rate, the essence of art is order, completion and fulfilment. Something is created out of nothing, order out of chaos; and as we succeed in shaping our intractable material into coherence and form, a relief comes to the mind (akin to the relief experienced at the remembrance of some forgotten thing) as a new accretion is added to that projection of oneself which, in metaphor, has been called 'Absalom's Place' or a coral reef or a 'cedar or shrubbe'.

Since he was a slow worker, he would need a long life to complete his projection. His few published works were only a start. 'Long may Absalom's pillar grow,' but in the event of his death he asked for Howard's advice on what remained – 'that, together with my dear Wife's judgement' should be sufficient.

He had the choice of a BBC job or one in the Ministry of War Transport. Arthur Bliss had come back from the States as assistant Overseas Music Director in the BBC, and Gerald saw him, but was suspicious that he would have left that job within six months. (In fact, Bliss succeeded Boult as Director of Music in 1942.) Gerald decided to have nothing to do with music rather than 'flounder about in something that is neither music nor organization'.[40] So he also went up before a Ministry of War Transport board, wearing his one and only suit, bought off the peg in a Harrods sale in the 1920s. He much preferred the interviewers there to the type of person he saw at the BBC; and though the other applicants, he told Toty de Navarro, were 'correctly educated, matriculated, school-certificated,' and he was without all those qualifications, he was found the most suitable. He was to be 'a sort of Herr Oberprofessor-trinkendanzenshnifflepopper'.[41]

In July he conducted four Newbury String Players concerts, at Ashmansworth, Kingsclere, Burghclere, and Newbury – all in churches. They added Grieg's Holberg and Warlock's Capriol suites, Bach's A minor Concerto and Double Violin Concerto (his old friend Sybil Eaton joining Rosie Roth), Purcell's 'Evening Hymn' and Handel's 'Bright Seraphim' for Sophie Wyss; Handel's B flat Organ Concerto, for a local player Gilbert Sellick, and Elgar's Elegy, in memory of a player who had just died. It didn't occur to him then that he could keep the group going when he was in London, and the thought of abandoning them saddened him, 'as they're getting quite a good ensemble (for amateurs, most of whom taken singly, are pretty poor players), and the regular weekly rehearsal does wonders'.[42] NSP had now been going six months, and had earned £100 in collections for bomb casualties.

A weekend neighbour at Ashmansworth was D. M. S. Watson, professor of zoology at University College London. His government war job could be done from his holiday cottage, and so his family London home, 14 Frognal Lane, was empty except for a housekeeper. Gerald was to lodge there: a perfect

---

[40] To A. Scott, 27? July 1941.
[41] 29 July 1941.
[42] To Iris Lemare, June 1941, Journal only.

arrangement, as the house needed to be kept aired, and Mrs Watson, a good amateur pianist, owned a lovely Blüthner. The night before Gerald left home the full incongruity of his position struck him: 'To think that I, who wrote Proud Songsters, Dies Natalis, Farewell to Arms, am to become a Principal in the Foreign Shipping relations department of the Ministry of War Transport. How fantastic — how unbelievably fantastic.' Next day, 30 July 1941, the Finzis went to London, Gerald to his office in Berkeley Square and Joy to take his luggage to Frognal Lane. I lay London shirts in a strange drawer and manuscripts on the work table . . . G like the smallest boy going to the largest college for the first time . She left with him, too, a drawing she had made in 1937 of their elder son, asleep.

CHAPTER EIGHT

At the Ministry

1941–45

The work was hard: 'papers & papers & telegrams & files', he told Robin Milford, and he did not get home till 8 or 9pm. By then he was too tired to compose, or even to read solidly. He found it a 'town life without the amenities', as he wrote to Edmund Rubbra (Joy copied the letter into her Journal); but he appreciated being treated as an adult, not having to 'clock in'. He had to change his views about civil servants. 'The higher grades are a first rate lot of people. I often wondered how one could "place" R. O. Morris, and now I realise that he is very typical of that type, with his all round brain, peculiar humour and many other qualities.'[1] He compared the civil service to the technical side of the creative mind; and within a few weeks was making comparisons, which Joy recorded: 'It seems as though the mind of the artist can encompass the other man's mind, but the other man is a stranger within the gates.' A composer could become a civil servant – could one imagine the reversed position – even a matter of comprehension without ability.

He had been considering, as he and his friends were uprooted from their chosen lives, what might be gained from the experience, and felt there might be some useful stimulus in mixing with 'tough company': 'there is a danger, with all of us,' he had written to Robin soon after the outbreak of war, 'of a sort of withering up from over-refinement – rather like a plant which hasn't enough soil for its roots to get down. In that sense tough company is a good antidote to the drawing room'[2] (though not everyone would rate civil servants 'tough'). As a composer, he admitted to Rubbra, 'you can live other people's lives, but they can never share yours'; and he found the strain of a divided personality exhausting.

To Robin, who was near breakdown after his little son's death, and whose doctor had recommended ten days' holiday from time to time, Gerald rather tartly replied: 'if only Joy & I cd feel assured of that, even in peace time!' – the Aldbourne days, with their Aran, Norfolk, and Dorset holidays, must have seemed far away! 'And if one suffers from Marvell's sense of "But at my back I always hear" . . .' he went on, quoting Andrew Marvell's To his Coy Mistress; but instead of 'time's wingèd chariot', he substituted 'hurrying footsteps'. It was curious, to favour a prosaic metaphor at the expense of a poetic one; but he was thinking as a composer ('away from my beloved books, so I may be

---

1   5 October 1941.
2   18 October 1939.

wrong').[3] In his music, any reference to time's passing, such as in 'So I have fared', brings inexorable footsteps – beating crotchets tolling the time away (Ex. 8.1). Always himself haunted by that chariot, his 'coy mistress' was music, his fear was that his 'echoing song' would be incomplete.

Ex. 8.1

R. O. Morris was in his mind, for early in May Mrs Morris had died. The Morrises had gone to live for the duration with the Vaughan Williamses in Dorking, and Vaughan Williams wrote to tell Gerald of her death. His mind must have gone back to his early student days, and, perhaps thinking to please RO a little, he dedicated to him his recently composed Prelude and Fugue for string trio, first played in Birmingham on 13 May at Queens College Chambers, and then at the National Gallery Concerts on 11 September 1941.

He managed to get home to Ashmansworth for three weekends out of four, but they flew by almost before he and Joy could get through music, letters, and talking. *What real bliss the quietness has meant to us,* Joy noted. *That I promise him when the shadow is lifted and the people gone.* He still conducted Newbury String Players – his 'only link with music', he told Robin. In September Arthur Bliss came for a weekend, missing his wife and family, still in California. *His same debonair self . . . His is a progressive spirit – forging ahead and in the vanguard of fashion – increasing age bringing a deepening of his perceptions.* They took him to a rehearsal of Robin's Oboe Suite (Gerald kindly reported this to Robin) *and the shadow lifted from him and we had a delightful evening of talking and music. He feels G's songs to be the only things of their kind in England with nothing to touch them.*

Newbury String Players gave two more concerts that December. Gerald added to their repertory Boyce's Symphony No. 7 from his Op. 2, Arensky's Tchaikovsky Variations, Bach's Giant Fugue (BWV 680, in the Vaughan Williams-Foster arrangement), Bach's 'Sighing, Weeping' (from cantata No. 21), and Haydn's Cello Concerto.

1941, AT ASHMANSWORTH

With Gerald living in London, Joy found nothing worth writing about in her Journal, and there is a two-year gap. As with the Wordsworths, whose Journal

___
3   15 August 1941.

Dorothy began 'because I shall give William pleasure by it', it would not have occurred to Joy to record any thoughts or activities Gerald did not share. Weekends when he was home were filled with NSP music-making. Apart from that, she found herself, a healthy young woman in her mid-thirties, in her ideal country home with two young sons and a succession of evacuees. Among these was little Ron Coomes, from London's East End, whose father was at war and whose mother was in hospital. Joy took him in, and even after he had been moved to a nearby cottage, he would 'hare back to Mrs Finzi's' every day after school. For a town boy it was glorious. She arranged for him to have tractor rides at the neighbouring farm, then to give more serious help with the harvest. She made learning into fun, so that he helped Gisa to cook and Frank Strawson to garden; there were chickens, Vera's ducks (and Francis the drake), the children's pony to look after. Joy paid him a little, but saved the money for him, and showed him how to put down a deposit for a bike. She was concerned at how pale and thin he was, and paid for an extra daily pint of milk at school. When he reached fourteen, she persuaded him to have another year at school, paid his bus-fare, then organized his getting a job on the Newbury newspaper. After a time she negotiated a rise for him from a weekly £1 to 25/-, enough extra, he found, for ginger beer and crisps. Overflowing with energy, generosity, and enthusiasm, she was to him 'a tall, smiling, happy, smashing lady'. (To Janet, however, the shy younger daughter of the Watsons, such confidence and animation seemed a little daunting and over-whelming.) The painter John Aldridge, stationed nearby, was another who found beauty and stimulus in Joy's open house. Joy taught him and his wife to make rag rugs, and that elderflower took off the taste of wartime artificial milk. When he was posted to Italy, she sent him the Penguin modern painters, *Horizon*, Lehmann's *New Writing*.

1941–42, IN LONDON

For Gerald, living alone in the Watsons' London house, there was 'an oasis in the desert',[4] he told Tony Scott, when during December 1941 Vaughan Williams invited him to hear Hubert Foss, head of OUP Music, and Alan Richardson play through the new Fifth Symphony. Apart from the wives of the two pianists and H. C. Colles, the *Times* critic, there was no-one else there, 'which I thought curious', Gerald was flattered enough to point out to several friends. 'I shd not say that it was quite up to the *Pastoral* or No. 4,'[5] he reported to Howard Ferguson. Though it had heavenly and magnificent stuff in it, he told Tony Scott that it was 'a more *reasonable* work than those other two & on that account suffers from the defects of its virtues. After all, one can't say that the excessive contemplation of the *Pastoral*, or the Royal Fury of No. 4 make for reasonableness.'[6]

4   27 December 1941.
5   23 December 1941.
6   27 December 1941.

Before long Gerald had run through the 'gamut of cafeteria experience'[7] and wrote to Toty de Navarro that 'after the war I want to lie in long, luscious, buttercuppy grass for days & days & days'.[8] London was dreary, battered, grey, shabby, though a performance of part of *Dies Natalis* by Suddaby under Boult at the Wigmore Hall in January 1942 must have been cheering. The prospect of a week's leave found him 'as excited as at end of term thirty years ago',[9] he told Tony Scott.

1942, NSP

Newbury String Players had again been invited to join in local festivals, at Newbury and Wokingham. Gerald asked Howard if he would play the Bach D minor with them. Howard demurred; while he would be amused to play 'in the charming obscurity of one of your local churches'[10] he could not cope with a festival in the small amount of practice time available. So Gerald asked the young Denis Matthews, and found it a 'joy to play with him & even my aged strings, white haired & hardly able to lift the bow, get quite a spirited performance'.[11]

The war had brought some professionals (including a double bass player) to live in the vicinity; they were glad to add their skill to the amateurs' enthusiasm. NSP gave another joint concert with Geoffrey Shaw and the combined choirs in the University Hall, Reading, and repeated it at Abingdon, both concerts during Gerald's leave. Sir George Dyson and Benjamin Britten came to their Bradfield concert – Britten was spending the weekend nearby with Sophie Wyss and her husband. He was unimpressed, writing to Peter Pears 'Sophy sang with an amateur (and how) orchestra under Finzi' and caricatured Finzi's attitude: ' "I prefer this to those horrible professionals" sort of thing – ugh!'[12] Then NSP played at Chieveley on 14 June. During the year they learnt Milford's Miniature Concerto and Sibelius's Romance, and also (in Gerald's scoring) Vaughan Williams's 'Orpheus with his lute', three Purcell songs for Sophie Wyss, and Parry's 'England', for massed choirs. In December they joined the Reading Madrigal Society (who sang Gerald's Bridges partsongs) to give a concert to the forces stationed in Berkshire, performing Boyce's Symphony No. 1, Moszkowski's Prelude and Fugue, and Bach's Peasant Cantata (Diack and Baker arrangement). Gerald asked Herbert Howells and Vaughan Williams for help to get a yearly grant and a small petrol allocation; and NSP was registered as a charity. Conducting in troop camps, schools, village halls, as well as in beautiful but cold churches, was Gerald's true war work.

---

7 25 January 1942.
8 11 April 1942.
9 27 December 1941.
10 11 January 1941.
11 de Navarro, 11 April 1942.
12 Donald Mitchell and Philip Reed, eds, *Letters from a Life: Selected Letters and Diaries of Benjamin Britten,* 1939–45 (London, 1991), p. 1056.

A week's leave in June 1942 passed with nothing accomplished but gardening: 'one simply can't start writing music with six months of arrears & only six days ahead',[13] he wrote to William Busch. All the same, during 1941 and 1942, even in dreary London, he heard (among much else) new music by his friends Sumsion and Bliss, and by Howard's friend Arnold van Wyk; he heard Howard, Denis Matthews, and Robert Irwin perform. He heard *Pierrot lunaire* and *Façade*; Pears and Britten in the *Michelangelo Sonnets*; and the first London performance of Walton's Violin Concerto. He saw exhibitions by Epstein, young Michael Rothenstein, Paul Nash, Edward Burra, Stanley Spencer; and also Sickert, whose mind, he wrote to Joy, was remarkable, 'with a greater power of inference and omission than anyone I can think of at the moment (you learn everything from what he doesn't say, not from what he says). It's lovely to see the mind keeping alive and unwithered right into old age.'[14]

As part of Vaughan Williams's seventieth birthday concert in October, Robert Irwin and Howard gave the first performance of Gerald's Shakespeare songs, 'for Ralph Vaughan Williams on his birthday'. Of the five, only 'O mistress mine' was new, and it had taken him more than three months to compose, he told Toty de Navarro – 'baulked, thwarted, fretted'[15] as he was with Ministry work. There was discussion over the title for the set, *Let us Garlands bring*, which Joy as usual had suggested. Gerald was afraid it might conjure up a 'middleaged man trying to trip it lightly with a wreath of roses on his head',[16] and Toty and his wife, appealed to, considered it 'too perilously elegant'.[17] But the printers had already begun to engrave. The Finzis gave a lunch party after the concert for the Vaughan Williamses, which included Denis Matthews and his wife and Ursula Wood; and Gerald presented 'Uncle Ralph' with the largest apple ever seen, which was admired for 'appearance, magnitude & taste – it fed five thousand & there are some broken pieces left',[18] Vaughan Williams told him. That evening he heard the broadcast of music written for the occasion by Vaughan Williams's pupils. He dismissed the Constant Lambert as 'balls', the Alan Bush as 'ghastly', thought little of Patrick Hadley and Gordon Jacob, rather more of Milford, Rubbra, and Maconchy. A week later his own Shakespeare songs were broadcast in his arrangement for strings.

At weekends when Gerald was due home, Joy would jump into her little Morris 8 (with Ron Coomes sometimes in the back for a treat) and, coasting all the way down the lane to save petrol, would collect him from the bus stop. In the five minutes' drive back she knew just how to unwind him so that he would happily go straight out to look at his watercress bed and the apple trees.

[13] 16 June 1942.
[14] 19 September 1941.
[15] 15 May 1942.
[16] 17 June 1942.
[17] 18 June 1942.
[18] 14 October 1942.

When he was at home, Ron remembered, the children didn't 'raggle-taggle' round the house so much. On the rare occasions when Joy was ill and Frank Strawson went to meet the bus, Ron sensed that Gerald was uneasy and uncertain until he saw Joy. But, apart from her asthma, Joy was strong and seldom ill.

At the Ministry Gerald became friendly with his chief, Gilmour Jenkins, a keen amateur singer and choir conductor. The relationship between the two was a little like that between Gerald and Bairstow, for when Gil sent for Gerald over some matter of work, Gerald might quite well say to his superior 'I don't believe a word of it. That's quite wrong.' In the end Gil concluded that Gerald was a hopeless civil servant but one of the most delightful people he knew. The opposite number to Gerald in another department was the organist of St Paul's, Knightsbridge, Richard Latham. When they first met, Gerald announced 'Since we're the only people who know what a crotchet is in these two ministries, we'd better get together.' As always with Gerald's friends, Dick was soon pressed into service. Gerald would come in and ask 'Are you busy?' 'Yes.' 'Surely not too busy to copy fiddle parts for NSP?' It was hard to say No to Gerald. His room-mate was Sir Charles Oman, head of ironwork at the Victoria and Albert Museum, who read Greek treatises during air-raids.

Gerald could not take ministry procedure seriously. Official files began to sprout extraneous leaflets, such as an advertisement for contraceptive pills (uncommon in those days). He persuaded Gil to see the funny side of writing minutes to each other when they worked in adjacent rooms. Gerald's job was to keep account of every enemy ship in neutral ports on the American continent, and collate it with information from the Navy (his shipbroking father would have been interested). Vaughan Williams used jokingly to say that Gerald spent his whole time turning one ship round South America. There was some truth in it, for the *Windhoek* occupied Dick Latham with its cargo, Gerald with its movements, all through the war. In fact, the work was heavy, the hours were long, and quite often, when telegrams were expected, the whole night had to be passed in the office.

In lunch hours Gerald and Dick would scour the bookshops. Mostly Gerald bought poetry, seldom books on music. He was even in those dreary days bubbling over with fun so that his colleagues called him Fizzy or Frenzy. He and Dick played a game, suggesting the best opening sentence for a detective story. Gerald offered 'I lifted the lid of the dustbin – and looked out,' which he gave as the perfect example of enharmonic change. He found time to read a little. He discovered Mervyn Peake; and Flora Thompson's *Lark Rise* – 'that sort of thing gives me more delight than all D. H. Lawrence put together',[19] he told Robin. He had also come across a 'good little book of verse' by Ursula Wood before he had met her at the Vaughan Williams's birthday lunch, and their

---

[19]   18 February 1942.

acquaintance developed. At the time she was living in a flat in the same building as the viola player, Jean Stewart. At Ursula's regular Wednesday evening gatherings Gerald found a welcome and respite from office life.

In January 1943 Pauline Juler and Howard Ferguson gave the first performance of Gerald's Clarinet Bagatelles (the first four) at the National Gallery. Writing to thank Howard, Gerald first commented on a broadcast by Myra Hess of Howard's fine sombre Piano Sonata – 'a grand work'. 'And after all, what big scale work of the last thirty or forty years have we got to touch it. Though I have a liking for some of the Ireland Sonata, you can have it, & the [Benjamin] Dale, & the numerous Bax ramblings – & the lot of them aren't worth a page of yours.'[20] (It was natural for him to think only of English music, and he probably didn't know Bridge's Sonata, even though it was dedicated, like Gerald's early Requiem, to Farrar.) The first performance of *Earth and Air and Rain* at the National Gallery on 24 March by Robert Irwin and Howard slipped by without comment in the letters – Howard was released from the RAF on 17 March. He had relented over NSP, and made time to play the C major Bach double with Denis Matthews for the 1943 Newbury Festival concert. Gerald also added Suk's *Bohemian Chorale* and a Vivaldi cello concerto to their repertory, and scored three of Gurney's 'Eliza' songs for Sophie Wyss.

But he could not compose. As to his own Bagatelles, they were indeed trifles, he thought, but their performance was one of the few good things in this 'interminable dreary waste land'. His fear was always that he might get bogged down. As he told Howard, 'at forty it's a bad thing to give up entirely'.[21] It was his constant refrain in the war, how he hated and resented the waste of his prime working years, 'in so utterly fruitless & sterile an occupation'.[22]

1943, THE BREAKDOWN

Gerald had begun working at the Ministry of War Transport on 30 July 1941. There is no Journal entry for 1942, and but one paragraph for 1943, on 1 June:

> G home on a months sick leave following prolonged collapse after Burghclere concert. He is too tired to do anything but work in the garden – too tired to sit at the piano – too tired to realise the extent of his exhaustion. Physically & mentally and what even the doctors can't see – spiritually. This dead life without chance of writing music means a suffering deeper than torn flesh or bruised bone. The passing of time at such a vital moment in his life, when he was just achieving an easier technique is a constant remorse and the fear of never recapturing it again. Tunes do not even come to trouble him now.

By conventional standards one could justifiably feel impatient with that, for

20 17 January 1943.
21 17 January 1943.
22 To Milford, 30 April 1942.

Gerald had had an easy time in the war. He and his wife were never more than sixty miles apart, and never for more than a few weeks. Though both worked hard, neither was in serious danger. Their sons were too young to fight. There were no casualties in their circle. Finzi may have been too tired to write music, but most weekends he had the chance to make it, in the countryside around his home. Countless men of his age might have envied him. He does not seem to have recalled, or linked to his own experience, the fact that the composing lives of both Holst and Vaughan Williams had been broken into by the Great War.

Reading the 'sickleave' paragraph in the Journal, an earlier sentence, for 16 October 1938, needs to be considered: 'I am incapable of bearing the suffering that I did.' Again, one might ask what suffering Gerald had endured, son of a well-to-do family, an indulgent mother, able to prolong his studentship till his mid-twenties, never forced to earn, able always to live in pleasant places, married to the perfect helpmeet and with two bonny sons. Even his brothers' deaths were brushed aside as of little account. Only the loss of Farrar touched him deeply, on a personal level.

But there is the nub of it. Finzi was not reacting to his war job on a personal level. Certainly there must have been medical concern about his health, particularly since he had a history of suspected tuberculosis. But the most likely diagnosis for the state he was in that June is clinical depression. His extreme tiredness was hardly physical – that can be put right with a couple of good nights' sleep. The deadly, sapping tiredness he felt, when responses are dulled, when past, present, and future are thick grey and each moment drags by wearily, is due to depression; and that is usually caused by conflict. Finzi was caught in the conflict of two ideals.

His letters show how deeply concerned he was to guard what Britain was fighting for against the Nazis. He had had to overcome his natural pacifism to reach the conclusion that he should serve the war effort – there was one conflict. Deeper than that, to him the fight was to preserve civilization; civilization meant above all the creative arts; and he was a creator. But while he was 'fighting' he was not creating. Finzi was not a conceited man. ('If he cannot bring a cedar, let him bring a shrubbe.') His concern was always to contribute to the commonwealth of the arts. But he knew that no-one but he himself could bring his own 'shrubbe'.

There may have been even more to it than that. On 19 May he conducted for the first time his scoring for strings of Gurney's 'Eliza' songs. It had been 'Sleep' that so profoundly affected him as a young man in York. Its great cry 'Oh, let my joys have some abiding!' had posed and solved his dilemma and reinforced his determination to create in lasting form. When he first heard the song, it was his brothers and Farrar who were recently dead, Farrar and Edgar in the Great War. Now Gurney too was dead. And here was he, engaged in his 'war' – which had to be fought, but was wasting his time. It was deadlock. He conducted the songs at the Newbury Festival on 19 May, and again on 29 May at Burghclere; then, as Joy noted, after Burghclere concert he collapsed.

Before his sickleave ended, however, he was battling on behalf of a fellow composer. Michael Tippett, as music director of Morley College, London, assisted by central European refugees, was reviving neglected early composers – Monteverdi, Purcell, Tallis – as well as giving contemporary music, much as was Gerald in his own way with NSP. Tippett had joined the pacifist Peace Pledge Union, and at his tribunals refused all the alternatives to joining the forces, in that way declaring it his moral duty to serve the community as a musician. On 21 June, in spite of Vaughan Williams's support, he was sentenced to three months in prison. Gerald sent a draft letter for the press to, among others, Bax, Berkeley, Ferguson, Howells, Lambert, Moeran, Rubbra, and Walton. Not all felt able to sign, for Gerald had confusingly dealt with conscientious objection together with the wider issues of creative artists in wartime. His reaction was typical of how John Amis saw him at that time, his dark face 'fulminating with rage at some injustice, a sort of walking *Manchester Guardian*'.[23]

After his leave, it was back to London and the Ministry. The Allies landed in Italy on 3 September, and in letters Gerald began to wonder 'How long, O Lord, How long'.[24] He and Joy ached to get away alone for a bit, even away from 'enchanting little Nigel',[25] but there was no hope till the end of the war. His only work was in getting a few odd jobs done. It took him seven or eight months to compose the Fughetta that completed the Clarinet Bagatelles, and he told Tony Scott that he was finding the greatest difficulty in scoring *The Fall of the Leaf*, drafted as early as 1926.

Prelude and Fugue, Op. 24; Elegy, Op. 22; Bagatelles, Op. 23

In fact, much of the work produced during the war was composed before it. Finzi was working on the Prelude and Fugue for string trio in the late summer of 1938. Like the earlier Oboe Interlude, it is a single movement of awkward length (the first, twelve minutes; the second, nine). Finzi would not publish single songs lest they got 'lost'. If only he had pushed himself into writing a complete trio or quartet! (He reserved his Op. 25 for a string trio, but no more than sketches exist.) The Prelude and Fugue is too individual a work to deserve neglect. It moves from a wan opening through an increasingly vigorous, bracing fugue to a splendidly assured conclusion. The Prelude has a pared-down quality of unusual pathos. There are two strains: the first of stretched dissonances, the second of swaying inversions round an internal pedal, all muted. The fugue subject is derived from the second strain, the counter-subject adding baroque-style figuration. The fugue unrolls formally, strict but lucid and lyrical. A stretto leads to a dominant pedal, over which

23 J. Amis, *Amiscellany: my Life, my Music* (London 1985) p. 84.
24 To Scott, 6 September 1943.
25 To Scott, November/December 1943.

'scrubbing' strings work up a crescendo, as in the later Clarinet Concerto. Finally the strings play the fugue subject boldly in octaves, then – mirroring the opening – crunch out the first strain from the Prelude, now masterly and grand.

The violin and piano Elegy, though published posthumously, belongs to the first summer of the war. The Introit, Elegy, and Eclogue were all meant as parts of larger wholes: Finzi's inspiration was most easily prompted in reflective mood, as the directions *Molto sereno*, *Andante espressivo*, and *Andante semplice* for the three movements suggest. They may sound simple, their regular tread and reassuring triads developing into ruminative Bachian figurations and romantic harmony. What is remarkable is Finzi's ability to spin out a melody. The piano presents the Elegy's first six bars. The violin begins the same tune, but soon diverges and carries it on – and on – for twenty-three seamless bars. Unpredictably, the entries of the theme cut across the steady footfall, shifting the metrical accent: the violin repeats its first bar at the *seventh* bar, the piano entry in the following bar is on the *second* beat, the violin's in the next bar is on the third beat. However, the piece is short for two triple *forte* climaxes, long for so little thematic contrast.

Finzi gave the date 1938 for the clarinet Bagatelles on the programme of the first performance, but the Carol began as an early song composed to Gurney's words (see pp. 35 and 176), and Finzi worked on the others between 1938 and 1942, using '20–year-old bits and pieces'.[26] Only the Fughetta (1943) was new. Each piece is clear in character, and the Romance and Carol are typically pensive, but the others are open to influences new for Finzi. Though his snorts about French 'piffle'[27] included Poulenc, his own high-spirited Prelude nods to the *Mouvements perpétuels* as well as to Bach two-part inventions, and the Forlana borrows more than just its title from Ravel. Its lilting rhythm and airy texture also share the dream-dance atmosphere of some of the Hardy songs. The Fughetta has some 'Portsmouth' points in common with Walton: a spirit and sheer cheekiness recovered perhaps from Finzi's early Violin Concerto, and foreshadowing the last movement of the Clarinet Concerto (1949) and the Toccata (1953). The influences are beneficially absorbed, giving his own lyrical warmth a welcome elegance and playfulness. The Bagatelles are very accomplished; seldom had he been so fluent and inventive.

Let us Garlands bring, Op. 18

Finzi sets Shakespeare as if he were the first composer ever to do so. *Let us Garlands bring* contains two of his most memorable songs. Any literate composer could think up the rhythm he chose for the words 'Come away, come away, death'; but to conclude the two little rises with what Gerald Moore[28] called

[26] To de Navarro, 7 March 1946.
[27] To Scott, 20 October 1943.
[28] G. Moore: *Singer and Accompanist* (London, 1953).

the 'lordly drop' on to the word 'death' was to find the inner truth of the words. The song shows Finzi's handling of dissonance at its most assured: the delayed resolutions in the second half of each verse not only drag mournfully but balance the processional opening; and the singer's wide leaps increase the tension. The song is rare in Finzi's output for the great melisma of twelve notes on the final 'weep'. A glance at the poem suggests how it probably came about. In verse 1 the brief line 'O, prepare it!' is end-stopped; but in the second verse its equivalent runs over – 'Lay me, O, where /Sad true lover . . .' so Finzi, too, carries his phrase over; then, needing six bars to balance his verses, gathers all the song's grief into one long Bachian winding phrase.

Finzi set 'Fear no more the heat o' the sun' in his twenties, about the time he composed the Milton Sonnets and the aria of *Farewell to Arms*. Running through them all is the thread of life's brevity: how could he, in that mood, have resisted 'Golden lads and girls all must, as chimney-sweepers, come to dust'? The poem is ambivalent. Is it comforting? – fear no more, it says, the sun's heat, the winter's rages, slander, censure; but relief that life can no longer scathe is negated by the thudding, disillusioned refrain '. . . come to dust'. Finzi contained the emotion in a formal, slow dance-measure; the voice arches over the hypnotic rhythm, and the dissonances in the generally diatonic chords stab to the heart. The incantation before the final tender resolution is chilling. It is a noble song.

Not so profound, more charming, are the three lighter songs. Comparison with Schubert rates Finzi's 'Who is Silvia' the less successful, despite the chuckle in the rhythm and the strummed coda (see p. 65). Finzi called 'O mistress mine' 'a pleasant light, troubadourish setting'.[29] It demonstrates how deftly in a strophic setting he responds to a new urgent implication in the second verse. Both verses are simple, in regular metre. Finzi plays with the words, setting quantity against stress to bring out their liveliness and meaning. He makes one *hear* the different position of the question mark in the first lines of each verse. Then, after dallying happily through the first verse, he slashes two bars out of second ('What's to come is still unsure: in delay there lies no plenty') yet paradoxically pulls out 'delay' into the longest mid-phrase note in the song. The song has a debonair lightness, and the springy 'dance of delight' relates it to the more intense 'Rapture' in *Dies Natalis*. The syncopation of 'It was a lover' is also jaunty, but Finzi catches the changing moods of the third line of each of the four verses: the first two heedless, the third thoughtful, the fourth triumphant.

He began a setting of 'Blow, blow, thou winter wind', asking Toty de Navarro if he would be called 'a heathen & debauchee'[30] if he omitted the chorus, but it remained unfinished. He composed *Garlands* for voice and piano, but scored them for strings at the same time. Clarence Raybould conducted the string version with Irwin and the BBC SO on 18 October. Howard

29 To de Navarro, 15 May 1942.
30 15 May 1942.

Ferguson, after the broadcast, considered them 'all too literally transcribed from piano'.[31] Finzi appealed to Clarence Raybould, who thought them 'with the possible exception of "To Sylvia", entirely satisfactory'.

Farewell to Arms, Op 9

In the 1920s Finzi set the first two verses of George Peele's poem from *Polyhymnia*, 'His golden locks time hath to silver turned', written on the retirement in 1590 of Queen Elizabeth's Master of Armoury and Champion of the annual tilting tournament. Finzi called it, as Peele had done, *Farewell to Arms*, whether or not he knew Hemingway's novel of 1929. He certainly knew Dowland's setting of the poem; and he owned Bullen's 1888 edition of Peele's *Works*. The Aria was first performed on its own, and in 1939 Boosey & Hawkes thought to publish it, but war broke out. When Finzi offered it again in 1941, Leslie Boosey felt the moment inappropriate. 'It refers to old age, rather than to war,' Finzi pointed out. Then he came across a poem by Ralph Knevet (1600–71) that seemed made to be an introduction to the Peele, picking up the idea of a soldier laying down his arms, turning to an old man's occupations, his helmet becoming a beehive. Finzi wrote to Norman Ault, in whose *Treasury of Unfamiliar Lyrics* (1938) he had found Knevet's poem, to check the pronunciation of 'ventriloquious', and also chased up variants of Peele's poem.

The complete *Farewell to Arms* is in the form of a baroque recitative and aria for tenor and small orchestra (or strings). The recitative has all Finzi's melancholy: softly rounded phrases easing on to deflected cadences. There are descriptive touches, too, of mice and drums; but the tenderest phrase is reserved for the old soldier's boastful memories. The aria is based, Bach-like, on a ritornello, first cousin to 'The salutation' in *Dies Natalis* (see p. 46). For all the twenty-odd years between them, recitative and aria belong faultlessly together. Finzi makes the connection plain by anticipating two bars of the aria-ritornello in the recitative, showing that the ornament on the Introduction's first chord is a contraction of the ritornello's first three notes.

He briefly breaks the ritornello pattern as the old soldier leaves the court for the 'six-eight' countryside. The phrase is related to the Introduction, being a variant of 'Now all recruits . . .', both over block chords (Ex. 8.2).

Ex. 8.2

Now all re - - - - cruits, But those of fruits. —

But though from court to cot-tage he de - part, — His saint is sure of his un-spot-ted heart. —

The Aria's ritornello is continuous, patterned, and self-contained, given vitality by the accented passing notes and ties across the regular bass beat. Over it Finzi floats an independent vocal line, articulating the meaning by stress and duration. The texture is mostly two-part, and there is not an accidental in the whole aria. Voice and instruments interlock perfectly. So the aria functions on two planes, the ritornello symbolising time 'never-ceasing', the voice carrying the anguished perception of its passing, to such intensity that Finzi is driven to repeat (rare practice for him) the opening couplet at the end: 'O time too swift, O swiftness never ceasing'. Lyrical but tightly structured, Farewell to Arms has a rare poise.

Over Christmas 1943 Joy had flu, and Lydia, their Czech refugee, was laid up too. Gerald, like many another, spent his leave fetching coal and wood, feeding ducks and chickens. But the baritone Robert Irwin broadcast Garlands on 18 December. On 21 December Eric Greene and Boyd Neel gave the first broadcast of Dies Natalis. Herbert Howells, who listened, wrote to tell Gerald 'it was strangely comforting: and (it seemed to me) it all gives one back a standard of beauty that virtuosity has so nearly wrecked in so much contemporary music'.[32] On 18 January, when Dies was given at the Wigmore Hall by Mary Linde and the Jacques orchestra, The Times considered it established in the repertory.

At the end of that month the single Journal entry for 1944 occurs: Day after day the only hope now is that the end of the war is in sight. In the spring, raids began again on London: 'I really don't like them,' Gerald told Tony Scott, 'but don't think I shd feel so jumpy if I were not so tired. Earlier on, when I was in one or two bigger ones, I felt less nervy than I do in these lesser ones & I can only put it down to the double life I'm trying to lead (rather unsuccessfully in both cases, I'm afraid, with M[inistry] O[f] W[ar] T[ransport] and music).'[33] The teen-age Janet Watson, spending the occasional night in her parents' London home to go to the ballet, breakfasted with Gerald in the big old-fashioned kitchen. Though it was a time when she found most adults difficult to communicate with, they chatted away together happily, as he put her at her ease with no apparent trouble.

Then in June came the flying bombs. From his Hampstead room Gerald had a front-line view and saw 'dozens of the bloody little pests scudding along both day & night. Psychologically I think it was a mistake to do away with the AA guns,'[34] he wrote to Tony. 'The feeling of helplessness – (even though they are tackling the job far away) – is what gets people down.' Many of his letters of the time end 'so tired'. By June, just after the Allies landed in Normandy,

[32] 24 December 1943.
[33] 14 April 1944.
[34] 23 June 1944.

even his beloved home and orchards seemed a mill-stone round his neck: 'what a labour a garden & house are when there is no help or outside labour left,' he wrote to Toty de Navarro, 'I hadn't even time for proper spraying.'[35]

NSP

During that one year, 1944, however, NSP had given twelve concerts, all the work taking place in Gerald's sparse time off. At the 1943 Christmas concert they were joined by carol singers from Downe House School, just the other side of Newbury, arranged through Robin Milford's teaching there; the programme included the *Puer natus Variations* by Arthur Hutchings (who had so slated Finzi's Milton Sonnets in 1936) and ended with the *Canzoni ricertati* No. 6 of Gerald's old teacher, R. O. Morris. It was NSP's twenty-third concert. To their repertory they had now added the Overture and Chaconne from Purcell's *King Arthur*, and Mozart's *Eine kleine Nachtmusik*; scenes from Gluck's *Orpheus* (at Vaughan Williams's suggestion), Haydn's D major Piano Concerto (which Howard played), and more Purcell songs (sung by Eric Greene, already well-known as Bach's evangelist). Leon Goossens, no less, came to play Cimarosa's Oboe Concerto. They also added Vaughan Williams's Fantasias on Christmas Carols and Greensleeves, his 'The New Commonwealth' (with massed choirs for the festival), and Elgar's *Sospiri*. With the Reading Madrigal Society they performed Parry's *Blest Pair of Sirens* and Bach's cantata 'Sleepers, Wake!' Then early in December they played for the first time in Enborne church, sharing the concert again with the Downe House girls, who sang a group of carols. There they gave – complete – Corelli's Christmas Concerto, and, with Eric Greene, *Dies Natalis*. Since hiring fees for parts were so large, they were beginning to build their own library, most of it, before Xeroxes, hand-copied. Gerald was also looking beyond the standard romantic or 'arranged' repertory, and searched during his London lunch hours for lesser-known eighteenth-century music.

One of their concerts was at Cheam School, 'an unheard of event', Gerald told Robin Milford, hoping that a light might be lit 'in the spirit of some small boy, perhaps as unhappy & lonely as I was in my school days'.[36] Education was much in his mind. ('Thank God I never was sent to school, to be flogged into following the style of a fool,' he had written to Vera Strawson in 1921.[37]) After some heart-searching the Finzis had decided to send their sons away to Bedales in Hampshire. Gerald wanted them to have the companionship he had lacked, and music was important there. More than that, with his suspicion of imposed discipline, he was appalled by accounts of traditional public schools. Childhood, for the composer of *Dies Natalis*, should be untrammelled. When his little boys fought and broke a window, there were no recriminations: Joy and Gerald merely got some hardboard and patched it up.

---

[35] June 1944.
[36] 6 April 1944.
[37] 12 May 1921.

The children were so beautiful and attractive that they would have melted anyone's heart. Some visitors were shocked at their outspokenness, others merely noted that they had no automatic deference to their elders. The villagers thought them over-indulged and might have delivered a few good clouts, but Mrs Watson – she of the lovely Blüthner – observed that if there was music the boys were silent, attentive, and still.

The ethos of Bedales appealed to Gerald and Joy in its reaction against Victorianism: it taught both sexes together to be self-reliant, to use their hands, to cultivate the land, and to make a place in the midst of all this for the arts. The classes were small and non-competitive. Moreover, Justin Brooke, Gerald's admired fruit-growing friend, was an old Bedalian. So Kiffer was sent to the junior school, Dunhurst. It turned out to be just what they hoped for. 'All the same,' Gerald confided to Tony Scott, whose own son had also started school, 'I'm doubtful about the wisdom of our having sent Kiffer away at nine. I wish we cd have kept him at home till eleven. The point is that once a child leaves home his growth, development & future are entirely out of one's control and nothing will convince me that there is any substitute for the back-ground of a happy home life. Maybe that, as seven to eleven is a distinct period in a child's life it's better to go at seven rather than in the middle of the period, as I did.'[38] He bitterly resented having been unable to see much of them during the war years (though he had been home most weekends). 'Paternity & maternity are, I'm sure, "induced" & the excitement of watching children grow up – quite as exciting as tending bulbs & apple trees' (he was writing to Toty de Navarro, an enthusiastic daffodil cultivator) 'is unimaginable to people who have never had any.'[39]

As 1945 opened Gerald was chafing at his job. The end of the war was in sight and his colleagues were being released to their peacetime work. Vaughan Williams wrote to Joy 'Could you send me on a card the name and address of Gerald's chief?'[40] On 30 January William Busch died suddenly of pneumonia, only days after the birth of a longed-for daughter. Gerald went to his In Memoriam concert, and begged the BBC to broadcast his Theme and Variations for piano. Writing to tell Robin, he modified his views of youth and age. It was the capacity to feel that mattered, and the 'power to bear tenseness & excitement . . . Many young people never experience it, except, perhaps, when they fall in love, & many old people never lose it.'[41] Gerald was past forty.

His Farewell to Arms (on the subject of swords being beaten into plough-shares) was broadcast on 1 April, and a week later so were the Clarinet Baga-telles. On 8 May the end of the war in Europe was celebrated; but in the Far East it was dragging on. For the Newbury Festival Concert he persuaded Vaughan Williams to conduct the choral works, and he himself, with his 'old ladies' increased from twenty-five to forty-five players for the occasion,

[38] 20 October 1943.
[39] June 1944.
[40] Undated.
[41] 3 March 1945.

conducted the *Tallis Fantasia* – in spite of Vaughan Williams having warned him not to, since it needs 'thirteen players before you *start* on the full orchestra'.[42] But after the concert Vaughan Williams had to admit 'your orchestra is really splendid'; Gerald had 'absolutely got hold of the music & the tempi were always right'.[43] Sybil Eaton, Jean Stewart, and Amaryllis Fleming were among the soloists. *Earth and Air and Rain* was down for a performance by Robert Irwin and Gerald Moore at the National Gallery on 2 July. Altogether Gerald had good cause to feel that his own post-war work was more necessary than 'putting the shipping lines on the map again or feathering the nests of wealthy ship-owners'[44] as he wrote to Cedric Thorpe Davie. He laid a copy of *Farewell to Arms* on his chief's desk; and on 1 June 1945 (four weeks ahead of his official release!) walked out of the Ministry.

[42] 23 December 1944.
[43] ?20 May 1945.
[44] 11 March 1945.

CHAPTER NINE

For St Cecilia
1945–47

When Finzi's Milton Sonnets were published in 1936, his attitude to words was examined and his temerity in setting such well-known poems was challenged (see p. 87). But on 15, 22, and 29 July 1945 Ernest Newman wrote articles in the *Sunday Times* on Words and Music in which he praised Finzi and brought his name to a wider public. Newman began by looking at the tensions between words and music, in their Cain and Abel struggle. He found that on the whole music had had the better of it, and quoted, as a climax of absurdity, the false accents and stresses of the Gypsy Chorus of Balfe's *Bohemian Girl*. Now, he went on, there had been a revolt against that kind of thing; and he cited Britten's *Serenade* (1944) and Finzi's *Dies Natalis* (1939) as examples of settings where the composers preserved the natural speech-flow of the poem, at the same time making real music, not simply correct declamation. He commended *Dies Natalis*, in particular the final 'Salutation', to the reader's study, drawing attention to the chorale-prelude derivation, and came to the conclusion:

> Mr Finzi has proved that if a composer goes about it in the right way, with the requisite blend in himself of musical imagination and poetic sensitivity, a vast amount of our finest poetry that has hitherto evaded musical treatment becomes susceptible to it.

That was heartening encouragement to come at the moment of Gerald's return to full-time composition.

Slowly he and Joy picked up the threads of life. Their evacuees left. A weekend with Toty and Dorothy de Navarro at their Broadway home was Joy's 'first chance of resting . . . for years & years',[1] he told Toty. In September the Finzis took their younger son, Nigel, to start at the Bedales preparatory school, and came home to live alone in an empty house: *the first time since we had built it, recorded Joy in her Journal, and the first time without children since eleven and a half years.* '*These are the conditions I have always longed for, this is what I have always wanted*' (not minus the children but minus the strangers in the house! G.F.)

Though Gerald forgot the Ministry within days, he found it a struggle to get his mind back into musical order, he admitted to Tony Scott. 'It's a difficult thing to write music,'[2] he told Robin Milford fiercely, and the following year

[1]   25 July 1945.
[2]   11 July 1945.

'ideas don't come just by whistling for them!'[3] His lost years at Berkeley Square had left him with 'such a political inertia' that he could not get interested in the election, when a Labour landslide ousted Churchill (Gerald considered himself a strong Liberal). It was a wrong attitude, he admitted, for 'nothing was ever more truly said than "the price of Liberty is eternal vigilance"' which 'John Bright or one of those fine Victorian ethically-minded rebels'[4] had said, he told Robin (who pointed out it was John Philpot Curran).

Once the children's summer holidays were over, Gerald turned his attention again to Gurney. He wrote reminding Edmund Blunden of his contribution to the *Music & Letters* symposium of 1938, and reported that two volumes of songs had since been published. Remembering how Blunden had rescued the poet John Clare from obscurity, Gerald now asked his help over Gurney's verse, which had been set in order and typed (he modestly did not say by himself, Joy, and Vaughan Williams's typist). He doubted whether Gurney had composed much worthwhile music after 1922, but his poetical faculties seemed to have lasted longer. Perhaps it was the influence of Gerard Manley Hopkins, together with Gurney's own mental state, that produced the terrific things, and it was not easy to know where incoherence set in. Since the Flanders background was familiar to Blunden, might Gerald visit him for an hour? They met on 10 October 1945 at *The Times Literary Supplement* office, where Blunden was then working. It was their first meeting.

1945, VAUGHAN WILLIAMS

Ever since he saw it in 1924 Gerald had been deeply moved by *The Shepherds of the Delectable Mountains*. A BBC commission in 1942 for incidental music spurred Vaughan Williams into amplifying it and in October 1945 he sent a libretto for *The Pilgrim's Progress* to Gerald: 'I shd be glad of any criticisms literary or dramatic!' Gerald took him at his word, though admitting his inexperience and rightly feeling that in opera text and music could not be divorced. He would prefer a straightforward fight without blackouts between Pilgrim and Apollyon's shadow; would have omitted Mr and Mrs By-Ends; and – 'Now comes the point where you may turn on me like Apollyon!' – considered Bunyan's re-appearance at the end 'a barbarous intrusion!'[5] 'Food for thought,'[6] Vaughan Williams replied. He wanted By-Ends, he said, as the third obstacle in Pilgrim's way; and the Epilogue for the very purpose of bringing the audience back to earth. But Gerald's letter had been frank and – for all his admiration for the older composer – not in the least sycophantic. Joy copied it into her Journal.

So that part of the Journal ends, as it began, with Vaughan Williams: it spans the distance between *The Poisoned Kiss* and the libretto of *The Pilgrim's Progress*. Then the Journal is blank for nearly six years. The war was over, Gerald

---

[3]   31 March 1946.
[4]   10 July 1945.
[5]   5 November 1945.
[6]   8 November 1945.

was home, and life was for living. At first, since the USA now withdrew lend-lease, living was in some ways harder than during the war. Shortages were more acute: bread and flour, for instance, were not rationed till a year after VE Day. Manuscript paper and paper clips were hard to find. There was no longer the anticipation of peace for encouragement; peace had arrived, but not plenty, and a tired nation was easily irritated. During February 1946 Gerald was laid up, and the following month found him still in a 'moth-eaten state' with a cough, and spending every spare second on some 'ridiculous' household job, for they had little help. He was, however, taking more and more a long view of things. Tony Scott, having had a domestic tiff with his wife, turned to Gerald for sympathy. How absurd it was, wrote Gerald after comforting him, 'when one thinks of all we have come through to be here at all. The only survivor out of millions of spermatozoa, then one of the infants or children who didn't die. Then we escaped being one of the millions who were killed or died as a result of the Nazis. And after all that we get in a frenzy because a plug won't pull, or a man hammers a nail in or a pencil gets mislaid!'[7]

1945–53, APPLES

He lost no time in improving his orchards. In December 1945 he and Joy went to a pruning demonstration at Wisley (calling in on the way to see Tony in his new house near Slough). The following March he had sixty trees sent from Cheals Nursery and in 1947 thirty sets of scions from Switzerland and France. He thought it disastrous the way old slow-bearing varieties were gradually being shoved out of existence by the inevitable Cox's Orange Pippin and Laxtons Superb. 'Both are wonderful apples,' he had written in 1942 to Toty de Navarro, who was being gathered into the apple fellowship, 'but a single D'arcy Spice, Court Pendu Plat, Orleans Reinette, Margil, Wyken Pippin, Claygate Pearmain, Adam's Pearmain, Sturmer, Ribston etc shd be in every orchard, if they only give a few pounds a year, just for the joy of variety.'[8]

It was variety of flavour he prized above all, and then the variety of season, so that, if skilfully planted, an orchard could produce fruit that could be eaten from the end of July 'till apples come again'. Commercial growers have to choose reliably cropping trees, producing large uniform fruit which travel well. Gerald was concerned with taste and individuality. Between March 1945 and December 1952 he sent scions of thirty varieties to the National Fruit Collection at Brogdale in Kent. (Though some of these were found to be falsely named, and some were already present under a synonym, in the 1980s trees of his were still growing there of Morris's Russet, Roxbury Russet, Welford Park Nonsuch, Baxter's Pearmain, Golden Non Pareil, Mead's Broading, Norman's Pippin and Haggerstone Pippin.) 'My orchard is going to

[7] 17 March 1946.
[8] 13 October 1942.

be a treasure house!'[9] he told Toty. Ultimately he grew 386 varieties as full standards, glorious in blossom. He bought many from the old-established Scotts Nurseries in Merriott, Somerset (and in due course Michael Wallace there did his grafting for him). The Scotts catalogue was illustrated with drawings by the fine artist Robin Tanner, and by 1953 Gerald was able to contribute an article on *Alternatives to Cox's Orange*, which began characteristically 'The amateur apple grower has at least one advantage over the commercial grower in that he is free from official advice (which may often be as bad as it is good).' His attitude to Cox's Orange came to be like his attitude to Handel: both were good but overpowering: Cox had overshadowed Golden Harvey, as Handel had overshadowed John Stanley. His friends enjoyed his enthusiasm without enjoying every single apple they were pressed to sample: 'some of them *needn't* have been rescued', remarked John Sumsion dryly.

NSP, 1945–46

Gerald had celebrated peace by giving a Newbury String Players concert (Chieveley, 8 July 1945) with an all-new repertory: Respighi's Ancient Airs and Dances, Mozart's Divertimento K. 136, Boccherini's Cello Concerto and, with Joan Elwes, three hymns from Bach's Schemelli hymnbook, his 'Welcome Lord' from cantata No. 61, and Purcell's Morning as well as Evening Hymn. By now they had a professional leader, May Hope; and Jean Stewart, who had enjoyed playing in the *Tallis Fantasia* with them, came as often as she could to lead the violas. They kept close links with Downe House School. They gave a concert there on 14 July, and again Downe's carol singers joined NSP for Enborne on 15 December, when they gave the first performance of Robin Milford's Te Deum, composed for the school. They also added Barber's Adagio, Vaughan Williams's *Concerto Accademico*, and Boyce's Symphony No. 8. For the first time there were printed programme notes.

    Finzi was now getting more performances. *Dies Natalis* was broadcast in August 1945 and given in Winchester Cathedral that November. The Introit was broadcast in 1945, and in February 1946 Finzi enjoyed conducting it at the Oxford Subscription Concerts and meeting Thomas Armstrong, Balfour Gardiner, and Norman Ault. Henry Holst played it, and Gerald quickly pressed him into service for the Newbury Festival. In 1946 the Festival returned to something like its pre-war format. At one concert Keith Falkner sang a Bach aria with NSP and Bernard Brown played Purcell's Trumpet Sonata (Z. 850), Gerald's first modern revival from manuscript. They added Purcell's Chaconne and music from his anthems. Jean Stewart came to play the viola part in Howells's *Elegy*, written in memory of Francis Purcell Warren, a composer killed in Farrar's war. In his excitement Gerald was becoming naively ambitious, and Howard Ferguson had to tell him he must not do Mozart's K. 488 with strings only, nor ask Myra Hess, then a national idol, to perform with NSP. So Gerald asked Kathleen Long to play K. 449, and completely fell for her:

'She's so without pomposity & I can't imagine certain other famous pianists saying "A kitchen chair is all I want for playing the piano".'[10] She no doubt suggested Bloch's Concerto Grosso, which was in her repertory and, as a Fauré specialist, Fauré's Nocturne (Shylock). Monica Sinclair, two years before her opera debut, came to sing in Bach's Magnificat. Also that year there was more Purcell (Rival Sisters and Dido overtures), two Bach Sinfonias (with Rutland Boughton's oboist daughter Joy), Dunhill and Corelli concertos for the local organist Gilbert Sellick, a Handel Concerto Grosso (Op. 6, No. 12), and Leonardo Leo's Cello Concerto with Anna Shuttleworth. As he had done for Robin Milford, Gerald now encouraged Tony Scott by performing his Prelude and Fugue. The Christmas concert in Enborne Church was personal, with Vaughan Williams's Four Hymns, and Finzi's own Farewell to Arms. Gerald made a point of not including his own music, except on special occasions.

1945–46, BRITTEN

In July 1946 Gerald and Joy went to Glyndebourne, since their old Aldbourne friends the Foxes lived nearby, to see Britten's The Rape of Lucretia, of which Gerald dryly remarked to Cedric Thorpe Davie that 'any rape on the stage must be exciting'.[11] But he could hear nothing in Britten's music. The previous year Tony Scott had heard the Sinfonia da Requiem, and had little time for it. 'I didn't listen in to the Britten,' Gerald wrote back,

> as I heard the first performance, & it's one of the few works that has ever got me to sleep. But then I'm "allergic" to Britten's music! It's beyond me, the Britten boom. See Mrs Behrend's eyes [dedicatee of works by Britten and Tippett] light up at the very name! It's very difficult to say in public what one thinks about one's contemporaries, as it's so often mistaken for jealousy! I still go on getting his works as they come out, in the hope of finding a spark, but up till now, with the exception of 'Peter Grimes', [which he had seen in June 1945] they've struck me as being derelict & dead. Rubbra's description of them as having 'no central core' struck me as being good. My first impression of soap-bubble music still holds good. Wonderful iridescent colours & then, puff, & it all disappears into thin air. [He had described Les Illuminations as 'soap-bubbles' in 1940.] I think he has technically, a most brilliant flair, a gift for placing notes & bringing things off, but as a rule what he brings off isn't worth a rats dropping.
> How odd it is to find quite a number of people who think Walton a mere nothing next to the most wonderful Benjamin. 'The first English composer of international reputation' as they are now saying as they said of Walton ten years ago, Bliss fifteen years ago, VW twenty years ago & Elgar thirty years ago.
> However, there's always the chance that Britten may develop into something better & that he may grow out of his arid opportunism. And Peter

10 To Milford, 18 May/June 1946.
11 21 July 1946.

> Grimes *was* a good opera, though I know that opera doesn't postulate good
> music (any more than it postulates good drama).[12]

That makes sorry reading! Though in style and technique Britten and Finzi
could scarcely be more different, they were at one – did they but realize it – in
their passionate sympathy with minorities and victims of prejudice, in their
pacific outlook, their love of England, and of English poetry. Finzi had just
been at the first performance of Britten's Donne Sonnets, but it seems that
'behind the notes' he had been unable to hear the rage against sickness,
cruelty, and death that was their source, composed as they were in reaction to
Britten's visit to Belsen. No-one could have been more alert to the German
atrocities than Finzi: among his newspaper cuttings are those on the Belsen
trials at Nuremberg in the autumn of 1945, sickening to read. It is a fine irony
that he was deaf to the same concern in Britten's music.

Of course he was not alone. While many of us can never forget the shock of
delight at each new Britten work, there were plenty of people in the early days
who sniffed in disapproval, and there was always the pejorative 'clever'. Finzi's
whole cast of mind was the reverse of Britten's. For instance, he was not
attracted to Mozart; and would probably have agreed with Hans Keller's
pairing in 1948 of Britten with Mozart (though not in the way Keller
intended). It would be unjust to attribute jealousy to Finzi, though he was not
the only composer of his generation – Walton suffered more – to be eclipsed
by the dazzling young Benjamin. In Finzi's case, he shared Britten's publisher,
who naturally promoted the glamorous newcomer: *Dies Natalis* had nearly been
shouldered aside to make way for *Our Hunting Fathers*. (Could there be a stronger
contrast, in style and aesthetic, than that between the singer's opening phrases
of Finzi's 'Rhapsody' and Britten's 'Rats away!'?) But Finzi had formed his
opinion of Britten earlier than 1939; and he was frank and independent
enough to stick to his views. As he had written to Robin Milford in 1939: 'I've
long since given up trying to understand peoples likes & dislikes – why, for
instance, one person loves Berlioz & Liszt, another loves Busoni & Bellini,
another Van Dieren & Weber, not one of whose music I can appreciate at all!'[13]

In 1946 Britten and Finzi were brought together in Bacharach's *British Music
of our Time*. Britten had his own chapter. In the last, Robin Hull appraised
Ferguson, Finzi, Jacob, Berkeley, Rawsthorne, Maconchy, Bush, and Tippett. He
described Finzi's style as 'fastidious, yet rarely over-refined', instanced the
Interlude and Prelude and Fugue as more vigorous and impassioned, spoke of
Finzi's 'astonishing capacity for identifying himself' with his poet in Shakespeare and Hardy, placing *Earth and Air and Rain* above even *Dies Natalis*. The same
year Boosey & Hawkes' house journal *Tempo* published a useful article by N. G.
Long on Finzi's vocal music, concentrating on *Dies*.

[12] 16 December 1945.
[13] 11 May 1939.

In July Finzi wrote to Tony Scott: 'At the moment I'm doing a short anthem for that remarkable parson, Walter Hussey of Northampton, who annually commissions composers & artists to do works for his church. Britten's 'Rejoice in the Lamb', & an awful thing of Berkeley's (rather like a still-born turd) [Op 21/2, Herbert and Vaughan] & a decent motet of Rubbra's ['The Revival'] have been the previous commissions.'[14] By August he was still working, and Joy and the boys went mackerel fishing in Cornwall without him, while an SOS went to Howard Ferguson who came to help with the scoring. The anthem, Lo, the Full, Final Sacrifice turned out bigger than he expected.

In September Dies Natalis took its rightful place at the Hereford Three Choirs. It went 'all right', he reported to Tony Scott, though he noted the difference between the strings of an orchestra and a string orchestra. He conducted it himself on 13 September (he'd already conducted it at Vaughan Williams's Leith Hill during May), and Elsie Suddaby sang. His work with Newbury String Players had been excellent preparation, except for one thing: 'I can't pretend that the whole Three Choirs Festival was dependent on your morning suit,' he wrote to Tony, 'but I certainly was! It was a perfect fit & what with Tom Scott's [their doctor's] shirt & collar, & John's [Sumsion's] tie – together with John and four assistants to help me put the things on in the right order – I got through it all right.'[15] Alice Sumsion, a 'marvel of organization', had taken the old Deanery for a house-party of about twenty-five.

Then on 21 September they went up to St Matthew's, Northampton, for the first performance of Lo, the Full, Final Sacrifice, under Alec Wyton. Hussey's first commission, Britten's anthem, had been for the fiftieth anniversary of the church's dedication in 1943. Then came a Madonna and Child from Henry Moore, a Crucifixion from Graham Sutherland, and a Litany and Anthem from W. H. Auden – images in stone, paint, and sound. The Finzis lunched with a bevy of bishops, and were highly entertained when one accused another of the deadliest sin, sloth. Tony, who went with them, noted Gerald and Joy 'sitting so good and well behaved one on either side of the bishop'.[16] But Gerald was musing on 'what a curious spectacle' it all was, he told Tony, 'and how like Anthony Trollope the secular side of it, and how like a pagan ceremony the religious side'. Casting back to his cargo ship voyage, he found he could not see much difference between the 'dressings up and goings on of all the various sects and communities. They all seem equally fantastic whether in Cairo or Northampton.' But music was the thing, and he recalled A. C. Ward's comment about Leonardo da Vinci, that though he was 'not what would ordinarily be called a religious man, the Last Supper shows he could understand what Christian Faith meant to others, and respect and minister to it.'[17]

14 7 July 1946.
15 16 September 1946.
16 29 September 1946.
17 22 September 1946.

Lo, the Full, Final Sacrifice, Op. 26

Hussey suggested the theme of the Eucharist, and approved Finzi's eventual choice of words by Richard Crashaw (he had considered going back to Vaughan's 'Up to those bright and gladsome hills'). Crashaw's 'Hymn in adoration of the Blessed Sacrament' is a translation of 'Adoro Te' and 'Lauda Sion salvatorem' by St Thomas Aquinas, and contains 'involutions and obscurities not found in the original 13th-century Latin', as Finzi wrote in his programme note; he selected verses from both poems to make his composite text, where Crashaw reaches 'an ecstasy hardly surpassed in English poetry'. Plainly Finzi was not drawn to the poem for its Christian content, but for its intensity, imagery, and passionate language. He matched it with glowing, rapturous music.

He began with lines taken from the last three stanzas of 'Lauda Sion', the picture of the final sacrifice – 'On which all figures fix't their eyes'. After the hushed introduction, the chorus enters unaccompanied with quiet concentrated awe, the sound fanning out from a low-pitched unison; the lightened texture and the super-imposed fifths on '*ransomed*' are curiously austere, as is the Phrygian harmony. Many of the motifs are related by pitch or rhythm, unifying the whole work, but the variety of texture is striking. As well as brooding unaccompanied passages, there are curving melodies ('O dear Memorial'); a psalm-like reciting-tone ('Help Lord, my Faith'); haunting calls, close imitations. In this his first mature choral work, lasting over fifteen minutes, Finzi's control of pace and form is firmer than in anything he had yet composed. The paragraphs starting 'Jesu Master' and 'Rise, Royal Sion!' are each gathered into excitingly graded *crescendos*, and the bright homophonic passage 'Lo the Bread of Life' is perfectly placed as the anthem's climax.

Finzi's image for the sacrament of communion (. . . 'drink the same wine' . . .) seems to dissolve tonality and time: pedals and bass outline a whole-tone augmented fifth, alto voice and keyboard move in canon up and down a syncopated major arpeggio. A harmonic echo of that passage, now sensuously relaxed, underlies the calls 'Come Love, Come Lord'. (Finzi would have known Crashaw's poem, if not otherwise, from this passage in the third of Vaughan Williams's Four Hymns.) That then builds to a thrilling high bright second inversion for the sight of 'Glory's sun'. The controlled descent from this (Ex. 9.1) – the lower voices trailing the higher, the gradual lessening of assurance in dynamic, pitch, tonality, and rhythm – is pure Finzi in its suggestion of glory glimpsed, then fading.

The opening words, now for male voices only, are repeated; and the melismas of the eight-part Amen attain a Palestrina-like serenity, but for the dissonant stab in the final bar – reminder perhaps of the sacrifice. The anthem breathes an atmosphere of fervent private devotion and is one of Finzi's finest, most original works.

Ex. 9.1

When   Glo - ry's   sun   faith's _____   shades ____   shall   chase,

Love's Labour's Lost, Op. 28 (I)

At the end of 1946 Finzi became involved in a new activity. Noel Iliffe was to produce Love's Labour's Lost, arranged for broadcasting by his wife Simona Pakenham (who later wrote a book on Vaughan Williams). They asked Finzi for incidental music, scored for sixteen instrumentalists. By the nature of the medium it had to make an immediate impact but always take second place. Finzi had to work fast, for a given performance, and in the knowledge that what he composed might be cut, pulled about, or patched up − stimulating conditions. Coming so soon after his enforced wartime silence, the commission was both encouragement and discipline. There would be no space for his ruminative style, since fragments need a sharp profile.

In his London days Finzi had been an avid theatre-goer, and with Howard Ferguson saw most of the famous Shakespeare productions. In the 1930s they had both toyed with the idea of writing an opera, even drafting librettos for Nicholas Udall's Ralph Roister Doister (?1552). More recently Gerald and Joy had gone to Stratford-on-Avon whenever they could. Love's Labour's Lost, one of Shakespeare's earliest plays and bristling with topical references, has not been a favourite among composers, though it cries out for music. At first Finzi found it hard to get hold of, he wrote to Robin Milford, but 'after a couple of rehearsals, when I cd see who was who, it cleared itself up & I really enjoyed it'.[18] He had to get the job done in three weeks, finishing the scoring at four in the morning on the day before the performance. 'I'm just not made that way but I rather wanted to do it, just to show myself that I cd. do it.' There is little doubt that the experience loosened his sinews. Many of his contemporaries − Vaughan Williams, Walton, Britten − had been composing for the films: this was his equivalent.

He set the songs 'When daisies pied . . .' for Hiems and 'When icicles hang . . .' for Ver. He was excited to find an anonymous but 'heavenly little mediaeval poem' in Hawkins' History (book IX, chapter LXXIX) for Moth's 'Concolinel' (the obscure name of a lost lyric). After the broadcast, to make a group of four songs, he also set Moth's 'If she be made of white and red'. Noble and gracious music was needed for the two royal groups; pipe and tabor for the rustics; hunting sounds; dances; and 'gesture' music for the

---

18 22 December 1946.

masque. His innovation was to imagine the three lovers' sonnets in Act 4 Scene 3 with background music – 'it's quite reasonable to suppose these wd be read to "soft music" ',[19] he wrote to Toty de Navarro. So for these he composed three self-contained pieces.

The play was broadcast on the Home Service on 16 December 1946; Paul Scofield was Berowne. Leslie Boosey wrote wondering whether the 'charming' music could be published. Only the songs at present, they decided, but Boosey suggested making a suite, adding that he would like an orchestral work in the catalogue. Finzi promptly sent him his old *New Year Music*.

Then *Dies Natalis* was recorded. This record, many people's introduction to a love of Finzi's music, gave him little pleasure. It was not British Council policy to consult composers over the choice of singer or conductor, and he considered both unfortunate. In his mind Joan Cross was too connected with opera and with Britten; and Boyd Neel too much the slick professional and the Handelian. There were three recording sessions, two in October 1946, one on 29 January 1947. In the first two, four movements were completed, leaving the 'Rhapsody' for January. It began snowing on 25 January, and the 29th was the coldest day for fifty years: not a day for 'sweetness and unusual beauty'. There were power reductions which gave the engineers hideous problems, as Joan Cross recalled – 'I don't think I did justice to that piece alas!'[20] At one of the three sessions Boyd Neel was unwell and Finzi had to take over; after his death, no-one could discover which. It seems likely that it was on the cold day, so possibly the 'Rhapsody' was in fact composer-conducted.

NSP AND RESEARCH

Pondering the direction his post-war life was taking, Gerald considered the future of Newbury String Players. He might hand them over, he told Robin Milford in October 1946, if the right man could be found in the neighbourhood. 'But I'm afraid it also implies another Joy! That's harder to find than another conductor. Only a few people like yourself realize the enormous amount of time & work involved, not so much by the music side of things as by the organization side, the eternal letter writing, phone calls, the finding of substitutes at the last moment, the engaging of artists.'[21] The following year, prompted by the marriage of the viola player Jean Stewart, he continued to Robin: 'it's this damnable daily round, the life of cook, housemaid, secretary, wife, mother, nurse all in one, that makes any professional life impossible for a woman in these days'.[22]

He was always wanting to expand NSP's repertory beyond the 'war-horses'

[19] 8 January 1947.
[20] Letter of 29 April 1959.
[21] 31 October 1946.
[22] 5 January 1947.

of St Paul's, Capriol, Holberg Suites, and Elgar's Serenade, and was on the look-out for works simple enough for amateurs, particularly with solo instrument and strings, which were not romantic arrangements such as Tartini's 'clarinet concerto' by Gordon Jacob and Vivaldi's Cello Sonata by d'Indy. Hubert Langley's *Doctor Arne* (1938) led him to Thomas Arne's six concertos. About the same time Ruth Dyson, a young keyboard player Gerald had met through Vaughan Williams at Dorking, wrote submitting Arne's Fifth Concerto in Julian Herbage's edition. She played it with NSP several times during the autumn of 1946, and Hubert Langley came to a performance. Gerald encouraged her to borrow the keyboard scores from Langley and to reconstruct the other five concertos, and he himself made inquiries for parts to the British Museum, the Bodleian, and the Fitwilliam Museums. He found them in the Bodleian and ordered photostats.

In 1945 Cedric Thorpe Davie was appointed master of music at St Andrews University, which held one of the copyright libraries. Because of paper salvage, Ceddie had not kept Gerald's wartime letters; in autumn 1946 he wrote saying that he was making an edition of the Arne concertos (he was establishing a student orchestra). Gerald replied that he was delighted, and hoped OUP would allow an edition that was not only practical for performers but also 'correct'. He cited Constant Lambert's pioneering edition (1928) of the Boyce symphonies as a valuable example (though later he found it wanting). 'In the last few years I have rather changed my mind about a lot of eighteenth-century stuff – Boyce and Arne in particular – and feel that we have been rather viewing the scene from the wrong hillock, if you know what I mean. So, although I don't think they are *great* works – (and are the bogus cello Haydn & Boccherini great works?) – once one gets back to their idiom and background I think they are extremely delightful works.' He had recently seen a suite of Boyce pieces edited by Parry, which he found completely insensitive to their period. He was sure the only edition of Arne worth having was 'what Arne wrote; no more and no less'.[23] 'The eighteenth century knew perfectly well what it was doing.'[24] Were cadenzas needed, he wondered, asking advice from Ceddie and Howard Ferguson. (When Thurston Dart came for a weekend in 1950, he told Gerald there should be a proper candenza in the Arne, not merely a flourish.) Ceddie sent his edition for Gerald's opinion, and problems cropped up about dynamics and phrase marks, ornaments, and continuo. Gerald reacted from his NSP experience: 'about ornaments. For heavens sake don't say "a moments consideration will determine which is intended in each individual instance". These are easy works and will be played by amateurs as well as professionals, to some of whom not a twelve months consideration will determine anything. Simply say "the acciacatura should be played thus . . .".'[25]

23 11 November 1946.
24 19 November 1946.
25 6 January 1947.

During 1947 Gerald added three Vivaldi concertos to NSP's repertory and wrote to Robin Milford: 'I realise what a lot we miss by not performing Vivaldi exactly as he intended. We did the original version, with continuo . . . & no attempt to dress the old chap up . . . it was a real experience.'[26] Gerald had added three more Boyce symphonies to NSP's repertory (when Robin had introduced him to No. 4 in 1940 he bought full scores of them all). Then in 1947 Mollie Sands began to take over and extend Sophie Wyss's repertory with NSP. Her *Invitation to Ranelagh* had just been published (1946), and her interest in English eighteenth-century music, especially in Arne and Greene, coincided with Gerald's. She checked various points in the BM for him.

BOOK COLLECTION

The late 1940s were, as Gerald described them to Cedric Thorpe Davie, 'the very "lean years" with the boys at school'. 'Books remain my only vice.'[27] To some of their friends his collecting *did* at the time seem rather a vice. People noticed that Joy went really short − 'hadn't a sou to buy a dress or a handkerchief', John Sumsion recalled − and was pretty near being short of money even for food. But if a book of poems or an apple tree was needed for Gerald's collections, it was bought without hesitation − and friends who loved Joy could not help but remember that the money that paid for it was largely hers. For her, however, there was no problem. They had made the decision to educate the boys well, they would be short of money, and it was part of Gerald's moral dictum, which she endorsed, that if one had a shilling, ninepence of it went on books. Many of the books were, of course, second-hand. Gerald was an inveterate bookhunter, especially at the Three Choirs Festival; he was on the list for catalogues of dozens of dealers, and circulated his friends with his wants. But he kept up too with recent publications, and would order whatever he felt he needed from the *Times Literary Supplement* reviews.

As his letters to Vera Strawson show, he had begun collecting as a teenager in Harrogate. Then he and Rupert Erlebach exchanged dealers' catalogues in his Painswick days. At Ashmansworth, in the groundfloor room below his music-room, he had floor-to-ceiling shelves built, with free-standing stacks at right-angles. By his death this non-musical library comprised three thousand books. One would expect substantial holdings − texts and critical commentaries − on Wordsworth (thirty-eight volumes), Blake (forty volumes), Clare, Cobbett, Hardy, Bridges (thirty volumes), and Blunden (sixty-three volumes). There are over eighty volumes devoted to Shakespeare, including the twenty-nine edited by Quiller-Couch and Dover Wilson. Less predictable are the complete publications of the Early English Text Society, and the Percy Society's *Early English Poetry, Ballads, and Popular Literature*. There are fine nineteenth-century printings of, among others, Beaumont, Fletcher, and Quarles. There is

[26] 13 February 1947.
[27] 2 February 1947.

much verse of his own time and generation. Of the forty poets published in the 'Georgian' volumes (1911–22) thirty-five in four hundred and fifty volumes are in Finzi's library. Even writers he did not much admire – Eliot, Auden, Roy Campbell – are represented. This was not a 'musician's library', not collected by a composer looking for texts. These books were read for their own sake, by a man of consuming curiosity who loved literature. Much is poetry, but there are also pamphlets, diaries, letters, novels, plays, and translations from European and Classical literature. The library is particularly rich in minor figures, not only in the anthologies but in slight volumes which add to its idiosyncrasy and enhance its value to critics and historians.

From his Harrogate days onwards Finzi also gathered individual poems, some as cuttings, some copied. There is a hand-written Commonplace Book, undated but early, into which, he told Joy in 1934–35, 'from time to time I put down lovely things as I come across them'. There is a typed collection, arranged alphabetically by author; and a book of pasted-in cuttings of poems mostly from The Times, The Times Literary Supplement, The Listener, and the New Statesman, between 1937 and 1946 – though poignantly the last, about a mother's death, is dated 26 June 1955, soon after his own mother died. He frequently quoted from these anthologies in letters, so many extracts are already in this book.

MONEY

As a result of Gerald's lodging during the war in Professor Watson's house, where there was a complete Bach Gesellschaft edition and an electric coffee grinder, the Finzis decided they too must have both. The grinder could be afforded, but the outlay for the Bach – £107 – was considerable. Gerald thought of selling the famous gold watch (a twenty-first birthday present from his much disliked uncle), and was cross but not surprised to find it wasn't worth as much as he'd hoped – 'trust your uncle, the old sod'[28] wrote Howard, when reporting on the estimate for him. However, they bought the Bach.

Though Gerald and Joy were quite different in their day-to-day handling of money – he thrifty, drawing out the same amount each week, she extravagant when she was able – they were at one in their basic ideals. They never had the kind of hotel holiday or restaurant meal that middle-class people took for granted – they stayed with friends, and had them back in turn. They never drank gin or other spirits. Gerald took to making his own wines, and gave up smoking his pipe. Their car was always modest and utilitarian; in time they bought a Bedford van, better for mixed loads of children, instruments, music stands, garden produce; 'and to solve the hotel problem we can sleep in it!'[29]

However, Gerald never did things by halves. In 1948, after much discussion with Howard, he settled on the kind of manuscript paper he wanted, then

[28] 22 September 1947.
[29] To Milford, 17 September 1949.

ordered twelve hundred sheets at one go. 'Strike me pink!'[30] was Howard's mild reaction. In ordinary ways the Finzis were not lavish, but by careful management they made it seem to visitors that money was never a problem. (In any case, in Joy's view, money had nothing to do with making music.) Gerald earned very little from his compositions: right up to his death, if his annual income was £150 it was a remarkably good year (£10 – £12 a week was a living wage in 1950). They borrowed money to build Ashmansworth, and as time passed had to sell shares each year to pay taxes. If the Finzis seemed privileged to those in nine-to-five jobs, not many people who have their opportunities have the temperament and dedication to use them as productively.

In 1947 the St Cecilia's Day Festival Committee commissioned a choral and orchestral work for their celebration concert from Finzi and the text from Blunden. Finzi of course knew and liked Blunden's poems, and as early as 1931 had set 'To Joy', which he considered one of his best songs (it was published after his death only because he had hoped to complete a Blunden set). He had met Blunden about Gurney. Also he had quoted Blunden in the Introduction to his Catalogue. On the whole, however, Blunden's poetry did not 'spark him off' musically, Joy later recalled, and he was more apprehensive than excited at the prospect. He proposed a meeting at Ashmansworth, but Blunden was too busy for a visit, and suggested sending a draft of the verses 'when I have had a happy thought for them. I have fancied a little catalogue of Saints with their special attributes, and so to herself,' he wrote, 'and I think some humour and emotional variety would be proper to this kind of Ode, – no doubt I am old-fashioned but I have the tradition of Dryden & Collins in hearing, and without attempting their range would like to sustain the suggestion of it.'[31]

So on 13 June he sent the first draft of verses, modestly telling Gerald to be 'quite decisive if they won't do' but being willing to make 'minor alterations'. He pointed out the strophe and antistrophe principle, and the compromise in the final verse. (The poem is printed on p. 162.) Gerald replied with delight that he would certainly not wish (as Blunden had suggested he might if his own poem would not do) to revert to an old one in an 1857 collection he owned, ranging from Fishburn, Oldham, and Tate to Christopher Smart. His small suggestions were musical, not criticisms of the Ode. In Verse I he asked for 'sing out' in the last line. In Verse II he questioned 'charming' – which had become 'so corrupted as to give almost a simper to Cecily!' 'Modern Britain' he himself associated with 'publishers' series, railway hoardings & technical

---

[30] 30 January 1948.
[31] 15 May 1947.

magazines'. In Verse IV, in spite of his respect for Arne and Wesley, what about Gibbons and Purcell? '(That enchanting last couplet about Handel is going to be a problem, but I wouldn't have it away for anything!)'[32]

The serious, musical difficulty lay in VI. 'The last verse must build up, but after the first six lines the musical "catalogue" suddenly brings it down to an intimate level, from which it wd be impossible to build up again in the last four lines.' He was sorry to lose the organ – though he didn't like organs, St Cecilia did! – but could the catalogue be cut, and the first six and last four lines run on? (Unlike Purcell, who relished Brady's 'musical' text, Finzi would praise music but not its instruments.) 'Whom men slew' again 'put a spanner into the jubilation'; if, in devising another end to that line, Blunden could rhyme it to 'who lives in minstrelsy throughout the world', the open vowel would be better – 'through' was not easy for the last word. Finally, in Verse II, was he correct in applying 'mysterious' to 'next star' rather than to 'man'? (He was.)

It was not an effusive letter, but that of a responsible professional craftsman. Blunden thanked him for his 'great care over the details'. A little ruefully perhaps, he admitted that he often tried to catch 'the ungrimed sense' of a word such as 'charming'. As to the instruments: 'the reader might not object to this by-concert, the eighteenth-century might have approved, but now it will indeed be taken as too much of an excursus. But can you not manage "whom men slew"? for that takes up the note from the opening of III, and I feel that the triumph of St C is so much deeper if the imagination perceives it through the disaster of her mortal life. Then, man's martyrdom is connected.'[33]

Gerald's reply is missing; but he must have asked for an extra couplet for the end, and also made some comment on apples, for Blunden sent:

> The gift of Saint Cecilia whose young voice
> Man doomed to death, and who could yet rejoice,
> Sure of her dream, her choral empire won,
> And minstrelsy for all time travelling on.

and ended: 'I have eaten better crab-apples since 1930 than the apples one is sometimes compelled to buy'.[34]

'I think it's nearly there,' replied Gerald, but – wanting a broader vowel than 'won' – suggested the final line 'Gathered to praise in universal song'. 'I feel rather an idiot,' he went on, 'making suggestions of this sort, after hours of cogitation, when your practised mind can do better in a couple of minutes, but there it is. I hope this musician's view doesn't clash too awkwardly with the poet's view. (How often I've regretted those occasional jars which make certain poems to which one is attracted impossible to set. I instanced that "idola" in your early "Water Moment"' [the poem is 'A Waterpiece' and the lines are '. . . the immemorial bream/ . . . Glide on; idola that forgotten

32 17 June 1947.
33 19 June 1947.
34 25 June 1947.

plan,/Incomparably wise, the doom of man.'] Gerald goes on: 'or the last line in that most touching poem of Hardy's "Childhood among the ferns" which is made impossible by 'and this afar world perambulate'. How I love that man.'[35]

(Writing of the Hardy must have spurred him to overcome the difficulty within the year; the set containing the poem was published in 1949. Hardy was in his mind, for that July of 1947 Robert Irwin broadcast *Earth and Air and Rain* – 'as lovely a performance as I have ever heard', Gerald wrote to him.[36] This prompted Gerald to write to Tony Scott (and Robin Milford) that he wished he could get on with the other two or three songs needed to finish another baritone set (which became *Before and after Summer*). 'Seven sleep in the drawer. But I can't. I'm completely bogged up.'[37] He was still struggling to score his organ anthem, *Lo, the Full, Final Sacrifice*, for the Three Choirs. Parts for that and for the Gurney 'Eliza' songs had to be made and checked, and he had barely begun the Cecilia work.)

Ending his letter to Blunden, he had hoped, he said, that the apple expert Morton Shand would write a book on the varieties that had been lost in recent years; and then asked Blunden not to omit his poem 'Seagrave's Death', which he had read in some periodical, from his collected volume. Blunden found it 'strange & pleasant' to hear Finzi speak of the little piece on Seagrave's Death. He returned the Cecilia typescript, amended, and declared:

> An essay on 'Words & Music' should be available to all bards who may be called on to provide verse to be set, and one day you should publish one . . .
> T. Hy. would have enjoyed talking over his 'songs' with you in respect of their problems for the musician.[38]

Blunden's small changes seemed to Gerald most happy. 'I only hope that I shall justify all the trouble to which you have been put & to which you have responded with such tolerance.'

> Yes, 'words and music' interest me a lot & I only wish they interested more musicians, as well as poets. But there are as many schools in music as in poetics; & perhaps, in the end, practise and affection on both sides will bring a habit of thought which no amount of essaying can do![39]

By 14 September he had made some progress '& rather like what I've been doing'. But he found the Handel couplet in Verse IV 'rather stumps me'. 'I love it in itself'; however, with ' "their looks turned listening to that faultless face" you come to a state of quiet rapture', which continued through Verse V. But 'old Handel breaks into the mood'. Would it be possible to stop at the eighth line of the stanza, though it meant leaving out the English composers?

[35] 29 June 1947.
[36] 21 July 1947.
[37] 27 July 1947.
[38] I July 1947.
[39] 4 July 1947.

'The only demur on the writer's part,' responded Blunden, 'is that the Ode loses individuality – the mild venturousness which was in the passage on musical instruments & is in this on English musicians is natural to me. I would forego the little joke on Handel (though Dryden's Ode had its jests), & keep him in a little less corporeally'; and he sent the revised couplet. He was soon to set out to Tokyo as a cultural adviser so must 'leave all Odes in good order'.[40]

Gerald was sorry to think of him in Japan, but hoped it would give him refreshment. 'I never get away, but I do know how greatly the landscape is revivified when one sees it upside down.' He would like to change Gibbons to Dowland, the 'most exquisite of our lutenists', in Verse IV. 'Indeed, I had thought of quoting his song – so apt it is – "Time stands still with gazing on her face" after "Their looks turned listening . . .".' Above all he was anxious to keep the rapt state. He accepted the revised Handel couplet, with the suggestion 'Handel is here' instead of 'And chief be Handel here' to avoid the weak opening stress. ('Incidentally, I don't know that "chief" is quite right, with Byrd & others around him! In any case, as Blake said "There's no competition in Heaven".'[41])

The patient Blunden replied 'I quite agree with the modifications you have in mind'. (In 1954, in answer to a query, he approved 'transcends' rather than 'ascends' in verse V.) 'Perhaps in course of time you could let me have a copy of the old version, which would make a good foundation for a reflection on what does & what does not suit a musical setting. In general, I had supposed a virtue in a variousness of allusions & "materials" – but then it does not fall to me to make the music.'[42] (He commented on the glut of apples that autumn.)

His letter crossed one of Gerald's, making the same suggestion, that the original Handel couplet, and any other excisions or changes, should go back into the Ode when Blunden published it. 'I can see no reason why a poem shd not have its "poetical" form as distinct from its "musical" form.' He had in mind Robert Bridges' Ode, written for Parry's *Invocation to Music*. Also, in Parry's *A Song of Darkness and Light* (Bridges' Ode *A Hymn of Nature*) certain lines & even a stanza are bracketed at the beginning of the score as being "omitted in the musical setting". 'So for heaven's sake don't feel that any of my suggestions are hampering or that musical demands are permanently emasculating the Ode. Though you wrote it for music it has its own life as well.'[43] (Blunden published his original Ode, and a poem in memory of Finzi, in *A Hong Kong House*, London, 1962.)

Finzi agreed about 'the virtue in a variousness'; but 'the danger there lies in following a poem line by line & perhaps missing an "over-all" form'.[44] There was nothing now, he said, presenting him with yet another couple of trifles,

[40] 17 September 1947.
[41] 18 September 1947.
[42] 24 September 1947.
[43] 24 September 1947.
[44] 25 September 1947.

to which Blunden couldn't reply on a postcard. (His own apple trees were too young to give a glut, and his growing sons ate about 6lbs a day!) Blunden, his mind turning to Japan, replied that 'so long as you can produce your total musical expression I shall be happy'. The Ode would go into his 'old ragbag of verse. One way and another even though the time has been against me I find quite a miscellany gathering there.'[45]

FINZI AND FERGUSON

The Three Choirs Festival that year, 1947, was at Gloucester. As well as Gerald's *Lo, the Full, Final Sacrifice* and his orchestration of the Gurney songs, there was *Dies Natalis*, which he conducted and Eric Greene sang. The week after the festival he wrote desperately to Cedric Thorpe Davie, bluntly asking him if he could come south for a week, to help with the scoring of *For St Cecilia*. When Ceddie, too busy with his own deadlines, was unable to comply, Howard Ferguson once again stepped into the breach, and spent ten days at Ashmansworth, on hand to advise. Gerald, grateful not only for this but for a lifetime's support, dedicated the work to him. Gerald used to consult Howard on everything from where to get thick blotting paper or good looseleaf books to points of etiquette such as 'do I write Dear Boult or Dear Sir Adrian Boult', and how to word a change-of-address card. Each always asked the other to read proofs; to the end of Gerald's life they consulted each other on musical problems. But about this time Howard, moving house, stopped keeping Gerald's letters, so that the correspondence becomes one-sided. Also, Gerald and Joy, having always regarded Howard as an incorrigible bachelor, began to understand that he was homosexual. For all Gerald's theories of tolerance, this was to him – as indeed it would have been to many of his generation – a considerable shock. Nothing could disturb their basic firm friendship, but there was now something in it of constraint.

Gerald posted the *Cecilia* vocal score to Boosey & Hawkes on 30 September, though by 17 October he was still struggling frantically with the scoring. To both Tony Scott and Toty de Navarro, before the performance, he deprecatingly played down the ceremonial side – 'bits you'll find a bit noisy'. Adrian Boult conducted the Ode on 22 November 1947 at the Albert Hall, with René Soames as the soloist. By then the Blundens were on their voyage to Tokyo. Gerald wrote wishing Edmund had been there to share the generous reception, and reported an appreciation of the poem: ' "an altogether admirable subject for composition, not too elaborate, but with plenty of suggestive images and allusions to stimulate the composer's inspiration." Who cd be more grateful for this than the composer.'[46] When the vocal score was published, Gerald sent one to Japan, with a warning not to judge the work from a piano performance, and a wish for a new book of verse from EB. Thanking him, Blunden reported a small one coming soon: 'I wish I could

[45] 27 September 1947.
[46] 28 November 1947.

have some ample vision one day, for I believe I might answer with the expression.'[47]

For St Cecilia, Op. 30

Though Blunden's Augustan-shaded poem is not great or visionary, it offers scope to a composer. For this Ceremonial Ode Finzi used a full orchestra for the first time since New Year Music (1926): the large forces and the music's brave demeanour were expected for the festal occasion in a big hall. In this, Finzi–Blunden is nearer to Purcell–Brady, Handel–Dryden, and Parry–Pope, than to Britten–Auden (1942). Bairstow's pupil had learnt his lesson well: the occasional strenuousness of the early motets is here turned to stirring account, and the choral sound is varied and assured.

As with Lo, the Full, Final Sacrifice, the text's opening words – 'Delightful Goddess' – prompt the rhythm: shining fanfares cleave the silence; then the burst of bright choral sound settles into a melody of Parry–Elgar breadth, leading swiftly to the dedication to St Cecilia, 'Thine be our first devotion'. Finzi highlights the important words – 'Thine be our first . . .' and 'Sing out . . .' – with diatonic triads (as in Dies Natalis, see p. 45). Besides brilliance, the Ode has reserved and tender moods. 'Changed is the age' brings about one, and the solo tenor's expressive entry, piano on an off-beat, is typical of Finzi's dislike of show. (The tenor's entry in the coming Intimations of Immortality is similarly self-effacing.)

The caressing phrase (Ex. 9.2) introducing the personal, rather than the symbolic, aspect of the saint is made up of two of Finzi's fingerprints (see Ex. 3.3, 10.3, and 1.1)

Ex. 9.2

after which the semi-chorus, awe-struck, echoes her name, as though to banish any presumption that her inspiration may be taken for granted. The 'host of mortals' through the ages join Cecily's disciples in a quiet 'march of time' (Finzi's most overt acknowledgement of Holst's 'sad procession' in A

[47] 23 November 1947.

Dirge for Two Veterans). Then time is stilled in the hushed invocation to the great composers of the past ('Stand with us, Merbecke' . . .) set to a reciting-tone in octaves, which broadens into sweeping parallel chords of poetic depth and remoteness, picked up near the end at 'and music's calm'. There is a similar passage in *Lo, the Full, Final Sacrifice* ('Help Lord, my Faith) and both may derive from Vaughan Williams's *Tallis Fantasia*, which Finzi had conducted with NSP in spring 1945 (perhaps, too, from the Litany in *Gerontius*). In the tenor's 'How smilingly the saint' the first phrase is of four bars, the second is spun out, freely developing, to eleven. The song moves through melting modulations, and asks that 'Cecily's delights sustain Song's later-comers' in a musical phrase of such intensity that it might come from Finzi's own heart – he himself, in the span since Purcell, being a conservative 'late-comer'.

This solo brings the 'dance of delight' (Ex. 9.3), instrumental upper phrases twining over a regular thrummed bass, the voice floating above – a gentler cousin of 'The rapture' in *Dies Natalis*. These passages are, from his early Requiem onwards, unique to Finzi. His steadily changing chords, making a rhythmic-harmonic framework, allow such free interplay, with the solo poised above.

Ex. 9.3

The negative side of his regular harmonic pace is that in the nobler strains Finzi's movement is stiff, compared with, say, Elgar's, or Parry's at his best. In the opening nine bars of the Ode, for instance, Finzi changes his chord on practically every beat, whereas Elgar's habitual progress is more relaxed, his frequent accented harmonic appoggiaturas giving alternate tension and release. (The four bars before cue 10, however, are pure, dreamy *Wand of Youth* Elgar.)

Though Finzi showed himself aware of the dangers of 'following a poem line by line', he has not escaped them. His respect for his poet means that his underlay is syllabic, with no words repeated. This gives individuality to his songs and solo writing. In choral writing, he holds to the same principle. The only syllable in *Lo, the Full, Final sacrifice* that extends over half a dozen notes is the 'A . . .' of Amen. In that work and in this he repeats very few verbal phrases, so that any vocal line read on its own makes grammatical sense. There are, however, drawbacks to this. Once the music becomes contrapuntal, words are bound to overlap between parts. More seriously, the composer's means of expansion are limited. Finzi the conscientious word-setter could not easily become Finzi the musical architect. This is noticeable especially in the second and last stanzas, when the sections seem short and one climax follows another quickly. If only Finzi had on occasion allowed the musical demands to override the pace of the words! Comparisons with Purcell and Handel are irrelevant, since both used baroque closed forms. For St Cecilia has most in common, in style and in themes, with Blest Pair of Sirens, which Finzi much admired. Parry however had no scruples in drawing out 'sing everlastingly and 'sing in endless morn' to build long paragraphs of mounting intensity in his eleven-minute piece, and Milton's poem has only twenty-eight lines. Finzi allowed Blunden to write fifty-nine lines for a continuous work lasting about eighteen minutes!

Finzi does allow repetition between one part and another for saints Valentine, George, Dunstan, and Swithin, much as Walton did in Belshazzar's Feast for 'praise ye . . . gold, iron . . .' (and with side-drum, muted trumpet, piccolo 'droplets', Finzi vividly points up the saints' attributes). Walton's passage must have been, if only subconsciously, Finzi's model here. But Walton builds up a ferocious paean of praise; Finzi – granted in his shorter work – illustrates each image in turn, and moves on, missing a structural opportunity. There is some unease, too, in the long-range tonality. Finzi's Ode is in E flat major, but much of the opening and ending leans to the flatter side, to A flat and even D flat – the swerve in the fifth bar through B natural, even when familiar, seems a wrench. There is an air of deliberate striving for the big occasion in For St Cecilia, not so much in the ceremonial fanfares that jubilantly open and close the work, as in the prominent percussion and the dutiful contrapuntal entries, as at 'wherefore we bid you' (cue 23). Finzi's distrust of virtuosity must have demanded a deliberate defiance of inhibition: it shows, for instance, in the need for the direction grandioso for the final peroration. The moments to treasure in For St Cecilia are delicate ones: the pure sustained wind overlapping the women's entry 'Straight, by the beautiful inventress'; the celesta dissolving into silence after the chorus repeats 'Her blue eyes bless'. Those are Cecilia's magical sounds.

The work marked a turning point. Until then Finzi had been a fairly private man, known for short movements with small forces. His previous big London première, the Violin Concerto, had been a failure. The commission for the Albert Hall made him an official composer, history at his back: he shared the concert with Purcell and Handel. The Musical Times placed the work squarely in 'the finest English tradition . . . In its spacious design and strong writing there are moments of real nobility, and the composer has succeeded in obtaining his effects without undue striving.' Frank Howes in The Times considered the tenor air 'one of the loveliest things in contemporary music'. Finzi was proud enough of collaborating with a living poet to have Blunden's letters bound into a slim hard-cover book, gold-lettered on the spine. Music was Finzi's life: that his imagination was profoundly stirred by music's saint cannot be doubted. Whether his technique quite matched his imagination is less sure. But in sum *For St Cecilia*, as Howard Ferguson wrote to Finzi after the first performance, 'seems so much larger in musical scope and intention than anything you have yet written! . . . Beauty and sensitivity were always there, and to spare; but now you've added real size to them.'[48]

[Original in roman, changes in *italic*]

I

Delightful Goddess, in whose fashionings
    And fables Truth still goes adorned,
Resourceful Legend, taught by whom Time sings
    Of what had else been lost or scorned,
Thine be our first devotion, while we throng
    On this returning day to reverence one,
Thy fairest, and herself Time's Sweetest song; —
Speak but Cecilia's name, and earth is new-begun.
Sing

II

Changed is the age, mysterious man's next star,
But Legend's children share his calendar,
And are beloved in modern Britain here,
        though change on change appear,
The due companions of the fleeting year;
St Valentine for love's adventure beams,
St George is with us in war's iron gleams,
St Dunstan whose red tongs clipt Satan's powers,
St Swithin with his forty days of showers,
And many another saint, are fondly ours.
But where in all the saintly company
Is one beloved so much as charming Cecily?
        beyond melodious

III

How came you, lady of fierce martyrdom,
    How came you by your manifold skill?
You found the soul of music yet half dumb,
    Deep-chained the utterance that should fill
The high-carved roofs of life with tides of tone.
    Then in a rapture conscious of all these
You threw the palace open, and the throne
    Blazed forth dominion of infinities.

IV

Straight, by this beautiful inventress given
Art's clue, a studious angel alit from heaven,
And in good time a host of mortals too
As Cecily's disciples saw the clue,

48 23 November 1947.

Till through the West melodious genius vied
re-echoing
In making music where her clear notes guide;
In England too men marked Cecilia's race
grace
Their looks turned listening to that faultless face:
Stand with us, Merbeck, and be Byrde close by,
And Arne, and Wesley, lift the theme on high
Dowland and Purcell
Even let old Handel in the midst announce
Handel is here, the friend and generous guest
Himself a Briton every inch and ounce!
With morning airs for her, and choral zest

V

How smilingly the saint among her friends
  Sits, and with fingers white and long
Awakes her own praeludium, which ascends
  The union of all other song!
For ever those the first in arts remain
  And their original blooms on winterless,
For ever Cecily's delights sustain
  Song's later-comers, and her blue eyes bless.

VI

Wherefore we bid you to the full concent
Of St Cecilia's joyous argument,
And in her host we congregate each form
Her Music takes when it would lull, or storm;
And every means that grew beneath her hand
To witch man's thought far past the ground he spanned
  wing
From the lake-boatman's flute, the twanged spinet
To Malines carillons, or castanet;
From the camp bugle under the cold moon
To the French horn, the pipes, the 'loud bassoon';
And last to that chief work of Cecily's,
The mighty organ, her's the day and his,
Whom she built stern as mountains and sublime
Or gentle as the brook's or grange-clock's chime;
Ocean of music's strife and music's calm,
For all man's martyrdom the crowning psalm.
The gift of St Cecilia whom men slew,
Who lives in minstrelsy the whole world through.
Exult in music's strife and music's calm,
For all man's martyrdom the crowning psalm,
The gift of St Cecilia whose young voice
Man doomed to death, and yet who could rejoice,
Sure of her dream that bears the world along
Blest in the life of universal song.

CHAPTER TEN

Consolidation

1947–48

In October 1947 the Royal Academy of Music invited Gerald to return there to teach. He refused, courteously; but must have been pleased, and even more so when it bestowed honorary membership on him. Joy's drawings, too, were beginning to attract attention. Vaughan Williams's old Cambridge college, Trinity, wanted a portrait to add to their collection of honorary fellows by contemporary artists. Vaughan Williams had not enjoyed the traumatic experience of being drawn by William Rothenstein when he had to sit absolutely still without speaking, so he asked Joy. In December 1947, taking with them Ashmansworth honey and medlar jelly, the Finzis went to Dorking for two nights. In the morning Vaughan Williams alarmed them by appearing wearing a tie and with brushed hair; but Gerald talked and laughed with him till he forgot he was being drawn. Joy had to work quickly, and felt she had caught only his public aspect. After supper as they sat round the fire, Vaughan Williams slumped down in his old armchair opposite his wife, Joy drew him without his knowing, the private man in repose. She gave that drawing to Gerald. Perhaps the experience eased Vaughan Williams's fears, for the following year he sat for Epstein's portrait.

For Christmas 1947 Robin Milford sent Gerald his Organ Meditations and – as always when anyone gave him music – Gerald played them immediately. He wished he had more sympathy with the instrument. 'It's really the lack of limitation which I dislike. Actual organ (diapason) tone, in a few clear lines, is very lovely, but since it became the king of instruments it has grown a mane and lost its modesty.'[1] A pity, he thought, when there was so much glorious music written for it. At the turn of the year his *New Year Music* was broadcast. He had sent it hopefully in 1945 to Charles Groves – 'a very rough diamond' but 'he at least will not patronize'.[2] Groves performed it on 2 January 1948 with his BBC Northern Orchestra, and Finzi went up for the rehearsal, then dashed back to hear a try-through of Tony Scott's Fugue.

1948, PARRY

The centenary of Parry's birth fell on 27 February, and Gerald gave a twenty-minute broadcast, with illustrations played by Howard Ferguson, to introduce a Third Programme concert. (He also provided a linking script for

[1]   11 January 1948.
[2]   To Milford, 24 November 1945.

an overseas concert.) He was amused to hear that members of the Royal College of Music staff were asking 'Why is this fellow Finzi talking about Parry when he never knew him?' The answer, Gerald told Robin, 'is that I'm talking about him precisely because I didn't know him! (and incidentally no one else offered to do it)'.[3]

The talk was printed, slightly revised, in the periodical Making Music No. 10, 1949. Finzi admitted that he never knew Parry, the 'personality of remarkable vitality and warmth' summed up in Robert Bridges' lines on his memorial tablet in Gloucester Cathedral (. . . 'this Stone remember thy bounteous gaiety . . .'). Parry's direct influence passed with the generation that knew him; it was his creative work that mattered. He developed early but matured late; and his achievements were hard won. Finzi discerned two strains in him: the man of feeling (Prometheus Unbound) and the Puritan (Grosses Duo for two pianos), which ultimately became unified. Blest Pair of Sirens stands 'acknowledged as one of the supreme fusions of voice and verse'. Finzi passed quickly over the instrumental music (but singled out the last twenty pages of the E minor symphony as 'gold'; and The Birds as happy and buoyant) for he found 'the complete man' in the choral works. However, it did Parry no service to pretend they were all equally good, nor to be blind to 'the defects of his integrity'. Job was packed with imagination and feeling; but some other works had a curious flatness or 'festival bustle'. Among the finest he rated the motet De Profundis, the Nativity Ode, and the series of 'personal' cantatas in which Parry attempted to fuse his ethical and musical ideas, writing or selecting his own texts.

Then Finzi began applying his own premises. Parry's mind was 'fundamentally religious while avoiding every form of religious dogma'. He 'cared for the thing itself rather than for the appearance of the thing'. One must look 'behind Parry's notes' to the distillation of his mind. The eclipse of his music at that time was partly owing to 'a failure to distinguish between the thing said and the language in which it is written'. And (with an echo of his own Absalom's Place) men are 'great or small not according to their language but according to their stature'.

To Tony Scott he wrote: 'After listening again to A Child of our Time, which tries to do the same thing as Parry spent his time doing, I can't help feeling how dreadfully inferior Tippett's work is to, say, Beyond these voices there is peace. I find it almost embarrassing to listen to . . . [Tippett's] string concerto is another matter.'[4] Robin Milford challenged him on his ideas of Parry's religion. He replied 'I don't really think the test is the actual belief so much as the intensity of the belief – Blake's "A firm persuasion that a thing is so makes it so."' Robin was cross with the 'mean-spirited' RCM professors; but Gerald more temperately replied: 'I don't like to think of how much worse I shd have been if I had not been a comparatively free man, for I cd never have earned my

3   22 February 1948.
4   7 March 1948.

living as a musician, not even as a pedagogue; and how sour that might have turned me.'[5]

His interest brought him into correspondence with Parry's daughter, Lady Ponsonby, then elderly. Novello's list of Parry's work in print was inaccurate; the RCM did not give easy access to the manuscripts she had lent them; and Gerald was disturbed that much of the music was unavailable for performance. Parry's library was still at his old home, 17 Kensington Square, London, which had suffered from bombs and dry rot. Lady Ponsonby asked Gerald if he would take what scores he needed, and recommend good homes for the rest. Delighted, he sent some to Howard, the Purcell Society volumes to Thornton Lofthouse for Reading University, and other volumes to Cedric Thorpe Davie for St Andrews (where in 1947 Ceddie had founded a department of music). Then Gerald began listing the whereabouts of Parry's own works, in print and in manuscript. 'So many promise, but don't perform,' wrote Lady Ponsonby, in gratitude, agreeing to search her home, Shulbrede Priory near Hindhead, for further manuscripts. Acting on his own dislike of the organ, and his wish to identify himself with what he loved, Gerald scored Parry's organ fantasia 'When I survey the wondrous cross' for strings.

Robin Milford, who had moved to Butcombe, near Bristol, told him that the Stinchcombe Festival at Stroud was in danger of collapsing. Gerald wondered whether Diana Oldridge, its guiding spirit, was having to give it up, for 'it's always the individual, the person with just that extra energy, enthusiasm or vision – or "firm persuasion" – who seems able to keep [such enterprises] alive'.[6] He himself was busy keeping Newbury String Players alive. It was natural that he should add Parry's *English Suite* and his own arrangement of 'When I survey' to their repertory. With his recent Northampton connection, it was also natural that NSP should give a concert there at St Matthews, and for the organist Alec Wyton to play a Handel concerto with them. It was more surprising to find them playing at Blenheim Palace.

He broadcast another talk on 1 May 1948, a review of the week's music on the Third Programme, in a series 'Critic on the Air'. Schütz's St Matthew Passion gave him a chance to praise the BBC's *History in Sound of European Music*, as musical education was far too much a matter of reading about music: Fayrfax and Taverner were the giants of their age. However, he found little to admire in Bruckner's E Minor Mass, nothing in some Grieg songs, nor yet in a Weber clarinet concerto, and heard not much more than 'Sparkenbroke-ish romanticism' in Berlioz's superb *Les Nuits d'été*. But in a recital of Wolf's songs 'the musical worth stood out', even to one who wasn't familiar with German; and he was surprised to find Spohr's Nonet delightful. He loyally praised chamber music by people he knew, Arnold van Wyk and Benjamin Frankel, and (perhaps thinking of 'how sour that might have turned me') praised the Norwegian government for giving Fartein Valen a grant to compose. But as for

5   8 March 1948.
6   8 March 1948.

likes and dislikes, 'Time lays the lion down with the lamb. Mr Gladstone and Disraeli share equal honours in Westminster Abbey and the world has room for the manifold varieties of human experience.'

In December 1948 Gerald's old teacher R. O. Morris died. Gerald was enraged by The Times obituary, which gave no idea, he wrote to Cedric Thorpe Davie, of the 'strange fantastic creature'.[7] He sent a supplementary letter to The Times and then, recommended to the editor by Vaughan Williams, wrote in the RCM Magazine (vol. xlv, no. 2). He stressed that Morris taught well because he was a composer, and (as he had just said about Parry) that it was to his work one must look, for personality disappears with those who knew him. Morris's creative period lasted only some ten years, and thereafter was a topic that could not be mentioned to him. Composition was one of many subjects he mastered, then lost interest in. In his early days he had written some of the soundest music criticism of the time. The OUP had published an edition (1920) of Lorna Doone with an introduction and notes by him. His reserve and reticence, Gerald guessed, were a defensive armour. But 'his scholarship and erudition were combined with a fantastic humour' (the Bugsworthy hoax), a 'faun-like sensuousness' (a phrase Vaughan Williams's wife Adeline hesitated over), and 'a tender devotion to cats'. Gerald singled out 'Corinna's Maying', the Concerto piccolo, the Suite for chamber orchestra, and the six Canzoni Ricertati as most approachable; at the other extreme was the Toccata and Fugue for orchestra, and halfway between came the Symphony. He admitted a lack of presentation in the music, and 'disdain of display' (a quality Morris may have encouraged in Gerald); but stressed the distinction of his mind, quoting Landor: 'I shall dine late; but the dining room will be well lighted, the guests few and select.' Morris had been one of Vaughan Williams's executors. Vaughan Williams asked Gerald to take his place, and with Bliss to decide what should be done with any manuscripts unpublished at his death. He told Gerald he was leaving to him Beethoven's tuning fork which he had had from Holst, 'to be passed on to anyone I consider worthy'.[8] It was a laying-on of hands. (The tuning fork is now in the British Museum.)

ASHMANSWORTH

Although the Finzis had never been without domestic help, it was now scanty compared with their Aldbourne days. In 1947 Gerald had thought it unlikely that they could afford any resident staff until the boys' education was complete, but the demands on his and Joy's time were increasing as commissions came in and Newbury String Players flourished. Joy, in spite of all her reserves and resources, was finally driven to say 'look here, what about having two more wives?' It became obvious that skilled and reliable help was needed on the land. They advertised in an agricultural paper, and in October 1948 Jack and Olive Theyer came to live in the gardener's cottage. On their arrival, 'all

7   December 1948.
8   5 June 1949.

Mr Finzi was worried about was where was the cat?' Once it was found, safely curled in the watering can for the journey, he went off to rehearsal. Olive cleaned the house every morning, and Jack took over the fowls, the kitchen garden, and the orchard. This became extensive: apart from the usual fruit trees, there were peaches, quinces, nuts, figs, and medlars.

While at kindergarten, Gerald's sons had brought home their friends. Among them was Richard Shirley Smith, showing promise of the artist he was to become. He found 'a centre of civilisation and the arts where imagination, scholarship and skill were urgently employed with integrity'. The Finzis 'inspired his life's direction'.[9] A later visitor was the young composer Jeremy Dale Roberts, Kiffer's friend at the Royal Academy of Music. For these boys, as for old friends and new, Ashmansworth was an enchanted place. There was endless hospitality for waifs and strays. Nobody fussed. Vaughan Williams recalled that there were no clocks except one in the kitchen, and that wrong. There was a delightful informality. The long living-room was always in a state of flux, with Joy's knitting or sewing all over the sofa, music spread over the two pianos, perhaps a new book of verse and another on apple trees on the arm of a chair. The doors were nearly always open, with people coming in and out. Beyond its wide windows (Vaughan Williams's favourite views were from Ashmansworth and Mycenae) there was the terrace to sit on, or to walk up and down. There was so much going on that it was surprising meals ever arrived, but they did, on time, and full of delicious garden produce. Either round the circular table that sat twelve, or in the kitchen by the Esse, talk flowed on. Last thing at night there was the ritual of peppermint tea by the dying fire, and the smell of wood ash. For all that, the house was a place of achievement. Gerald would work in his study, palisaded round in silence and safety.

In January 1949 both *A Young Man's Exhortation* and *Earth and Air and Rain* were broadcast, and perhaps that prompted Finzi to complete the waiting Hardy set of baritone and piano songs. Though *Before and After Summer* (as he called it) was published after *For St Cecilia*, Op. 30, he gave it the early number of Op. 16 because many of the ten songs had been composed during the 1930s – 'Amabel', for example, was performed in 1932 by a tenor. Only four – 'Childhood among the ferns', 'The self-unseeing', 'The too short time', and 'Channel firing' – belong for certain to the 1940s. Some songs had probably been considered for *Earth and Air and Rain* thirteen years before; and several more were considered for the present set, then put aside. Robert Irwin spent some time at Ashmansworth in May, going through the songs with the composer.

9   R. Shirley Smith, *The Paintings & Collages* (London, 2002), pp. 3 and 140.

Before and After Summer, Op. 16

Finzi placed 'Childhood among the ferns' first. For Hardy, the memory of the boy who did not wish to grow up was so potent that he used it three times, in his 'autobiography', in Jude's childhood, and in this poem. Finzi could identify with that (see p. 10), remembering his own make-believe house in the bushes, the bursting sun, the withdrawal from the world into childhood. The line 'Why should I have to grow to man's estate,/ And this afar-noised world perambulate?' may have held him up, as he had told Blunden in 1947, but it must have been only for the technical reason of setting the awkward words. The happy first four verses have generous melody, with accompanying rain-drops or rivulets. But at the resistance to change in the fifth, the harmonies move from major modes to static parallel triads without propulsive dominants, and the song ends in the dominant minor of the opening E flat major. The interplay between piano and voice is a delight. The opening piano motif reaches the voice only at the significant words 'the sun then burst'. The *staccato* piano figure of the first stanza is smoothed out for the second, then reaches into and shapes the voice. An incidental broken chord bass figure at 'ferns spread' and the running quavers in the treble at 'luxuriantly' in the first stanza, are expanded to make the accompaniment for the middle stanzas.

The toccata-like *allegro* accompaniment of 'Before and after summer' gives it a stinging sleety quality, bracing except for the intrusive minor seventh (C flat) in the second bar, suggesting worse to come. The opening figure augmented, and an enharmonic shift, C flat to B minor, bring October shadows, and with them Finzi's *andante* mourning march of time (so like Ex. 8.1). The *allegro* and the *andante* are apparently unrelated; yet the outline of 'these later shafts of sleet' (*allegro*) is traced in 'these happy suns are past' (*andante*). Sad chromatic distortions of the 'looking forward' figure reach the unanswered question, so the D flat major song closes on C sharp minor. In the third song, 'The self-unseeing', Hardy looks back on an exquisite scene from his childhood and realizes that only now, too late, can he appreciate that past joy. The conceit forces sinister chords from Finzi, but with, crucially, a ghostly 'dance of delight' for 'Childlike, I danced in a dream'; and an unresolved ending indicates how unsettling memory can be.

These first three poems have regular and equal line-lengths. In the songs, however, there is no sense of metrical sameness, so skilfully does Finzi juggle with verbal stress. 'Overlooking the river', a poem he often thought of longingly, cooped-up in wartime London, breaks that pattern for it is a rondel – the first two and last two lines of each verse being the same – but continues the emotional pattern. There are three verses of drowsy riverside idyll, which Finzi clothes in easy-going melody and Bach–Parry accompaniment; but then once again comes 'alack!' A critic writing in 1923 about *By Footpath and Stile* noted that Hardy's lyrics 'often depend for their peculiarly subjective pathos on the sudden turn to the last line or sentence, a serious difficulty for the composer to overcome who works in a less direct medium than speech and requires elbow-room at the very moment when his song must come to an end'.[10] It was a difficulty Finzi set himself often, and dealt with by unconventional tonality. Here the emotional graph directs a sunny E flat major song to end on a sad F minor chord, so matching the inconclusive mood. It is among the most poetic examples of his 'deflected' cadences. But four songs of regret in sequence – before and after summer indeed, never summer now! One can only marvel at Finzi's varied shadings of similar emotions.

The fifth song, 'Channel firing', deals in colloquial, grisly language with the idea that religion is powerless against man's stupidity and evil. The words are spoken by the dead, who mistake gunnery practice for Judgment Day, and are reassured by a sympathetic but helpless God. Finzi composed it during the first year of the war (see p. 115). It would seem, on reading, to be impossible to set; even Finzi wrote 'If only God didn't say "Ha, Ha". That's a great difficulty!!'[11] The song is through-composed but has elements of a rondo, for the nine verses are rhythmically gripped together with the angry mutter of the guns (Ex. 10.1).

Ex. 10.1

This develops into a muscular Brahmsian figure (Ex. 10.2) as God speaks.

Ex. 10.2

Finzi binds the otherwise freely developing melody with his finger-print (Ex. 10.3); compare in this song 'broke the chancel window-squares', 'arose the howl of wakened hounds', 'as far inland as Stourton Tower'):

---

[10] H. E. W. in *The Music Bulletin*, November 1923.
[11] To Toty de Navarro, 26 April 1939.

Ex. 10.3

"Will the world e - ver sa - ner be."

Another binding figure invites speculation. It has the rhythm of 'threatening', but begins to invade the accompaniment eleven bars before that word occurs. Not until the recapitulation before 'Again the guns' does it meld with Example 10.1. Easy to suppose that the phrase 'for so much threatening' was one of the earliest in Finzi's sketches, and that he then worked backward and forward from that point.

'Channel firing' lasts almost seven minutes, a dramatic arioso or a tone-poem, as ambitious as Wolf's 'Prometheus'. It is Finzi's denunciation of war on the innocent. His anger is shown in the first line when he abruptly throws the word 'unawares' on to a high accented note, his compassion at the words 'for you are men, And rest eternal sorely need,' set to his Ur-phrase (compare Examples 1.1 and 9.2). At the end Hardy contrasts man's madness with the monuments of perished civilizations – Stourton Tower, Camelot, Stonehenge; and Finzi, taking his cue from Hardy's unexpected, vulnerable 'starlit', gives the music historical perspective by stilling the voice and thinning the accompaniment, distancing the savage human emotion to a cool impersonal poetry. Finzi was asked by a singer, James Atkins, whether he would score the song for orchestra. He replied that it would be impossible to get the balance right between the medium and low registers of voice and orchestra. 'Not that I don't prefer almost any song with orchestra accpt. to piano accpt.!'[12]

The sixth song, 'In the mind's eye', is also among Finzi's greatest. It is a vision, and the dissolving modulations powerfully suggest the shifting visual planes – 'now, as then, I see her'. The opening five-note figure sounds first in octaves; then harmonized, half-speed, as if itself a phantom; then with hollow chording ('foremost in my vision'); and finally stabilized over a pedal ('shape so sweet and shy'), as the singer accepts his dear ghost. 'The too short time' begins as recitative arioso; in the song's structured second half the imperturbable accompaniment mirrors the sun's and birds' denial of winter's approach. Hardy's rueful pessimism is perfectly caught. Then come two lighter songs. 'Epeisodia' begins with a formal eighteenth-century air; its depressing second verse has a low tessitura from which the piano climbs to dance above the voice. Hardy's unusual chain-rhymes go from country courtship – 'caressed we' – to the greyness of town life – 'pressed we' – to the grave – 'rest we', Finzi's Amen cadence making the sudden solemn point. In 'Amabel', as in 'To Lizbie Brown' (see p. 79) the name chimes as a refrain through the verses. Here 'Time the tyrant fell' has brought 'custom-straitened views' and 'ruined

12   13 April 1951.

hues' to poor Amabel. Did it never occur to Hardy that time has its effect on men, too, turning some of them paunchy, balding, smug? Perhaps it did to Finzi, for the song has a sly humour and the ending is a mite theatrical.

He completes the set with a big dramatic scena. 'He abjures Love' is a gaunt poem, severe in thought, compact and tough in language: the disillusioned answer to the first song in the set, the logical consequence of denying God in 'Channel Firing' and denying lasting love in 'Amabel'. For the dismissive energy it needs Finzi turns again to his Brahmsian piano dotted rhythm; the impetus sweeps him right through Hardy's first two verses – a single angry sentence. There is another Brahmsian figure – a tolling-bell – for the two dark episodes, 'I was as children be . . .' and 'I speak as one . . .'. The variety of pace and figuration in this four-minute song is remarkable; even more striking is Finzi's assurance in the transition from one sentiment to another, as between 'I did not sicken' and 'fever-stricken'. Though every note is inspired by the poem, the structure could almost stand as a piano piece without voice, so strong it is. In the penultimate verse Finzi meets a problem he will meet again in *Intimations of Immortality*: how to celebrate a negative. No longer will the poet see life transfigured by love. Finzi responds with his now familiar D major vein (Ex. 10.4) – compare the endings of 'A young man's exhortation' (p. 40) and 'Proud songsters' (p. 80) – to express longing for something past, timeless, or precious:

Ex. 10.4

Such a simple harmonic statement might be deemed naive, but, as always with Finzi, its placing in the context gives it grace. Here, it is brief and immediately contradicted; then comes the thudding curtain.

HARDY AND BLUNDEN

In 1941 Toty de Navarro, encouraged by his wife and Howard Ferguson, copied out and sent Gerald – unattributed – the poem by Hardy that begins 'Nine leaves a minute' and wrote underneath 'what about it?' At the time Toty was regularly sending Gerald his own poems, and Gerald was half caught out:

'you must be prepared for people to say not only "This is not 100% Toty" but also "this is 70% Hardy".' It at once roused musical ideas in him 'as Hardy invariably does'. There was amusement all round when the hoax was admitted: 'It's difficult to know which to admire most,' wrote Gerald, 'the judgement of you three that it might strike music out of me, or my own honesty & sound critical sense.'[13] It is pleasant that *Before and After Summer*, of which 'Nine leaves a minute' (called 'The too short time'; see p. 171) became the seventh song, had its first private performance at Toty's Broadway home on his birthday in 1949. Robert Irwin and Howard then performed the new set to Leslie Boosey: 'There can be no-one else in the world quite like Boosey,' Gerald wrote to Toty, for he pronounced the set (which included 'Channel firing') to be 'very charming' and added that his problem was to know how much to charge for the volume. In spite of such 'encouragement' Gerald still felt that there were perhaps another hundred Hardy poems that attracted him – so 'I shall go to my grave with most of them unset!'[14]

For his birthday that year (1949) Joy found the copy of Edmund Blunden's early collection of poems, *The Waggoner*, which Blunden himself had given to Hardy in September 1920. Gerald wrote to Tokyo to tell Edmund that though he was not a relic hunter and disliked the trade in association values, he admitted to a 'great pleasure when the association is linked with affection or admiration. Alas, I never knew TH, except through his work and that has been to me what the Bible must have been to Bunyan! You, I know, will forgive such idolatry. As for EB, well, I have my own copy of *The Waggoner* dated, in an illformed hand, 1920, which tells of a fidelity from the age of eighteen or nineteen to this very day.'[15] That suggested another link: might he put Blunden's name at the top of his new Hardy volume? So *Before and After Summer* was dedicated 'To Edmund Blunden'.

'. . . what the Bible must have been to Bunyan!' What drew Finzi to Hardy so compulsively that he left over fifty completed song settings of the poems? Hardy is no obvious choice for a lyrical composer. Few of his verses offer a spare word: there are no bland descriptions, but keen, precise observations; no mellifluous easy-running metres, but intricate rhyme schemes, lines often packed with hard crusty sounds. Finzi admired Hardy's dignity, his compassion, what he considered to be his rationalism, and above all his freedom from religious bigotry. In 1938 he singled out from William Rutland's just-published *Life of Hardy* a quotation to illustrate why, as he said, '*I have always loved him so much and from earliest days responded, not so much to an influence as to a kinship with him. (I don't mean kinship with his genius, alas, but with his mental make-up).*' The quotation reads: 'The first, manifest, characteristic of the man who wrote *The Dynasts* is his detestation of all useless suffering, and his loathing of cruelty. The suffering that fills the world, and the thought that it is unnecessary, are to him a nightmare. This was the long tribulation of Hardy's life.'

[13] 25 September 1941.
[14] 7 June 1949.

Yet, on the face of it, the two men were so different. Both loved the old country ways, and the slow rhythms of the seasons; but Hardy lived where he was born, and was rooted to his childhood landmarks. Finzi's country home-life was self-chosen and self-created. Hardy was brought up an Anglican, intended to take holy orders, and even after the upheaval of losing his belief remained a 'churchy' man. Finzi was an agnostic, and never went into the church opposite his home except to give concerts there. For Hardy, the past was a quarry: poem after poem celebrates a memory, more precious and vivid than the present; among his greatest poems are those inspired by his return journey after Emma's death to his Lyonnesse. Finzi in his life apparently never looked back, never wanted to revisit old haunts, was eager to grasp each moment and press on to the next. Hardy would seem to have more in common with Elgar than with Finzi. Yet Finzi again and again sets Hardy poems concerned with the power of memory to crystallize the past.

Finzi marked another sentence in his copy of Rutland: 'There is nothing more remarkable about Hardy's life than the tremendous tenacity of purpose with which he made for himself this career in letters upon which he had set his heart.' Finzi could identify with that. And another: 'It is an interesting paradox that Hardy should have placed so high a value upon intellectual reason, while his own mental life was almost entirely governed by emotion.' Perhaps Finzi recognized himself there, perhaps not. 'The truth is,' he once wrote, 'I'm fundamentally a rationalist (a Hardyite, if you like, – disbelieving in Beliefs and accepting only ideas and feelings. In this respect Hardy's compassionate outlook is the one, above all, that I appreciate).'[16] Finzi's setting of 'The oxen' (see p. 23) is too early for it to do justice to the poem; but he shared its experience. Once, being driven home late after a carol concert by Mrs Stein, an NSP violinist, he said wistfully 'Wouldn't it have been wonderful had it been true!,' echoing Hardy's 'hoping it might be so'.

Finzi and Hardy shared a love and respect for the language of the great religious poets and particularly for the Bible. They shared too a horror of the constrictions of social convention. They were alike in valuing traditional virtues, but with free-thinking minds. It was always the thought in a poem, never just beautiful words, that attracted Finzi. In sum, they had in common three main preoccupations: the futility of war, an obsession with time's passing, and the beauty of the natural world and its indifference to man. Both rejected their relatives with some brutality. But Hardy remained close enough to his background to remember its ugliness, so that his nostalgia contains a bitter self-correcting element; Finzi was a displaced person. There is nothing in his music to match the fierceness with which Hardy drives Tess and Jude to destruction against the rigid code of society's behaviour. Finzi's search for salvation in green hills and apples makes for a less complicated kind of regret, which turned itself into a romantic rescue of the neglected, the obscure, the

---

[15] 22 August 1949.
[16] To W. Busch, 10 October 1940.

unfulfilled, the disadvantaged – whether apple trees, eighteenth-century worthies, young artists struggling in unhelpful circumstances, or killed before their prime.

WORKING METHODS

Finzi probably never set out to compose a song; but when he read a poem, one line – often not the first – would call up music unbidden. John Russell, visiting, found Finzi reading a Vaughan poem. 'He looked up, smiled, and by way of humorous greeting, sang, and at once wrote down, "O rose of Sharon! O the lily of the valley! How art thou now" – the last lines but the prime musical motif of "Welcome Sweet and Sacred Feast".'[17] He liked then to have the poem typed, and crossed out each line as he set it. Once the starting line of melody had come, he composed more or less continuously at the piano, as if the sound itself was a generating force. He was not a good pianist – not even a respectable one, according to John Sumsion, who occasionally helped him to shape the piano parts – 'you'll get the same result if you do it this way, and it's twice as easy'. Hearing him play, Cedric Thorpe Davie was reminded 'of RVW, struggling and fumbling'. Some of Finzi's closest friends never heard him sing; some who did described his voice as a 'bari-tenor'. Others called it a growl! Yet his songs are a singer's delight, they are so vocal. They are never dedicated to performers, and he never composed 'on' a known voice. He had no Rubini, Bernac, Pears. In his early days he gave scarcely any directions – dynamics or phrasing – saying 'any musical person would know how it should go'. When he began conducting, he realized how much performers' time that wasted. Newbury String Players became his instrument.

Working in isolation, he forged musical friendships as his support. Closest of all was Howard Ferguson, from their meeting in 1926 for the rest of Gerald's life. As a colleague Gerald was both demanding and generous. He called on his friends (pestered them, almost) for advice, sometimes on what struck them as extraordinary details – whether a D should be flat or natural, whether to use an oboe or a clarinet, or the best accentuation of a word. His friends sometimes discussed this among themselves, humorously; but it was as though the gathered opinions served to focus his own ideas. He then needed a performance, to check the work. Once a work was finished, he said he lost interest in it: it was a problem solved.

He kept to a working routine learnt from Vaughan Williams, who taught him to be ready for the fertile moment when it came. Once the post was dealt with, 9.00 till 12.30 was earmarked for composing. At Aldbourne, half-an-hour's badminton before lunch gave him the maximum exercise in the shortest time. At Ashmansworth, after lunch and a quick cat-nap when he liked to be read to, he generally worked in the garden. Between tea and a late dinner was often his best composing time. Afterwards, he read, listened to music, talked, wrote letters, but tried not to compose as it disturbed his sleep;

[17] *Musical Times* (December 1956), p. 630.

but if he had reached an impasse, he would consciously consider his problem, and often found on waking that it was resolved. Sometimes, however, sketches were left for years, to form part of much later works. 'It's my bad habit,' he wrote to Herbert Howells, 'working on so many things over so long a period and never quite knowing which is going to be the next to take charge of things and get itself finished.'[18] Howard Ferguson saw it as a very bad habit indeed: he could see 'no harm in using-up self-contained slabs of old stuff, provided they are not mixed up with stuff of a much later vintage. When there is such a mixture, difficulties start crowding in. The chief of these in your case, it seems to me, being the amount of time you have to spend tinkering at the old stuff in an attempt (unavailing) to make it fit with the new.'[19]

One small piece of 'tinkering' was self-contained and the original exists. The carol 'Winter now has bared the trees', composed on 16. xii, 1925 at Churchdown for Howells's daughter, Ursula, became Carol, number three of the Five Bagatelles for clarinet. What strikes in comparing the two is how bare the old manuscript is: not one direction to the performer, no tempo, dynamic, expression or phrase mark. Ursula's carol (in G) has four verses, the clarinet's (in B flat) has three. The tune is the same in both, but in the early piece voice and piano cling timidly together in unison, with none of the piano's later descanting and changes from line to chord. In both final verses the piano has the melody, 'Christus natus hodie!' stimulating a new vocal phrase, and 'Hodie' is the little repeated refrain in the Bagatelle. Absent in the song of course is the clarinet's taking over in the last verse the piano's high tonic from the first verse. Finzi had learnt much about texture, register, and spacing, and about integrating a piece with small but sure touches.

AN 'INTERESTING EXPERIMENT'

In August 1947 Gerald Abraham of the BBC Third Programme wrote to tell him that six poets had been commissioned to write a poem 'specially for musical setting'. All six would be sent, anonymously, to six composers, for each to choose one, to give reasons for their choice, and to answer a question-naire. This would make a couple of programmes, which might illumine the suitability of words for music, musicians' approach to poetry, even inspiration. Would Finzi take part in this 'interesting experiment'?

Though the idea went right against Finzi's principles, he was the only composer to complete the commission (Rubbra, Berkeley, and Rawsthorne were among those invited). He didn't hesitate to express his views: 'It would have hardly been possible to have a worse collection of poems expressly got together for the purpose of being set to music,' and he refused to answer the questionnaire. However, the poem he chose, by George Barker (1913–91) struck him as a fine piece of work with 'something of the magnificence and fury which one associates with, say, Dylan Thomas'. He changed the poem's

---

[18] 21 May 1940.
[19] 2 January 1954.

title from 'Ode against St Cecilia's Day' to 'Ode on the rejection of St Cecilia';
and pointed out that it could only be treated as a declamatory song which
needed a 'vocalising movement to pair with it; but I doubt whether such a
point as the distinction between the two styles has ever occurred to any of the
poets!'[20] He rose to the challenge with a big dramatic scena, the initial octave
leap on the command 'Rise' indicating the operatic style and scope – it is the
only one of his songs where voice and piano begin together. Barker's rhetoric
provokes equal displays from Finzi: thunderbolts, a midnight march, a
melisma on 'sigh', a violent recitative for the 'killer in the skull', Elgarian
tenderness for Cecilia herself (For the Fallen?), broken phrases and silences: all
grandly summed up in a massive eleven-bar peroration, con passione. Finzi may
not have had much use for 'Gerald Abraham's parlour game'[21] but he has in
fact ably combined the declamatory and vocalising styles in this one fine song.

[20] To John Lowe, 6 December 1948.
[21] To John Lowe, 8 March 1948.

CHAPTER ELEVEN

Intimations of Immortality

1948–50

At the 1948 Three Choirs Festival Gerald was informally asked to produce a new work for the following year. He had enjoyed composing the Clarinet Bagatelles, but been irritated because he felt their success was greater than their worth (the edition sold out within the year). The clarinet was in his mind, since Stephen Trier had begun to play with Newbury String Players; so (perhaps thinking he could at least match Weber) he offered a concerto for clarinet and strings. He discussed with Howard Ferguson whether to ask Pauline Juler to play it, but Howard pointed out practically that Miss Juler was just about to marry 'so a simple sum in arithmetic . . .'[1] So Gerald wrote to Frederick Thurston, and 1949 was largely given up to the composition of the concerto.

Gerald's sons Kiffer and Nigel were becoming 'delicious distractions'. In their teens, they were 'still enchanting enough', he wrote to Edmund Blunden, 'to make me often think of Robert Bridges' *Pater Filio*':

> [Sense with keenest edge unusèd,
> Yet unsteel'd by scathing fire;
> Lovely feet as yet unbruisèd
> On the ways of dark desire;
> Sweetest hope that lookest smiling
> O'er the wilderness defiling!]

(Among his papers is an undated sketch of music for the last verse.) 'What a terrible doctrine is that of original sin to one who believes that perception starts at birth and constantly declines thereafter: and how embarrassing to read Wordsworth's later apologetics for the "Theology" of the Intimations.'[2] There was a debit side: after Easter 1949 he told Tony Scott 'the holidays were devastating . . . no work'.[3] So much so that when August came and the Clarinet Concerto was still unfinished, Joy took the boys on holiday to Cornwall and left him at home. In a way they were working too, taking part in a film, *The Starfish*, directed by the young John Schlesinger, whose mother played in NSP. The Finzi boys were striking enough with their fiery Celtic looks to attract anybody's attention. They could, however, be maddening. Ursula Wood, on holiday with them, found them so contrary she would happily have knocked their heads together!

[1]   4 September 1948.
[2]   1 January 1950.

Ursula was with the family too at Hereford for the first performance of the Clarinet Concerto, which Finzi conducted on 9 September; Vaughan Williams was at the Festival conducting his *Pastoral Symphony*. 'Afterwards,' she recalled, 'we drove out to Weobly' [it was there that Vaughan Williams had collected the carol 'The Truth sent from above', the subject of Gerald's first letter to him] '. . . It was a shining afternoon, apples glistening on the trees, the country quiet and fulfilled, summer moving into autumn.'[4] Gerald was pleased with the performance; and the next month was feeling 'as if I'd like to write another clarinet concerto, but saying something completely different'.[5]

Clarinet Concerto, Op. 31

The Concerto for Clarinet and Strings is Finzi's first mature three-movement instrumental work. By 1949 he had been conducting Newbury String Players for eight years; he had behind him the experience of writing against time for *Love's Labour's Lost*, and of composing the choral–orchestral *For St Cecilia*. Life at Ashmansworth seemed good, settled, and fruitful. He wrote in the programme for Hereford that the mood of the Concerto grew out of 'the warm and romantic qualities . . . and natural fluidity' of the instrument.

The Concerto opens, however, with bold octaves in two parts grating in canon (Ex. 11.1a), a direct confrontation at Finzi's personal point of extreme dissonance, sevenths and ninths at their starkest – and with a nod to the opening of Vaughan Williams's Fourth Symphony. The short orchestral exposition ends dramatically, also with octaves, but on the dominant G, so establishing a firm C minor. This strong overall tonic-dominant structure, unusual in Finzi, allows for a freely developing solo part: an outpouring of beautiful, sinuous melody. The clarinet, which here seems always to return a soft answer, first enters with an expressive version of Example 11.1a (recalling Walton's Violin Concerto of 1939); its second phrase ends with a 'tail' of semitones, C, D flat, C etc. (Ex. 11.1b), derived horizontally from the opening octaves. Through this 'tail' Finzi explores such distant romantic regions as Example 11.1c, before cue 3, which reaches towards private dreams.

Finzi's way of reshaping intervals, expanding or contracting them, sends his tunes slyly on to unexpected chords, so that the chromatic side-slips and twisting modulations seem directed by the melody rather than harmonically propelled. Also, a figure from one theme may insinuate itself into another, all the material seeming to belong generically together. The phrases in Example 11.2 come from (a) bars 7–8; (b) bar 10 (exposition); (c) bar 2–3 after cue 1 (clarinet's entry); (d) bar 13 after cue 2 (second subject); and (e) – from the Adagio – at cue 4.

3   2 May 1949.
4   U. Vaughan Williams, *R.V.W: a Biography* (London, 1964), p. 294.
5   To Milford, 4 October 1949.

Ex. 11.1

a)

b)

c)

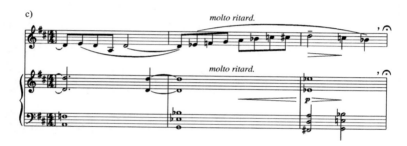

Ex. 11.2

a)

b)

c)

d)

e)

A severe view might judge that all this undermines the first movement's structure: the clarinet evades rather than faces the confrontation implicit in the opening, and never fully engages with the orchestra, so that the listener is cheated of a true concerto, and the material is all too similar. A sympathetic listener (and the Concerto is very popular) is seduced into following the improvisatory lone voice towards intimate poetic visions. At such times the string writing is spare and delicate; at others throughout the Concerto it is dense and rich, with divided and double-stopped strings, and energising triplets runs and trills.

For all the clarinet's rhapsodizing, the first movement is succinct: the development is brief; a reprise of the original C minor clarinet theme falls contentedly into D major, then the opening octaves clash over B flat – keys a tone to either side of the tonic C minor. The final climax, however, when a 'scrubbing' crescendo over a dominant pedal again bursts con furia on to bare octaves, can seem frenetic rather than powerful. After a cadenza, leaping octave trills for clarinet and tolling triads for orchestra pound out eight bars over a tonic pedal, so balancing the opening, and – after the internal waywardness – re-establishing the tonality. (This ending recalls that of the Oboe Interlude – both highly charged emotionally.) At the first performance there was no cadenza. The Observer critic commented that the end came as a surprise. So, apparently, did Vaughan Williams, for Finzi then wrote to Thurston that he would send 'the little cadenza which we can try out at Oxford [in November]. Actually it doesn't want to be more than half a dozen bars, but it's not easy to do, though I think VW was right on that point.'[6]

The Adagio attains a still, tranced state. It begins, like the first movement, with single lines marked by a semitone – three notes rising, then falling, first and second violins answering each other. The main theme, at cue 1, is a hushed chain of inversions; at cue 3 these become an oscillation of two becalmed chords: a rapt sound, floating and time-cancelling – recalling By Footpath and Stile (see p. 24) and A Severn Rhapsody (see p. 29). The clarinet weaves self-communing arabesques, twice reaching (poco tenuto) towards the visionary world of Example 11.1c. More intense emotions extend (Ex. 11.2e) the initial three-note figure, which builds passionately and painfully to the 'Angel of the Agony' discord at cue 5. Still more pervasive than Gerontius is the influence of Elgar's Violin Concerto: both Elgar and Finzi knew how to make their soloist's decorations thematically expressive; and the lusingando passage in the first movement after cue 2 is pure Elgar. The particular mood, of innocence and gravity, however, is Finzi's own.

The Rondo, after an introduction that recalls harmonic asperities from the first movement, takes off with an infectious tune (first sketched in the 1930s). Finzi is such a noted song-writer that there is a special pleasure in hearing the clarinet range happily through, say, Ferrier to Baillie, in carefree tunes that need pay no heed to verbal values or a singer's compass. The theme begins

6   15 September 1949.

decorously with a four-bar phrase; but the answer flows on and up for another eighteen bars, juggling its sequences and extensions across the beat (compare the more reflective violin and piano Elegy, and the tenor's solo in *For St Cecilia*). There are two melodious, inconsequential episodes. Then a slightly awkward join leads back to the Rondo's introduction, now grand and full, which transforms itself for a couple of bars back into the first movement, so proving the music's thematic integration. Trills adorning the rondo theme also reflect the first movement, and smartly bring the Concerto to a brilliant end.

During 1949 Gerald continued to add to Newbury String Players repertory (see Appendix 3), most ambitiously with Elgar's Introduction and Allegro. NSP were now giving eight to ten concerts a year, and travelling further afield. They played their first open-air midsummer serenade concert at Bucklebury, in a little theatre once the kitchen of a burnt-out manor. That December at Enborne Gerald gave the first performance of a Symphony for Strings, Op. 3, by Kenneth Leighton. Gerald reported to Robin Milford that Leighton was 'a young man up at Oxford (a pupil of Bernard Rose, who asked us to do it) & I've seldom come across an early work of such achievement'.[7] Immediately he wrote to Howard Ferguson, asking for information about the Mendelssohn Composition Scholarship for Leighton.

Gerald had been to see Britten's realization of *The Beggar's Opera* (1948), which he admitted to Cedric Thorpe Davie was brilliantly done. But he saw no justification in 'dishing-up' other periods in 'up-to-date-dress'. 'It's possible to make Byrd sound like Strauss and Boyce like Stravinksy, but that isn't shedding new light on Byrd and Strauss . . . it merely misunderstands what they were driving at.'[8] He recalled the Victorian editors who thought they were bringing Byrd, Gibbons, Weelkes up to date. NSP was playing the 'Cimarosa' oboe concerto, which was, he told Ceddie, really by Arthur Benjamin, with quite as much Benjamin in it as Cimarosa. But he found it a beautiful little work, 'if you consider it a *re-creation*'.[9] He was all the time teaching himself such distinctions.

That was the background against which he made his first edition. He turned his attention to the blind organist and composer John Stanley (1712–86). In 1947 NSP had played Stanley's trumpet tune (Philip Jones the soloist) and in 1948 they played the concertos Nos 2 and 3 from the set of six for strings and continuo published as his Op. 2. These had no modern editions – Gerald owned the parts of the Walsh set of c. 1745. Eagerly he seized his chance and persuaded Boosey & Hawkes to publish a couple of the concertos

7   June 1949.
8   3 October 1948.
9   21 February 1949.

if he edited them, to see how they sold. In his introduction, Gerald disputed the accepted idea that English composers of the eighteenth century were mere imitators of Handel. He considered Boyce, Arne, Roseingrave, Avison and others to be fine composers in their own right. Though little of Stanley's music was known in the 1940s, his contemporaries had regarded him highly. Gerald aimed simply to make Stanley's original text available: 'it is not always remembered that composers of earlier generations knew perfectly well what they wanted'. In 1949 Boosey & Hawkes brought out Concerto No. 3 in G major, the first of his Stanley editions, as either a string concerto with continuo, or a keyboard concerto with strings.

He began to seek others working in his field: Adam Carse, who edited early symphonies in addition to writing his classic studies of the orchestra; William C. Smith, whose bibliography of John Walsh's publications, 1695–1720, came out in 1948. Smith was happy to share his knowledge, realising that he had found a genuine fellow researcher. In thanking him, Gerald ruefully admitted that Smith's information 'makes my sporadic attempts at research during the last four or five years look very silly!'[10] Smith provided him with a publication date (1742) for the Stanley concertos, which differed from Barclay Squire's in the British Museum's catalogue. Next there was the problem of dating the two sets of 'six cantatas', to words by Sir John Hawkins; Gerald's research at Stationers Hall made nonsense of the dating in Grove. He was, he told Smith, sharing his information with Mollie Sands, who was revising the entry on Stanley for the 1954 edition of Grove.

Then came Gerald's big discovery. Constant Lambert in 1937 had published the overtures to The Power of Music and Pan and Syrinx as being by Boyce. Gerald had acquired photostats of the Stanley oratorios held by the British Museum, which showed that the overture to Stanley's The Fall of Egypt (performed in 1774) was the same as that for 'Boyce's' The Power of Music. How could that be? This was real excitement, to overturn a mis-attribution. Joyfully Gerald shared the news (which earned him a footnote in the 1954 Grove entry on Boyce, though the Lambert entry in the 2001 Grove still attributes the overtures to Boyce) with Carse, Sands, and Thorpe Davie. Then he was after librettists, of Stanley's oratorio Jephtha and his opera Teraminta. There was confusion about Teraminta. Was it muddled with J. C. Smith's opera of the same name? Then came songs. Did Finzi know, asked W. C. Smith, that Stanley issued Twelve English Songs in 1741 as his Op. 3? Might that be a collection of earlier sheet music, asked Gerald and – following another of Smith's hints – shot off a letter to the Library of Congress, which had a copy. Gerald at once ordered a photostat, which 'would be available for you or anyone else who wants to borrow it'. Next he wanted to know how the 'Charles' had crept into John Stanley's name. At Smith's suggestion he checked the lists of Oxford graduates and investigated Stanley's coat of arms. Again, what were the publication dates of Stanley's sets of organ voluntaries?

10 7 October 1949.

One composer led naturally to another. In a sale Gerald found a work by Jackson of Exeter, bound in with an Arnold edition of Handel. Who knew about Jackson? Could Ceddie help him find scores of Avison? What did Smith know about Charles Wesley or William Felton? All this was initially prompted by Gerald's work with NSP.

1949–50, NSP

The little orchestra was changing the Finzis' lives. It involved them in administration and research, making life at Ashmansworth unlike pre-war Aldbourne. Apart from Gerald's growing reputation as a composer, he now had some status as an organizer. He became the first chairman of the Berkshire County Music Committee, setting up an instrument loan fund, and on 9 February 1950 the *Newbury Weekly News* printed a letter from him in that capacity welcoming a junior orchestra. Gerald had encouraged Michael Shiner, an amateur singer, to found this, partly as a resource from which to replace the 'dear greying heads' in his own. Newbury had two orchestras, the Amateur Orchestral Union, which had been going seventy-one years, and the ten-year-old NSP: both relied in the main on older players.

NSP however was now attracting young professionals from outside its area. Students leaving the colleges who needed experience and a little money (three guineas and expenses) loved playing with them. Among these was Anna Shuttleworth, a cello student at the Royal College of Music in the mid-1940s, when – still suffering from post-war restrictions – it was in some ways a dry and competitive place. The flautist Alex Murray, also from the RCM; the clarinettist Stephen Trier, whom Gerald befriended while he was at Marlborough; James Brown the oboist and William Waterhouse the bassoonist were the chief wind players at the end of the 1940s and early in the 1950s.

The adolescence of these young people had been dulled and darkened by the war. Ashmansworth came as a revelation to them. From the moment of arrival, to be greeted by 'what's the news? what's been exciting you lately?', a visitor felt the most important person in the world – gathered in, swept up, made a part of whatever was going on. Everyone was welcomed with warmth and encouragement for whatever individual offering he could bring. Gerald and Joy had great sympathy and respect for the half-formed ideas of young people, especially if they were misfits in their own home; and were always keen to lend moral support if families were opposed to a life in the arts.

One of the young players encountered Joy's passing craze for garlic, and never forgot eating garlic sandwiches. Another remembered a picnic on the Downs, with real country food off proper china plates. Another remembered his first night there, when the Finzis got out *Meet Yourself as you really are*, a book of questions designed to reveal personality, which everyone answered with such frankness that he was amazed. Anything and everybody was discussed, and at great length. Nobody ever took umbrage. Arguments begun late at night spread over the next morning's breakfast, always with good humour.

Herma Fiedler, then the secretary of the Oxford Orchestral Society, drove over every Saturday to play and ferried undergraduates in her car. One of these, John Wood, found his attitude to music changing, but

> it was by osmosis rather than as a result of anything that was said: one just gathered that music was a very important thing (though musicians weren't: I can't imagine anyone who was less of a VIP in his own evident estimation than Gerald) and that work and concentration were needed and expected. The fun was there: rehearsals were enjoyable and there were riotous tea-parties afterwards at the Bandarlog cafe in Newbury . . . it was just that one's priorities got re-arranged.[11]

Gerald struck these young people as a deep person, quiet and direct; and his gimlet eyes and cultivated voice impressed them. He hardly mentioned his own work. They thought of Ashmansworth as a farmhouse (it was when the orchards were young and needing care), as he liked to give the impression he composed in his spare time. Gerald learnt conducting as he went along. At the start he had no technique and not much ability. He had a way of holding his baton from underneath, which lost him authority, until Jean Stewart demonstrated during a meal with a carving knife to show him how it should be held! John Sumsion taught him how to split beats and click sounds off. But he had the musician's gift of finding the right tempo (a far cry from his early London days when Sybil Eaton could never get him to strike the same tempo twice). And he learnt to be succinct: Sybil, who wrote asking if the upbeat in a concerto should be short or long, and what length dress she should wear for an NSP concert, got back a postcard: 'Both short'.

The Players found him gentle, perhaps not always forceful enough. They felt he conducted as a composer, absorbed in the music: his mind more on how it was made than how best to display it. This may have meant the concerts were less effective for an audience, but for thoughtful musicians they were an experience worth sharing. Gerald never had much sense of presentation, and did not enjoy conducting his music at the Three Choirs, but accepted the invitations because it saved rehearsal time.

Joy was orchestra manager, stand-shifter, chauffeur, librarian, copier of parts, provider of picnic food for rehearsals and concerts. Timelessly dressed, she wore longish skirts, blouses or little jackets with interesting buttons, and latterly, indoors or out, a headscarf. For all her air of fey other-worldliness, she had the logistics under control. She was the benign dispenser of boiled sweets in the rehearsal break, even of hot water bottles in cold weather for the old ladies whose fingers shrivelled on the strings. With little domestic help and food still short she provided meals and beds for all but the local players. On top of this she played in the second fiddles. There were those who asked themselves why, talented and beautiful as she was, she should always play 'second fiddle' to Gerald. They missed the point that she loved Gerald because

---

[11] Letter of 13 March 1984.

he demanded so much; she enjoyed the stimulus, the activity, feeling herself the hub and the pivot – in every sense 'pulling the strings'. If sometimes she ruefully recalled her family's remark before her marriage, 'Old Gerald, he'll be a rod to break your back,' she had wished it that way, and she was never a martyr.

To many of the young players, Gerald became a confidant and a father-figure. Sensitive shy adolescents grew deeply attached to him. But there was also a quality about him that could be discomfiting: his penetrating X-ray eyes saw through to one's core. People could be dismissed for lack of artistic integrity, and a non-creative person was of no consequence. Such purity was hard to face.

WORDSWORTH

This was the man who set Wordsworth's *Intimations of Immortality*. In 1950 he said it had 'simmered sixteen years',[12] which took its inception back to 1934, the year after his marriage. As early as 1931 he asked Jack Haines (his poet friend in Gloucestershire) where the stress should fall in 'Shout round me'. Howard Ferguson's Christmas wish in 1936 was 'may *Intimations* flourish'. In 1938 Finzi was able to tell William Busch 'I'm halfway through my choral work,'[13] and knew it would be for tenor, chorus and orchestra. During the war it lay dormant. In 1942 he told Vaughan Williams that the longish work he had intended to dedicate to him for his seventieth birthday lay 'on the stocks at home, two thirds finished'[14] (in the end he dedicated it to Vaughan Williams's wife Adeline). On 19 May 1950 he wrote to Cedric Thorpe Davie 'Today I've finished *Intimations*. It's a forty-minute work, eighty to ninety pages of vocal score, & all to be scored within the next two months.' He got up at six every morning and did nothing else all day. On 16 August he had fifty-six more bars to go. It was just ready in time, with the help of the copyist Ronald Finch.

Finch went with him to the London rehearsals. They took the tube, and a black ticket collector made some remark that attracted Gerald's attention. (Howard's friend the South African composer Arnold van Wyk had been staying at Ashmansworth.) Gerald spent half an hour with the man, listening carefully to what he had to say about apartheid – reasoning, explaining, expressing his own sympathy. As a result he was late for the rehearsal. At the next, Vaughan Williams was present, and Finch heard him begin to rumble with laughter. On page forty-four of the vocal score, just below the words 'the pansy at my feet', the title had been misprinted 'Intimations of Immorality'.

The first performance, under Sumsion and with Eric Greene as soloist, was at Gloucester on 5 September. The Finzis packed the boys off to the Cowley Manor music party, and stayed the whole week. It was a glorious festival, every

[12] To Thorpe Davie, 14 September.
[13] 14 February 1938.
[14] 11 April.

minute of the day filled, one of them with buying a Bland and Weller 1795 full score of *Messiah* for seven shillings and sixpence. Gerald's work was in the company of friends: Parry's organ Prelude in his own arrangement, Holst's *Hymn of Jesus*, Vaughan Williams's *Tallis Fantasia* and Sixth Symphony, and the first performance of Howells's *Hymnus Paradisi*.

In his programme note Finzi wrote that *Intimations*

> 'finished itself', if any justification is needed for the setting of a poem which, both in its philosophical content and poetic expression, is one of the greatest in the English language. It is sometimes argued that certain poems, complete and wonderful in themselves, are in no need of a musical setting, and that the composer should confine himself to words primarily intended for music. Such a view may express personal feelings but not necessarily the feelings of the composer, who is driven to composition by the impact of the words.

Intimations of Immortality, Op. 29

'Driven to composition by the impact of the words.' It was inevitable that Finzi should set the *Ode: Intimations of Immortality, from Recollections of Early Childhood*. All his life – his feelings, his thought, theories, reading, compositions – had been leading to this point. He had to identify himself with the words through his own music. However, the Ode poses problems for a composer. It is descriptive and reflective, with no dialogue and no dramatic events. There is a narrator who at times speaks personally and at others is a commentator. Unlike so many British choral works, it is not drawn from the Bible; it is not religious; it is not an anthology of texts round a central subject. But in the 1920s Finzi was directed to the *Ode* through Dobell's Introduction to Traherne (see p. 28), and in 1933 he looked back at his own childhood through Wordsworthian eyes (see p. 70). His ideas on education damned the 'shades of the prison-house' in favour of 'delight and liberty'. The life the Finzis made for themselves – rural, natural, simple – resounds to the shout of the happy shepherd-boy.

If his music reveals the truth, however, Finzi's inner life was shot through with melancholy. *Intimations* opens with a solo horn call (Ex. 11.3), epitome since Weber of romantic nature, here a symbol for the mystery of pre-existence.

Ex. 11.3

That theme is repeated over a web of pianissimo strings, *Apostles*- and

Ex. 11.4

[Andante sosenuto]

Tallis-wise. Then comes one of Finzi's most melodious, gracious tunes (Ex. 11.4), standing in varied renewals for natural delights. Lovely – but a little predictable, a little comfortable. What lifts this opening prelude out of the ordinary is the third bar of Example 11.3; the consecutive augmented fourths for woodwind, under the horn's final sustained note, are gawky in interval, hollow in placement and scoring. The effect is neither romantic nor gracious, but uneasy. The implications of this sad hint are realized in, among other places, the *lontano* woodwind chords following '. . . something that is gone' (six bars before cue 21); and they inform the whole passage between cues 20 and 22. Through much of *Intimations* and of Finzi's other work this chill wind blows. To hear his music only as euphonious and benign is to miss the desolation in its depth.

Bleakness lies at the heart of Wordsworth's poem, which is loss, but for the assuaging power of memory. To him, the intensity and intuitions of pre-existence and childhood are dimmed by the insidious process through which life is tarnished and 'fades into the light of common day'. The poem recalls a *past* visionary gleam: 'There *was* a time . . .'. So the challenge to the composer is how to celebrate in music (which exists in its own, present, time-span) what the poet is celebrating in memory: to express at one and the same moment remembered radiance and exile from it. The level of consciousness, of perspective, shifts continuously. Music has no tenses to make such feelings explicit, but it has powers of association, as when Finzi recalls the horn motif (Ex. 11.3) in the *major* as the tenor sings of the 'imperial palace whence he came' (nine bars before cue 25; also five bars before cue 30) – scholars think 'imperial' was Wordsworth's spelling of 'empyreal' or celestial. There is too in the sound of Finzi's scoring melancholy mixed with grandeur. Not only in *Intimations*, but in many of his compositions are to be found climaxes, which die away slowly in overlapping imitations, a metaphor for 'trailing clouds of glory': such is the end of the first choral paragraph before cue 5 '. . . the freshness of a dream' (see also Example 9.1, from *Lo, the Full, Final Sacrifice*).

In spite of these regrets, no-one could catch more tenderly than Finzi the natural beauties of this world. *Intimations* is full of ravishing sounds, many of them for unaccompanied voices. Quite why the grace-note – rare for him – on 'love-ly is the rose' is so touching it is hard to say. The whole passage between cues 7 ('The Rainbow comes and goes') and 9 is magical: the beauty of women's voices, solo tenor and rocking horn notes; the high held violins shimmering above 'waters on a starry night'; the bright trumpets at 'glorious birth', all are points of delicate and poetic scoring.

The Ode is in what has become known as Three Choirs genre, lofty in sentiment and style. ('Delightful goddess' was enough, Finzi noted wryly, to ban For St Cecilia from the Cathedrals.[15]) He set the poem complete, except for stanzas seven and eight, which omission he considered did not detract from the train of thought. Wordsworth's Ode is an English Pindaric, each stanza having its own shape, rhyme-scheme, varying lengths of line, though most stanzas close with slow-moving iambics. Finzi set it as a single span, with an orchestral prelude and interludes; chorus and tenor soloist are frequently meshed and intertwined. One soloist was a modest demand; possibly Finzi felt the need for an individual voice. Wordsworth uses both the personal 'I' and the philosophic 'We', though he insisted that he spoke undogmatically, as poet not philosopher. Similarly, Finzi does not treat the words schematically, as he could have done by reserving the chorus for 'We' and the soloist for 'I'. It is strange, all the same, to hear the choral basses, imitated by the altos and tenors, confide that 'To me alone there came a thought of grief'. Perhaps this is why it is one of the uneasy musical joins in the Ode. Once or twice Finzi even allows the moment to override its context. For instance, he ignores the negative in 'Not for these I raise The song of thanks and praise', setting it joyously; and he ignores the subjunctive in 'if I were sullen', darkly illustrating 'Oh evil day!'

There are obvious enough influences behind *Intimations*. The *giojoso* orchestral gathering dance, with hammered dissonant triads, pursuing brass calls, syncopations, and a catchy xylophone tune, owes something to *The Hymn of Jesus* and to *Belshazzar's Feast*. Pervasive throughout *Intimations* is the major/minor clashing third of Walton's Viola Concerto. There is Brahms, too, particularly in Finzi's sombre transformation of Example 11.3 into a funeral march (cue 22), a startling musical image of 'our birth' as exile from an earlier, more perfect state. Compare 'Denn alles Fleisch es ist wie Gras' from the *Deutsches Requiem* – the same pedal note, triplet, key, and tessitura. Possibly Finzi made a subconscious link through his quotation in *A Young Man's Exhortation* ('all flesh is as the grass'). Since Brahms's Requiem was for the living, irrespective of creed, this brief reference to a lament for transitoriness was fitting. The comparison between Brahms and Finzi however raises a critical point. For Brahms, the theme was the opening of a ternary scheme. For Finzi, it forms only one phrase, at once abandoned in deference to fresh words – illustration rather than construction. His response to the rise and fall of emotion is generous and spontaneous, but a forty-three-minute-long continuous piece needs a strong command of form. Especially in Stanza V the music sounds sectional, with awkward joins, and climaxes too close together. Such attention to detail allows the music to lose vitality; but repetition of lines to make a larger musical paragraph would have been as much against Finzi's principles as it was natural for Brahms. The problems are the same as in *For St Cecilia* (see p. 160). Syllabic setting, valid in vocal solos, is less helpful in complicated madrigalian imita-

15 To Scott, 15 February 1949.

tions, when different words are uttered simultaneously. Not of course that Finzi never uses a homophonic style: 'We in thought will join your throng' is almost simplistic. So would be the tenor solo 'And the Children are culling' but for the loving extension on 'fresh flowers' (this music came to him as he was driving through Surrey one spring).

However, Finzi's imagery here and elsewhere for the riddle of man's existence is mysterious and potent (Ex. 11.5a, b, c). The great phrases, 'And that imperial palace whence he came', 'That hath kept watch o'er man's mortality', 'And can immense Mortality but throw So small a shade' (from 'At a lunar eclipse') all in Finzi's music accept the littleness of man, all grow in aspiration but end with a fall.

Ex. 11.5

As the tenor faces eternity, an other-worldly light shimmers round him: the eerie accompanying discord – B, C sharp, E sharp, G, D natural, F sharp – is scored so as to allow his voice through and above it, and the rolled cymbals add awe (Ex. 11.6). Time is suspended and music becomes silence.

Ex. 11.6

His final solo lines in the Ode ('another race hath been . . .') match the compassion and the sweetness of 'Everything was at rest, free and immortal' from *Dies Natalis*.

Wordsworth came to believe that the Soul *can* 'in a moment travel' to the rapt, visionary state, not only through real-life childhood, but by imaginative grasp. Finzi sets 'Hence in a season of calm weather' simply and clearly, as though the words were the heart of the poem, in C major block chords (echoing 'sing a joyous song'). Then he touches his most profound (cues 31–32) in a series of grand harmonies (C major, B flat major, E minor, G major, B minor, E flat minor, G minor, A flat major, E flat minor, A flat major, G major, D flat major, E minor): plain triads all, but by their disposition – related or unrelated, rooted or inverted – visionary: 'Our Souls have sight of that immortal sea', and clinched by a great melodic phrase rolling in stretto through them. That sea is a symbol in Wordsworth for the imagination and in Jung and Freud for the submerging of the personal human psyche in the collective unconscious: the 'oceanic' experience of being at one with the world. Such passages, together with Example 11.6, have the potency of archetypes, and seem to be 'intimations' – signs or tokens, intuitive glimpses without reasoning – of immortality. These moments justify Finzi's ambition in setting this poem. If he does not match them throughout nor altogether sustain the eloquence of the first two stanzas, his *Intimations* is nonetheless an intensely personal statement.

After that, the work's ending is inconclusive, both in Wordsworth and in Finzi: not unison, nor homophony, but five-fold imitations and a foreign accidental in the final vocal bars reflect uncertainty rather than affirmation or conviction. Both men could see only the possible consolations, seldom the achievements, of old age. It would be naive to suppose that Finzi took this view too literally; the child can stand for the artist, whose vision must be held clear and single through the adult daily round.

Some early press notices were appreciative. The following year when *Intimations* was repeated at Worcester *The Times* invoked Parry, 'who first attempted the setting of metaphysical poetry in the form of a choral cantata'. Parry would have rejoiced to hear this 'finely wrought, deeply felt, and, as far as scoring goes, more skilful inheritance from his pioneering. The composer's chief difficulty is to depict all the joys and beauties of life which the poet resolutely places second to the doubts and the shades of the prison house of mortality. Finzi kept the threads intact and in perfect balance . . . made a profound impression.'

However, the tide was turning. For the first time, Finzi began to be dubbed irrelevant. Martin Cooper, in the 1950 October *Musical Times*, wrote:

> To use, as Finzi does, an idiom compiled not from those of the great masters of the past but from a selection of our own native (and confessedly lesser) composers of the last half century, is to incur the charge of being the epigone of an already epigonic generation. This harmless and derivative music, not very happily orchestrated, was wedded to Wordsworth's finest poetry. Such

words would beggar even the greatest music and they showed the inadequacy of Finzi's painfully clearly.

When the score was published some of the reviews, if less trenchant, also concentrated on the music's derivative style.

CHAPTER TWELVE

. . . and of Mortality

1950–51

Edmund Blunden arrived home from Tokyo in mid-June 1950, to work again for the *Times Literary Supplement*, and found it hard to adjust. Gerald, from the security of Ashmansworth, stood amazed at what he saw as the grind of Blunden's life. (How shocked he would have been had he known that some of Blunden's productivity depended on his Japanese mistress-secretary!) To Edmund himself he wrote: 'it is beyond me how you have managed to keep your imaginative & sensuous faculties, your friendly scholarship and "four days at the office" all going together'.[1] To Robin Milford he was explicit: 'what a difficult life he has, slaving four days a week at the Times Lit office, with three children under five, in his mid-fifties, no rest, no repose, not even a room to work in his little four roomed house – No. 326 Strode Rd [Virginia Water] explains it – yet never a complaint or a loss of serenity or of integrity or concentration.'[2]

He could not leave it there, but tried to arrange a civil list pension for Blunden. Failing in that, he wrote to enlist Vaughan Williams's help in organizing financial aid from admirers. Ursula Wood replied on his behalf, after 'consultation and advice', pointing out that 'unless you can give him as much money as he is *earning*, it's no good'. She thought that there was a difference between accepting money in an emergency and living on it. 'Charles Lamb did earn *his*, didn't he? I know that both you & I & Bob [Trevelyan] are more or less lilies of the field, so it's very hard not to wish equal freedom available to all others.' She suggested collecting money to give Blunden a long holiday to help his bronchial trouble, but Ralph thought 'it would be wrong & unfair to make him throw up a good job' and that to try to change the course of his life might be difficult and 'verging on the impertinent'.[3]

NSP

During 1950 Newbury String Players gave thirteen concerts, more than ever before in one year, round the now traditional midsummer concert at Bucklebury and Christmas at Enborne. A local harpist made it possible to do Britten's *Ceremony of Carols*, Elgar's *Sospiri* and Vaughan Williams's *Greensleeves*. A local flautist, Catherine Powell, daughter of the past senior-master at Bedales, joined them for Quantz and Haydn concertos; through her teacher the distin-

[1]   17 September 1950.
[2]   22 May 1951.
[3]   18 December 1950.

guished Dutch flautist Johannes Feltkamp came to play. Gerald revived Stanley's Overture to *The Fall of Egypt* (the first performance since 1774) and his Concertos Nos. 4 and 5. The young John Constable played Walter Leigh's piano Concertino with them. The following year NSP went for the first time to Laverstoke Mills, the house of Lord and Lady Portal.

1951 opened cheerfully, with a full diary ahead. Worcester had agreed to repeat *Intimations* in September, and Gerald had no big work on the stocks. If he seemed a little tired, it was not to be wondered at: 'I'm not surprised the *Intimations* took it out of you,'[4] wrote Robin in April.

May was a month of culmination. On 5 May NSP performed Kenneth Leighton's *Veris Gratia*, composed for them and dedicated to Gerald and Joy. By now many young composers had heard of the little orchestra and its composer–conductor, always ready to read new scores and give a performance if at all possible. Among them was Stephen Dodgson, who had recently left the RCM. Catherine Powell suggested that he should write something for her, so he composed a Divertimento for flute and strings; and came down for a run-through, 'suffering torments of self-doubt'. 'GF struck me as instantly kindly, but reserved & (perhaps) a bit shy.' His conducting was 'more of the encouraging than dominating kind'. It was Joy who was most vividly in evidence, as the day-to-day organizer. What impressed Dodgson most about the whole event was that 'they all belonged very closely together – friction between players & conductor was unthinkable. GF was careful, conscientious & pleasant to me, but didn't actually particularly encourage me (I don't think he too much cared for the music – I don't blame him!) or discourage me.'[5] Dodgson was quite right. 'Interesting but rather ungrateful writing,' Gerald told Robin, 'which no-one except the composer, a nice chap, enjoyed!'[6]

RESEARCH

On 8 May 1951 Finzi read a paper to the Royal Musical Association summing up his Stanley researches. To illustrate how context changes perception, he began with his favourite story (see p. 112) of the Frenchman who found the writings of Seneca exaggerated, but on rereading them during the revolution found them to be reasonable and true. 'Such a re-orientation' was needed for English music of the mid-eighteenth century. Addressing the Royal Musical Association, the senior research body in the country, Finzi deplored the complete lack of biographical and critical literature for the period 1710–80. 'Works remain uncollected and judgments are still based on nineteenth-century estimates.' Most new editions were stylistically bad and texturally incorrect. He did not deny that Arne, Boyce, Avison, Felton, and Stanley were not of Handel's stature, but too often they were dismissed as his imitators. 'We should remember Francis Quarles's "if he cannot bring a cedar, let him bring a shrub".' Avison, whose later revisions of his earlier concertos were of partic-

4   14 April 1951.
5   Letter of 10 December 1980.
6   22 May 1951.

ular interest, was not mentioned as a composer in the Oxford History of Music. The 1927 *Grove* repeated inaccuracies about Felton copied from Rimbault in 1869, in turn copied from Busby in 1819 and Burney in 1789. 'This is not research: it is pure village gossip.' The name of Boyce, 'a far bigger man', is not 'even to be found in the index of the Royal Musical Association. His work remains scattered and uncollected.'

'And so to John Stanley.' Here Finzi gathers up his own research, with tributes to Mollie Sands and W. C. Smith. First he disposes of Handel. The Oxford History told us that Stanley's eighth organ voluntary was in the style of Handel's organ concertos, but the 'rest show no special leaning to the Handelian manner'. Stanley wrote thirty voluntaries, says Finzi. 'Apparently twenty-nine of them are like himself, and one is like Handel; so why bring in Handel?' Then he fills out Stanley's life with new detail, taking a swipe or two at Sir John Hawkins's daughter Laetitia, 'this vinegarish woman', whose memoirs he considered unreliable. He corrects and amplifies the publication dates given in the British Museum catalogue. He was not uncritical, even damning *Jephtha* as 'lifeless'. Speaking of Stanley's cantatas, he comments that the eighteenth-century cantata carried within it 'the seeds of perfection'. 'Unity of subject-matter was conveyed in diversity of vocal treatment, the recitative, either stromentato or secco, and the aria.' (Was he by any chance thinking of *Dies Natalis*?) Then he reveals his great discovery: that the overtures to *The Power of Music* and *Pan and Syrinx*, long attributed to Boyce, were in fact composed by Stanley.

With its new facts and new estimates based on wide, practical knowledge, the lecture reads extremely well: challenging, but full of wit and charm. Even better, it was illustrated. Finzi had gathered students from the Guildhall School of Music to play the whole of Stanley's First Concerto from Op. 2, and to sing 'By the moon's soft beaming light' from Cantata No. 2 of the second set; the duet 'Ah! to be guilty and to die' from *Zimri*; 'The turtle lamenting the loss of her mate' and 'Welcome death' from *Teraminta*; and the duet 'The gliding stream' from *The Fall of Egypt*.

Despite Gerald's dislike of prejudice, his attitude to Handel did strike some of his friends as prejudiced. Naturally he felt vexed that critical opinion had allowed Handel to overshadow his contemporaries, Gerald's chosen composers. But there was a moral element in his reaction: he was strongly influenced by Sedley Taylor's *The Indebtedness of Handel to Works by other Composers* (1906), and felt that in his 'borrowings' Handel was at best unscrupulous. For all Gerald's admiration for Boyce, he could not agree with him that, according to Stafford Smith (1750–1836), Handel 'takes Pebbles and turns them into Diamonds'. In 1954 he told Cedric Thorpe Davie 'I still feel Puritanical after Sedley Taylor's book and Max Seiffert's article on the Telemann thefts, and don't find any excuses for Handel are justified.'[7]

---

7   28 April 1954.

BLUNDEN AND GURNEY

Back from Tokyo, Edmund Blunden, with his wife Claire and their three children, stayed at Ashmansworth during May 1951 to select poems for a Gurney volume. Gerald and Edmund had laid plans for this at the 1950 repeat of *For St Cecilia* (when owing to the Albert Hall's echo poor Edmund heard none of his words). Interest in Gurney had been revived by an American student, Don Ray, who wanted to write a thesis on him. 'Can one really get the background of G's mind, the innumerable places & people, poets & composers, who went to his making – from Los Angeles?'[8] wondered Gerald. But his reply to Ray was long and helpful.

During the week Blunden (fiercely confined by Gerald to the book-room) selected the poems and wrote the elegant sympathetic Memoir. By the end Gerald liked the man as much as he admired his work. John Betjeman, whom Gerald had sounded out in 1951 about a civil list pension for Edmund, came over from Wantage for a meal, finding his host 'a shock-headed man and an agreeable presence'.[9] Gerald showed them some of Ann Bowes-Lyon's verse, sad, he told Toty de Navarro, that she had been discouraged by that 'pontifical, withering T. S. Eliot'. 'No words can express the excellent memory into which our stay with you is now graduated,' wrote Edmund in thanks. 'I fear we were a tumultuous crew. It was a sort of voyage, the bright sea of passing spring played all its colours and lights and breezy fragmentary melodies all round the ark.' He reported that Sidgwick & Jackson (the publishers of Gurney's early volumes) considered that generous financial support would be needed for any book showing his later work – 'a "sheaf" *might* be selected but his curious way of writing along until the sudden great word arises makes that hard to be content with'.[10] He hoped that Marion Scott would strengthen his Memoir, though Gerald warned him that she was a 'remarkable little person, in her combination of fragility, iron will & propriety: but she can drive one crazy with delays and postponements'.[11]

Then on 14 July 1951 Gerald was fifty. The Royal Academy of Music arranged a special concert of his music. On 8 July Scott Goddard broadcast about him in *Music Magazine*. But it must have seemed ironic to Gerald, for by then he had been forced to add a postscript to the introduction, Absalom's Place (see p. 122), to his Catalogue of Works:

> Since the preceding pages were written, ten years ago, a good deal more work has been written. Performances, publication & some kindly and generous notice, have all taken place, which I hope my development has justified.
>
> But a serious, & possibly fatal, illness has now been confirmed by the Doctors. At forty-nine I feel I have hardly begun my work.

---

[8]   10 October 1950.
[9]   Letter of 29 July 1982.
[10] 26 May 1951.
[11] 14 June 1951.

My thread is cut, and yet it is not spun;
And now I live, and now my life is done.[12]

As usually happens, it is likely that new ideas, new fashions & the pressing
forward of new generations, will soon obliterate my small contribution. Yet I
like to think that in each generation may be found a few responsive minds,
and for them I shd still like the work to be available. To shake hands with a
good friend over the centuries is a pleasant thing, and the affection which an
individual may retain after his departure is perhaps the only thing which
guarantees an ultimate life to his work.

He signed it, Gerald Finzi, June 1951.

THE BLACK BOOK

What had happened can best be told in Finzi's own words. He had a scholar's
instinct for preservation. He had been employing it for poor distracted
Gurney; for dying-out apple breeds; for neglected English composers. Now, he
turned it on to himself. He took a strong black hard-covered ledger-sized
book. On the opening left-hand page he wrote the Vaughan quotation in
Latin, which he had already used (englished by Blunden) in the introduction
to his Catalogue in 1941, and repeated now with painful force:

To After Ages
Time soon forgets; and yet I would not have
The present wholly mouldering in the grave.
Hear then, posterity.

He numbered the pages up to thirty-seven. On the first page he wrote information about his father. On the fourth page are comments on his sister Kate,
with the chilling dismissal:

I at least learnt from her that the world can be divided into two types:– those
who care for the thing itself & those who care for the appearance of the
thing. As she belongs to the latter category & I to the former I have not found
it possible to be very interested in her activities.

Then each page has a single, heavy roman numeral heading. Most of them are
blank. Some pages have been cut away. On page VI is a note about his associations with Ivor Gurney's work. On loose separate sheets tucked into the book
are a first draft of the page on his father, and a note on his father's father
(drawn on in earlier chapters). There is also the following:

Felix John Finzi 11/8/1893 – 3/8/1913
Douglas Louis Finzi 17/2/1897 – 7/7/1912
Edgar Cecil Finzi 17/12/1898 – 5/9/1918
Gerald Raphael Finzi 14/7/1901 – ?
Katie Finzi 28/2/1890

[12] Chidiock Tichborne (?1558–86), from his poem that begins 'My prime of youth is but a
frost of cares', written in the Tower three days before his execution for complicity in the
Babington conspiracy to free Mary Queen of Scots.

though the handwriting here is much earlier, and might date from before he
went into Midhurst Sanatorium.

On page 2 is 'A note on my illness', written with many crossings-out and
second thoughts. He was, he wrote, in his mid-forties (1946) when he first
noticed a very small lump in the back of his neck, which for at least a year he
took to be a boil or a spot. Later, glands in his chin began to swell rapidly.

> Then I thought it time to see our great friend & Doctor Tom Scott. I was then
> forty-nine. Controlled & detached as doctors are (or shd be) it was perhaps
> because of our personal friendship that I sensed at once that he took a
> serious view of what I thought to be . . . [the sentence is incomplete]

At hospital a small gland from his neck and marrow from his chest bone were
removed, and the diagnosis was one of the reticuloses that had then only
recently been separated from Hodgkins Disease – as Finzi wrote in the Black
Book: 'Giant follikular reticuloses'.

Dr Scott arranged for him to see Professor Leslie Witts, the occupant of the
Nuffield Chair of Medicine at Oxford, and an authority on that group of
diseases, 'for him to give me the verdict, having told him that I cd stand the
truth. Joy came with me. After several minutes of turning over of papers &
side glances he said "Well, what can I do for you." I replied:

> I shd like to know the truth. Is it serious.
> W. It's bad, but it's not the worst.
> F. Wd my life be insurable
> W. No.
> F. Do you give five years
> W. Possibly, at the very most ten.

AFTER THE VERDICT

They were able to cope only by disregarding the verdict. Lymphoid-follicular
reticulosis can be described as cancer of the lymph nodes (the modern name
for it is non-Hodgkins lymphoma). The sentence was long enough for it to
become part of life. As Professor Witts got to know Gerald, he told him he
might even live fifteen years, he was such a strong and resilient man. Gerald
had always had a sense of the shortness and pressure of time – intimations of
mortality – so that in a way the verdict only confirmed something he had
already known. For Joy, it was almost a relief to have the matter clarified, as for
some time she had been worried. They both felt that the quality of life, not its
length, was what mattered. 'The great thing now was to do as much as you
could before you went.'

For Gerald's sake, it was essential that no-one should know. He had to keep
his privacy. He could not have stood pity, or questions, or covert looks: he
would have been constantly reminded of his condition. But Gerald and Joy
told their sons, hoping that as they were young and growing the news would
fade into the background: five or ten years is a long time when you are seven-

teen and fifteen. To begin with, there was no apparent change in Gerald; he had a course of radiotherapy to reduce the swelling of the lymphatic glands. He was not exactly ill; and life had to go on. That was the summer of 1951.

In September that year David Willcocks (in his first festival at Worcester) 'got a superb performance of *Intimations* and William Herbert sang *Farewell to Arms* like an angel',[13] Gerald wrote to Cedric Thorpe Davie, noting with pleasure that he had had a work performed at the Three Choirs for each of the past six years. He continued his efforts on other men's behalf. With Edmund Blunden he went to see Rupert Hart-Davis about the Gurney poems. Robin Milford directed the first performance of his *The Forsaken Merman* with NSP and Downe House choir, and Gerald persuaded Vaughan Williams to hear a run-through of Tony Scott's *Sinfonietta* and Kenneth Leighton's *Violin Concerto* (played by Frederick Grinke and Howard Ferguson). Robin wrote to thank Gerald 'for all the selfless & loving work that went into my "Merman" . . . unpaid work is indeed giving . . . You & Joy give so much to so many.'[14] He told him that Tony too had said how 'marvellously painstaking & kind' Gerald had been. Rubbra reported that Gerald's NSP work 'was spoken of in the highest terms' at an Arts Council Meeting. Coming at this moment, such gratitude must have warmed his heart.

A younger man, John Russell, had been to hear Elgar's *The Apostles* at the 1947 Three Choirs. Meaning to leave when it ended, he was trapped by the crowded audience into hearing *Dies Natalis*, and (like Herbert Howells with *Tallis* in 1910) lost his heart. Russell became music adviser to Reading Education Committee, and met Gerald, who in 1948 recommended him as conductor of Newbury Choral Society. He used to call at Ashmansworth for tea on his way to his weekly rehearsal, when his admiration quickly warmed to devotion. In 1951 he persuaded Gerald to allow him to give the first performance at Reading of an old Romance of 1928. Gerald dedicated it to 'John Russell, Musician'.

1951, JOURNAL RESUMED

That autumn, 1951, after a gap of six years, Joy took up her Journal again, with one laconic introductory sentence: *After the verdict and first course Xray treatment.* On 15 November she records *Finished slow movement of cello concerto.* Gerald filled no more pages of his Black Book; since none was dated, it is impossible to do more than speculate that he began it soon after the verdict. It is speculation, too, that the time he might have spent filling the blank pages went instead into his Cello Concerto, Grand Fantasia and Toccata, and *In Terra Pax*. 'Being is the great explainer,' he quoted from Thoreau to Tony Scott[15] a few months later. Composing was the centre of his life. The simple accolade he had admired on Parry's memorial and had just bestowed on the young John Russell was what

---

[13] 8 September 1951.
[14] 9 October 1951.
[15] 11 January 1952.

he most wanted for himself: musician. From then on Joy kept her Journal fairly regularly; but the content and manner changed. It is more of an exterior record of events. The progress of Gerald's compositions and of his health is charted unemotionally. There are few references to world events, for there was no war looming. Far more names cross the pages. Since Gerald had left the Ministry, his Ashmansworth home had become a centre: the nucleus of constant old friends had many new rings round it, of young performers, composers, and researchers. Still basically a shy man, Gerald had become accustomed to people. During the war he had worked among strangers and his house was filled with evacuees; then his growing children brought in their own friends. He could always escape to his private end of the house, safe behind his double doors; but the security of his marriage had stilled many apprehensions. Joy too had altered. She occasionally records one of Gerald's letters, and often his opinions, but seldom his words, more often her own paraphrase. In the war, apart from him, she had grown independent. On occasion, whether she realized it or not, she was surely writing for the eye of a stranger.

The first performance of Gerald's anthem 'God is gone up', for the St Cecilia's Day service, was on 22 November. After the rehearsal they went as Dick Latham's guests to the Madrigal Society's dinner (Latham was the musical director). The next day Gerald went to the luncheon after the service, then dashed back to conduct an NSP concert at Andover where he revived, after a hundred and fifty years, Charles Wesley's fourth Piano Concerto, which the seventeen-year-old John Constable played.

Edmund Blunden had come to the rehearsal of the anthem, and Joy noted that he looked overworked. He had just found Gurney's manuscript draft of Clare's 'Ploughman Singing', which he had dedicated to Blunden. Gerald managed to get the dedication into the proofs of the third book of songs, published in 1952 – a happy association in view of Blunden's rediscovery of Clare. For this volume Marion Scott added her and Herbert Howells's recollections of Gurney's performance of his own songs. Edmund was being drawn into Gerald's eighteenth-century research. He gave him a Foundling Hospital book with three unknown Stanley hymns (Gerald had now handed over his Stanley material to Mollie Sands). A verse by Hawkesworth in the book shocked Gerald: 'what blind spots amongst a civilized people to expect children to sing about themselves:

> Left on the worlds bleak waste forlorn,
> In sin conceiv'd, to sorrow born
> By guilt and shame foredoom'd to share
> No mother's love, no father's care.'[16]

Edmund replied cheerfully that at Christ's Hospital 'in the old days the young

---

[16] 28 November 1951.

had to sing about their miserable condition etc, but it doesn't seem to have depressed them a bit'.[17]

Finzi and Britten shared the conviction that no poem need be outside a composer's range of choice: both set Wordsworth, Britten set Eliot and Finzi set Hardy, each collaborated with a living poet, Britten with Auden, Finzi with Blunden. Though Finzi did not admire Britten's music, he kept up with it. The first performance of Britten's *Billy Budd* was broadcast on 1 December. Gerald realized it was unfair to judge a broadcast of a stage work; but the music struck him as *almost worthless though brilliantly presented*, Joy noted in the Journal: *There are some exciting things such as the battle, the sailors' pseudo shanty, and many novelties, even novelties of banality, but he feels him to be the Meyerbeer of this age* [how much Meyerbeer had Finzi heard? Maybe this was Parry's influence?]. *Rubbra phoned up in between the acts completely exasperated by it.* The next morning's papers hailed it *as the greatest musical event since the war . . . It is odd how these fashionable hysterias can overwhelm the public in every decade*, mused Gerald, wondering how the musical world could take seriously *as a profound work a piece of flimsy mysticism covering a homosexual story!!* They wished they could know the verdict of 1990. *In fairness G feels that there may be some deficiency in himself which makes him unable to appreciate opera as a whole because he found Bliss's* The Olympians *an unsatisfactory work and VW's* Pilgrim's Progress *a failure – in this case perhaps production.*

He was, it seems, thinking of contemporary opera, for Benjamin's *The Devil Take Her* and *Prima Donna* and Menotti's *The Consul* were *'recent works which have delighted and moved him the most'*. (He came also to admire Walton's *Troilus and Cressida*.) A week later they went to Wellesz's *Incognita* at Oxford, but it received no critical comment. Vaughan Williams and Ursula were there too, and the Finzis brought them home to *ovaltine and bread and cheese in the kitchen warmth and then sat over the wood fire talking*, Joy recorded. *Cats perched on VW. At 3.30 he said 'I hope I am not keeping you young people up.' He was first up next morning and walking to see the day while I made breakfast.*

The first performance of Gerald's Christmas anthem 'All this night' at St Paul's Cathedral *sounded very well and trumpet like*; and the London visit gave him a chance to collect more of Parry's manuscripts to bring home to sort. Since 1948 he had kept up with Lady Ponsonby. They had exchanged visits, he finding at Shulbrede Priory two apple trees not in the National Collection – 'music, children & apples! What could be nicer,'[18] she wrote to him. He had listed Parry's manuscripts at the RCM (where he ran up against Dyson's bureaucracy – Henry Havergal *should succeed Dyson at the College* – his *warmth and vitality to redeem it*). He rounded up further manuscripts from Emily Daymond and Susan Lushington, persuaded Curwens to publish the two Intermezzi for string trio of 1884, and searched for the Parry letters of the Bridges–Parry correspondence. In April 1950 Lady Ponsonby sent him a cheque in gratitude, which he insisted on putting towards a Parry reprinting fund. He was keen to have at least extracts (including 'To everything there is a season'!) from the choral works in print, to keep Parry's music in performance at this time when he was neither a contemporary nor a historical figure.

In December Gerald and Joy drove to Somerset and stayed overnight with Arthur Bliss. *In his delightful way he put forward alien views — recognition and performance are entirely result of social contacts — that he cared nothing for his posthumous reputation only what it brought in for his descendants.* Perhaps Joy was taking his teasing too literally. She thought that the subject of his *Adam Zero* ballet (an allegory of the cycle of man's life) ran through his thought and had *done much to mellow the brilliant figure of thirty years ago, so that now he realizes that each generation is a repeating wave with a different twist in its manner.* Next morning, *when a red sun rose over the frosted wood like a chinese painting,* they drove to Merriott to meet Michael Wallace of Scotts Nursery, *gathered plants and home through frost under the moon. A lovely break. G very happy.*

The following day, however, an examination at Oxford found Gerald's glands again active. The Finzis had tea afterwards with Percy Scholes, and liked his dry humour and admired his music library *indexed and cross referenced in a wonderful method.* There were more treatments on the spleen and the arms; and though Gerald, sending a copy of 'All this night' in a Christmas letter to Toty de Navarro, wrote 'I've nothing much to report; a couple of male voice part-songs; an anthem for the St Cecilia service at St Sepulchre's last month; this unaccompanied motet,'[19] Joy's last Journal entry for 1951 notes *increasing awareness of the possible shortness of time left.*

[19] 23 December 1951.

CHAPTER THIRTEEN

Speculation

1952–53

In the dark days of January 1952, encouraged by John Russell, Gerald began scoring the slow movement (Eclogue, see p. 221) of his early Piano Concerto, and then the slow movement of a Cello Concerto, which Anna Shuttleworth tried over with him. His positive reaction to the X-ray treatment was cheering, so was their sons' playing for the first time with Newbury String Players, well enough to make a real contribution.

Gerald was at a piano run-through of Vaughan Williams's Sinfonia Antartica on 25 January. He was not totally impressed: the very fact that it falls back on texts for each movement shows some of its weakness, Joy recorded in her Journal. After the 1953 Oxford performance under Barbirolli he wrote to Vaughan Williams that there was a huge audience and standing room only. As with Marie Lloyd — hundreds turned away! Vaughan Williams took him and Kiffer to the dress rehearsal of Wozzeck. They were told that the orchestral playing was bad and the vocal lines nowhere near accurate at times but to Gerald, noted Joy blandly, neither of these things would have been apparent. He had heard Boult's concert performance in 1934 and felt that seeing the work was less impressive than hearing it, and being one's own stage. He had found Billy Budd, listened to as music, unbearably tawdry, whereas Wozzeck had made a tremendous impression. Then Vaughan Williams gave them seats for the revised Pilgrim's Progress for which there was, the Journal notes rather naively, an entirely different audience from Wozzeck. Gerald still felt the weakest part to be after the release from prison where instead of moving on the Pilgrim has a long dissertation of not the best VW and it becomes a bore. (It comes as a shock to find Gerald calling Vaughan Williams a bore!)

They attended a concert in London in February 1952, as Vaughan Williams had persuaded and subsidised Boyd Neel to perform some of the composers Gerald championed; Vaughan Williams described Tony Scott's Sinfonietta 'as being like the Grosse Fugue with knobs on'; the Journal considered it an extraordinary powerful work — the result of frustration and difficulty . . . Lacking all technical facility the work makes up for it with an inward fury. Both the other pieces had already had first performances by NSP. Leighton's Veris Gratia — mellifluous and beautiful — gave Gerald the chance to contrast Leighton's flowering genius at twenty-two with Scott's thwarted inarticulate talent at forty-two, and make a favourite comment: Talent allied to character is often more powerful and effective than natural genius. He cited Bax, Bantock, and Britten as examples of natural genius, in that way outshining the natural ability of Vaughan Williams who had to struggle with force of character for articulation. The third work, Milford's Elegiac Meditation, had, they thought, a poor performance. A few weeks later Jean Stewart and NSP played it in Stockcross church, with *a passion and intensity which quite put the dead, disinterested* [sic] *Boyd Neel performance into the shade.* On that occasion the Finzis may well have been right. But their disdain of professionalism and technical efficiency, going back in Gerald's case at least as far as Boughton and the Glastonbury Festival in 1920, was part of their anti-establishment attitude and the complement to their amateur activities.

Gerald's views on the amateur linked into his views on heredity and environment. In the magazine *Mercury* (Spring 1950) he wrote: 'We are told that genius will always out. There is no greater fallacy than this cliché. It is easy enough to point to some isolated figure and to overlook the mute inglorious Miltons. . . . Civilization consists of the finest things of the finest minds and not only drain pipes and refrigerators.' With his experience in playing to schools with NSP, he deplored the early division of children into musical and unmusical. The introduction of peacetime compulsory national service in 1948 for men between eighteen and twenty-six distressed him unbearably; it had 'a devastating effect on a boy who has kept an instrument going through all the difficulties of school life, and then, in his late teens, is obliged to give it up completely'. Supported by Lady Ponsonby, he rounded up his friends to sign with him a letter to *The Times.* As to his feelings in general, 'the last eight lines of "Summer" in [Vita] Sackville-West's *Land* says all that there is to be said about it'.[1] He had known the poem since 1927, when he had commented on it to Jack Haines:

> Much goes to little making, – law and skill,
> Tradition's usage, each man's separate gift;
> Till the slow worker sees that he has wrought
> More than he knew of builded truth,
> As one who slips through years of youth,
> Leaving his young indignant rage,
> And finds the years' insensible drift
> Brings him achievement with the truce of age.

Writing to Tony Scott after the Boyd Neel concert, Gerald picked up the point Joy had made in the Journal. 'I often feel,' he wrote, 'if life were long enough (which it won't be) that I shd like to develope the text which I used in the Parry talk, "Men are great or small, not by the language they use, but by their stature." It's a failure to grasp such an obvious fact which lies at the back of all the second-rate, schoolboy level musical criticism which floods the world.'[2]

1952–53, NSP AND RESEARCH

Perhaps the Boyd Neel concert prompted Joy to ponder on what had become by its very success a real problem. Newbury String Players, started in the war to keep *spiritual activities alive locally*, meant that Gerald was tied every weekend,

---

[1]   To Scott, June 1950.
[2]   22 February 1952.

save at Christmas and for a six-week summer break. Players could miss an odd rehearsal, but he never could. After twelve years, Joy longed for someone to *share the work and take over entirely*. It was too valuable to drop, but there was no money for a salaried conductor. Besides, it needed an exceptional person to deal with *twenty-five or so self-centred amateurs*, who for all their keenness and loyalty had *to put their musical interest second to personal ones*; and the conductor would need to keep adding fresh works, old and new, to hold the players' attention. Joy thought back over the first chances given to young composers and instrumentalists, and concluded that such an organization had more than local importance. In her last sentence for that Journal entry one can see what had prompted the speculation of this impersonal and far-sighted woman: there *was no likely successor in the event of G suddenly having to give up.*

Since giving his Royal Musical Association talk on Stanley, Gerald had become sought after as well as being a seeker. Charles Cudworth, the Cambridge librarian, brought to his attention another later (1780) set of concertos, in the Rowe Music Library. Gerald was able to incorporate this information when he revised his lecture for publication in *Tempo*. Denis Stevens, then a BBC producer, suggested some Stanley broadcasts for 1953. Gerald was now digging deeper into his chosen period. He had come across some keyboard concertos by the young Charles Wesley (1757–1834), brother of Samuel. They had one foot in the world of Boyce (whose pupil he was), he told Cedric Thorpe Davie, and the other in the world of Mozart. Gerald edited three little Wesley string quartets, which he thought simple enough to be useful for inexperienced players before they approached Haydn, and was disappointed when Boosey & Hawkes refused to publish them, though they took the Stanley concertos Nos. 1 and 2 during 1952. In 1953 Hinrichsen accepted the Wesleys, and also published Stanley's aria 'Welcome Death'. Gerald was now discovering the composers John Garth (c. 1722–c. 1810) and Mudge (1718–63). W. C. Smith was asked about Mudge, and was able to supply his first name, Richard, which had eluded Gerald. Gerald sent some Festing concertos to Adam Carse, who was looking for works for a series he was editing. This promoted a discussion on how far solo parts were embellished. Gerald sent Carse extracts from Avison's 1752 *Essay*, and he and Joy visited him, old, ill and housebound, in July 1952.

Gerald's main energy, however, was directed to William Boyce. In 1951 he had asked Ceddie about parts for Boyce's Twelve Overtures of 1770, as the British Museum set lacked second trumpet parts. The search took him to visit Leslie Bridgewater, the theatre musical director, who was adept at eighteenth-century pastiche. Bridgewater owned a set, but it was incomplete. He surprised Gerald by disclosing an interest in twelve-tone music, and had analysed Schoenberg's Piano Concerto bar by bar. Then Gerald's letter to Ceddie on 23 January 1952 describes the moment any researcher longs for: 'I was over at the Bodleian recently and asked to see a shelf number concerned with Boyce and found myself faced with a complete truck of fifty manuscript volumes of Odes fifty ditto of original parts and fifty ditto of vocal parts.' Here was the missing trumpet part, but also much else. On 13 February 1952 Joy recorded in her Journal that Gerald had spent a day at the Bodleian. *He feels despair at the amount of music which lies unpublished.* There was, she said, a vast quantity of Boyce there, including all the Birthday and New Year Odes and instrumental works, some very fine. (The Master of the King's Band was expected to produce odes annually, though they were heard by few and never repeated.) *The vocal aspect is another problem for all the words are rubbish. Perhaps if they were sung in a foreign language there wd be less difficulty in accepting the odes nowadays, but it is a dreadful thing that such a figure regarded in his lifetime as second only to Handel & thro whose work a great personality exudes, shd remain unpublished and well nigh unrecognised except for a piece here & there.*

With so many varied interests, however did Gerald find time to compose? One activity fed another. There were house gatherings at concert weekends when a string quartet might be present, and would try over anything Gerald wanted to hear. The young professionals playing with NSP were helpful in many ways. Stephen Trier made suggestions for the solo part of the Clarinet Concerto. Anna Shuttleworth tried over the Garth cello concertos (a rare form in England in 1760), then performed them with NSP. The bassoonist William Waterhouse, studying the historical development of his instrument, became useful in the eighteenth-century research, and as a second pair of eyes in proof-reading Gerald's own compositions. It was for Bill that Gerald revived 'Softly rise, O southern breeze' with a bassoon solo from Boyce's *Solomon*. He and Gerald exchanged catalogue information: Bill was exploring the repertory, and was glad to hear of Parry's Nonet.

Gerald was now in demand for writing articles and giving lectures. In April 1952 he went to Liverpool to talk to the National Union of Students on 'Some Aspects of English Eighteenth-century Music'. He had stipulated a small body of strings, a pianist, and some singers to perform his illustrations, but he had overestimated their capacity. At 7p.m. Joy had an SOS by phone, and in half an hour she and the boys were on the road with sleeping bags, instruments, and food. She drove till 2.30a.m. *Stoke-on-Trent was a disappointment — no flaring furnaces — electric kilns making a pink cloud over.* They tried to sleep in a field — *laughed too much — rather cold and not very comfortable*. Rising at five — *lovely dawn* — they arrived in time to join the rehearsal at 10a.m. for Gerald's lecture at 11.30. After lunch they set off south, to stay overnight with the Sumsions. The next morning the family visited Gerald's mother, now living in an old people's home near Gloucester.

1952, ST ANDREWS

In September 1951 came an official invitation to be external examiner for three years at St Andrews University, where Cedric Thorpe Davie was professor. After consulting Dr Witts, Gerald accepted with some confidence, though he told Ceddie that 'for me to travel to St Andrews is about as great an event as Livingstone travelling to darkest Africa or a dairy maid setting off for fairest Polynesia'.[3] With a nice touch of self-mockery he asked 'Does one need DDT

3   8 September 1951.

in third class sleepers? I imagine that Border raids are a thing of the past & that no revolver or blunderbuss is necessary!'[4] He prepared the written examination papers with Ceddie. Two of his suggested questions came very near home. He gave his favourite quotation from Quiller-Couch: ' "There are streams which suddenly dive into chasms and are lost – to emerge into daylight at long distance, having pierced their own way through subterranean channels." Apply this analogy to any composer whose reputation was lost and subsequently revived.' What meaning this had for Finzi, so shortly after finding the 'truck' of Boyce's unpublished manuscripts! The other question shows that the memory of his tobacco merchant uncles still rankled. 'An imaginary uncle, who strongly disapproves of the idea that you should take up music as a profession, writes you his reasons. Give his letter in not more than two hundred and fifty words.'

So in May 1952 Gerald and Joy went off to St Andrews, both travelling third class on Gerald's first class allowance. *Scarlet cloaks of the university students made lovely colour.* Gerald was impressed with Ceddie's wide musical teaching, and enjoyed the university choir and Scottish country dancing. *They all lack aesthetic awareness or taste,* Joy thought about the Scots, *but are very kindly welcoming people with lovely voices. Returned laden with plants.*

Early summer brought Vaughan Williams's *Oxford Elegy* at Oxford, and after the concert the Finzis took Vaughan Williams and Ursula home 'to the evening scents of their garden, with jasmine fully out over their welcoming door'. Vaughan Williams was amazed that Gerald knew he had cited a quotation from Matthew Arnold's poem in his early unpublished work, *Harnham Down*. Ernest Farrar had conducted it at South Shields in 1912 and introduced it to Gerald. *Then VW was the rising young composer and the order of the day was 'out-of-door' music, Whitman, Norfolk jackets, pastoral impressions* . NSP gave their hundred and fifteenth concert, at High Wycombe, where Wilfred Brown (who had taught Gerald's sons at Bedales) sang *Dies Natalis* for the first time under its composer's direction and Edmund Rubbra played Bloch's Concerto Grosso and Walter Leigh's Concertino. Afterwards, the Finzis went back to the Rubbras' cottage near Speen in the Chilterns – *summer evening – summer garden – and lovely grown over little valley.* Rubbra played them his Violin Concerto, which they admired.

1952, BLUNDEN, SASSOON, LETHABY

They picked up the Blundens at Reading on the way home and took them back for a week. Gerald was by now *devoted to Edmund and a great admirer of his mind.* While he was there, Edmund's old friend Siegfried Sassoon came over for an evening, and the two First War poets revived memories of Passchendaele on its anniversary. *It was a curious experience for Gerald* to meet one of *the daring young poets* of his early manhood, now going on for seventy, Joy recorded; did she perhaps notice the similarity between the ancestrally foreign Sassoon and Finzi, both with quintessentially English personas? Sassoon she found to be *a*

---

4   23 March 1952.

shy nervous egotistical man — much absorbed by his devotion to his young sixteen-year-old son. A rapid delightful talker — soon at his ease. But it was Blunden — over-worked — asthmatical — strained to the last degree but beautifully serene who struck Gerald as having the more penetrating mind.

Gerald consulted him on behalf of old Alfred Powell, architect and potter, brother of Oswald, Second Master at Bedales. Powell had been a life-long friend of the designer W. R. Lethaby, the first principal of the Central School of Arts and Crafts, and a founder of the Art Workers' Guild. He had some 'aphorisms' of his, and asked Gerald's advice. Gerald and Edmund proposed that an extract should be published in the Times Literary Supplement (which it eventually was, on 17 April 1953). Gerald wanted Edmund to meet Powell: 'Old age is nearly always dust & ashes, but here is rather a glorious one.'[5] Soon afterwards Edmund was looking at some letters from Leigh Hunt to Vincent Novello, and considered that Novello's circle 'wants its book, but it needs a musician'.[6] 'Of course V. Novello needs a biographer,'[7] replied Gerald. He had seen a Boyce Concerto, which Novello had presented to the British Museum as a tribute to Dr Boyce, 'who, in my estimation, in purity of melody, solidity of harmony, and skillfull refinement in the construction of his sterling counterpoint, was one of the very best composers of the genuine English school'. Gerald sent Edmund a reprint of his RMA lecture on Stanley, to which Edmund responded, 'Please produce some companions to it on Jackson, Avison, Smith, and "little Hudson" [1732-1815] who made Coleridge and Lamb sing up, at C[hrist's] H[ospital].'[8] He had broken it to Gerald that he was shortly to go to Hong Kong. 'I can't help feeling a bit melancholy about the next gap of three years'[9] wrote Gerald, and — knowing his own chances — quoted (not quite accurately) Hardy's and his 'Summer schemes': 'But who shall say Of what may chance before that day.'

He had submitted his *Love's Labour's Lost* suite, including the songs, to the 1952 BBC Light Music Festival at Cheltenham, and it was gladly accepted. He had worked on it during April, on holiday in East Anglia at a windmill lent to the Scotts; the Scott and Finzi boys going sailing. The Suite was given on 20 July in a programme with two pieces from Eric Coates's *The Four Centuries*, about which Joy noted *absolute saccharine sentiment! He rolled away in a vast car — so much for sentiment!*

At the end of August Gerald and his elder son, old enough now to share his musical life, travelled to St Andrews to examine again. (Considering Kiffer's passion for Stravinsky and Bartók, 'he's extremely nice to me',[10] Gerald told Ceddie.) They saw *Highland Fair*, produced by Tyrone Guthrie, for which Ceddie had composed the music, and found it delightful, full of enchanting Scotch

5   11 July 1952.
6   8 July 1952.
7   11 July 1952.
8   14 July 1954.
9   17 July 1952.
10   1 October 1951.

tunes. Gerald and Joy went on to Hereford, though that year he had no work of his own performed at the festival. Vaughan Williams admired John Gardner's Symphony, but felt that his *Cantiones Sacrae* was written to order. Gerald pointed out that there was nothing wrong in that: Vaughan Williams did it himself (and Gerald had just completed an 'ordered' Magnificat). *V W: Yes: I quite agree so long as they don't sound as if they were written to order.* Joy noted that Herbert Howells *has very sweetly included G[erald] in his new clavichord book* (perhaps he told her of his intention; Howells composed two pieces 'for Gerald': 'Finzi's Rest', dated the day after his death, was published in 1961).

One concert at the Three Choirs prompted Gerald to speculate: *How reputations grow. The Mystical Songs and Tallis Fantasia were always what they are, but how few performances they got forty years ago.* He developed the thought in a letter (which Joy recorded) to the young composer, Bryan Kelly, who had brought him some work for an opinion. *'Nothing is more embarrassing than to see quite able composers trying to be in the swim.'* He instanced Frank Bridge, as a superb technician with little to say, successful when he used a language natural to him, but when he tried to adopt the 'middle European' style, *sterile beyond words. . . . Dont be too sure*, Gerald told Kelly, *that there is such a thing as 'progress' in music. There is only change and a difference of per- spective and style.* Was Mahler an improvement on Byrd? or J. C. Bach on J. S. Bach? or Schubert on Beethoven? It was equally necessary not to be preju- diced, *and to realise that the twelve-tone scale was as capable of moving us as any other idiom.* Blunden sent him the *Times Literary Supplement* fiftieth anniversary number, which reprinted reviews contemporary with earlier books' publication. It was another reminder 'that the ups & downs are the same in every generation', he wrote to Blunden. It was odd to read that the de la Mare poems 'were "often too harsh and clumsy and lacking in charm", but it remains to be seen whether the original slating of T. S. Eliot's "Prufrock" wasn't more justified than the present day would allow. (But then, I never fell. Not even the O M convinced me. Duveen [the Edwardian art dealer] got a peerage.)'[11]

Magnificat, Op. 36; Anthems, Op. 27; short choral pieces

During 1951 Gerald met the 'delightful Miss Dee Hiatt, who runs the [choral] music at Smith College, Massachusetts',[12] as he told Cedric Thorpe Davie. She brought her Chamber Singers on European tours in 1951 and 1952. Gerald did not care for American culture, and used to irritate Alice Sumsion and Trudy Bliss (both American-born) by his dismissive remarks. But he did admire Roy Harris, Copland, and Menotti; and a private recording of *Dies Natalis* made in 1943 by the American William Ventura under Bernard

---

[11] 24 July 1952.
[12] 20 August 1951.

Herrmann set him thinking of that work, up till then sung always by a soprano, sung by a tenor.

Iva Dee Hiatt asked him in 1950 for a non-liturgical Magnificat with organ. It was his first overseas commission, but not something he wished to compose: years in Bairstow's organ loft had made him over-familiar with *innumerable dreary automatic magnificats*, Joy noted in July 1952. He found it hard to *throw any new light on the words*, and was pressed for time. Possibly working against the grain forced a more athletic style on him. His setting is straightforward, strong, and direct. Unusually, he repeats words, even verses. The fine, striding opening theme returns refrain-like, on the third occasion sung meditatively by two women in turn (Dee Hiatt had asked that soloists could be drawn from the choir). He did not set the 'Gloria'; there is, however, a blissful Amen, written in the car on the way to the post office, which *followed the zero hour post to* the publishers.

Dee Hiatt spent a night with the Finzis, *trying to extract press notices from G's scanty collection for advertisement in America.* She conducted the Magnificat at the candlelit Christmas Vespers on 12 December 1952, with the organist Vernon Gotwals: it was, she believed, the first British work composed for an American college. There were two more performances that weekend, it was also broadcast, and made into a private record, so that altogether four thousand five hundred people heard it. 'The men of Amherst College [under Robert Beckwith], seven miles away, "hitch hiked" over to Smith College for the mixed chorus rehearsals and then "hitch hiked" home again in the frosty midnight air,'[13] which perhaps explains why Dee Hiatt originally had asked for a work for eighty women's voices only. Finzi scored the Magnificat for orchestra in 1956.

As a result of *For St Cecilia*, Finzi was invited to compose an anthem with organ for the 1951 St Cecilia Festival Service. His choice of the poet Edward Taylor (1644–1729) was that of a widely read man. Taylor, a Puritan in the metaphysical tradition, was born in England and emigrated to Boston, studying at Harvard; his devotional poems were not printed until 1937. Finzi's 'God is gone up' (Op. 27 No. 2) comprises two stanzas (the first repeated after the second) from Taylor's Meditation No. 20. The bold opening reflects, in the Elgar–Walton tradition, the ceremonial fanfares of *For St Cecilia*. Familiar Finzi moods, such as the haunting calls at 'mixing their music . . .' and the purity of 'More to enravish as they this tune sing . . .' beautifully endorse Taylor's 'heart-cramping notes of melody'. The marriage anthem 'My lovely one' (Op. 27 No. 1) was composed for Joy's sister Mags's wedding to Joseph Neate on 2 September 1946. Again to Taylor's words, from Meditation 12, it is inward and expressive, even a little sentimental, the dynamics never rising above a mezzo-forte. Dick Latham teased Finzi that the bride might at first be embarrassed at 'Oh, let thy Beauty give a glorious touch' and then be piqued to discover it was the Lord (and not her) being so praised. The longest of the three Op. 27 anthems is 'Welcome Sweet and Sacred Feast' (No. 3), composed

13 From Iva Dee Hiatt to Finzi, 17 December 1952.

at the invitation of the BBC Religious Broadcasting Department. Finzi went back to Henry Vaughan for the poem, 'The Holy Communion' (making brief cuts). The anthem is clearly by the inspired composer of *Lo, the Full, Final Sacrifice*, though the material is less memorable, and the piece is perhaps too sectional for its length. These shorter pieces, less ambitious than *For St Cecilia* and *Intimations of Immortality*, are in their modest way more perfectly realised. Finzi seems relaxed about allowing the occasional melisma and repeats for structure's sake. The music flows surely and easily.

'All this night' was composed for Charles Thornton Lofthouse (who had collaborated with NSP) and his University of London Musical Society. The poem appeared (No. 123) in the *Oxford Book of Carols*, but little was then known of the poet of slender output, William Austin (1587–1634), whom Traherne admired. Composed for four hundred unaccompanied mixed young voices to sing at Christmas at St Paul's Cathedral, the motet is vigorous and jubilant, demanding and effective. It has much *divisi* but almost no counterpoint, little imitation, Finzi no doubt taking into account the acoustics of the building. From the opening 'cock-crow' the chording is high and bright; a single dark moment leads to a thrilling climax that greets the sun's rising, the coming of Christ. The piece is as brilliant as it is brief.

The unison song 'Muses and graces' Op. 34, the words by Ursula Wood [VW], was composed for the twenty-first anniversary of Overstone School, Northamptonshire, in 1950. Cedric Glover was the chairman, and thought of Finzi and Ursula Wood as a school-song team – 'a beautifully mad idea in its way', Ursula recalled. A little charmer of a song, it was performed in the school grounds and directed by Vally Lasker, who had worked with Holst. Finzi loved the Ecclesiasticus passage praising 'such as found out musical tunes'. He waited a decent interval after Vaughan Williams composed his setting, then in 1952 produced his own sturdy 'Let us now praise famous men' (Op. 35) for two-part male voices. Also for men's voices, unaccompanied, is 'Thou dids't delight mine eyes' (Op. 32 No. 1 – he had hoped to complete a group), much in the style of his 1930s Bridges settings for mixed voices.

Although in July Gerald had been given a cheering medical report and sent away for nine months – *every month is a precious asset in time* – glands in his groin swelled in September and needed treatment. By now he had overcome his family prejudice enough to meet his older cousin Neville, the cancer specialist, whose study Gerald's father had subsidized. Neville suggested the use of oblique X-rays for investigating the rib cage. This was done, and showed a shadow, probably of enlarged glands. *G tired and down* – *'That I, of all people, should have to die so soon when I have the seeds of growth in me'*, runs a Journal entry on 11 September. The previous day Gerald had written to Robin, to condole with him on his father's (Humphrey Milford's) death: 'It is always the loss of a lifetime of knowledge & experience, now never to be passed on, which seems so dreadful to me. . . . If C. S. Lewis thinks there is a solution to "the problem of pain" I'm afraid I don't, at least, not in life as we at present think we understand it.'[14]

For Vaughan Williams's eightieth birthday in October 1952 Gerald broadcast in Music Magazine and wrote an article 'The Roots and the Tree', for the *Philharmonic Post*. Writing and speaking about Vaughan Williams here and at Leith Hill the following year, pressed for time he fell back on his familiar stories and tags of verse. But he stressed the music's spiritual adventure and range of expression, denying any charge of narrow moods. It is indicative of his outlook, however, and of the period, that he found the suggestion of Debussy's influence on the *London Symphony* to be absurd.

On the way to Dorking for the celebrations, the Finzis lunched with Neville to show him the latest X-rays. They found *him full of ideas about everything*. One of these, that soap was harmful since it was better to preserve the natural body oils, appealed to Joy, who promptly bought loofahs and dark towels for her family − 'why should one accept conventions?' They went next day to the Royal Festival Hall, where they found it pleasant that Vaughan Williams had the kind of reception *usually given to politicians and boxers*. The Sons of Light was in the programme, which Gerald thought a very bad work, and since Vaughan Williams had asked for his honest opinion, wrote at some length to him: *Even L von B wrote the Choral Fantasia, so don't feel too abashed at my taking you at your word . . . not memorable in any way . . . I wonder whether it was written too easily?* 'This flop, if it is one, has made me lose my self-confidence,' Vaughan Williams replied. He wanted his friends to tell him, 'like the policeman did to Mrs Sheldon Amos at Piccadilly Circus, whether I ought to go home as being too old for the job.'[15] But he wrote to his old friend S. P. Waddington: 'I feel lost without you and Gustav to look over my things and tell me where I get off. Nobody else has *both* the skill and the patience to tell me what I want to know.'[16] However frank Finzi felt able to be with his senior, and however fond Vaughan Williams was of his younger colleague, there remained always a little feeling of teacher and pupil. Herbert Howells was sixty that month. Gerald sent him a photograph of Joy's portrait of Uncle Ralph, and a letter saying 'If I had written [the Viola Elegy, the Piano Quartet and *Hymnus Paradisi*] I cd say Nunc Dimittis all right.'[17] 'It's queer to be sixty,' replied Herbert, 'but grand (I should imagine) to be eighty.'[18]

That autumn Edmund Blunden made two quick visits to Ashmansworth for Joy to draw him. 'Her portrait drawings are as they say distinctive,' Edmund wrote afterwards, 'like Sharaku's of Japanese actors, or some of those heads in

14 10 September 1952.
15 19 October 1952. Sarah McLardie Amos, active in women's rights.
16 M. Kennedy, *The Works of Ralph Vaughan Williams* (London, 1964), p. 321.
17 15 October 1952.
18 17 October 1952.

Norman churches. Claire will say, in a realistic approach, that Joy sees me in a Hardyesque way and so perhaps I acquire age in the impression (& tragedy!). But I was looking suspicious of the Deity while sitting.'[19]

WHITE-FLOWERING DAYS

Finzi was commissioned by the Arts Council to contribute to the new 'Triumphs of Oriana', an anthology of ten 'songs for mixed voices' for the Queen's coronation. Both words and music were to be new, and since Blunden was on the list of suggested poets, Finzi asked him to collaborate again. 'Amazing to relate T. S. God aint included in the twenty-four contemporary poets.'[20] Blunden agreed, but *rather hilariously chanted 'as I stood at the corner of Piccadilly plying my trade'*. In December he sent two poems: 'You will tell me what you think, and if I must try again.'[21] 'It's odd,' replied Finzi, who chose 'White-Flowering Days', 'although it may have been rather a bore for you & valuable only for the cash price . . . you can't help doing something worthwhile & showing a few of your fingerprints.' From a musician's point of view, the closed vowels – 'tune', 'gleam', 'green' and so on, in the middle verse, all demanded a low tessitura. 'Don't worry overmuch, but if your craftsmanly mind thought of an alternative rhyme scheme I shdnt complain. "Old romance". Shades of Marcus Stone?' And what about Avilion? Was it Blunden's own variation of Avalon? Since the verses were not strophic, he asked for an optional couplet suitable for a refrain. 'Not quite T. H.'s "Fill full your cups; feel no distress/ That thoughts so great shd now be less!" . . . And what about a title? (no, I'm not offering you the knighthood).'[22] Replying, Blunden gave Wordsworth's 'Sole sitting by the shores of old romance' and Tennyson's 'island valley of Avilion' as his authorities (Finzi was later enchanted to discover that one meaning of 'Avilion' was Isle of Apples). Blunden offered a refrain and made revisions. In the end Finzi did not use the refrain, but asked for an extra stanza in the rhythm of the first to allow him to devise his musical unity.

Gerald was reacting less quickly now to treatment, and there was *sickness and mouldiness all night and next day. . . . The suffering of life such as is seen in any hospital waiting room harrows G unbearably*. On the last day of the year he went out after elevenses with his sons to dig up and replant the peppermint bed. He worked in the evening on his forthcoming broadcast on Stanley, and when the bells began to ring he, Joy, and the boys *went over into the church and saw Stan Cope and Mr Lunn ring in the New Year*.

[19] 19 December 1952.
[20] 15 November 1952.
[21] 19 December 1952.
[22] 26 December 1952.

CHAPTER FOURTEEN

Men of Goodwill

1953–54

All through January and February 1953 Gerald had X-ray treatment in Oxford, for the glands inside his rib cage. He dreaded it, fearful of the old tuberculosis threat; and his cough was breaking his sleep. Early in March Professor Witts declared his condition just about stationary. It was twenty months since Gerald had first seen him. *Needless to say*, Joy wrote wearily, *knowledge of the illness is still where it was.*

Gerald had always kept in touch with Ernest Farrar's widow, Olive. In January he wrote to ask her whether she would give Ernest's manuscripts to the Literary and Philosophical Society of Newcastle-on-Tyne, or the Durham County or Newcastle Public Libraries. Joy copied the letter into her Journal. 'Nothing is clearer than the fact that if arrangements aren't made about these things mss have a habit of getting scattered and ultimately lost beyond recall. The generation immediately following is nearly always neglectful and has little place for its predecessors.' He told her he was sorting Parry's autographs, and how when one was completed 'I send it to the Bodleian and so, thirty years after his death, some attempt is being made to get a collection of his mss work together under one roof for the benefit of posterity.' It was amazing how quickly reputations disappeared. He told her of his work on Stanley, and on Garth (with his favourite Quiller-Couch 'subterranean stream' quotation); and commended Imogen Holst for handing her father's autographs to the British Museum. 'It would be absurd,' he went on, 'to pretend that Ernest lived long enough to be a Parry or a Holst, as he well might have been, but in time to come, when the history of those years is considered by future musical scholars, it may well be that his name will come up from the underground river.'

Edmund Rubbra stayed overnight with the Finzis and played them his *Song of the Soul — its single mood of Catholic religious ecstasy perhaps rather the hothouse type, but a more complete whole than many of his works,* they thought. He told them that Richard Arnell's father had died leaving him £200,000 — Rubbra *seemed rather indignant with Arnell about this — a very human jealousy.* In March the Finzis went to Dorking to hear Vaughan Williams's celebrated but controversial performance of the St Matthew Passion, *an unique interpretation of JSB as seen through VW's mind.* Gerald thought even the much-criticized continuo part for piano fell into place. He was torn between his veneration for Vaughan Williams, who regarded the *score as something to work from,* and his experience now as an editor, seeing the danger when the *innumerable smaller men think the same. Thus the damage done by well meaning, but*

Fruit gatherers at Ashmansworth. Kiffer, Nigel, and Gerald harvesting pears growing on the south side of the house outside the bookroom. Gerald's apple orchards contained over 350 varieties.

Finzi after conducting the first performance of his Clarinet Concerto at Hereford in 1949: Frederick Thurston, Ursula Wood [Vaughan Williams], Kiffer, Vaughan Williams, Gerald Finzi, Joy Finzi.

The only known photograph of Newbury String Players with Finzi conducting. At the Corn Exchange, Hungerford, on 26 February 1950, when the programme included the revival of Stanley's overture to *The Fall of Egypt* and Robert Irwin sang Finzi's *Let us Garlands Bring*.

Howard Ferguson drawn by Joy
Finzi in 1948: 'he was staying
with us at Ashmansworth when I
did this drawing – adding the firm
outline to express his ivory tower
containedness.'

After the first performance of Finzi's
Cello Concerto at the Cheltenham
Festival in 1955: Barbirolli, Finzi,
and (right) Robin Milford

Finzi in July 1956, a few weeks
before he died, with William
Waterhouse.

The sexton's cottage and church
at Chosen Hill, between
Cheltenham and Gloucester.
Here Gerald listened as the bells
rang in the New Year at the end
of 1926, a memory which
shaped the *Nocturne* and *In Terra
Pax*. Here he brought the
Vaughan Williamses in 1956,
and from the sexton's children
caught the virus that killed him.

ignorant or blinkered performers and editors. The Finzis went back in April for the Leith Hill Festival, when Gerald conducted his *Dies Natalis* and presented the banners to the winning choirs. They stayed with Vaughan Williams who, despite his eighty years, was up at six but got more agitated than he used to over details — *burst into a rage all in a minute about nothing.* He showed them his new Christmas work *Hodie* (Gerald had begun work on his *In Terra Pax*).

1953, RETURN TO YORKSHIRE

That year Gerald returned to Yorkshire because Malcolm Sargent was performing *Intimations* in Leeds Town Hall on 25 March. Gerald told the choir that the first choral concert he had ever heard had been in that hall. He and Joy met a pupil of Farrar's, H. P. Dixon, who wrote the words of 'In Memoriam', the music composed by another Farrar pupil, Harry Gill — a song Gerald would have included in the anthology he always wanted to compile of outstanding single songs. They spent an evening talking about Farrar, Bairstow, and R. O. Morris. Gerald raised the question of Farrar's unpublished work, wrote to enlist the conductor Maurice Miles's interest, and arranged with Ernest Bullock, director of the RCM, to house the manuscripts there. The next day Gerald lunched with his old apple correspondent, Miss Halliday. He was surprised to find the Yorkshire people *affectionate, humorous and warm-hearted*; his subjective recollections were of *an unpleasant place and people.* It becomes noticeable how often, now that Gerald's life was becoming wider, he was able to revise his ideas. Even public schools are no longer wholly black: after judging the music competition at Wellington College, *where every niche has a bust of a general, the music,* they thought, *showed up quite well.*

On their way home from Leeds they called on Kenneth Leighton's mother at Wakefield. Realizing the modesty of his home — a *back-to-back four roomed house in a cobbled street* — Joy tactfully stayed in the car in another road and Gerald walked alone to the door. *Pleasant to think that in these days outstanding genius, born in such surroundings, can through State Aid fulfil itself.* What was needed now, they thought, *was help to enable the uncommon person to be free to be uncommon.* Gerald had done his share, acting as Leighton's sponsor, writing testimonials for him, sending his scores to people who might play them; further, he had suggested that Leighton should enter for the Royal Philharmonic Society prize (which he won), and had extracted £100 from the Butterworth Trust for copying his orchestral parts.

The NSP Stockcross concert in April 1953 was one of their best. The three eighteenth-century revivals were *Mudge, immensely serious-minded, Garth, serious but happy and the really enchanting Wesley organ concerto.* Frank Howes was there for *The Times,* but in Gerald's opinion took the uninformed view that the eighteenth century in England consisted of Handel's followers, though he credited Finzi with demonstrating that the period was not as dark as had been painted, and praised the 'confident and competent' playing. Charles Cudworth, the faculty music librarian at Cambridge, with a specialist's interest in the period, described the concert as 'sheer, unalloyed delight' and 'a revelation of what treasures of English music still lie buried under the accretion of neglect and misunderstanding'.[1] He stayed overnight and the whole household took to his *mellow and kindly disposition*, despite his having left school at fourteen and in his early days earning two shillings and sixpence a week in a bookshop, and being *married early to a cripple* (Joy had misunderstood: Mrs Cudworth suffered ill-health, but was not disabled). *Like G. he has never won a prize or passed an exam*, which in his case meant that he could never advance economically – *a cause for sadness – only on account of not being able to give his wife greater comforts.* Some time later Cudworth brought a student, Stanley Sadie, *to look up things in G's library and discuss points about eighteenth-century interpretation. Sadie turns out to be a very knowledgeable young man, there is hardly an English eighteenth-century work he doesn't know.* For the Newbury Festival, Julian Bream played – *a delightful unspoilt tough little cockney* – and gave them a *fascinating serenade in the garden.* He was having a bad time doing his National Service in the army. At a coronation concert in Andover, Gerald *did his best* with Stanford's *Revenge*, but found it *difficult to be sympathetic towards its and Tennyson's heroes.* Difficult too to be sympathetic towards Delius's early *Irmelin* at Oxford: *unless the Delius Trust had too much money to spend*, was the severe but sound judgment, *there was absolutely no justification for the production.*

During their May visit to St Andrews the Finzis took tea with the Earl of Crawford and Balcarres – *house hidden in lovely grounds . . . interior a mass of lovely things. The Crawfords people of genuine taste and culture.* (Lord Crawford held appointments for the National Gallery, the British Museum, and the National Trust, among other arts institutions.) The Finzis admired the library, and found *Crawford clearly knew every book in intimate detail . . . A first rate and delightful character.* They came back for a Finzi-Milford concert under Richard Latham at St Paul's, Knightsbridge, and then, at the Wigmore Hall, the first English performance of Gerald's *Magnificat*. On 1 June there was the coronation eve concert at the Royal Festival Hall, with 'White-flowering days' in *A Garland for the Queen*. After the concert Gerald (true to his long-held dislike of ceremony) set out for home and a day's rest, leaving central London *matted with thousands upon thousands of people in cold, showery weather settling down for the night in the streets, for the next day's sights.*

Love's Labour's Lost, *Op. 28 (II)*

A young architect, Michael Greenwood, had heard the broadcast of *Love's Labour's Lost* (see pp. 149 and 208). He was producing the play for the coronation with the Southend Shakespeare Society at Chalkhill Park, and wrote asking to use Finzi's music. Since the performance was to be in the open air, more was needed for entr'actes and to cover entrances and exits. Finzi wanted all this timed, then supplied the extra music: fanfares, flourishes, the Hunt, and a Nocturne. He made no charge, but asked that he and Howard Ferguson should attend. So they arrived by car, 'HF smoking cigars and GF chewing mints'.

---

[1] *Newbury Weekly News*, 16 April 1953.

Gerald was 'particularly kind' about the performance, and Joy noted his view that the production by the *brilliant young architect* was unusually good, although the orchestra was out of tune.

Finzi considered that any future producer could 'take or leave what he wants, and to begin and end where he likes': the short pieces were 'a patchwork to be unpicked, a quarry from which to dig'.[2] However, there now existed an independent body of music. Howard had criticized the Suite broadcast from Cheltenham as having too little variety, and thought the songs out of place. With his Southend additions, Finzi made an instrumental suite of ten pieces, lasting nearly half an hour. Since in the suite the play's chronology is lost, a few points are gained by knowing the music's origins. There are two royal groups, the King of Navarre and the Princess of France, each with their courtiers. The Introduction opens with her flourish, then comes the noble, gracious music for his court. The twisting, divided cello theme in the Introduction (1) belongs to the fantastical Spaniard Armado. Finzi thought of Armado's page, Moth (2), as 'that strutting, independent small creature'; he is sharply characterized – almost caricatured – in three solo clarinet bars (Ex. 14.1).

Ex. 14.1

His witty scherzando is set off by the melancholy tune Finzi composed for Moth's Concolinel, 'Is it not sure a deadly pain', given here to a solo viola. The sombre opening of the Nocturne (3) brought news of the King of France's death. The Hunt (4), lent romance because it takes place far off, is fleet and airy, and shows how brilliantly Finzi could write by now, uninhibited by words. The Dance (5) has a touch of artifice about it: the dancers are masked and mocking. The Quodlibet (6) is music from the entertainment of Worthies (Alexander, Hercules, etc. – Finzi quotes from 'The British Grenadiers') presented for the royals by the 'pedant, the braggart, the hedge-priest, the fool, and the boy'. The final chord of the Quodlibet, surprisingly soft and gentle after the horseplay, parallels that moment of truth when old Holofernes reproaches his 'betters' – 'this is not generous, not gentle, not humble'. The Finale (10) concerns the 'Russians' and their dance.

The three Soliloquies (7, 8, 9) are open-textured enough to allow a spoken voice to sound over them. No.1 ('So sweet a kiss') has the melodic fingerprint that occurred as early as 1929 in the C. Rossetti song 'Oh fair to see' (see Ex. 3.3). Finzi often used it, memorably in 'Channel firing' (see Ex. 10.3), and For St Cecilia (Ex. 9.2) and in Intimations of Immortality ('Those shadowy recollections,

---

2   Introduction to ms score.

which, *be they what they may*'). Simple, yet characteristic of that tender, quizzical expression his friends knew so well.

Altogether the incidental music is enchanting – Finzi's *Wand of Youth*: and, as in Elgar, the miniatures are touching as well as pretty. The Suite shows a new and welcome concentration and vividness. It is deftly scored with solos and unisons, and much *pizzicato, staccato*, and *spiccato*, as though Finzi were thinking about what would come through the microphone well. Shakespeare's play, for all its mockery and fun, has a serious, poetic strain, personified in the courtier Berowne ('love . . . gives to every power a double power'). The grander moments of Finzi's score are worthy of this. (In June 1954 a Royal College of Music student orchestra, conducted by James Lockhart, *an able young conductor*, Joy noted, ran through the Suite. *VW and Howard came and seemed pleased with the work*. John Russell broadcast it with the LSO on 26 July 1955.)

In July the Blunden family stayed at Ashmansworth before leaving for Hong Kong. Gerald had tried but failed to secure Edmund work in England, and had prodded Vaughan Williams into putting forward his name as Poet Laureate to Edward Bridges, the poet's son and Secretary to the Treasury; but to no avail. Interested in the history of Christ's Hospital, Blunden was covering the same period as Gerald in his revivals, and sent useful items out of the *Gentleman's Magazine*. Gerald asked him to keep a look-out for references to Mr Mudge. 'You must have seen all that is given in edns of Fanny Burney's Diary concerning Stanley,'[3] queried Edmund. Gerald had; and rather agreed with a recent *Times Literary Supplement* review about John Hawkins's dullness. 'And Laetitia' [Hawkins's daughter and biographer] 'a most unpleasant, untruthful, simpering scarecrow, is hardly worth the attention given to her.'[4]

The day before they sailed, Edmund sent 'a farewell squeak', telling Gerald that he and Joy had 'constantly enriched our years since Japan'.[5] 'Though you hold out the prospect of a meeting in 1957 & the Chances are all in its favour,' replied Gerald, 'the Changes wreak such cruel & continual havoc that I never have far from my mind TH's "but who shall say . . .".' Gurney's poems, refused by a round of publishers, were finally accepted by Richard Church of Hutchinson. As for Marion Scott, 'prodding people is not a pleasant job, but I have had to do it to her for twenty years or so. Yet G[urney] had no more devoted friend & wd-be comforter.' It would be wise to warn Richard Church of her dilatoriness (Gerald seemed unaware that she had been compiling her forty-page Haydn catalogue for the 1954 *Grove*). 'Yet she has befriended many generations of RCM students in the past.' In the days when he first heard of

---

3   25 February 1953.
4   27 February.
5   20 August 1953.

her from Ernest Farrar 'she was young, delightful & even said to have love affairs!'[6]

In June X-ray treatment began again, but in mid-October Gerald was shocked to be told that his blood count was not satisfactory enough for more. The time was coming for the removal of his spleen. In desperation, the Finzis turned to a non-medical therapy popular at the time, radiothesia (or the 'black box'). This was supposed to effect cures at long distance: the operator 'tuned in' to the patient's vibration, and treated him by long wave. Joy was not impressed by the operator (aptly called Miss Ray) but thought anything was better than nothing. *G sceptical too, but felt they had got hold of something of enormous potential importance which might, in the hands of genius, revolutionise medicine: scientists and doctors ridicule the whole thing without bothering to examine it.* (Towards the end of her own life Joy took to consulting a pendulum for her health.) A brief holiday in Ireland, arranged by Joy's sister Mags to visit their cousins, came providentially two days after the bad news. It was the Finzis' first flight, and thrilled them both – *nothing could be more beautiful in the Himalayas than rising from a dark foggy day into the brilliant world of sun and limitless horizon of clouds.* Gerald's colour improved. Every day he received radiothesia from Oxford. *Absolute quiet only the peacocks cry.*

Soon after that Robin Milford had to undergo electrical shock treatment for his worsening depression. Gerald wrote reassuringly, praising the recent broadcast of Robin's *Days and Moments*, and wondered if the so-called 'normal' people were not, more often than not, the real 'mental' cases. 'Just look', he said, 'at your ribbon development on the Bath road or any other main arterial road, or man's inhumanity to man, or bull-fighting or Littlewoods pools. Surely the world is one gigantic asylum!'[7] Their own activities that autumn were more wholesome: 'gathering apples, garnering nuts, giving concerts, writing music',[8] he told Blunden, now in Hong Kong.

John Russell, without saying a word to Gerald, and knowing nothing of his illness, persuaded the Newbury Choral Society to mount an all-Finzi concert of *Intimations*, *For St Cecilia*, and the Grand Fantasia and Toccata, this last on the strength of his having seen the manuscript of the early Fantasia and hearing that Gerald thought of one day adding a Toccata. Since composing the Fantasia, Finzi had changed his mind about the work several times. At some point during or before 1947 he had composed a 'weighty introduction' to it. That year he mentioned a piano concerto with strings to Ivor Atkins, and sketches for the outer movements exist. For some years he kept the Fantasia and the Piano Concerto separate in his mind, but goaded and encouraged by Russell he now used ideas from both.

Russell would not forget the first time he played the Fantasia through 'from

6   23 August 1953.
7   10 November 1953.
8   16 October 1953.

the closely-packed pages of forbidding unbarred manuscript'. 'It seemed all wrong. The piano writing is brutal and static; the harmonies revolve a great deal round savage false relations; the orchestra deserts after the second phrase, and the pianist is left alone in midstream to make his way over rocks and through a swirling torrent to the other side. . . . But it all came right, so right that it was obvious that it must straightway be given its Toccata and performed to show a new Finzi.'[9] Finzi himself, not dreaming the Newbury concert was a serious possibility, suddenly realized the programme was settled; so between the Irish holiday in October and the concert on 9 December he revised the Fantasia, and composed the Toccata. He conducted and Russell played the solo part.

Grand Fantasia and Toccata, Op. 38

It seems extraordinary that in 1953 Finzi could match a Toccata to a Fantasia composed about 1928, even though in his Catalogue he stated that the Fantasia was 'considerably revised, re-written and scored in 1953'. The obsessive, craggy quality of the Fantasia (see p. 58) belongs to his earlier years, when he could not have achieved the confidence, speed, and lightness of the Toccata. In fact the pairing sounds effective and inevitable, in spite of the out-of-joint relationship, which keeps the orchestra waiting silently through seven of the piece's fifteen minutes. It works by imbalance, precariously. In the thirty bars from the point (cue 1) where the orchestra joins the piano in the Fantasia to the Toccata subject, Finzi compresses a rare power and passion. The inquiring spirit, insistent searching, and build-up of tension in the Fantasia demand exactly the release provided by the linear, athletic Toccata, linked to the Fantasia by the rhythm of the first-beat 'knock'.

That subject is lightly worked as if in fugato, with insouciant syncopated episodes. The piano writing, unlike anything else in Finzi, is motoric, percussive, spare, with witty passage work, idiomatic in a Ravel–Prokofiev–Walton style (in particular, Walton's *Sinfonia Concertante*, which Finzi admired, seems an influence). Just when the Toccata begins to feel too lightweight, too flippant even, to balance the gravity of the Fantasia, a *molto allargando* effects a return to the opening of the Fantasia (cue 15) – the bass thundering down in whole tones, the piano's original free improvisation usurped by the brass, grandly augmented to a measured chorale. Briefly the piano, over shuddering, violent strings and rolled cymbal, looks back to the chordal, expressive Fantasia. Great menace is compressed into these few bars, before the brief, clipped end.

The Grand Fantasia and Toccata is completely individual, unless it could be compared with Beethoven's Chorale Fantasia or Vaughan Williams's 'Old 104th' (though both these use a chorus as well). It is startling in its jump

---

[9]   *Tempo*, No. 33.

across the centuries, from the baroque Fantasia to the twentieth century, leap-frogging over Finzi's generally more conservative idiom. He was amused to find it called eccentric. 'Well, one doesn't always know oneself,' he wrote to Lady Ponsonby, pointing out that 'it was based on forms which wd have seemed quite reasonable to J.S.B.'[10] Of course it is eccentric; but because it grew from such internal pressures, it has a power and individuality that many more polished pieces lack; and achieves the genuine confrontation missing in the Clarinet Concerto. Howard Ferguson never came to like it, but Finzi wrote in his Catalogue 'I feel it achieves what I wanted.'

Eclogue, Op. 10; Romance, Op. 11

Finzi originally intended to follow the Fantasia with a slow movement, described by Rubbra in 1929 as having 'the same untroubled serenity' as the Introit. Finzi revised it in 1952, and it was published as Eclogue after his death. Serene the opening certainly is. The piano's first paragraph is entirely diatonic, moving with quiet grace in baroque pattern-making: *almost* predict-able, but constantly evolving, and so lyrical that is sounds self-communing. The first bars are the most contrapuntally controlled – three tonic subject-entries at half-bar intervals; after that, the imitations relax. The limpid twelve-eight section might almost be Fauré in Mozartian mood, though there are Finzian turns of phrase – 'my entrance into the world' from *Dies Natalis* for one. In the reprise two of the themes run over each other, making a comment, not a repeat. Towards the end the mood turns questioning: the bass drops away (at the same position as in the earlier Introit), as if facing uncertainty; there is a tiny cadenza, a brief ambiguous tonal excursion – tonic minor or flat submediant? – and tolling chords add a sense of farewell to that of benedic-tion. A short piece, awkward for programme-planners, Finzi's Eclogue is large and serious in spirit, a rapt but not untroubled meditation.

The Romance for strings was published only in 1952, though in 1951 Finzi described it to Robin Milford as 'antiquated', and dated it 1928 on the score. However, it seems unlikely that, with his Newbury String Players experi-ence, he left it unrevised, though it must be remembered that *Dies Natalis*, with its exquisite string writing, was published before he founded NSP. In turn of phrase and texture the Romance recalls Elgar's early Serenade; but the most Elgarian passage – the surging, cantabile lower strings either side of cue 8 – devolves onto pure Finzi for the climactic passage – thirds and sixths over tremolando – either side of cue 9.

During 1952–54 Newbury String Players gave Britten's Simple Symphony for the first time, Colin Davis played Gerald's Clarinet Concerto with them, and John Carol Case sang *Let us Garlands Bring*. Robin Milford had recommended

10 14 July 1954.

Carol Case to the Finzis, who then went to hear him sing *Garlands* at the Festival Hall in 1951. So began their friendship with one of Finzi's finest interpreters.

Gerald had now revived four of John Garth's Cello Concertos with NSP. Max Hinrichsen came to a concert, and agreed to publish one. The performance in June 1953 by William Pleeth and NSP of the Fourth Concerto prompted Joy to assess Gerald's revivals in her Journal. *He gradually found that by eliminating nearly everything that was added by editors, keeping to the notes that were written in the first place, trying to adhere and understand the intentions of the age and the composer, (including the necessity for a continuo) quite a different picture of the eighteenth-century school appeared.* Joy admitted that these ideas had been recognized by others for many years, but the main source of the instrumental music was practically untapped. *Having gone through an immense amount of stuff, good and bad, [Gerald's] outstanding revivals have been Stanley, Garth and early Charles Wesley. CW if only on account of his boyish keyboard concertos, Garth for his remarkably fresh and happy cello concertos, but Stanley, above all, who takes on quite a different perspective and becomes one of the major composers of his period — becomes the equal, and in some ways, superior to Arne and splendid old Boyce. So in its small way some valuable work has been done in this direction, but it has taken up a lot of time.* The following year she noted: *G's test is always one of performance and without that it is never really possible to say whether a work is dead or alive.* So NSP was not only his instrument, but his research tool as well.

To mark the Festival of Britain in 1951 the Royal Musical Association had founded *Musica Britannica*, a national collection of the classics of English Music. Gerald was on to it like a flash, suggesting to Cedric Thorpe Davie that he should submit his Arne editions; they were not accepted, as Arne's *Comus* was already in the series. Gerald was then invited to edit Boyce's trio sonatas, but — though he much admired them — he felt obliged to refuse, as he had been responsible for Herbert Murrill's starting to prepare them for Hinrichsen. In February 1954 he lunched with Anthony Lewis, the editor, and agreed instead to prepare a volume of Boyce's unpublished overtures to the choral court odes. *G knows these overtures pretty well and has already revived one or two of them with the String Players.* The following month he handed his edition of Stanley's Fifth Concerto to Boosey & Hawkes. *After the first publication (No. 3), Joy recorded, there was much debating on the wisdom of doing any more. They were unable to see the possibilities. Roth himself is an intelligent musician, but publishers as a whole in G's opinion is that they are extraordinarily shortsighted and far less practical than the average composer.*[11]

In November 1954 Finzi finished his edition of Charles Wesley's fourth keyboard Concerto from his Op. 20. *The Wesley has meant a good deal of work,* noted Joy. Gerald had just filled in some gaps with microfilms, he told Ceddie, with Shield, William Flacton, Avison, and Thomas Tremain. He came across some quite good bassoon concertos by the unknown Henry Hargrave. He was looking out for something for Bill Waterhouse to play, and found a charming work by Capel Bond (1730–90), the sixth concerto of the 1766 set. Since Gerald was again wondering whether to give up NSP — he was beginning his fifteenth year with them — Bill suggested a possible conductor, but he wasn't

---

[11] Finzi's editions held their ground until John Caldwell's for OUP in 1987.

local. Gerald pointed out that NSP needed someone on the spot to deal with
the mixed personalities, and to understand that the concert calendar had to be
fixed round Easter and point-to-points! Also, there could be no fee or travel
expenses. 'I've benefited enormously from all I've had to do with them,'[12] he
added. Though he didn't say so, it also needed someone with a library as large
and specialized as his. His collection of rare printed music, photostats, microfilms, hand-copied autographs and parts was by now unique.

'Uncle Ralph' and Ursula Wood, married in 1953 and set up in their
London house, came to the traditional Christmas concert at Enborne when
that year Gerald revived Boyce's Overture from the 1772 New Year Ode. The
Vaughan Williamses took back with them an Ashmansworth small black kitten
called Crispin – 'intelligent, amusing, and affectionate' – also a poet of sorts.
Vaughan Williams teasingly sent 'Lines by Crispin':

> I know I'm no judge, but the works of Rev Mudge
> Seem nothing but fudge, and you wont make me budge
> In spite of his herald, to wit our friend Gerald.[13]

Cats were a major part of the Finzi household. Howard wrote on behalf of a
friend asking for 'a kitten (male, either dehydrated or not)'.[14] About this time
Gerald was best man at the wedding of Cynthia Freeman, who played the viola
in NSP. A superb cake was made in the Ashmansworth kitchen and laid on the
spare room bed. Very few people knew that one of the cats had found it comfortable enough to curl up on, and had to be shooed off in a hurry. All the cats
ate from a large and beautiful platter in the kitchen, which, incidentally, was
enlarged at the end of 1953 when Gerald's life insurance matured.

GURNEY AND MARION SCOTT

Hutchinsons had the Gurney Poems well in hand, but Marion Scott was ill –
'now it is the real thing', Gerald wrote to Blunden. He had tried to persuade
her to write her memories. Even though 'she would not have known any of
the cruder aspects, which a man wd best know, & her understanding wd be
limited to a more "genteel" aspect', her 'intense devotion' to Gurney made it
possible for his work to be gathered.[15] She had, however, completed a beautifully written and judged entry on Gurney for Grove 5. On Christmas Eve 1953
Herbert Howells telephoned to say she had died. The Letters of Administration
now reverted to Gurney's family ('who were', Gerald wrote to Edmund, 'his
greatest enemies'[16]). In her Will, however, she left Gerald a debt she had
incurred in aiding Ivor's upkeep, so that it could still legally be his business.

---

12 25 July 1954.
13 December 1954.
14 7 December 1952.
15 12 December 1953.
16 7 January 1954.

He sent a dedication to her of the Poems for Edmund to approve, telling him that the hostile Gurney family were demanding all the manuscripts (Gerald had spent twenty-five years adding to the collection), and were refusing to meet both Gerald and Vaughan Williams. What happens now to royalties, asked Edmund, who thought the 'power and difference' of the poems would make some critics speak out for them. Remembering his earlier editing, he wrote 'It is, then, not so easy as John Clare!'[17]

Anxious to heal the rift, Gerald and Joy drove to Gloucester to see Gurney's brother Ronald and his wife, finding them, Joy noted, *hospitable with parlour tea and homemade everything with butter*. They sensed in him an obsessive hatred towards a non-earning brother who wasted money on buying music paper. 'If you were to explain to him, in Goethe's words', Gerald reported to Edmund, 'that the work of art is greater than the artist, it would mean nothing at all.'[18] But he persuaded Ronald not to destroy the manuscripts. Alice Sumsion commiserated on the time it all took. 'Yes, of course these things are a worry, take up one's time & interfere with one's work,' replied Gerald. 'But who else will do it? And if it ought to be done, can one comfortably step aside or leave it undone?'[19] In October 1954 Gerald was able to tell Edmund the book was out. He wished it could have contained more of the coherent lyrical poems, but understood that Edmund wanted to avoid antagonizing a younger generation, thinking the book would do better on the 'rough power' of the wilder, stranger poems.[20]

Gerald reported to Blunden his interest in Robert Gittings' *John Keats – the Living Year*. 'Keats still seems to me as good a man as ever lived. I know you dispute this,' he went on. 'But even if he did go a-drinking & a-whoring & loathed parsons, his wisdom, humour, integrity & affection are surely what make a good man.'[21] He had also read James Pope-Hennessy's volumes on Monckton Milnes, and 'my hat goes off to Pope-Hennessy for the way he has dealt with such a mass of stuff'. He was delighted with Milnes's 'liberalism, tolerance, political & literary prescience. Even his collection of Erotica makes him more companionable than many of his time!' In spite of it all, though, they might have found him rather a *bore*. But Edmund couldn't deeply praise Milnes's work on Keats: 'he idled where he should have passionately seized the transient gift'.[22]

Gerald approached Cecil Day Lewis, a reader for Chatto & Windus, about the poems of a new friend, Averil Morley (who later married the ecologist Frank Fraser Darling). Gerald found the *young revolutionary is now very much the*

---

[17] 10 March 1954.
[18] 8 May 1954.
[19] 4 March ?1954.
[20] P. J. Kavanagh, checking against the autographs for his *Collected Poems of Ivor Gurney* (Oxford, 1982), found that typing errors had produced some of the 'queernesses'; but paid tribute to the Finzis' perception and industry.
[21] 22 March 1954.
[22] 2 April 1954.

conformer. Gerald asked him whether his respect of the law was respect or fear: without hesitation he answered 'oh fear'. Other people were changing too, Gerald found. A visit to the Vaughan Williamses in March was rather a challenge to his views. They found Ursula looking after him wonderfully. It was interesting to see Vaughan Williams accepting whatever environment was given him so long as he is allowed to get on with his work. Nowadays everything is wealth, ease and comfort, and much going about (they were just off to Rome and then to the Grand Canyon). Gerald's 'inbred puritanism', as Ursula later put it, was a trifle upset.

At their now annual Stockcross concert in 1954 Gerald conducted R. O. Morris's *Concerto piccolo*. He had recently conducted Gordon Jacobs's Bassoon Concerto, and written to Olive Farrar about Ernest's manuscripts: it was as though he were consciously and loyally discharging his debts to his teachers.

In May the Finzis went again to St Andrews, going on with the Thorpe Davies for a wonderful week (fifteen hours sunshine a day) to Iona and Fingal's Cave, the country brilliant with spring flowers and long light. Some alarm at Gerald's indigestion was allayed when it was traced to Scotch tea and not further symptoms! He described to Blunden the 'sharp spikes of mountains which made you wonder why anyone wanted to go to south America, and seas of a fantastic colour. And all the time we were blessed with blazing sun, whilst the rest of Scotland and England was drenched with rain.'[23] His mind going back to Gloucestershire, after visiting his mother, now in a home at Painswick, he added 'As an old woman whom I used to know, who lived in a cottage halfway up May Hill, said when there was a shower, "Isn't the Lord wonderful. He watered my potatoes, when the neighbours had none at all." '

'Who should be on the train [coming back] but little Herbert Howells,' which made the journey much quicker. Herbert and Gerald had been in touch again, since Martin Cooper had asked Gerald to write an article on Howells for the *Musical Times*. Gerald wrote to Herbert saying that he would only select works, and not attempt to cover his entire output. 'Your letter to me is sane and courageous and frank,'[24] replied Herbert, but dilly-dallied in sending him scores. The article was published in April 1954, and Gerald explained to Herbert that he had dealt mostly with the past 'because H. *Paradisi* is getting something of the attention it deserves. . . . I haven't embarrassed you by saying that everything is marvellous . . . uncritical, adulatory articles do much more harm than good.'[25] His is a thorough and well-informed survey of Howells's published work, alive to his 'diamond-cut brilliance', sympathetic to the demands of earning a living, aware that the complicated mind that produced the burning contrapuntal climaxes could lapse into note-spinning. All the same, it is odd, when he was so short of time, and with his ambivalent feelings, that Gerald took on such a task; and strange that he said so little about

23 11 June 1954.
24 11 August 1953.
25 5 March 1954.

Hymnus. (After Finzi's death, Howells confided that 'GF didn't begin to understand me at all.')

John Russell and his wife came unexpectedly into a sum of money. Their first thought was 'to buy a new egg whisk'; their second, to repeat the Newbury all-Finzi concert in London. Russell was making his way as a conductor, and chose to use an LSO date in this way, guaranteeing any loss. Gerald, with no false optimism, foresaw a nearly empty hall, but, backed by Vaughan Williams, Russell went ahead, added *Dies Natalis* to the programme (*For St Cecilia*, Grand Fantasia and Toccata, *Intimations of Immortality*), and engaged Richard Lewis to sing and Peter Katin to play. The Festival Hall on 8 July was three parts full – *an extraordinarily warm and enthusiastic audience* – and all Gerald's friends were there. He was delighted that Russell's 'courage, enterprise & enthusiasm were rewarded'.[26] It seemed a great occasion, though the press, apart from The Times, rather patronizing. 'It was really all rather a strange & curious thing to happen to one!'[27] Gerald wrote to Herbert Howells, who had congratulated him rather ambiguously on a 'long flow of music courageous in the least fashionable way'.[28] The Finzis returned for their annual midsummer NSP concert at Bucklebury, when Anna Shuttleworth played the last of the Garth concertos to be revived (No. 1) and they gave Roy Teed's 'Such were the Joys': *a lovely summer evening and full house and everyone happy.*

The Journal entries at this time get shorter, but are so frequent that they seem to spin like a top – or a dance of death. 'I've had a really frightful time, without a day to myself,'[29] wrote Gerald to Cedric Thorpe Davie. Apart from his composing, he was chairing committees and adjudicating. Though there was no social entertaining at Ashmansworth (and their sons now felt hardly able to bring their young friends home) many people were in and out for work. In July and August 1954 alone the Vaughan Williamses came to hear Rubbra play his Sixth Symphony; Robin Milford and Bryan Kelly each brought their compositions; Iva Dee Hiatt from the USA stayed a night; Ceddie with his family, down to collect his OBE, camped in the garden; and Steuart Wilson and Charles Lofthouse came over from Downe House summer school. People meeting Gerald casually, perhaps for the first time, were 'haunted by his eyes – so intense – almost mad'. The sheer activity would be striking for a fit man: for a dying man it becomes frightening.

---

26 To L. Clark, 16 July 1954.
27 11 July 1954.
28 9 July 1954.
29 25 June 1954.

In Terra Pax, Op. 39

The Newbury String Players' annual Christmas concert at Enborne, with a choir, had become special – the church candle-lit, the atmosphere warm, intimate, with a sense of dedication and tradition. For all his agnosticism, Gerald loved the family Christmas, when with local friends they went carol singing round the village, there were candles in the windows and a gorgeous tree; then the younger children shouted up the chimney to Father Christmas and Gerald (upstairs) shouted down. Most of all he loved the 'time of silence', as he had told Robin Milford in 1940; and the turn of the year – the symbolism of rebirth – touched him deeply.

During 1951 he took out his Bridges Collected Poems, and set 'Thou didst delight my eyes' for male voices. Another poem 'Noel: Christmas Eve, 1913' had long been one of his favourites (he had quoted from it in the preface to his *New Year Music*, when that was published in 1950). Now he thought of framing St Luke's account of the angel bringing the news of Christ's birth to the shepherds within Bridges' poem. He subtitled *In Terra Pax* 'A Christmas Scene', but there is no Virgin, no Child, no crib. In his programme note Finzi says the Nativity 'becomes a vision seen by a wanderer on a dark and frosty Christmas Eve, in our own familiar landscape'. Possibly his idea came from a Christmas card in 1940 from Winifred Blow drawn by Detmar, with the crucifixion set on the Gloucestershire hills. This setting of a Biblical scene in the English countryside inevitably recalls Samuel Palmer and Stanley Spencer, who in their turn were re-creating the Virgilian eclogue. *In Terra Pax* was not commissioned, so came from internal compulsion. It is the summation of Finzi's Paradise in pastoral England, of his quest for roots and continuity, for spiritual and enduring verities in a Romantic image of a united past and present.

In April 1951 he sent two drafts of the text to Howard Ferguson, who criticised the first because of 'the repetition of the fourth verse at the end; and the excitement and climax of the third verse, which would kill the Luke extract stone dead. Furthermore, four verses delays Luke too long and turns it from a centrepiece (which it should be) into an afterthought.' Version II, in which Finzi omits Bridges' third verse, made, thought Howard, 'a most lovely little work and is perfect as it stands – with the possible addition ". . . on earth peace, goodwill towards men" for pp women's voices at the very end'.[30] (Was he thinking of *Dona Nobis Pacem?*) During 1954 Finzi worked at version II.

As *In Terra Pax* begins, the poet stands alone on a hill thinking of the first Christmas; and the sound of church bells seem to become the angels' song. The verse Finzi omitted, describing the ringers 'With arms lifted to clutch/the rattling ropes that race/Into the dark above', links the music with his experience as a young man (see p. 36) when he shared the bell-ringing on Chosen Hill. That memory would have been strengthened one Christmas when,

[30] 14 April 1951.

staying at Joy's home before they married, they heard bells and scrambled two miles across snow-filled fields to get closer; and as recently as 1952 he heard the New Year rung in at Ashmansworth church.

So In Terra Pax was born from images deeply laid down in Finzi's consciousness. It was the only work he composed for his own NSP, with added voices, harp, and cymbals (he scored it fully for the 1956 Three Choirs Festival). It shares with Vaughan Williams's Serenade to Music, also composed for known, loved performers, a peculiar intimacy. All through the piece run two musical ideas, inherited and traditional, part of everyone's memory. There is the pentatonic bell or chime motto, and the refrain of 'The first Nowell'. A welcoming, all-embracing gesture, the carol refrain brings associations of the 'alleluia' of the hymn-tune 'Lasst uns erfreuen' (1623) ('Ye watchers and ye holy ones') and phrases in Vaughan Williams's Serenade and the Romanza of his Fifth Symphony. Finzi is of course not the only composer to draw on associations for emotional effect: Elgar in The Starlight Express also used 'The first Nowell', and Britten was about to quote 'Eternal Father, strong to save' in Noye's Fludde. Another reference might be to Mahler's Adagietto in his Fifth Symphony, which Finzi had recently conducted with NSP. Finzi, as Mahler, scores for harp and strings, and uses the harp to prick through the texture as the stars 'spangle' the dark sky.

Unlike his practice in Intimations, Finzi here assigns definite roles: the solo baritone has Bridges' poem, the chorus the Biblical narrative, the solo soprano the angel's words. Harmonically, there are telling moments. The Angel reassures the shepherds in six flats, but at the momentous words 'which is Christ the Lord' the music lifts into a clear C major for one bar. Later, as the baritone reflects in E flat on what has happened, the words 'Angel's song' echo for one bar the same C major (four bars after cue 15): in both cases, the effect is to shine light on the words. The baritone's first words 'A frosty Christmas Eve' are foreshadowed (before cue 3) in D major (Ex. 14.2a), but after the Angel's words, which have 'changed' everything, the chords supporting the same melody (before cue 15) are enharmonically 'changed' too (Ex. 14.2b) Such details, though slight, are powerful.

Ex. 14.2

There is uneasy expectancy in the instrumental interlude derived from 'keeping watch over the flock in the fields'; then the rolled cymbal creates excitement and awe. (How touching it is to recall the young Finzi asking his teacher

Farrar how to notate rolled cymbals!) The chorus, with the men's voices tense in high register on 'lo' and 'Lord', is released into melismas at 'glo. . .ry' which 'shone. . . .' round them. Finzi is less strict here than in his early days, and allows other melismas too, such as the baritone's ecstatic 'sing. . .ing'. A buffeting in the strings is like the beating of angels' wings; then 'Glory to God' peals out dramatically on voices alone, the opening pentatonic theme chiming above sturdy basses ringing down the scale. The strings strike in with 'Nowell', which gradually fills all the voices singing 'and on earth peace'. Bethlehem fades. Bridges' watcher is again alone, and in his final phrase searches the 'eternal silence' between the strings' five bare octaves (Ex. 14.3): man set against his naked birth and his solitary end. Here Finzi, gazing from his hilltop at the starry infinity, joins hands across the centuries with that fifteenth-century astronomer, Mordecai Finzi.

Ex. 14.3

Gently the chorus repeats the angels' message of peace, and for the first time the strings play the carol's first line.

Peace on earth was what Finzi wished for most passionately. No subject however noble, no intention however sincere, can guarantee memorable music; but In Terra Pax, though heart-felt, is unpretentious. It is, like Dies Natalis, a luminous and poetic masterpiece.

There was difficulty over the title. In 1951 Howard replied to Gerald's suggestions: ' "Noel" is apt, but suggests Walford Davies or Eric Thiman; "Pax hominibus" possible; "Fared I forth alone" not very indicative; "A frosty Christmas Eve" too wordy.'[31] In Finzi's copy of Bridges' Poems he placed a letter from a newspaper concerning the translation of 'Pax hominibus bonae voluntatis' (Bridges' subtitle), which the writer felt should mean 'peace on earth to men of goodwill' rather than 'goodwill towards men'. Perhaps that prompted Finzi's title. A work so associated with the countryside round Gloucester could have only one dedicatee, but John Sumsion did not know it was to be his until he was given the printed copy.

[31] 14 April 1951.

∽

While Gerald was working on In Terra Pax, Barbirolli invited him to compose a major work for the following year's Cheltenham Festival: it was his first commission from a conductor of international standing. In 1940 Gerald had told William Busch that a cello concerto had 'long been at the back of my mind, one of the many things started and then put into cold storage'.[32] The autumn after Professor Witts's Verdict, 1951, Joy noted in her Journal finished slow movement of Cello Concerto. So during the later part of 1954 he was at work on both In Terra Pax and the Cello Concerto.

Few friends guessed that he was terminally ill, and he dropped few clues. When John Carol Case suggested he compose a baritone Dies Natalis, he replied with a sweet smile 'I'm afraid there isn't time'. Thea King, when her husband Frederick Thurston died of cancer in 1953, found Gerald exceptionally sympathetic and knowledgeable. He was now looking drawn and yellow, and his crisp hair was limp; he had such a horror of being an invalid that it was kindest to ignore his appearance. Through September and October 1954 he had another course of X-ray treatment and was very mouldy as a result. It affected his activity; unable to do anything during the week. Under the strain he became irritable and sometimes showed signs of losing his temper, though Joy could nearly always steer him away from a dangerous subject and make him laugh. The pressure on her became almost more than he had any right to expect, thought friends not in the know.

At this point, with his Boyce editing and NSP commitments on top of his creative work, he accepted an invitation from the Royal College of Music to give the Crees lectures, established in 1950. At first glance it seems absurd. But he could choose his subject, and had written on words and music for the Oxford Guardian (5 October 1950). For years he had gathered material on that topic (the earliest was an article by V. C. Clinton-Baddeley from The Listener, 29 September 1938), so the lectures would give him a chance to formulate and share his views. Then there is the passage he had written about Vaughan Williams the previous year to Robin Milford: 'We often lose as much as we gain with maturity. . . . I would give ten Sinfonia Antartica or Sons of Light, for one Wenlock Edge, Tallis Fantasia or Five Mystical Songs.'[33] Did he apply it to himself? He was now middle-aged. Was he apprehensive that his own lyrical gift might run dry? He was facing death: was he packing his life so tightly that he would not have time to think?

At all events a holiday was much needed, and so after the Three Choirs and a last quick examining trip to St Andrews, the Finzis took four days in late October and stayed at the coastguard cottages at Abbotsbury in Dorset. Rough

[32] 19 November 1940.
[33] 18 September 1953.

magnificent seas, noted Joy. They visited old friends in their new homes: Robin and Kirstie Milford, just settled at Lyme Regis, the engraver Reynolds Stone and his wife, who had lived some time in Ashmansworth, at Lytton Cheney. In the evenings Gerald and Kiffer worked at the Capel Bond Bassoon Concerto.

The holiday gave Gerald time to write to a new acquaintance. Leonard Clark had been at the Festival Hall concert, and wrote a heartening letter to Gerald afterwards, sending too his newly published poems *English Morning.* Gerald had heard of Clark from Jack Haines in his early Gloucestershire days. Sadly Haines was now old and practically blind, reported Gerald, who had visited him not long before. As he always did with a new friend, Gerald asked about Clark's earlier work. A schools inspector, Clark had not been prolific, but he sent Gerald his collection *The Mirror.* They exchanged literary news and views, Gerald on Gurney and Blunden, Clark describing de la Mare – 'though ill he sparkled – outshone everybody' – and Edith Sitwell – 'so pleased to be a Dame';[34] Gerald now preferring Masefield's prose to his verse – 'such lovely things' as the autobiographical *So Long to Learn.* From Abbotsbury, Gerald wrote to Clark of showing his 'eldest son places like Maiden Castle, which I first knew when I was about his age. And I'm still romantic enough to have visited the site of the original Fleet church,' the source of Meade Falkner's novel *Moonfleet.* 'I read that when I was about ten years old & almost every decade afterwards with equal delight. . . . Tomorrow to Stinsford & Bockhampton & then my sentimental journey ends.'[35]

On their return there was a pile of some forty letters. They did not notice that one from Professor Witts to his doctor was addressed in error to Ashmansworth. In it Gerald read that he was *going downhill very rapidly.* With his fine manners he was most concerned at the doctors' and secretary's embarrassment; so he destroyed the letter and said nothing. But after an examination it was decided that he should enter hospital for a week, to be treated under observation.

Before that Arthur and Trudy Bliss stayed at Ashmansworth, for Joy to draw Arthur: *Gerald much enjoyed his wine-like conversation.* Impressed with Gerald's library and wide knowledge, Arthur confided that he was going to try his hand 'at some orchestral variations on an English theme (Elizabethan, Restoration, early Victorian?). Now to find a pliable tune & not too square!'[36] and asked Gerald's help in looking for one. (The problem solved itself when Bliss received Blow's Coronation Anthems in the *Musica Britannica* series, and composed his *Meditations on a Theme of John Blow.*) Bliss was proud, he wrote later, to have Joy's 'idealised' portraits, and hoped he could be as 'thoughtful and "civilised" '[37] as she had made him.

On 28 November Gerald went in to the Radcliffe Infirmary in Oxford. *G very depressed in spite of the beautiful sister in charge.* It had been intended to give him a

34 3 November 1954.
35 28 October 1954.
36 7 November 1954.
37 6 March 1955.

drug that acted on the whole lymphatic system, but tests showed that though the glands were enlarged, the blood count was better. Since the drug had side effects, it was decided he might be better without it for the moment. *G very impressed by the organization of the hospital, the care and attention given by the doctors*. He scored In Terra Pax for ten hours on the first day, which astonished the nurses but was for him *a lovely chance of work without interruption*.

1954, CHRISTMAS

He was home and well enough to conduct the Christmas NSP concerts. *Ashmansworth church was a lovely Christmas sight and scene. Tea for all by candle light afterwards.* Boosey & Hawkes had brought out a hundred copies of the In Terra Pax vocal score without a price on it, and Gerald gave one to each performer. Perhaps it was the juxtaposition of his time in hospital, Kiffer's coming National Service tribunal, and the refrain of his own music, 'And on earth peace, goodwill toward men', that caused him to write to Edmund Blunden in Hong Kong about patriotism. They had been trying to trace, for Howard Ferguson, a Purcell manuscript previously in the W. H. Cummings collection of over four thousand rare items, bought mostly by the Nanki Library of Tokyo. 'How sad it is that the Cummings collection, like another equally fine musical library, the Arkwright collection, was ever allowed to be scattered. It is strange how someone who imagines himself to be a patriot, doing all the right things, perhaps with six uniforms, a sword & a VC, will think nothing of selling a Shakespeare folio, a Constable or a Purcell ms, which will then be lost to the country for ever.'[38] And what *were* they to do about 'the whole beastly business of conscripting young men to carry out Government policy, right or wrong? . . . The real difficulty is to know at what point the individual is justified in parting company from orthodox society, as the Pilgrim Fathers did.' To Lady Ponsonby, widow of a radical Liberal MP, he confided his distrust of 'statesmen, politicians, policies, wars', and that his only hope lay 'in the anarchy of the individual . . . to retain complete freedom of thought and action, whatever his government may do'.[39] He comforted himself with Blunden's poem 'The Long Truce':

> And gravely as I go I reach that Grove
> Where once the Cavalier and Roundhead strove,
> And think, this peace rewards their rival love:
>
> I see them now at truce eternal lying,
> With no hoarse trumpet summoning, none replying –
> Only in sweet content for England vying.

[38] 18 December 1954.
[39] 17 May 1956.

CHAPTER FIFTEEN

Return to Chosen Hill

1955–56

He took a turn for the worse, and in January 1955 Dr Witts pressed for the immediate removal of his spleen. Gerald, with the Crees lectures to prepare for May and the Cello Concerto to complete for July, begged for the operation to be delayed. He was *terribly apprehensive*, noted Joy in her Journal: *That this should have come to me at the prime of my mental powers, with all my work before me.* The decision had to be made, however, and on 24 January 1955 Joy drove him to the Radcliffe Infirmary. *I feel as if I'm going to be guillotined*, and Joy felt as she did when she took him to the Ministry of War Transport in 1941. But the day after the operation Gerald was dictating letters, and the Vaughan Williamses, visiting, found him 'under an enormous pile of scoring paper, which seemed to take up all the room on his bed'. Joy noted that the removed spleen weighed four and a half pounds instead of a healthy four ounces, with the same unemotional precision as she had recorded the differing weights of the ice-covered and melted twigs in the Great Freeze. After a fortnight, Gerald was allowed home. He was not warned that from now on his resistance to infection would be low. The operation and blood transfusion had gained him a respite – that was all. It simply meant that he could stand further weekly X-ray treatments. They told their friends that the operation had been for appendicitis, and Gerald looked so much better that they were believed. Not even to Howard, who sent an 'ever-so-gentle and discreet imploring to take things easily for a bit',[1] did Gerald confide that his illness was fatal. He missed only one NSP rehearsal and one concert. But on 11 February he signed his Will.

Now the Cello Concerto was his prime concern. Barbirolli had chosen Christopher Bunting, a Casals pupil, to play it, and Gerald invited Bunting to Ashmansworth for a weekend in March, as the slow movement and most of the first were finished. The Finzis were impressed with his *powerful mind and great sensitivity* and the *grand manner* of his playing. Suddenly, after a long period with no songs, Gerald set Hardy's 'Life laughs onwards', its wry conclusion all too apt to his own state: 'I saw that Old succumbed to Young / 'Twas well. My too regretful mood / Died on my tongue.'

Then they went to London to stay with the Vaughan Williamses, as Kathleen Long was giving a recital in their house. *Lovely playing and interesting programme*, noted Joy, but Kathleen found Gerald's manner hard to take that evening; tense and anxious as he was, he seemed to have 'a chip on his shoul-

---

[1] 9 February 1955.

der'. Gerald contributed a variation to a set of 'Diabelleries', the tune by Alfred Scott-Gatty – 'Where's my little basket gone' – suggested by Vaughan Williams, to raise money for the Mcnaghten concerts. Gerald was puzzled by Vaughan Williams's new life. He was now a wealthy man, and gleefully talked of accountants as *the men he gets to cheat the government* (he was setting up his Trust). The Journal notes that twenty years earlier his *moral propriety would have been outraged*. Gerald's was perhaps a little outraged then: *truly there are many men in one man*. Bunting came to the house to rehearse the Concerto, and, as is customary for the soloist, showed Gerald how to make trills and double stopping more effective. Vaughan Williams suggested lengthening the cadenza, and Bunting made another visit to Ashmansworth to work at this, which *by the end of the day he & G had extended considerably*. The Finzis found him *a magnificent player and a very tortured person*. He needed work, and Gerald used Herbert Howells as an intermediary to ask for a teaching post at the Royal College of Music – but there was no vacancy.

The Finzis were part of the 'committee' to hear Vaughan Williams's Eighth Symphony, which, as Gerald had predicted, was his most light-hearted. Vaughan Williams came to their Stockcross Easter concert; the next day they took *a picnic lunch in warm sunshine on to the top of Inkpen* (the beacon on the Ridgeway). Gerald – thinking of who knows what – asked Ralph what he felt about ghosts. He replied *partly through upbringing (Wedgwoods and Darwins) and partly personal inclination he disliked anything supernatural, but that so many people seemed to have had experience of them that he couldn't pass judgement.*

PRISON AND PACIFISM

During those post-atomic bomb years Gerald was involved first with the Musicians' Organization for Peace, then with the National Peace Council. His son Kiffer had gone to the Royal Academy of Music in 1952 on a major County scholarship. He had registered as a conscientious objector, and in April 1955 he went to prison for three months, for refusing either to do National Service or to appeal on religious grounds. The Finzis found that many people admired his courage – *it is easy to see how dictators or governments can control by fear* – but Gerald privately admitted that it was not a dilemma he should like to face and that he might not have gone so far. 'Joy & Nigel went down to see Kiffer in Lewes prison,'[2] Gerald wrote to Robin Milford. 'He has lost about two stone, as they made no attempt to supplement his veg. diet.' He was in bad company, 'mostly the worst & most vicious types', and was glad to have a warder about. He asked his father to send him the score of Vaughan Williams's Sixth Symphony and Morris's *Contrapuntal Technique* to study. (Just as, nearly thirty years before, Gerald had asked Howard to bring him miniature scores to Midhurst Sanatorium.)

Kiffer came out, Gerald told Blunden, 'looking rather like a Belsen creature. But he has a kindly nature & is tolerant and good humoured and mostly thinks

2   28 May 1955.

that people are very stupid'[3] (not everybody's definition of tolerance?). Gerald
greeted his son's return by copying a verse of Blunden's from 'Return' and
laying it on his desk:

> Return; how stands that man enchanted
> Who, after seas and mountains crossed,
> Finds his old threshold, so long scanted,
> With not a rose or robin lost!

People from the great past now flit through the pages of the Journal. Gerald
had become a member of Elgar's Birthplace Trust and looked eagerly at Elgar's
daughter, hoping to see a resemblance between her and her father – but *all one
finds are the ashes of a great burnt tree*. At the next Trust meeting Arthur Bliss, *in his
usual exhilarating form*, persuaded Mrs Elgar Blake to donate a covenant *which she
ought to have done from the very beginning with her ten thousand pound fees a year. As it is a covenant for five hundred pounds is not nearly as generous as the committee pretended it was*. Parry's
elder daughter, Lady Ponsonby, came for a night, and *delighted us with her liberal
views and stories of the political past* (her husband Arthur had been elected an MP in
1908). Gerald owned the score of Parry's two-viola quintet in E flat, but
lacked the parts. These he found during alterations at the RCM, and he organized the first public performance on 12 February 1955 at Exeter College,
Oxford, through Nevill Coghill, translator and dramatic producer, fellow of
Exeter, Parry's old college.

The Finzis lunched at Ham Spray House (where Lytton Strachey had lived)
with Ralph and Frances Partridge; they found Ralph a *delightful and completely civilized man*, and talked of Kiffer's being in prison and of pacifism, *about which
[Ralph] was ardent* (he had successfully appealed to the Tribunal for Conscientious Objectors). In her turn Frances Partridge, after a summer evening's
supper at Ashmansworth, found that household 'efficient, broadminded, prosperous, somewhat Bedalian',[4] and admired the elegance of the cold meal set
out for them, and also Joy's 'splendid pre-Raphaelite looks'.

In June 1954 the Society of Women Musicians commemorated the life of
its founder Marion Margaret Scott. There were reminders of women musicians' low status when the Society was founded in 1911; tributes to her work
as a critic (Kathleen Dale) and as an authority on Haydn (Rosemary Hughes).
Gerald spoke of her as 'Champion of Genius'. All personal irritation laid aside,
and his own efforts not mentioned, he generously acknowledged her devotion
and care for Gurney, incidentally giving his own fullest assessment of Gurney's
difficult character and 'burning lyrical impulse'. In 1955 Gerald reported to
Edmund Blunden on Ronald Gurney's intransigence over a fourth volume of
Ivor's songs. Gerald had persuaded Vaughan Williams to write to Ronald,
offering to buy the manuscripts. Ronald implied that he *might* give them to
Gloucester Public Library; and Vaughan Williams quickly wrote taking this for

---

[3]   2 August 1955.
[4]   Letter of 14 March 1984.

granted: 'it might make that pathetic paranoiac feel unable to draw back'.[5] 'The quaint egotism of Ronald Gurney,'[6] replied Edmund, always readier with commiseration than wrath. Gerald had hoped Edmund might apply for a vacant Leeds University post; 'we all want you back where you really belong'.[7] It was inconceivable to Gerald that anyone would choose to work outside England. But Edmund replied 'at my age apart from other considerations I should not have been given the job, and perhaps I could not manage it'.[8]

During May 1955 Gerald gave his Crees lectures[9] at the Royal College of Music on *The Composer's Use of Words: a discussion of words and music, fusion and conflict, problems of composers and poets, vocal forms and many theories, all of which leave the birds still singing and Pilate's question unanswered.* He began with a warning from Professor Gilbert Murray, who, asked as an undergraduate to write an essay on the difference between right and wrong, found that fifty years later 'he was still going on with it'. Finzi's conclusion to his third lecture is lyrical: 'as surely as birds must sing, so long as words exist and man is capable of feeling, there will be song'. In between, he summed up his wide reading – with firm principles, strong opinions, and long historical perspective – in more measured and relaxed tones than he'd used among his friends. He gave his most compelling exposition of the changes in reputation brought about by fashion. 'The sense of one generation becomes the nonsense of the next . . . we, not they, change.' He illustrated this too from verse, comparing anthologies of 1898, 1920, and the 1950s, each preface contradicting the last: 'not all things can be bad simply because they are succeeded by something else'. He demonstrated the influence of the cultural climate on idiom by contrasting the eighteenth-century Maurice Greene's setting of Spenser's 'What guyle is this' with Rubbra's. (His performers were Norman Tattersall, Kenneth Byles, Gaynor Lewis, Valda Pluckett, and Roy Teed.) He gave an example of polarities and prejudices: 'When Sir Michael Costa heard the last Amen chorus in Messiah, he turned to Dr. W. H. Cummings and said "Now, this is the most magnificent thing ever written". Dr. Cummings agreed with him. And when Berlioz heard the same chorus he turned to his neighbour, a Mr G. A. Osborne, and said "It seems to me that they are all gargling their throats". Mr. Osborne agreed with him. Straightway you can see two incipient schools, Costa and Cummings, Berlioz and Osborne.'

He declared that his own methods were too personal to be a guide, and told only indirectly of his own creative processes. So there is no mention of Hardy, nor of his collaboration with Blunden, but much on Parry and Bridges, Stanford and Graves. However, he did draw on his own past, choosing songs by Farrar and Gurney, Stanley's 'Welcome death', Dowland's 'Time stands still', and mentioning Felton. Many of his opinions and quotations are already

5 2 August 1955.
6 18 August 1955.
7 12 March 1955.
8 13 April 1955.
9 The Crees lectures are available on www.geraldfinzi.co.uk.

familiar, and his sources are in his 'words and music' cuttings, collected over the years and now coherently assembled. His themes are the importance of the environment on the creative artist, and that native song should grow out of native language (remembering that Parry in his young days set Shakespeare in German translation!). He is good on occasional music, pointing out working to order can generate its own excitement. The BBC song experiment comes in for some stick. He quotes from Housman and Yeats, but also from Jackson of Exeter and from the Foreword to Schoenberg's *Pierrot lunaire*. Some of his prejudices sneak through: he accuses Handel of plagiarism, has a dig at Christie's Glyndebourne and at Britten, but is fair to Stravinsky and illustrates syllabic setting with Ravel's spell-binding 'Le martin-pêcheur'.

With gusto, good historical examples, and his engaging personality shining through, he gave a stimulating overview of the subject dearest to his heart (opera lay outside his field). On the whole the lectures were a passionate exposition of his 'bilge and bunkum' letter of 1936 (see p. 88). More notice was taken of them than he expected, with long reports in *The Observer* and *The Times*. Frank Howes summed it up: 'Finzi's main contention was to claim for the composer the right to range over all literature, ancient and modern, poetic or prosaic, for anything that would kindle the flame in him.'[10] *Tempo* asked for publication, but Gerald realised how much editing that would need at a time when he was sorely pressed over his Cello Concerto.

RESEARCH

In *Terra Pax* was broadcast on 27 February under John Russell, with Stanley's First Concerto, Mudge's Fourth, and Boyce's duet for tenor and bass, 'Now shall soft charity repair', which Gerald considered outstandingly good: *all G's discoveries*, noted Joy. Between going to London for the rehearsal and listening to the broadcast, Gerald conducted the first modern performance of Capel Bond's Bassoon Concerto with William Waterhouse. Gerald had checked Bond's birth-date at Gloucester and his tombstone at Binley near Coventry, discovering that he was 'an indulgent husband'. On 12 June Gerald revived Stanley's cantata *Pan and Syrinx* at Bucklebury with NSP. 'We were enchanted with the work, & every one of the arias is lovely,'[11] he told Cedric Thorpe Davie. But his tenor was a bit weak, hardly 'a gay Pan galloping thro' the glades with designs on Syrinx!' Gerald thought a work like this, to say nothing of the six concertos, ought to show that Stanley was no insignificant person. There were four portraits of him painted, engraved, and published in his lifetime; evidence that his worth had then been recognised – Gerald owned a 1784 engraving.

All this time he was having X-ray treatment, and though he had stood up well to the continuous and intensive work, he knew the facts. Ceddie asked him to return to St Andrews as external examiner when Howard Ferguson had finished his three-year stint, but Gerald replied 'that's 1958–60. I'm

10 *The Times*, 20 May 1955.
11 13 June 1955.

approaching old age, you know.'[12] On 22 June Joy wrote thankfully in her Journal: *This day Gerald finished the Cello Concerto.*

The Cello Concerto is Finzi's most ambitious instrumental work, traditional in its three movements, the first in sonata form, the second slow, the third a fast rondo. Sketches date back to the 1930s. What is new is the despatch of the start and the finish ('I feel as if I'm going to be guillotined') – the brusque slice through two contrary motion discords to reach the tonic A minor at the start, the disconcerting scamper at the end of the Rondo. The power and turbulence of the orchestral opening come from the steep dynamics and violent percussion, the rhythmic scotch-snap and trills – not decorative, but coils of energy. The low register, close chording, blunt trombones, and tam-tam make the main theme dark and compact, except for the unexpected swing to the major chord formed by the intrusive F sharp in its second bar. Gathering speed and weight, the music rushes upscale to a bar's climax in which chords holding E and F naturals grind against each other. In Finzi's songs such a stab usually occurs under a poignant word, with striking but momentary effect. Here in the Cello Concerto he hurls the dissonance as the climax of the orchestral exposition: emotion and construction are authentically at one, and the mood is disconsolate fury. The orchestra breaks onto a hollow octave dominant, crouches and springs three times, then subsides sullenly for the soloist's entry. His part is on the whole mollifying, with questing arabesques. But three times he lands, high and exposed, on a semitone clash with the orchestra. Bleak woodwinds blow over pedal points leading to the development. If there be a weakness, it is the undistinguished second subject, which has a too easily gained lyricism, and relaxes without recharging the energy. However, it yields unexpected riches in the long, complex cadenza, virtually another development. At the end there is no escape. The chords of the opening, heavy with menace, threaten the soloist whose bravura flights are finally pinned down to a single desperate note. In this movement Finzi achieves a finer lyrical and dramatic integration than in any previous work; the close thematic fabric is swung along by the lilting compound time, and the surges of tenderness and of frustration are convincing. Surely, whether consciously or not, it was the working-out of a personal and tragic situation that gave him authority over a form that might not have been suited to his temperament. That urgency tore down any inhibitions and made it possible for him to assimilate the conflict and bravura of a big first movement into his personal style.

At the time the critics, thinking perhaps of passages such as that between cues 10 and 11, remarked on the influence of Elgar. Two other presences brood over the first movement. The violent opening of Vaughan Williams's

[12] 6 June 1955.

Fourth Symphony (C/D flat, D flat/C) has surely fertilized Finzi's F/E, E/F
confrontation (three bars before cue 2). More surprising is Sibelius's Fourth
(in his early days Finzi had made a piano duet reduction of the opening). Both
works are in A minor. Finzi's brusque opening echoes the savage chords at
letter B in Sibelius's first movement. His opening A–F sharp outline follows
Sibelius; the fact that Sibelius – in a symphony – in the sixth bar gives a theme
to a solo cello suggests that Finzi might have remembered this sound-world
for his Concerto. More generally, Finzi's sometimes chilly scoring for woodwind, a feature of his melancholy moods, sounds less English than Nordic
pastoral. At a deeper level, it might seem that, in expanding his emotional
range, Finzi learnt profitably from the fury of Vaughan Williams and the foreboding of Sibelius, in two symphonies he much admired.

The opening of the *Andante quieto* is music of the utmost simplicity, in which
Finzi trusts to the plainest, most common-tongued idiom of his period (see
Ex. 16.4). It is a summation of a mood met with before, in his Introit (see
p. 52), Elegy (p. 134), and Eclogue (p. 221). The opening four-bar phrase in
D major twists in the eighth bar into C sharp minor; throbbing dotted
rhythms propel the melody on and on for twenty-eight bars before it reaches
a full close: a glorious melody formed from diatonic harmony with regular
pulse, occasional suspensions, a little imitation. As the slow movement
continues it becomes an anthology of Finzi idioms, with turn after familiar
turn of phrase. To point out a few: his way of making a climax of dotted
chords over a syncopated repeated bass note – the nine bars before cue 6 in
the Concerto, the sixteen bars before cue 24 in *Intimations of Immortality*. The
chains of thirds over a *pizzicato* bass, seven bars before cue 10 in the Concerto,
throughout 'The Rapture' in *Dies Natalis*, particularly three bars before cue 3.
Characteristic figuration: two bars before cue 1 in the *Andante* (Ex. 15.1a), two
bars before cue 4 in the Intrada from *Dies Natalis* (Ex. 15.1b)

Ex. 15.1

a)

b)

Then the orchestral climaxes formed from Example 15.1a, thickened by parallel sixths and increased dynamics, in the *Andante* before cue 13 and in the Intrada after cue 10.

Poignantly, the movement's flow is twice checked (cue 6 and five bars before cue 9) with a questioning recitative-like phrase for the cello (Ex. 15.2a) which recalls 'From dust I rise', cue 3 in 'The salutation' from *Dies Natalis* (Ex. 15.2b). In that, the words continue 'and out of Nothing now awake'. What meaning might that association have had for the dying Finzi?

Ex. 15.2

For those who love Finzi's music, recognition of these old friends in the *Andante* is welcome. However, falling back on familiar idioms might suggest a failure of invention. Also, the movement sounds long, not simply because it lasts about thirteen minutes, but because of its uncertain structure. Finzi does not really develop his themes, or show them to be changed by what happens to them: the build-up between cues 11 and 12 and the fff climax after cue 13 have already been suggested at the *allargando* between 8 and 9 (both derived from cue 1). That simple dotted figure is inflated to carry a great deal of weight. Howard Ferguson put his finger on it when he considered the movement 'heart-breakingly beautiful' but that 'formally and emotionally' it over-balanced the rest of the work. He suggested cutting the second climax and a 'largish wad of music', which he felt to be redundant. He guessed that Finzi would not do this, for he had 'the impression that the movement means something special to you'.[13] At the time he wondered if it was a tribute to Joy

[13] 21 July 1955.

and their marriage; after Gerald's death he came to believe it was his reaction to the Verdict. However, close though the movement's idiom may be to *Dies Natalis*, it does sound different. With *Intimations* behind him, and a full orchestra at his command, Finzi infuses the Concerto with a melancholy grandeur; with brief but evocative horn solos, and trombones held in reserve for the first 'from dust' phrase. To the freshness of *Dies* is now added experience, even tragedy. In the final bars, marked *morendo*, the soloist seems to vanish into thin air, in valedictory resignation.

The Rondo tune is eerily foreshadowed by the cello in *pizzicato* double octaves and chords. When the *allegro* sets off, it is a jaunty polonaise; on one of its returns the oboe gives it an enchanting counter-melody. There is what begins as a light dancing episode, but its trill relates back to the energy and urgency of the first movement. A *meno mosso* allows the soloist a regretful backward glance. Then, as the music seems to be working towards a cadenza with a familiar pedal note and 'scrubbing' figuration, it surprisingly clears into the relative C major with the Rondo theme grandly augmented, chorale-like on brass (much like what happens in the Toccata). It is a striking but curious episode; in its place in the *giocoso* Rondo it seems inappropriate. As a summing-up of the earlier weighty movements and the skittish Rondo it is too late, too brief. Did Finzi lose his nerve at this point? Was there something he dared not contemplate? The passage is marked *molto maestoso*, but sounds more defiant than commanding. The movement ends with a flick and a scamper. For all its jollity, the Rondo has a hectic air.

The Cello Concerto was first performed at the Cheltenham Festival on 19 July 1955. Gerald was delighted with Bunting, who played from memory, and with Barbirolli. Arthur Bliss thought it the 'finest score you have yet written, but I admit I lean more enthusiastically to your instrumental works . . . than I do to your choral works. Somehow in the former you seem to let go more easily. I liked the drama of the first movement. I knew the elegiac second would sound beautiful & moving, and it *did*, but I was surprised at the friskiness of the finale – and its final bow (genuflection not stroke) was beautifully timed. Bravo.'[14]

The day after Joy and Gerald got home they entertained eighteen Swedish students, touring England to hear some amateur music-making. *Jolly lunch on the loggia and dining room.* The students attended a Newbury String Players rehearsal, had tea with the players, and heard the concert: Purcell, Mudge, Capel Bond, Garth, Elgar, Walter Leigh, and Francis Baines – characteristic of NSP, though perhaps not of English music elsewhere in England at that time. *There was nothing like our band in Sweden,* they said.

[14] 20 July 1955.

Gerald's mother, aged ninety, and in a nursing home in Painswick, had seen
the press notices of his Cello Concerto with intense pleasure. '*I am so happy I
really want to die.*' She was bed-ridden, and looked like Mrs Tiggy Winkle with
her fuzzy hair and little cap. The Finzis had visited her regularly and dutifully.
On 6 August Gerald was called to her side, and the next morning she died. Joy
in the Journal summed her up: *Though she was a simple and rather silly little woman, in
whom life-long deafness, and a fundamental lack of brain, had created permanent illusions about
everything, G always owed a deep debt of gratitude to her for having made him independent, in a
small way, as a young man, thus enabling him to take up music.* 'And now I feel that the
Egyptians were so right to bury possessions with an owner!' Gerald wrote to
Lady Ponsonby. 'The little bits & pieces, letters, photos etc which were so
much a part of her background for as long as I can remember, become so
much junk & there's nothing to be done but destroy them, but I hate doing
it.'[15]

A quick trip to Dorset to see Reynolds and Janet Stone allowed the Finzis to
visit the novelist Sylvia Townsend Warner at Maiden Newton, as Gerald
wanted to ask her opinion on an early music problem (in the 1920s she had
worked for *Tudor Church Music*). In her diary she described 'Tiber-eyed' Gerald,
and Joy 'with her Saracen nose': how charming he was – 'and how Italian. His
sturdy upright carriage, and his round green eyes.'[16] A performance at the
Hereford Three Choirs Festival of *Dies Natalis* pleased him. Joy used to organize
daily games of rounders between the afternoon concert and evensong, to
allow the young people to let off steam: Gerald was invariably backstop, Eric
Greene the bowler. Gerald struck people as less shy and retiring these days,
though he always had Joy beside him. Quiet in crowds, he was a delightful
conversationalist in small groups. Afterwards the Finzis drove to St David's, *this
wonderful Land's End of Wales*, where they spent five days in a borrowed caravan –
sleeping long and bathing in sunfilled bays. 'Breakfast about 10 in sunshine shook
Gerald's sense of morality,'[17] Joy reported to Alice Sumsion. It was the first
holiday they'd had as a family since their sons were grown. They called on
Peter Boorman – *an unusual and delightful find for a Cathedral organist*, they recorded.

Later that autumn Gerald and Joy drove over to the Rubbras to hear
Edmund's new Piano Concerto, but found it less arresting than they had hoped
after his Sixth Symphony. They rejoiced in his widening personality and (as it
seemed to them at the time) happy home life. He reminded them how as a
student he had innocently given an orchestral work the title 'The Call of
Nature'. They had all been highly amused at the time but *he took himself so seriously
that one could never have said anything about it.* (Gerald had avoided calling *By Footpath
and Stile* by the title of its first poem, 'Paying calls'.)

On 29 October the Music Teachers Association presented a concert of

[15] 12 August 1955.
[16] Claire Harman, ed., *The Diaries of Sylvia Townsend Warner* (London, 1994), pp. 218, 248.
[17] 20 September 1955.

Gerald's music at the Royal Academy of Music. It was *a nice gesture*, and Howard Ferguson, John Carol Case, Thea King, James Brown, and John Russell were the best performers he could want. But the audience, *mostly female of misty moth-eaten music teachers*, depressed them. Their own next NSP concert on 5 November was in Magdalen College Chapel, Oxford, and Robin Milford and Francis Baines came to hear their own works. By chance the poet Ian Davie heard music and stayed to listen. Davie had previously sent Gerald his poem *Piers Prodigal*, composed after hearing *Dies Natalis*, hoping Gerald might set it. Gerald responded with his usual care and encouragement, and discussion over the Parry–Bridges letters followed.

On an annual visit Robin Milford, *wan and fragile . . . his fundamental melancholy making birth rather than death the tragedy*, had shown Gerald his new *Fishing by Moonlight*. Gerald interested Max Hinrichsen in it; Robin then dedicated it to Gerald, in spite of Gerald's saying he would get more performances under someone like Reginald Jacques, who had a professional orchestra. So on 30 November 1955 NSP gave the work's first performance. Gerald was upset when Robin said he could not attend – unaware that because of financial problems his wife had taken a job, which meant using their car. Gerald's comments give his own view of a composer's obligations. 'If I didn't know you very well & was a proper conductor doing a proper concert, I might reasonably think "RHM is not very interested in his own work or what happens to it." '[18] He ought, thought Gerald, 'as part of the job of being a composer', to hear what performances he could. Else when the score was printed he would always be saying that he wanted to revise this page or that.

As part of his 'quiet, but endlessly active'[19] life, as he described it to Blunden, Gerald gave *In Terra Pax* at their NSP Enborne concert, with the Marlborough Singers under Peter Godfrey. It was the first of four performances that December, in some ways a rounding of the circle. The year ended with a party at the home of Gilbert Spencer, brother of the painter Stanley. *G's duet Sleighbells brought the roof down. Mad charades. Came home at midnight as dancing started. Lovely moon.*

But 1956 opened wretchedly. *Here endeth the year of grace*, wrote Joy in her Journal, *with G looking so much better that people continually remark on it*. After treatment at Oxford on 2 January, Gerald ran a high temperature and felt nausea for several days. The next week, and the next, there were treatments, and nausea, but on each Oxford day he worked on Boyce autographs at the Bodleian. By the third week he was *feeling dead and very depressed*. His only comment in his letters was an oblique one, and the more poignant. Cedric Thorpe Davie's wife had developed cancer. Gerald wrote to him encouragingly, saying she was right that the X-ray treatment would leave her depressed, but wrong that it would do no good. 'All those whom we have known' had had the radiotherapy. 'But one must be very patient with anyone who has had intimations,

---

18 25 November 1955.
19 7 December 1955.

even if not real ones, of death, and who from being a "well" person finds themselves on the other side of the curtain amongst the ill and sick. It's a horrible experience which the "well" find difficult to understand.'[20] It was altogether a sad month, with ominous presentiments.

Even then he came out fighting. The Arts Council had decided to close its regional offices. Gerald, always against centralization and in favour of amateur music, enlisted the support of Nevill Coghill, and together they rounded up John Betjeman, Cecil Day Lewis, and Vaughan Williams. Their letter deploring the decision was printed on 21 January 1956 in *The Times*.

HARDY

Suddenly he finished a Hardy song. He called it 'In five-score summers' (its first line), but Hardy, writing in 1867, had called it 1967 and looked ahead to 'new eyes, New minds, new modes, new fools, new wise'. Finzi, in January 1956, knew that by 1967 there would be nothing 'beyond a pinch of dust or two' left of him, and did not shirk from setting words that seem more macabre now than they would have to, say, John Donne. Joy all the same noted that Gerald considered the song an extract from a diary. 'For I would only ask thereof That thy worm should be my worm, Love' made it unsuitable for public performance.

It was a bitter February. The Sumsions came to visit, and Alice spent a morning in bed, looking out at the sprinkled snow and the feeding birds and loved the idleness with books. Gerald completed another early draft, 'At Middle-Field gate in February', again sadly apt to his condition. In weather too frosty for outside work, two days later he opened his Hardy again and on reading 'It never looks like summer here' instantly set it. That evening, looking through old sketches, he came across a draft of that first line. The line written today had the same shape and fall as the previous germ and was obviously the completed idea after twenty-odd years. 'If one doesn't live long enough one can't complete the hundreds of musical lines waiting final shape.' 'What makes one suddenly write a song.'

The two Hardy poems presented textual problems. Gerald turned to Toty de Navarro, as in the pre-war days when Toty had sent his own poems for Gerald's criticism. Hardy had revised 'Middle-Field Gate' and in so doing had left the original verb 'lie' to agree with the new noun 'ploughland';[21] and in 'It never looks like summer now', how did Toty think the last word, 'elsewhere', should be stressed? Typical, of Gerald's scrupulousness, and of his way of using his friends' judgment as a touchstone.

RESEARCH

His main work for the past six months had been the preparation of the *Musica Britannica* volume of Boyce overtures. His realizations were invariably 'basic' ones, he told Cedric Thorpe Davie; 'not only do I like them better than florid

[20] 11 January 1956.
[21] 6 February 1956.

ones, but they can be done in the van or in the train!'[22] Kiffer had helped by searching, copying, and realizing figured basses, and his 'care and endurance' were acknowledged by Gerald in the edition. But it had meant [writing] continuo parts, and constant research and the following up of every clue, checking of various copies, compar - ing original parts with the score and so on. He had had to reduce the number of over- tures, he told Ceddie, as he had over-run by forty pages; there would still remain the published eight symphonies of 1760 and twelve overtures of 1770 to be reprinted and properly edited. 'Isn't it extraordinary that the old chap became completely forgotten as an orchestral composer.'[23] He had been back in touch with W. C. Smith asking for composition dates of the 1760 Sympho- nies. The British Museum gave 1750, but Squire didn't then know that two of them were birthday odes for 1756. What about dates for The Chaplet and The Shepherd's Lottery? The Twelve Overtures were one of the few dated (1770) sets, so Grove had no excuse for 1720. Next Gerald was after the date for the Cam- bridge Installation Ode, and pointing Smith towards a Musical Times article for 1 August 1901, which suggested that the twelve voluntaries for organ or harpsi- chord, supposed to be by Greene, were probably by Boyce.[24]

All this went into the ten-page Preface to his chosen eighteen overtures, fourteen from Royal Birthday and New Year Odes, one from the masque Peleus & Thetis, two from St Cecilia Odes (how Blunden's collaborator must have chuckled!) and one from an anthem. Gerald lists the instrumental music published during Boyce's lifetime, then all the manuscript works with their dates. He summed up: 'the virtues of Boyce's contribution will be mainly found, not in innovations, but in his melodic freshness and in a fully inte- grated personality, every bar of whose work bears the mark of a manly and direct style, a style which, though belonging to an age that eschewed emotional subtlety, yet ranged from buoyancy and gaiety to moments of simple beauty. Of his mastery there can be no question.' Who but Gerald would have managed to link Boyce with his beloved Hardy (p. xvi), in that both used the strange phrase 'my back begins to open and shut' to show the effect of emotion! In February 1956 the Finzis celebrated the finish of the volume, and drank a toast to Boyce. It is a good job done & a good deed done for a great man characteristically neglected for nearly two hundred years. How pleased he would have been to know that in 1990 his efforts would be described as 'trail-blazing'.[25]

On 11 March the Cello Concerto had its first London performance at the Royal Festival Hall. Gerald wrote to thank Barbirolli, who replied: 'The Dies Natalis, & the Concerto will be there when much else of "contemporary" will have fallen into well deserved oblivion.'[26] He hoped Boosey & Hawkes would

[22] 28 February 1955.
[23] 6 March 1956.
[24] Letters to Smith, 28 September, 12 October, 14 November, 6 December 1955.
[25] The Eighteenth Century, ed. Diack Johnstone and Roger Fiske, The Blackwell History of Music in Britain (Oxford 1990), p. xiii. The future revival of Boyce is charted by Ian Bartlett in 'Lambert, Finzi and the anatomy of the Boyce revival', Musical Times, vol. 144, no. 1884 (2003).
[26] 21 March 1956.

send copies to leading European cellists. They did, and when Casals wrote to thank him it was, Gerald told Cedric Thorpe Davie, like hearing from Paganini or Sarasate.

NSP

Elizabeth Maconchy came to hear Jim Brown and NSP play through her Suite for oboe and strings, composed for them. At the rehearsal, Kiffer conducted the Bach Double Concerto, which his younger brother Nigel, now at the Guildhall School of Music, played with the leader. Kiffer was ready for some conducting experience; but there was, too, always at the back of Joy's and Gerald's minds the question of who might take over NSP in an emergency. A few days later NSP went to play at Lymington – *a happy outing*. They ate sandwiches on the sea wall behind a windbreak then *walked out towards the channel and were loathe to return*. Nigel again played in the Double Bach (at a later concert, nervous but thrilled, he played it with Frederick Grinke). This family involvement made it easy to recapture the atmosphere as the Players moved from place to place. The audience was partly drawn from the immediate parish, but some followed the little orchestra round throughout the year. One of these, a sixth-form schoolgirl called Marianne Atkinson, remembered that at one concert when it came to the Bach, Finzi 'waxed quite lyrical in a very intense way' saying that the slow movement was perhaps the most beautiful piece of music ever written: 'if this means nothing to you, you can go out, there is nothing else for it'. She and her friends had not met this kind of direct involvement before:

> I see him as smallish, neat and trim, with much sprinkling of grey in the curly black hair, and with an intent look, usually but not always serious. He might have been a little shy; there was a certain solemnity, but suppressed gaiety as well as strong feelings could also be guessed at. The voice and gestures were rather quick and precise; in the last year or so he wore steel-rimmed glasses to conduct.[27]

VISITORS, 1956

That Spring, Lady Ponsonby came for three days, *very crippled, but her mind still nice and vigorous and cantankerous.* John Betjeman came over from nearby Wantage. Laurence Whistler invited himself, and was amazed that Gerald knew his work well enough to charge him – 'in his rather aggressive, kindly way', as he later recalled – with leaving out a poem published in 1939 ('Now while destruction like an imbecile') from his *Collected Poems*. Their apple-growing friend Justin Brooke and his wife stayed, and there were great fruit talks. Frank and Averil [Morley] Fraser Darling came to supper and commented: '*It's not for nothing that someone called Finzi built this Roman villa.*' Howard Ferguson visited, after an Italian holiday, and went through Gerald's new songs and was *enthusiastic and helpful,* Joy noted; *did some nice cooking with me.*

[27] Letter of 1 October 1980.

By now many people sought Gerald's advice. Some were old friends, like Dick Latham, who invited himself to discuss the scoring of his Te Deum and was filled with remorse after Gerald's death, feeling he had taken up precious time. Young instrumentalists came for auditions, and were given a chance of concerto experience. Young composers submitted works for NSP. Some asked just for advice; one received a long and thoughtful letter (which Joy copied into her Journal), with the pill kindly sugared: 'Now I can honestly say that, *at this stage* it isn't possible to find anything characteristic in your work, but that's no reason why it shouldn't appear in due course. The only way to compose is by composing.' Others, such as Philip Cannon, gained a performance and found Finzi's letters useful as publicity material. Peter Cox came from Dartington Hall to discuss who should be the next music director there. In London, Finzi dined with Boult and Vaughan Williams to plan the programme for an all-Holst concert (10 December 1956, the first-fruit of the Vaughan Williams Trust – Gerald was on the committee). *G got his way with nearly all his suggestions, including* The Morning of the Year. *Boult amiable, agreeing with everything said, much to our annoyance!*

The Finzis loyally attended concerts of friends' music. They went to hear Rubbra's new Piano Concerto and Vaughan Williams's Eighth Symphony. With their interest in Marlborough since Gerald had adjudicated there, they went to an opera, *Circe*, written by Anthony Smith Masters for the boys. It was a *remarkable achievement, considering the small place music is allowed in a public school.* Because they had to be in London to hand over the Boyce edition, they went to Mozart's *Marriage of Figaro*, at Sadler's Wells. In June they saw Stanford's *The Critic* at the Guildhall with the Vaughan Williamses, who were to go back to Ashmansworth with them the next day. By the time they had finished supper it was late, and Vaughan Williams wanted to see the dawn. So at 1.15 they left London and drove through the night to Ashmansworth. On arrival Vaughan Williams ate two huge bowls of cornflakes and honey, then sat at a window with his hearing aid tuned to listen to the birds and watch the dawning sky. *They were grateful for the effort the eighty-four-year-old had spurred us to.*

They had a flock of sheep in the orchard during apple blossom time – a Samuel Palmer painting, Gerald told Edmund Blunden. *His last Bucklebury concert was all that a midsummer night concert should be.* Two days later a hundred and twenty people came to country dancing on the Ashmansworth lawn in aid of the village hall fund. *Lovely sight dancing against the distant view – long shadows and the children playing under the fir trees. Shush* [Richard Shirley Smith] *danced clumsily and rapturously the whole evening until dusk.*

As July opened, Gerald was rescoring *In Terra Pax* for full orchestra for the Gloucester Three Choirs Festival. Howard's *Amore Langueo*, dedicated to Joy and Gerald, was to have its first performance there, and Howard called in to lunch to discuss festival plans. Gerald seemed in reasonably good health; but for the first time Joy records Kiffer's birthday in the Journal on 12 July, and on 14 July *G's 55th birthday.* That day Gerald went through the Hardy songs finished over the last months. The fifth, completed on his son's birthday, and born of such outward happiness and inner despair, was Hardy's I said to Love: 'Mankind shall cease: so let it be.' A more violent one than some of the recent ones and therefore a help by way of contrast was Joy's cool comment in her Journal.

1956, ON CRITICS

After the success of Gerald's Cello Concerto at Cheltenham in 1955, the Finzis naturally went to the Festival in 1956, though Gerald had nothing in the programme. The only works they really enjoyed were Sibelius's Fifth, Vaughan Williams's Eighth, and Rubbra's Sixth symphonies; and, of the new works, Kenneth Leighton's Cello Concerto. Joy headed a paragraph Critics in her Journal, and recorded their joint opinion. As normal the press notices showed what a wide divergence exists between their way of thinking and as musicians think. Colin Mason had nothing but contempt for anything that was of a particular idiom. Peter Heyworth, another pipsqueak, had therefore nothing but contempt for Rubbra's Symphony and raved about the Iain Hamilton work. Colin Mason warned Kenneth Leighton about writing in a dead language! 'When deeply cast down by the harsh words of a review, [Gerald] first taught me to recognise the completely shallow and ephemeral nature of newspaper criticism,' Leighton later recalled.[28] Frank Howes found Edward German a pathetic oddity showing how bad the music was at the earlier part of the century! . . . The nicest thing . . . was the pleasure of meeting little Diana McVeagh [who was not on that occasion writing for the press, and so escaped censure]. We were charmed by her personality. A great character for one so apparently demure and young. Gerald expounded his views on criticism in letters to the composer Anthony Milner, deploring the pressure put on younger people to conform to a minority style. 'I take it to be one of the glories of the world that it can hold a Byrd at one end and a Berg at the other: that we can appreciate a Bartók . . . and a Parry. Surely conservatism and liberalism are states of mind, not languages.'[29]

MORE VISITORS

Cedric Thorpe Davie and his family came for their usual summer visit, then Robin Milford for his, leaving with a considerable regard for Kiffer's 'varied talents in wine-making, hen-house erection, croquet-playing etc (not perhaps in car-driving, for I found that rather alarming!)'.[30] The Finzis went over to Bernard Robinson's music camp at Bothamstead. This wonderful organization has now been going on for nearly thirty years and BR, a scientist, has been an example to professional musicians. But they had to sit through Berlioz's Harold in Italy, which they found unbelievable rubbish.

In August, Vaughan Williams and Ursula came to stay, he working on his Ninth Symphony. They drove him through the summer countryside to Avebury, and to Oare where he had composed part of Flos Campi. He belied Gerald's good advice to young composers by asking for scores of the astringent

[28] Finzi Trust Friends Newsletter, vol. 6, no. 1, 1988.
[29] 12 August 1956.
[30] 13 August 1956.

moderns to see if he could get some ideas from them! But he had always had, they concluded, the power of *changing his speech without ever altering his essential core.* While he was there, Gerald finished a setting of 'Harvest', Blunden's poem of regret for unfulfilment, which asks 'what honey combs have I to take, what sheaves to pile?' In 1923 the young man had written to the great composer for permission to quote a tune. Now they were reaching the end of their lives together.

Gerald was confident enough to accept an invitation from Herbert Howells, now professor at London University, to give three lectures during 1957. He also agreed to compose a new work for the Hallé Centenary in 1958. *Gerald was very thrilled by this,* Joy noted, *and I was so glad that he began to get excited by it and bought immense quantities of MS paper. I knew he would never be able to undertake a big scale work again.* He was touched that Barbirolli wrote to him on the eve of an operation that meant he would be unable to conduct the Cello Concerto at the Proms on 31 August. In London for a Three Choirs rehearsal Gerald met Edmund Blunden, over on a flying visit for a conference. He found him looking *frail and tired* and wondered about the future for this *lovable and most rare minded man of letters.*

At the end of August Gerald *was still in song way.* He took up and finished setting Bridges' poem 'Since we loved', a brief but serenely triumphant song:

> All my joys my hope excel,
> All my work hath prosper'd well,
> All my songs have happy been,
> O my love, my life, my queen.

Gerald never dedicated a work to Joy. They were so close, it would have seemed like dedicating his music to himself; but if ever a woman deserved that tribute, Joy did.

1956, LAST THREE CHOIRS

So the Finzi family went off to Gloucester, to *one of the happiest Three Choirs we have ever had.* They were in King's School house again, with the Vaughan Williamses, Howard Ferguson, Meredith Davies, David Willcocks, Peter Godfrey and his wife, Richard Shirley Smith, and Harold Brown; and friends such as Herbert Howells, Edmund Rubbra, and John Russell were constantly in and out – *exhilarated by the high spirits of the young people in the house party.* Alice Sumsion had persuaded Joy to exhibit her drawings of musicians, which were visited by about a thousand people. The Finzis rejoiced in Howard's success. *Amore Langueo had a fine shape with the climaxes marvellously placed. The general texture is continually moving and restless as perhaps befits such an erotic poem.* Gerald conducted the full orchestral version of his *In Terra Pax* and was delighted with the performance. The Vaughan Williamses and the Finzis visited Rutland Boughton, whose Glastonbury Festival had meant so much to the young Gerald. Now an old man, Boughton said contentedly that he had done all he wanted to in his life.

It was the most natural thing in the world for the Finzis to take the Vaughan Williamses up Chosen Hill, where Gerald had stood over thirty years before and heard the bells ring in the New Year: the starting point for In Terra Pax. 'This is where I got the idea,' he told them. While the two wives stood outside in the September sun, Gerald took Uncle Ralph into the sexton's cottage. It didn't seem at all important that one of the sexton's children had chickenpox.

This year, for their traditional break after the festival, Gerald and Joy went to East Anglia. Characteristically it was to help young people. They took Richard Shirley Smith to meet John Aldridge, the painter they had befriended during the war when he was stationed at Newbury. 'Shush' showed Aldridge his portfolio, and asked advice about the Slade. Next day the Finzis drove to Justin and Edith Brooke. They talked apples and apricots, and arranged that Justin should advise the Bliss's daughter, who, just married, was considering moving to the country to grow fruit.

Gerald was happy to be back in his loved East Anglia, driving through the golden cornfields. But he complained of pain in his chest. Once home, he *took dope and went soon to bed.* Next morning Joy diagnosed a rash as shingles. By Monday the pain was acute but he was able to get about. For that week he had morphia night and morning. On Wednesday, 19 September he wrote to Cedric Thorpe Davie:

> This week was planned to be our annual three or four days holiday and we were going down to Dorset & had some nice meetings with friends all fixed up. We even planned this good weather! Then on Friday I burst out into a most horrible and hideous complaint called shingles which means that I shall be immobile for about a fortnight, and pretty stupid too, as there is nothing for it but morphia and veganin every four hours. Still, I have managed to correct the last proofs of the Capel Bond with which you will be enchanted.

Then chickenpox, a virus-related illness, developed, and that Saturday Kiffer had to take the first of the new season's NSP rehearsals. *Boys greatly entertained G by playing through a salon piece for cello and violin on Sunday.* On Monday Gerald's temperature was normal, and he had a Pilsner beer and some salmon and peas for lunch. That afternoon Joy noticed his thinking was muddled; and he showed no interest when John Russell dropped in to see him. Their doctor called in a second opinion. By the Tuesday Gerald could not speak; and had a very restless night. On Wednesday morning Joy knew she could no longer look after him. He went by ambulance to the Radcliffe Infirmary in Oxford. Joy arranged for him to listen to his Cello Concerto, a recording of which from the Proms was broadcast that evening, but he made no reference to it. It was found that he had encephalitis, inflammation of the brain. That night he had a short convulsion. When Joy went to the hospital next day, 27 September 1956, he took some nourishment; and (she concluded the Journal) *as I sat and talked to him I became quite contented, even happy in feeling all was well with possibly the awareness of the end of his suffering. I stayed with him until the evening and shortly after I left he had another convulsion and died.*

CHAPTER SIXTEEN

Epilogue

Finzi was cremated privately on 2 October 1956. Frank Howes followed his *Times* obituary ('there is no knowing what he might have done') with a sepa-rate article about him. Other *Times* tributes came from, among others, Vaughan Williams, Arthur Bliss, Graham Hutton, Edmund Rubbra, John Russell, Gilbert Spencer ('this upright man'), and A[lan] W[ard]; and in the provincial papers from Ernest Bradbury, Arthur Milner, Tony Scott and John Sumsion.[1] Benjamin Frankel wrote in *The New Statesman* and in *Music and Musicians*. On 27 January 1957 there was a memorial concert at the Victoria and Albert Museum; it opened with Mudge's Fourth Concerto, Eric Greene sang *Dies Natalis*, and there were two first performances: Kathleen Long played the Eclogue and John Carol Case and Howard Ferguson performed *I Said to Love*. Both Gerald's sons played in the Kalmar orchestra, conducted by John Russell.

When Joy's sister Mags died in 1973, Joy scattered her ashes and Gerald's on May Hill, so returning him to the place he had long cherished. After Reynolds Stone had cut the memorial tablet for Vaughan Williams in West-minster Abbey, Joy asked him to cut one for Gerald. This stands in Ashmansworth churchyard, with classical lettering on a grey-green slate from a Somerset quarry. In 1976 Joy commissioned a window in the church porch from Laurence Whistler: a symbolic tree, whose buds are notes of music, draws life from the initials, among them GF, of fifty English composers, from Dunstable to Britten. It is thick glass, so that – engraved on both sides – it gives the illusion, as you pass by, that the ethereal tree moves across the land-scape behind.

Kiffer finished sorting Parry's manuscripts and saw the eighteenth-century proofs through the press. In 1957 he conducted Newbury String Players in a private recording, with John Russell on organ continuo, Nigel Finzi and Anna Shuttleworth in violin and cello solos, of four of Stanley's Op. 2 concertos in Gerald's editions. Anthony Lewis recorded six of the Boyce overtures on L'Oiseau-lyre SOL 60041. Joy gave Finzi's autographs to the Bodleian Library, where they joined Parry's. Joy and Howard saw to the publication in 1959 of a fourth volume of Ivor Gurney's songs, and that year lodged his manuscripts in Gloucester City Public Library. The eighteenth-century microfilms and scores, some from Parry's library, were valued by Albi Rosenthal, who described the collection as the finest of its period in private hands; Cedric Thorpe Davie

---

[1] Some obituaries are reprinted in *Finzi Trust Friends Newsletter*, vol. xii (*recte* xiii) 1995.

arranged for it to be bought by the University of St Andrews in 1966, with a £3,000 grant from the Pilgrim Trust (the material included correspondence, manuscripts, and Finzi's unpublished editions).

Leonard Clarke helped Joy list the three thousand books in Finzi's library of literature, and in 1974 she donated these to Reading University. Reynolds Stone had made a wood-engraving of Ashmansworth church with the young apple trees in the foreground, which Joy used as Finzi's bookplate. A handsome catalogue was produced in 1981. Also in 1981 Joy gave Gerald's music library to Reading, including – since NSP had come to a natural end – some seven hundred sets of orchestral parts. For more than thirty years the collection, with Finzi's furniture, memorabilia, and seven of Joy's portrait drawings, was housed in the Finzi Room. When Reading's music department was closed in 2005, it became part of the Special Collections. Toty de Navarro's *Collected Poems*, edited by his widow and Howard Ferguson, were privately printed in 1980. Blunden's poem, 'For a Musician's Monument: G.F.', was published in *A Hong Kong House, Poems of 1951–1961*. In 1997 came Stephen Banfield's fine study of Finzi.

In Finzi's Will (he left £8804. 8s. 6d) he asked for the 're-issue or furtherance in any way of my musical works'. During his life, recordings had been made of *Dies Natalis* (see p.150) and of the partsong 'White-flowering days', in *A Garland for the Queen*. After his death the first recording (1964) was of music by Holst and Finzi: Imogen conducted her father's music, and Kiffer conducted *Dies Natalis*. Has there ever been another such double generation partnership? Wilfred Brown's interpretation is among his finest: intelligent, poetic, and informed with his acute but gentle feeling for words. In 1969 Joy donated Finzi's royalties to a Trust which sponsored recordings, so generating an audience and earning further resources. First came Hardy songs performed by John Carol Case and Howard Ferguson. The Trust has since subsidised many recordings of Finzi, and also of music by Ferguson, Leighton, Gurney, and Michael Berkeley, among others. To mark the twenty-fifth anniversary of Finzi's death in 1981 the Trust promoted a song competition and a weekend of English music at Ellesmere College, Shropshire. Since the 1990s the Trust has, with Boosey & Hawkes, published new performing editions. These include the cello and clarinet concertos, edited by Jeremy Dale Roberts, and the early violin concerto, edited by Stephen Banfield; also vocal anthologies which make the song cycles available to both high and low voices. Following the centenary celebrations in 2001, a Finzi scholarship scheme (suggested by a concept in the Trust deed) has seen an average of five awards each year. In 1982 the Finzi Friends was formed, which hosts gatherings at the Three Choirs Festivals and at Ashmansworth, and in 2001 inaugurated the triennial Festival of English Song under Iain Burnside's direction, in Ludlow.

In 1974 Joy moved to Yew Tree Cottage, then later to Bushey Leaze, both near Newbury. In 1967 *A Point of Departure*, her poems with engravings by

Richard Shirley Smith, was published. In 1987, encouraged by the painter Richard Eurich, she published her portrait drawings, In that place. The mysterious title prompted the question 'in what place?' – some of the fifty-seven portraits having been drawn since she left Ashmansworth. 'In England' she replied majestically. Not only are her drawings remarkable for their finesse and vitality, they are a tribute to her friendships. Among the musicians are Bliss, Boult, Ferguson, Milford, Thorpe Davie and Vaughan Williams; among the writers and poets, Blunden, Ursula le Guin, Helen Thomas (the poet Edward's widow), and Sylvia Townsend Warner; among the artists, David Jones and Richard Eurich. The 'after supper' portrait of Vaughan Williams is in the National Portrait Gallery. Joy died on 14 June 1991 at Ashmansworth, aged eighty-four. Her vigorous, productive life was celebrated at St Martin's Church, East Woodhay, on 14 September 1991, and her name was added to Gerald's on the memorial stone at Ashmansworth. Below both was added 'This root, this stem, this flowering tree'. The Finzis' Ashmansworth home remained in the family. Kiffer, married to Hilary du Pré in 1961, stayed on, bringing up his family. Nigel, who became managing director of Belhasa Projects, died suddenly in Dubai on 25 June 2010.

Finzi had left a good deal unpublished. Some works were complete, others not, for though he was mortally ill, the end came unexpectedly. (In his catalogue he allocated opus numbers to unfinished and merely projected compositions.) From the twenty-six completed songs Joy, Howard, and Kiffer compiled four sets. Two are of Hardy poems, Till Earth Outwears, and I Said to Love, (both published in 1958). To a Poet (1965) and Oh Fair to See (1966) are each to words of various poets. Joy, as usual, singled out a phrase from a poem as a title. There are sketches that suggest that Finzi had hoped to compose groups on words by Blunden (including the poems 'Return', see p. 235 and 'The Long Truce', see p. 232), de la Mare, Drummond, Traherne; a Bestiary from de la Mare's anthologies, and perhaps a Hardy set for a woman's voice. There were three instrumental works (Prelude, Elegy, Eclogue) ready for publication. Finzi had worked on The Fall of the Leaf since the 1920s, borrowing the title from Martin Peerson's piece in the Fitzwilliam Virginal Book. It was complete as a piano duet, but only sixty-four of its one hundred and fifty-eight bars were fully scored. Howard Ferguson completed the orchestration for publication.

The two unpublished sets of songs for tenor were performed at Ashmansworth on 24 July 1957; Edmund Blunden read the poems before Wilfred Brown and John Sumsion performed them (Howard Ferguson was on tour abroad). Sylvia Townsend Warner, making her first visit to Finzi's home, recorded in her diary: 'It is a beautiful small modern house that already looks mature ... we had a grand supper in the hand with champagne ... it was one of the best, the most amiable & well-knit parties I have ever known. Candles all over.' She wondered whether there were twenty-one candles in celebration of Nigel's twenty-first birthday. Joy replied – with characteristic practicality – 'I bought six pounds'. 'Cascades of swallows, & pears ripening on the wall,' reflected Townsend Warner, 'Alas, poor Gerald!'[2]

'Old age is dust and ashes': that at least Finzi was spared. The adage is one of the leading ideas that ran through his life. 'Work is what matters.' 'Time on his shoulder.' 'All only constant is in constant change.' 'Much to be said for limitations.' 'The mute inglorious Miltons.' 'And that one talent which is death to hide.' 'To care for the thing itself rather than for the appearance of the thing.' 'Men are great or small not according to their language but to their stature.' And his creed: 'A song outlasts a dynasty.'

'It is the business of the artist *to get on with his job*', he wrote to Vera Strawson in May 1927. His sense of elevated dedication, of a vocation, was total. Robin Milford noted his 'terrific ideal of the importance of the Artist'. Although he could be ruthless towards those who were not creative, he was endlessly supportive of those who were. His first impulse when making a new friend was to get to know their 'collected works'. His birthday and Christmas greetings usually end 'and much work'. To Robin Milford: 'much work in 1950 (cd one wish, as a personal wish, for anything better)'. Such emphasis on work – which many artists take for granted – suggests some puritanical guilt, even fright. For all his censorious tone towards non-creative people, he was, after all, financed by investments, and living on wealth created by commerce and factories. After his death his friends described him – affectionately – as task-master, slave-driver, tyrant: 'that characteristic admonitory finger'; but he drove no-one more furiously than he drove himself.

Three times he had been a survivor. He was the only son left of four. He was too young by a few years to fight in the First War. Descended from European Jews, he escaped the Holocaust. For someone with his strong principles and conscience, there must have been a desire to atone. Once the Second War was inevitable, he was paying for his freedom. It must have struck him, the irony of moving into that house of privilege in 1939; he simply had to work hard to justify it. No wonder – for all his professions of tolerance in letters – that he felt so committed, so extreme, even violent. His life-long friend Howard Ferguson considered him most immoderate; whatever he did became an obsession. His sons cheerfully referred to 'Dad's fads'. 'I don't quite remember him resting at any moment,' recalled Edmund Blunden. No wonder, too, Finzi's passion for preservation, for the single fine poem or song; his sympathy for the young life cut short in glamorous potential, for the underdog and the neglected. He shared with Blunden this trait of siding with the less fortunate. Vaughan Williams declared that 'Gerald's swans sometimes had only two white feathers'. Occasionally Finzi's moral fervour over-rode his aesthetic judgment: how else can one account for his admiration of Menotti's

<hr>

2   *The Diaries of Sylvia Townsend Warner*, p. 238.

The Consul other than that his humanitarianism was prompted by the plight of the refugees? But his advocacy of Gurney engaged his judgment equally with his sympathy.

He held that Jewishness was a faith not a race: 'choice, not birth, made one Jewish', in Joy's opinion. But, as his large collection of cuttings on the subject shows, he made a very conscious choice. On one occasion he asked the NSP player Mrs Stein 'what is a Jew?' 'One who says he is,' she answered, and sensed Gerald's and Joy's relief at her reply. It must be remembered how very strong, socially acceptable even, anti-Semitism was in England between the wars: the Holocaust was in the future, not yet imaginable. Joy stressed that Finzi's Jewish descent was unimportant, and it was spoken of only after his death. But something unimportant may be referred to casually; Finzi's rigid self-censorship made him like a clam about his family. His closest ties were those elected (though he adored his own children). He would have been supported in rejecting his background by the two great anti-family books, Samuel Butler's *The Way of All Flesh* and Edmund Gosse's *Father and Son*, at their height of popularity in the 1920s. Many of Finzi's aphorisms recall those in Butler's Notebooks; if Butler was not the source, at least his maxims chimed with and encouraged Finzi's own. Howard Ferguson, a close friend of the Jewish Harold Samuel and Myra Hess, was surprised after Gerald's death to discover his antecedents, though any Italian would have known the name Finzi was Jewish. Herbert Howells knew, through Arthur Benjamin, but never mentioned race or religion to Gerald.

Was Finzi's reticence less to do with his Jewishness than with his foreign name? Vera Strawson recalled his fury at being politely asked 'and how do you like England, Mr Finzi?' Jean Stewart was astonished at his scorn when he was asked 'are you Italian?' His name (did he never think to change or anglicize it?) perhaps accounts for his being so insistently insular, by way of compensation. How else could a man of German and Italian descent turn himself into a model English countryman and composer? Much was suppressed, much inhibited, as is shown by the pursed lips in photographs that bothered Herbert Lambert. The issue need not be over-emphasized. Finzi was not like those deracinated composers during the last century – Russians fleeing from the Revolution, Jews fleeing from the Nazis – all having to make new lives in a new country. He severed his roots by choice. His life was self-created.

Ashmansworth was a tangible expression of the Finzis' principles. They built it for his work. Gerald being a vegetarian, growing crops made sense. The house provided a base for a function in the neighbourhood; unlike many village activities, Newbury String Players was a valid offering of the Finzis' talents to their locality. When Gerald died, having conducted 164 concerts, one rehearsal was cancelled; then Kiffer took over and conducted the remaining 215. It was business as usual.

Working alone, without the colleagues of any institution, Finzi became a prolific correspondent. Often the same passage appears in several of his letters. Although for him music had absolute, and relationships only relative value, he was a staunch friend. Howard Ferguson recalled how he embroiled people, bound them by the demands he made. His doctor Tom Scott stressed 'the number of people who put their roots into Gerald'. Edmund Blunden thought he rather cultivated gifted people. Some said he had his showy side, and saw in him 'a streak of self-importance' – 'rather affairé', Sybil Eaton thought he became. Some friends – John Sumsion among them – were troubled by his idealistic encouragement of lesser composers such as Tony Scott and Robin Milford, who lacked his financial independence; Ruth Scott feared her husband was in 'danger of hero-worship'.

With Howard Ferguson he forged a working relationship much like that between Vaughan Williams and Holst. Ferguson stressed his reliability in musical matters, in the grinding business of proof correction; and his integrity in the giving and taking of criticism. However kindly, he was quite unable to compromise himself: 'it looks a useful work of an amiable sort'[3] was the highest praise he could summon for Ceddie Thorpe Davie's *The Thistle and the Rose*. Vaughan Williams prized his 'warmth, vitality, energy'. Finzi at first felt adulation for the older composer, then came to respond to him with great frankness, and enlisted his wealth and influence in good causes. Sumsion was another friend of reciprocal worth who gave him practical help in conducting and in writing for the piano, and on occasion with a compositional problem; in return Finzi read scores and offered suggestions for the Three Choirs Festivals. Finzi was generous in writing to other artists to express his admiration: to Dag Wirén, for instance, after NSP played his Serenade in 1950, to Arthur Benjamin after hearing a broadcast of his *Prima Donna*; and he was scrupulous in thanking performers of his own music. He actively helped musicians down on their luck or just starting out, approaching the Musicians' Benevolent Fund in 1949 for the pianist Philip Levi, and the Butterworth Fund for Malcolm Williamson in 1956.

Vaughan Williams saw the Finzis' marriage as 'uncomplicated and perfect'; but it could not easily have been predicted. Joy's County upbringing gave her an authority – that loud voice! – surprising in one of such sensibility. A powerful, even formidable personality, she hid her deep feelings and shied away from sentiment. To greet her, thought Laurence Whistler, 'was like kissing a hollyhock'.[4] She came to uphold, even more vehemently, Gerald's disdain for conventions, for superficial living, for false priorities. Fastidious in taste, the Finzis were content to do without much that worldly people deem necessary, but what they had was of the first quality. Joy's poetic heart but practical hands, her tenderness for anything that grew, made it possible for Gerald to achieve his rural dream at Ashmansworth, where he could compose his idylls and eclogues. John Russell even felt he contaminated the innocent atmosphere there, but the Finzis never considered him an intimate friend.

---

3   15 March 1953.
4   Christopher Finzi, ed., *Joy Finzi 1907–1991: tributes from her friends* (Privately Printed, 1992) p. 47.

Joy's radical simplicity cut through problems as though they did not exist. Her magnetism, even more than Gerald's, attracted young people to their circle. Was her fierce and loving protection of him always beneficial? Some friends lamented the sacrifice of her own creative work, found her eternal patience with him nearer to over-indulgence, her relentlessly poetic attitudes affected. But she gave him what he needed – 'Joy *made* Gerald,' declared Barbara Gomperts, who knew him before his marriage; and Richard Shirley Smith summed it up: 'Gerald was the boss but Joy ran everything.' Theirs was a partnership of ideals and endeavour. At his death her first feeling was of relief that there had been no disintegration, no slow failure when he could no longer compose.

LATE HARVEST

'Bright is the ring of words/When the right man rings them.' There is little doubt that Finzi considered himself such a man. In the final year of his life he had a burst of song-writing.

Six of the songs were to words of his lifelong composition companion, Hardy. In 'It never looks like summer', the little song that he completed 'instantly' after a gap of many years (see p. 244), Hardy revisits Cornwall after Emma's death. Finzi captures past happiness – 'summer it seemed to me' – in the singer's conjunct seven-note rise in the first stanza; and present sadness in the second stanza by the six-note fall in the bass, the flattening keys, and the singer's broken phrases. 'Life laughs onwards' is another 'memory' poem, but longer, and Finzi treats it discursively with an anthology of his idioms. As old succumbs to young, it is poetically apt that the musical figure for 'looked for an old [abode]' should meditatively introduce the positive phrase 'Life laughed and moved on . . .'. In this song Finzi seems to acknowledge how rare in Hardy's poems is the summing-up ''Twas well' by setting those two words unaccompanied. So the singer accepts that the past is past, in the opening phrase, now augmented.

'For life I had never cared greatly' is a rondo, in style casual but vigorous, one of Finzi's best tunes. As it proceeds, Hardy's thought becomes grimmer, and Finzi's light accompaniment denser; but there is a shining moment when the piano is pitched above the voice in the little descant at 'uncloaked a star'. The resolute ending matches the poem's gritty optimism.

In 'At Middle-Field gate in February' the foggy droplets – 'as evenly spaced as if measured' – bring for the last time Finzi's alternating chords, now harmonically stark: memories of Holst's 'Saturn', perhaps, or Debussy's *Des Pas sur la neige*. In this saddest of songs the last verse has none of Finzi's usual melodic warmth. The piano's final comment – 'how dry it was' – might apply not only to the weather but to the withered memory. Hardy's title for 'In five-score summers' was '1967' (he wrote the poem in 1867) and Finzi added the sub-title 'Meditation'. But the song is restless rather than meditative; for once Finzi's illustrative images seem only to chop it up, the violent chromaticisms being at odds with the simpler inflections. In the defiant 'I said to love', Hardy attacks Cupid as a trickster, but to be defied only if 'mankind shall cease'. Finzi's insistent *allegro* takes in rhetorical declamation, running scale accompaniment, extreme chromatics, low thrumming chords, false relations, and a repeated melodic tag for the refrain 'I said to love' – familiar devices, but used here to violent effect. All this explodes in a virtuoso double octave piano cadenza. It is an extraordinary song, on the verge of toppling over into melodrama, but held in check by sheer power and energy. It was Finzi's last setting of Hardy, completed only weeks before his death. In the final 'so let it be' it is tempting to hear his angry acceptance of his fate.

Finzi is often praised for his word-setting, as though he did little more than transcribe verbal values into pitch. That suggests something mechanical, pernickety, and conscientious, rather than, in his case, a relish for sound and sense. Even in strophic songs he adapts the repeats to the new words, and he seldom re-structures a poem to fit his music (an exception is 'His golden locks'). His one-note-to-one-syllable style, common enough in English song before Britten and Tippett, in Finzi was 'an article of faith'. It is customary too in French *mélodie*, but Finzi's practice can only superficially be compared with that, for French is unaccented, and English heavily accented; a Finzi song would be devilish to translate to *any* other language, since rhythm – the common factor between verse and music – dictates such different profiles. In his Crees lectures Finzi describes how 'some composers', on a very first reading of a line, 'instantly' match it with a musical equivalent. Surely all the phrases from Dies Natalis in Example 3.4, once heard, are unforgettable. There are many other tuneful snatches that hug the memory: almost recitative, affectionate, conversational, often colloquial, sometimes poignant, words caught once and for all:

Ex. 16.1

Finzi does not always hold to the general principle that unimportant words should be unstressed. In 'Intrada' (p. 47), for instance, the words 'and' and 'but' are lengthened and syncopated. In 'Her Temple' the unexpected stress on 'that' draws attention to the preceding 'not' and the following 'forget'. Finzi checks the melodic flow just *around* an important word or words, so throwing emphasis on them. It is syncopation used as punctuation:

Ex. 16.2

He declared that he had no theories about word-setting. 'It comes just "natural-like" and I can't see why a melodic line should not be just as beautiful with a decent accentuation as without. If it were a question of sacrificing the music to verbal accentuation I shouldn't hesitate to be on the side of the music, but I have never in my life found it necessary.'[5] It was not in his temperament to demand it.

In spite of his sympathy for the poet, his Hardy songs are less spontaneous than some of his others. It is as if he felt himself a trustee of Hardy's words, with a highly developed awareness of his responsibility. His very scrupulousness tends to enforce uniformly moderate speeds. Of course he could write a broad swinging tune, a 'Rollicum-rorum', and a perfect single-span lyric such as 'Since we loved' (1956). But he would not, could not, have composed a vocal quicksilver scherzo like Britten's 'Queen and huntress' (*Serenade*), in which voice and horn vie instrumentally with each other. Indeed, Finzi was apt to call Britten's songs vulgar. Not for him either the all-consuming melody, the thrilling arabesques of Howells's 'Come sing and dance', or the ardent headlong impetus of Bridge's 'Love went a-riding' or Quilter's 'Love's philosophy'. His lyricism soars most gloriously in the 'Rhapsody' of *Dies*.

However, Finzi's concern for words goes deeper than declamation, to the poems' thoughts and feelings. Here modulation comes into play. Many of his songs begin and end in different keys. Such a song is 'The birthnight' (1956), Finzi's first completed setting of de la Mare since 1921. Though the poet's imagery is of the open countryside at night, the song's mood is enclosed, intimate, and loving. It begins as a lullaby, the tranquil syncopated rocking, derived from 'dearest', suggesting the waiting cradle. A rising scale reaches first for the stars, then for the Spring, and lastly, after a hushed, withdrawn enharmonic change – D flat to C sharp – it symbolises the birth, the singer's final unaccompanied note being naked as the child. The song begins in D flat, and ends in F sharp, as it welcomes new life in a new key – F sharp could have been spelt out as G flat, the song's initial sub-dominant, but as Finzi has approached it by A major/E major the relationship sounds newly-minted. Never has Finzi's progressive modulation been more apt and moving. This is setting not just words but emotions, something more profound, subtle, and poetic.

So a poem's current of feeling prompts fluctuating tonality. Not all his

---

5   To Thorpe Davie, 3 October 1948.

songs would stand firm – as most of Schubert's do – without the words (the structure of Finzi's instrumental music is not always logical). That is their weakness and their strength. While a point can be made swiftly in words, in music it takes longer and making it can unbalance a song, but in 'Overlooking the river' (p. 169) Finzi perfectly unites structure and expression. In the first two verses he establishes E flat major; in the final 'alack' verse he almost ends on an imperfect cadence, but just turns the harmony round under the singer's last note so that the song ends in F minor – if not with a question mark, then at least with doubt. Schumann's 'Im wunderschönen Monat Mai', in which longing finds no response, ends on an unresolved dominant seventh. Like Schumann, Finzi understood the suggestive power of tonality. In his Crees lectures, he cites the ending of Somervell's 'She came to the village church': 'he has left it in the air, so to speak, and by a change of key there comes a sudden illumination, and the last two bars, which leave the vocal phrase incomplete, tell us something beyond the words'.

Finzi often employs recitative, arioso, sustained melody all in one short song. Usually recitative suggests questioning, and cantilena confirms certainty, as in the early song 'A young man's exhortation' (p. 40). 'Harvest' (1956) is also discursive: it would seem unlikely that such a kaleidoscope of textures, figures, rhythms, and keys could combine into a unified song, philosophical as well as beautiful. It is a finer, more personal tribute to Blunden than For St Cecilia. The song opens as if in mid-conversation, thoughtful and confiding, as the poet sadly reviews his lack of achievement; the motif at 'so there's my year' returns as the piano postlude; and only at the very end is regret dispelled by the first tonic major chord in the song. Often in his music Finzi marks intensity by a semitone clash, as is so poignant in 'Since we loved' (1956) – 'loved' is after all past tense. In 'Harvest' he uses the semitone thematically as well: vertically for instant effect on 'thriftless' (Ex. 16.3a); elongated and in octave displacement at 'I peer' (b), clustered again at 'poison' (c); elongated and widened to introduce nature's consolation (d), then smoothed by passing notes for 'valleys sweet' (e), instant again for the piano's climactic chord in the bar after 'both feast and crown'.

There are two remarkable visual images, the stoop at 'I peer' (Ex. 16.3b); and the jagged, rising, widening leaps to outline 'spires'. The singer's highest notes are carefully graded, f" for 'gloated', g" for 'bright', finally a" flat for 'laughing'. The imperfect cadence at 'what sheaves [have I] to pile?' as the poet/composer laments his incomplete harvest is resolved at the final 'goes among her stooks'. The song relaxes into Finzi's cantilena (Ex. 16.3e) as the poet gains comfort from earth's beauty, accepting his part in nature. Those are some of the sophisticated but probably intuitive means by which Finzi integrates this late fine song.

❧

Ex. 16.3

a)

[Andante espressivo]

And thrift - less I mean - while,

b)

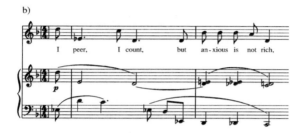

I peer, I count, but an - xious is not rich,

c)

deliberato

E - ven poi-son ber-ries

d)

e)

Earth's ___ val-leys sweet in lei-sure lie; ___

Finzi was nurtured by the pastoral and mystical strains in English music and poetry. He did not experiment with received language, but accepted an inherited tradition. A conservative with a limited range, he was sure of his own mind, for all his withdrawals and late starts. His way of developing an idea was by imitation, so making a web of sound. This was partly the influence of the Elizabethans: Bairstow was interested in Byrd, and Finzi's early London years coincided with the revivals by Terry and Fellowes. Tempered by his Bachian style, this imitation can produce contrapuntal elegance such as in Example 3.2.

Finzi had little use for Classical long-range tonality, for balanced repetition, or for the architecture of structured harmonic planes. That was one reason why he did not rate Mozart highly, and why he found it harder to compose quick or long movements than slow or short ones. The inexorable harmonic tension of Britten's song 'Before life and after' (Winter Words) was not his to sustain. He is reliant on the expressiveness of the suspension and the appoggiatura, and usually the peak of his dissonance is the simultaneous false relation. However supple his melody, his harmonic pace can be stiff. Occasionally he falls back on dotted figuration to give energy to his low-degree harmonic progressions. His climaxes, however grand-sounding, are usually achieved by dynamics and scoring; less often through thematic development. He distrusted virtuosity – 'the fatal facility' as he called it. He found little delight in it for its own sake (not allowing that it can be used to stir the emotions and that there is a real musical faculty involved). He took almost a pride in his 'slow mind' and admired late developers – Parry and Vaughan Williams – whose maturity was hard-won. He was just reaching a point where he had learnt to integrate virtuosity into his own style, as in his Cello Concerto.

Maybe a tougher musical apprenticeship would have stretched him; maybe it would have quenched him. He composed only a handful of lengthy works – no symphony, opera, or piano sonata. His style was compounded of Parry, Elgar, and Vaughan Williams; a little each of Walton and Bliss, some Bach, some folksong and possibly the lutenists; vocally he is descended from Dowland rather than from Purcell. But what he made of this fusion is his own; and within these bounds he expressed his interior life, his concerns with the first principles of being, time, and identity.

There are metaphors in his music, allied to words, which gather association and give it emotional depth. Taken abstractly they might seem repetitive, but as a whole they form a personal vocabulary of musical symbols. Some have already been noted. There is his upward expanding Elgarian phrase (see Ex. 1.1), to express warmth and aspiration. When he set words that indicate time's passing – to do with the seasons, generations, events across the ages – he uses an image based on a regular tread, scale, or ostinato (see Ex. 8.1). Sometimes it is serene, as though the passing of time is accepted as part of nature, healing and benign. Sometimes time is a thief, destructive, to be resisted. In happy contrast to this threatening march is his 'dance of delight' for something innocent, fair, and bright (see Ex. 2.1 and Ex. 9.3); often childlike – 'Childlike I danced in a dream' – or to do with human or divine love, 'winterless', in the present or the happy past. A third metaphor illustrates his sad perception of glory glimpsed, then fading, as in Example 9.1, and at the end of the first choral paragraph of *Intimations*. Another seems to suggest historical perspective: the close of 'Channel firing' and of the Cello Concerto's slow movement seem to acquire distance, withdrawing through time and space. Most characteristic of all is his 'benediction' music, which finds its fullest expression (Ex. 16.4) in the Cello Concerto.

Ex. 16.4

That music is itself a symbol: by being so 'out of time' it becomes timeless. The same mood occurs, if fleetingly but again often in D major, in songs whose words suggest acceptance of change – 'if I have seen one thing' (p. 40) – 'these are brand-new birds' (p. 80) – 'no more will I now rate the common rare' (p. 172). The idiom derives perhaps from Elgar's 'Softy and gently' (*The Dream of Gerontius*), and from 'Set me as a seal upon thine heart' (Vaughan Williams' *Flos Campi*). All have a quality of natural regeneration: change brings no end, only transformation. Lapped in the basic security of key, of the continuous unrolling of suspensions, imitations, and of unvarying tread, such passages in Finzi, like folksongs or lullabies, touch a need and a response deeper than reason. They offer a spiritual tranquillity only a hair's breadth away from valediction, noble comfort from a man who has gazed into 'the eternal silence'.

His music is shot through with visionary gleams: in *Dies natalis*, the sultry gold of 'the corn was orient and immortal wheat' or the bated breath of 'everything was at rest, free and immortal'; in *Intimations* 'another race hath been'. His songs can take in the sly, casual humour of 'The market-girl' or measure man's achievement against the universe with thrilling tension in 'At a lunar eclipse'. Not loud or commanding, Finzi's voice is lyrical, candid, and fastidious. No one else has quite his shades of shy rapture or melancholy, his characteristic radiance.

Finzi lived at a time when first Vaughan Williams and then Britten dominated English music. He and his reputation both suffered from being described as belonging to the school of the older composer and lacking the spectacular brilliance of the younger. In 1947 the Edinburgh International Festival was started, bringing continental musicians to the fore. In 1948 William Glock founded the Dartington Summer School, to which came

Hindemith, Stravinsky, Nono, Sessions, Elliott Carter; they wrote about their work in *The Score*. The Darmstadt School in the 1950s favoured serialism. Britain became aware of these adventurous new developments. Some of the older critics retired and were succeeded by a younger generation excited by the avant-garde. They were heady days. London audiences welcomed Mahler and Messiaen. A young group of English composers, born in the 1930s, led by Peter Maxwell Davies, began to attract attention. Vaughan Williams died in 1958. In 1959 Glock became BBC Controller of Music; as well as encouraging the new, he revived much that was old. Between Machaut and Boulez, good native composers like Berkeley, Rawsthorne, Rubbra, Walton, who did not write in one of the new fashionable idioms, found themselves cold-shouldered. This was as unhealthy as the previous conservatism had been. By the time taste had settled down again, and pluralism been accepted, Finzi's quiet subtle voice had temporarily been overlaid.

Most artists write for posterity and want their message to survive. In Finzi, the need was paramount. Early in his life he found it articulated in Flecker's 'To a Poet' − 'I send my soul through time and space'. In Joy he found his Boswell − his Cosima Wagner, Alice Elgar, Dorothy Wordsworth. Unlike his admired Hardy, who covered his tracks with bonfires and subterfuge, Finzi preserved letters, concert programmes, ephemera (but − curiously − few of his own sketches), and built up his libraries and his collections. Perhaps all this might seem self-important, as if his guardianship was disproportionate to what he had to give, his character even stronger than his ability. Yet all he asked for was affection. As he wrote in 1951:

> It is likely that new ideas, new fashions and the pressing forward of new generations, will soon obliterate my small contribution. Yet I like to think that in each generation may be found a few responsive minds. . . . To shake hands with a good friend over the centuries is a pleasant thing, and the affection which an individual may retain after his departure is perhaps the only thing which guarantees an ultimate life to his works.

Much of Finzi's career can be reconstructed, set out week by week on index cards or on a data-base. But the essential Finzi is not there. That is in the music, produced in the private time that is not revealed in diaries, from, in Gurney's words, 'the central fires of secret memory'. As Finzi's life drew to its close, his comments became starker. As he said to John Russell: 'You write your own music; you perform any music which you think people ought to hear; and you help other people to make music part of them.'[6] To Lady Ponsonby he wrote simply in 1954: 'In the end we all come down to Born − works − died & that's about all that's needed.'[7]

---

6   Note in programme for concert, Chelsea Chamber Orchestra, 22 October 1956.
7   22 June 1954.

Aug 3, 2021

APPENDICES

APPENDIX 1

Catalogue of Works

Boosey & Hawkes are now Finzi's publishers. His autograph manuscripts and sketches are in the Bodleian Library, Oxford.

opus **title** (author) date of composition; *date, performers, conductor/orchestra, place of first performance*; publishers, date of publication

EARLY SOLO AND CHORAL SONGS

Upon a child (Herrick) 1918; Stainer & Bell, 1922 (withdrawn)
A cradle song (P. Colum) 1919 (unpublished)
The twilit waters (F. Macleod) 1919 (unpublished)
The reed player with orchestra (F. Macleod), 1919 (unpublished)
The fairies (Herrick) 1919; *25 January 1924, John Booth, Harold Craxton, Wigmore Hall*; Curwen, 1923 (withdrawn)
The terrible robber man (P. Colum) 1920 (unpublished)
Tall nettles (E. Thomas) 1920 (unpublished)
Rondel (Chaucer) 1920 (unpublished)
Before the paling of the stars (C. Rossetti) 1920; *28 December 1920, York Minster* (unpublished)
Ceremonies (Herrick) 1920; *25 January 1924, John Booth, Harold Craxton, Wigmore Hall*; Curwen 1923 (withdrawn)
O dear me! (de la Mare) 1920 SS (unpublished)
The battle (W. H. Davies) 1921 (unpublished)
Some one (de la Mare) 1921; Stainer & Bell 1922 (withdrawn)
Time to rise (R. L. Stevenson) 1921; Stainer & Bell, 1922 (withdrawn)
My Spirit will not haunt the mound baritone and string quartet (T. Hardy) 1921 (incomplete)
Time was upon the wing baritone, female voices and piano (Herrick) 1922 (unpublished)
Epitaph: 'Even such is time' unison male voices (Raleigh) 1922 (unpublished)
English hills (J. Freeman) 1922 (unpublished)
The Cupboard (R. Graves) 1922; *9 May 1925, Ursula Greville, Royal Albert Hall*; Curwen, 1923
Days too short (W. H. Davies) 1925 (unpublished)
Winter now has bared the trees (I. Gurney) 1925 (unpublished)
The Temporary the All (T. Hardy) 1927 (revision incomplete)

SOLO SONG WITH PIANO OR INSTRUMENTS

2 **By Footpath and Stile** song-cycle for baritone and string quartet (T. Hardy) 1921–22

1 Paying calls (revised 1941)
2 Where the picnic was

3 The oxen (revised 1940)
4 The master and the leaves
5 Voices from things growing in a churchyard
8 Exeunt omnes
24 October 1923, Sumner Austin, Charles Woodhouse String Quartet, British Music Society, 6 Queen Square, London
J. Curwen, score 1925 (withdrawn); B&H, 1984, revised, and with piano reduction by Howard Ferguson

✓ 8 **Dies Natalis** cantata for tenor or soprano and strings (T. Traherne) 1, 2, 5, 1926; 3, 4, 1938–39

1 Intrada (strings only)
2 Rhapsody (recitativo stromentato)
3 The rapture (danza)
4 Wonder (arioso)
5 The salutation (aria)
26 January 1940, Elsie Suddaby, Maurice Miles/String Orchestra, Wigmore Hall, London; B&H, 1939

✓ 9 **Farewell to Arms** voice and small orchestra or strings

1 Introduction: ' The helmet now' (R. Knevet) 1944
2 Aria: 'His golden locks' (G. Peele) pre-1929
Aria only 6 February 1936, Steuart Wilson, Iris Lemare/orchestra, Mercury Theatre, London
complete 1 April 1945, Eric Greene, Charles Groves/BBC Northern Orchestra, Manchester broadcast; B&H, 1945

✓ 12 **Two Sonnets** tenor or soprano, small orchestra, by 1928

1 When I consider (Milton)
2 How soon hath time (Milton)
6 February 1936, Steuart Wilson, Iris Lemare/orchestra, Mercury Theatre, London; OUP, 1936

✓ 13a **To a Poet** low voice and piano

1 To a poet (J. E. Flecker) 1920s revised 1941
2 On parent knees (attrib. W. Jones) 1935
3 Intrada (T. Traherne) after 1951
4 The birthnight (de la Mare) 1956
5 June on Castle Hill (F. L. Lucas) 1940
6 Ode on the rejection of St Cecilia (G. Barker) 1948 15 March 1949, Bruce Boyce, BBC
complete 20 February 1959, John Carol Case, Howard Ferguson, Macnaghten Concerts, 4 St James's Square, London; B&H, 1965

✓ 13b **Oh Fair to See** high voice and piano

1 I say 'I'll seek her side' (T. Hardy) 1929
2 Oh fair to see (C. Rossetti) 1929
3 As I lay in the early sun (E. Shanks) 1921
4 Only the wanderer (I. Gurney) 1925
5 To Joy (E. Blunden) 1931; 17 February 1932, Frank Drew and Howard Ferguson, at OUP, London
6 Harvest (E. Blunden) 1956

7 Since we loved (R. Bridges) 1956
complete 8 November 1965, David Johnston, Courtney Kenny, Park Lane Group, 4 St James's Square, London; B&H, 1966

14 **A Young Man's Exhortation** tenor and piano (T. Hardy)

Part I *Mane floreat, et transeat* Ps. 89
1 A young man's exhortation 1926
2 Ditty 1928
3 Budmouth dears1929; with orchestra 17 June 1935, Leslie Woodgate, Jan van der Gucht, BBC
4 Her temple 1927
5 The comet at Yell'ham 1927

Part II *Vespere decidat, induret, et arescet* Ps. 89
6 Shortening days 1928
7 The sigh 1928
8 Former beauties 1927
9 Transformations 1929 17 February 1932, Frank Drew and Howard Ferguson, at OUP, London
10 The dance continued
complete in public 5 December 1933, Frank Drew, Augustus Lowe, Grotrian Hall, London: OUP, 1933

15 **Earth and Air and Rain** baritone and piano (T. Hardy)

1 Summer Schemes
2 When I set out for Lyonesse pre-1935, arranged for tenor and small orchestra; 6 February 1936, Steuart Wilson, Iris Lemare/orchestra, Mercury Theatre, London
3 Waiting both 1929
4 The phantom 1932
5 So I have fared 1928
6 Rollicum-Rorum
7 To Lizbie Brown
8 The Clock of the Years
9 In a churchyard 1932
10 Proud Songsters 1932 17 February 1932 Frank Drew, Howard Ferguson, at OUP
nos 1, 3, 6, 8, 10, 11 January 1937, Keith Falkner, Howard Ferguson, Mercury Theatre, London
1, 2, 3, 6, 7, 20 February 1937, Sinclair Logan, BBC
complete 24 March 1943, Robert Irwin, Howard Ferguson, National Gallery, London; B&H, 1936

16 **Before and after summer** baritone and piano (T. Hardy)

1 Childhood among the ferns 1947–48
2 Before and after summer 1949
3 The self-unseeing pre-1940
4 Overlooking the river 1940
5 Channel firing 1940
6 In the mind's eye
7 The too short time 1940
8 Epeisodia
9 Amabel F. Drew, H. Ferguson, 17 February 1932, at OUP, London
10 He abjures love 1938
complete 17 October 1949, Robert Irwin, Frederick Stone, BBC Third Programme; B&H, 1949

18 **Let us garlands bring** baritone and piano or strings (Shakespeare)

1 Come away, come away death 1928, 1938
2 Who is Sylvia? ?1932 *17 February 1932 Frank Drew and Howard Ferguson, at OUP London*
3 Fear no more the heat o' the sun 1929 *17 February 1932 Frank Drew and Howard Ferguson, at OUP*
4 Oh mistress mine 1942
5 It was a lover and his lass 1940

complete *12 October 1942, Robert Irwin, Howard Ferguson, National Gallery, London* (with piano)
18 October 1942, Robert Irwin, Clarence Raybould/BBC Orchestra, broadcast; B&H, 1942

19a **Till earth outwears** high voice and piano (T. Hardy)

1 Let me enjoy the earth 1936
2 In years defaced 1936
3 The market-girl 1927/1942
4 I look into my glass 1937
5 It never looks like summer here 1956
6 At a lunar eclipse 1929
7 Life laughs onwards 1956
21 February 1958, Wilfred Brown, Howard Ferguson, Macnaghten Concert, 4 St James's Square, London; B&H, 1958

19b **I said to Love** low voice and piano (T. Hardy)

1 I need not go 1930s
2 At Middle-Field gate 1956
3 Two lips 1928
4 In five-score summers 1956
5 For life I had never cared greatly 1956
6 I said to Love 1956
27 January 1957, John Carol Case, Howard Ferguson, Victoria & Albert Museum, London; B&H, 1958

CHORAL

Two motets
1 **Up to those bright and gladsome hills, Psalm 121** chorus and organ (H. Vaughan) 1922
10 March 1925, E. Bairstow/York Musical Society; Stainer & Bell 1925 (withdrawn)

2 **The Recovery (Sin! wilt thou vanquish me!)** chorus & orchestra or organ (T. Traherne) 1923
10 March 1925, E. Bairstow/York Musical Society; Stainer & Bell 1925 (withdrawn)

My God and King double chorus & keyboard (H. Vaughan) 1923 (unpublished)

The Search baritone, chorus, keyboard (Herbert) 1922–23 (unpublished)

The Brightness of this Day Christmas Hymn baritone, chorus, brass, strings and organ (or brass & organ, or strings and organ) or organ alone (H. Vaughan) 1922–23 score and parts lost
Christmas 1923, E. Bairstow/York Minster; Stainer & Bell 1925 (withdrawn)

4 **How shall a young man** unaccompanied SATB (Psalm cxix, words as from Byrd's Psalms, Sonnets, and Songs 1588); (unpublished)

Now Israel may say Psalm 130 (incomplete)

Requiem da camera baritone, chorus, or SATB solo voices, chamber orchestra 1924   7

1 Prelude
2 From 'August 1914' (J. Masefield)
3 'Only a man harrowing clods' 'In time of "The breaking of nations"' (2 versions 1)?1923 2) after 1928) (T. Hardy)
4 Lament (W. Gibson)

Prelude only, 1 December 1925, British Music Society, Anthony Bernard/London Chamber Orchestra, Court House, Marylebone Lane, London
Voices & piano 7 July 1985, Ian Caddy, Alan Cuckston, St Wilfrid's Church, Duchy Road, Harrogate
7 June 1990, Stephen Varcoe, R. Hickox/BBC Northern Singers, City of London Sinfonia, Christ Church, Spitalfields, London
Banks of York, edited by Philip Thomas 1990

1 **Ten Children's songs** unison and two-part voices with piano (C. Rossetti) 1920–21, later revised   7

1 The lily has a smooth stalk S
2 Dancing on the hilltops S
3 Lullaby, oh lullaby SS (or S)
4 Rosy Maiden Winifred SS
5 Dead in the cold SS
6 Margaret has a milking-pail SS
7 Ferry me across the water SS
8 There's snow on the fields SS
9 A linnet in a gilded cage SS
10 Boy Johnny SS (or S)
1–5 Stainer & Bell 1922 as School Songs; 6 -7 Curwen 1924; OUP 1936; 8–10 OUP 1936; 1–7 OUP 1954
nos 1, 2, 3, 5, revised, 4 rewritten

5 **Three Short Elegies** SATB (W. Drummond) 1926   7
1 Life a right shadow is
2 This world a hunting is
3 This life, which seems so fair
23 March 1936, Trevor Harvey/BBC Singers broadcast regional programme; OUP 1936

17 **Seven Unaccompanied Partsongs** (R. Bridges) 1931–37   ✓
1 I praise the tender flower SATB
2 I have loved flowers SAT
3 My spirit sang all day SATB
4 Clear and gentle stream SATB
5 Nightingales SSATB
6 Haste on, my joys! SSATB
7 Wherefore tonight so full of care SATB
complete 29 December 1938, Trevor Harvey/BBC Singers broadcast
OUP 1, 2, 4, 5, 1934; 7, 1936; 3,6, 1937; OUP complete 1939

✓ 26 **Lo, the full, final sacrifice** festival anthem (R. Crashaw) chorus and organ 1946,
orchestra 1947
with organ 21 *September 1946, Alec Wyton, St Matthew's Church, Northampton*
with orchestra 12 *September 1947, Finzi/London Symphony Orchestra, Three Choirs Festival,
Gloucester*
B&H, 1947

✓ 27 **Three anthems**

✓ 27, 1 **My lovely one** SATB and organ (E. Taylor) 1947; 2 *September 1946, Newbury;* B&H,
1948

✓ 27, 2 **God is gone up** SATB chorus with organ or strings and organ (E. Taylor) 1951
with organ 22 *November 1951, J. Dykes Bower, choristers from Chapels Royal, from St Paul's &
Canterbury Cathedrals, and from Westminster Abbey, St Sepulchre, Holborn Viaduct, London*
with organ and strings 20 *May 1952, J Dykes Bower, St Paul's Cathedral, London.*
B&H, 1952

✓ 27, 3 **Welcome sweet and sacred feast** SATB organ (H. Vaughan) 1953
11 *October 1953, G. Thalben Ball, BBC Singers, St Michael's, Cornhill, BBC broadcast*
B&H, 1954

✓ 29 **Intimations of Immortality (Ode)** tenor, chorus, orchestra (W. Wordsworth)
1936–50
5 *September 1950, Eric Greene, H. W. Sumsion/London Symphony Orchestra, Three Choirs Festival,
Gloucester*
B&H, 1950

✓ 30 **For St Cecilia (ceremonial ode)** tenor solo, chorus, orchestra (E. Blunden) 1947
22 *November 1947, René Soames, Adrian Boult/Luton Choral Society, BBC Symphony Orchestra, Royal
Albert Hall, London*
B&H 1947

✓ 32 **Thou dids't delight mine eyes** unaccompanied TBB (R. Bridges) 1951
Newbury Festival, 22 April 1953
B&H, 1952

Muses and Graces school song for unison treble voices, piano or strings (U. Wood)
10 *June 1950, Overstone School, Northamptonshire;* B&H, 1951

33 **All this night** motet unaccompanied SATB divisi (William Austin) 1951
6 *December 1951, C .Thornton Lofthouse, University of London Musical Society, St Paul's Cathedral, London*
B&H, 1951

✓ 35 **Let us now praise famous men** choral song for tenors/sopranos and basses/altos,
piano or piano and strings (Ecclesiasticus) 1951; B&H, 1952

✓ 36 **Magnificat** 1952, soloists ad lib, chorus and organ, 1956 orchestra
with organ 12 *December 1952, Iva Dee Hiatt/Vernon Gotwals/All-Smith choir and Amherst Glee Club,
Smith College, Northampton, Massachusetts, USA*
first English performance 29 May 1953, Audrey Langford/Bromley and Orpington
Choir

with orchestra 12 May 1956, Audrey Langford, Bromley and Orpington Choir and
    orchestra, Bromley
B&H, 1952

37 **White-flowering days** SATB (E. Blunden) 1952–53
2 June 1953, Boris Ord/Cambridge University Madrigal Society, Royal Festival Hall, London
Stainer & Bell, 1953; B&H, 1954

39 **In Terra Pax** Christmas Scene (St Luke, R Bridges) soprano, baritone, chorus
    (a) strings, harp/piano, cymbals, 1951–1954 (b) full orchestra, 1956
(a) 19 December 1954, Marion Milford, Charles O'Byrne, Finzi/NSP, Ashmansworth Church
(a) 27 February 1955, Myra Verney, Hervey Alan, John Russell/Goldsborough Orchestra, BBC broadcast
(b) 6 September 1956, Elsie Morison, Bruce Boyce, Finzi/London Symphony Orchestra, Three Choirs
    Festival, Gloucester
B&H, 1954

CHAMBER AND INSTRUMENTAL MUSIC

21 **Interlude** oboe and string quartet, or string orchestra 1932–36
24 March 1936, Leon Goossens, Menges Quartet, Wigmore Hall, London
B&H, 1936

22 **Elegy** violin and piano 1940
December 1954 Frederick Grinke, Wigmore Hall, London
B&H, 1983, edited Howard Ferguson

23 **Five Bagatelles** clarinet and piano 1938–43, 1–4 from early sketches
1 Prelude 1942
2 Romance 1941
3 Carol 1941
4 Forlana ?1941
5 Fughetta 1943
15 January 1943, Pauline Juler, Howard Ferguson, National Gallery, London (without Fughetta)
(complete) 8 April 1945, Pauline Juler, Howard Ferguson, BBC broadcast
B&H, 1945

24 **Prelude and Fugue** string trio 1938
13 May 1941, Breta Graham, Vincent Groves, Lilian Warmington, Queen's College Chambers, Birmingham
11 September 1941, David Martin, Max Gilbert, James Whitehead, National Gallery, London
B&H, 1942

SOLO INSTRUMENT WITH ORCHESTRA

6 **Violin Concerto** small orchestra and violin
        Allegro
        Molto sereno
        Hornpipe Rondo: *Allegro risoluto*

Introit (*Molto sereno*) small orchestra and solo violin 1925, revised 1935, 1942; violin &
    piano edited by Ferguson B&H
31 January 1933 (as separate work) Anne Macnaghten, Iris Lemare/orchestra, Ballet Theatre Club, London
OUP piano reduction 1935, full score 1943
Complete concerto, edited by S. Banfield, B&H, 2001

4 May 1927 (*second and third movements only*) Sybil Eaton, M. Sargent/British Women's Symphony Orchestra, Queen's Hall, London
1 February 1928, complete, S. Eaton, Vaughan Williams/London Symphony Orchestra, Queen's Hall, London
20 November 1999, Tasmin Little, Richard Hickox, Southampton University

10 **Eclogue** piano & strings, late 1920s, revised 1952
27 January 1957, Kathleen Long, John Russell/Kalmar Orchestra, Victoria and Albert Museum, London
B&H, 1957

31 **Clarinet Concerto** clarinet and string orchestra 1948–49
9 September 1949, Frederick Thurston, Finzi/London Symphony Orchestra, Three Choirs Festival, Hereford
B&H, 1951 piano reduction by Perry; 1953 and 2001 full score

38 **Grand Fantasia and Toccata** piano and orchestra, Fantasia 1928 (revised 1953), Toccata 1953
9 December 1953, John Russell, Gerald Finzi/Newbury Choral Society Orchestra, Corn Exchange, Newbury
8 July 1954 Pater Katin, Russell/London Symphony Orchestra, Royal Festival Hall, London
B&H, 1954

40 **Cello Concerto** cello and orchestra 1951–52, 1954–55 – cello part edited by C. Bunting
19 July 1955 Christopher Bunting, Barbirolli/Hallé Orchestra, Town Hall, Cheltenham Festival
B&H, 1956 and 2001

ORCHESTRAL

3 **A Severn Rhapsody** chamber orchestra 1923
4 June 1924, Dan Godfrey/Bournemouth Summer Symphony Concert Orchestra, Winter Gardens, Bournemouth
Stainer & Bell for the Carnegie Trust 1924

7 **New Year Music (Nocturne)** full orchestra 1926, 1928, revised 1940s
16 March 1932, Dan Godfrey/Bournemouth Municipal Orchestra, Winter Gardens, Bournemouth and broadcast [as Pavan]
B&H, 1950

11 **Romance** string orchestra 1928, revised 1941
11 October 1951, John Russell/Reading String Players, Town Hall, Reading
B&H, 1952

20 **The Fall of the Leaf (Elegy)** full orchestra 1926–29 revised 1941; orchestration completed by Howard Ferguson
11 December 1957, Barbirolli/Hallé Orchestra, Free Trade Hall, Manchester
B&H, 1958

25 **Prelude** string orchestra 1920s
27 April 1957, Christopher Finzi/Newbury String Players, St John's Church, Stockcross, Berks
B&H, 1958

DRAMATIC

28 **Music for Love's Labour's Lost** small orchestra, incidental Music for Shakespeare's play 1946

16 December 1946, Paul Scofield, Ernest Milton, Thea Holme, conductor Clifton Helliwell, play produced by Noel Iliff, BBC broadcast
(unpublished)

Three Soliloquies for small orchestra; B&H, 1952

28a **Songs from Love's Labour's Lost** voice and small orchestra or piano 1946–47
   (Shakespeare)

1 When daisies pied (Song of Ver)
2 When icicles hang (Song of Hiems)
3 If she be made of white and red (Riddle Song)
4 Is it not sure a deadly pain (False Concolinel, anon.)

7 July 1947 (in concert), Mollie Sands, Ruth Dyson, Wigmore Hall, London
B&H, 1947

28b **Suite from Love's Labour's Lost**, orchestra 1952, 1955
1 Introduction
2 Moth
3 Nocturne
4 The Hunt
5 Dance
6 Quodlibet (Clowns)
7 Soliloquy 1
8 Soliloquy 2
9 Soliloquy 3
10 Finale
without 3, 4, 6 but with songs 1 and 2, 20 July 1952, Gilbert Vinter/BBC Midland Light
   Orchestra, Town Hall, Cheltenham
complete 26 July 1955, John Russell/London Symphony Orchestra, BBC broadcast

MISCELLANEOUS unpublished

Waltz in the Finzi Weeklies (destroyed in fire)
A passer-by 1921, in piano score, based on Bridges' 'Whither, O splendid ship'
Allegro risoluto 1922 toy symphony orchestra
Jerusalem 1922 orchestrated
Lullaby 'Rock my baby' arranged for SATB (Greek folksong, English translation by
   Calvocoressi)
Short Fug(e) in praise of G. C. C. in 4 parts
A Grace for Hilles House (lost)
Cadenza for C. F. Abel's Concerto no. 5 from Six Concertos op. xi
The Blue bell of Scotland for chamber group 1944–45
A Latin Grace, 1945, SSA and piano
Two Chants for Richard Latham's chant book at St Paul's, Knightsbridge, 1948
Diabelleries a movement for the collection
Sleighbells (lost)
Unfinished movements, fragments, and sketches

ARRANGEMENTS AND EDITIONS

Bond, Capel: Concerto no. I for trumpet, strings and continuo (B&H, 1959)

Bond, Capel: Concerto no. 6 in B flat for bassoon and strings (B&H, 1956)

Boyce, William: Overtures for *Musica Britannica*, vol. XIII (Stainer and Bell, 1957)

Garth, John: Concerto no. 2 for cello in B flat (Hinrichsen, 1955)

Gurney, Ivor: songs 'Orpheus' 'Sleep' 'Spring' 'Under the greenwood tree' arranged for strings (B&H)

Mudge, Richard: Concerto no. 1 in B flat for trumpet and strings (B&H, 1975)

Mudge, Richard: Concerto no. 4 in D minor for strings (B&H, 1954)

Mudge, Richard: Concerto for organ and strings (B&H, 1957)

Parry, Hubert: chorale fantasia on an old English Tune 'When I survey the wondrous Cross'. Strings (Novello, 1950)

Stanley, John: 'Welcome Death' from *Teraminta* for bass and keyboard and/or strings (Hinrichsen, 1953)

Stanley, John: Concerto no. 5 in A minor for strings for keyboard and strings (B&H, 1954)

Stanley, John: Concerto no. 4 in D minor for strings or for keyboard and strings (B&H, 1954)

Stanley, John: Solo in for D flute and piano from Op. 4 No. 5 (Rudall Carte, 1954)

Stanley, John: Concerto no. 3 in G for strings or for keyboard and strings (B&H, 1949)

Stanley, John: Concerto in no. I in D for strings or for keyboard and strings (B&H, 1952)

Stanley, John: Concerto no. 2 in B minor for strings or for keyboard and strings (B&H, 1952)

Stanley, John: Concerto no. 6 in B flat for strings keyboard and strings B&H, 1955

Wesley, Charles: Concerto no. 4 in C for piano, strings, 2 oboes ad lib (Hinrichsen, 1956)

Wesley, Charles: quartets nos 1 in F, 2 in D, 5 in B flat (Hinrichsen, 1953)

Unpublished editions are at St Andrews University

WRITINGS

'Folk-Songs from Newfoundland' [review of Maud Karpeles], *Journal of the English Folk Dance and Song Society*, vol. 1, no. 4 (1935) p. 157

Linking script for overseas service concert of Parry's music on the hundredth anniversary of his birth, 27 February 1948 [typescript]

'Hubert Parry – a Revaluation', *Making Music*, no. 10 (1949), pp. 4–8 [revision of broadcast, BBC Third Programme, 27 February 1948]

'Critic on the Air', BBC Third Programme talk, 1 May 1948 [typescript]

'R. O. Morris – Obituary', *The RCM Magazine*, vol. xlv, no. 2 (1949), pp. 54–6

'My strongest musical impression of 1949', *The Music Teacher and Piano Student*, January and February 1950, p. 4

'A Junior Orchestra', Letter to *The Newbury Weekly News*, 9 February 1950

'Music and environment', *Mercury*, no. 7, Spring (1950), pp. 25–7

'Words and Music', *Oxford Guardian*, 5 October 1950, p. 13

'John Stanley (1713 [sic]–1786)', *Proceedings of the Royal Musical Association*, vol. lxxvii (1950–51), pp. 63–75

'Music and the Amateur' [book review], *Making Music*, no. 17 (1951), pp. 13–14

A Tribute broadcast on the occasion of Vaughan Williams's 80th birthday, 12 October 1952

'Vaughan Williams, The Roots and the Tree', Philharmonic Post, vol. vi, no. 6 (1952), pp. 64–5, 71

Address at Leith Hill Festival, 14 April 1953 [typescript]

'John Stanley', Tempo, no. 27 (1953), pp. 21–7 [revised reprint of PRMA lecture]

'The St John Passion in Dorking', Dorking Advertiser, 5 March 1954

'Herbert Howells', Musical Times, vol. xcv (1954), pp. 180–3 [reprinted, Musical Times, vol. cxxxviii, pp. 26–9]

'Guardian of Genius' [of Ivor Gurney], Society of Women Musicians conference, 25 and 26 June 1954; Marion Scott commemorative programme, pp. 8–11 (1954)

'The Composer's Use of Words', three Crees Lectures, Royal College of Music, 1955, The Finzi Journal, vol. 26, no. 1, 2009; vol. 27, nos 1 and 2, 2010

Prefaces and critical apparatus to editions

APPENDIX 2

Bibliography

Allenby, David, 'Finzi, Boosey & Hawkes and a Centenary', Finzi Friends Newsletter, vol. 19, no. 2 (2001)

Amis, John, Amiscellany, my Life, my Music (London and Boston, 1985), p. 84

Anderson, W. R., 'A Severn Rhapsody', New Works by Modern British Composers (London, 1928)

Banfield, Stephen, 'The Immortality Odes of Finzi and Somervell', Musical Times, vol. cxvi (1975) pp. 527–31

Banfield, Stephen, 'Time and Destiny, the Hardy songs of Gerald Finzi', Sensibility and English Song (Cambridge, 1985), pp. 275–300

Banfield, Stephen, note to recording of Finzi (EMI 7 49913 2, 1989)

Banfield, Stephen, 'Finzi and Wordsworth', Finzi Trust Friends Newsletter, vol. 10, no. 2 (1992), pp. 2–10

Banfield, Stephen, ed., Music in Britain, the Twentieth Century (Oxford, 1995)

Banfield, Stephen, Gerald Finzi, an English Composer (London, 1997)

Banfield, Stephen, 'Vaughan Williams and Gerald Finzi', Vaughan Williams in Perspective, ed. Lewis Foreman (London, 1998), pp. 202–21

Barsham, Eve, 'Parry's Manuscripts, a rediscovery', Musical Times, vol. ci (1960) pp. 86–7

Bartlett, Ian, 'Lambert, Finzi and the Anatomy of the Boyce Revival', Musical Times, vol. 144, no. 1884 (2003), pp. 54–9

Beechey, Gwilym, 'The Church Music of Gerald Finzi', Musical Times, vol. cxviii (1977), pp. 667–70

Bliss, Arthur, As I Remember (London, 1970)

Bliss, Arthur and S[cott], A[nthony], 'Gerald Finzi, an Appreciation', Tempo, no. 42 (1956–57), pp. 5–6

Blunden, Edmund, Thomas Hardy (London, 1942)

Blunden, Edmund, ed., Poems of Ivor Gurney (London, 1954)

Blunden, Edmund, A Hong Kong House, Poems of 1951–1962 (London, 1962)

Boden, Anthony, Three Choirs, a History of the Festival (Stroud, 1992)

Boyd, C. M., 'Gerald Finzi and the Solo Song', Tempo, no. 33 (1954), p. 15

Burn, Andrew, note to recording of English songs, Hyperion A66103, 1984

Burn, Andrew, Summer Weekend of English Music, Oxford, 20–22 July 1984, programme book (Liverpool, 1984)

Burn, Andrew, ed., Summer Weekend of English Music, 16–19 July 1987, Radley College, Abingdon, programme book (Liverpool, 1987)

Burn, Andrew, 'Quiet Composure', Country Life, vol. clxxxi, no. 29 (1987), pp. 118–19 [Finzi's library at Reading University]

Burn, Andrew, Foreword to Boosey & Hawkes catalogue of Finzi's works (London, 1994)

Burn, Andrew and McVeagh, Diana, eds, *Gerald Finzi, twenty-fifth anniversary celebration, Ellesmere College Weekend, 17–19 July*, programme book (Liverpool, 1981)

Burn, Andrew and Rees, Henry, eds, *Summer Festival of British Music 1990, Radley College, Abingdon, 11–15 July*, programme book (Liverpool, 1990)

Caesar, Adrian, Introduction to the Finzi Bookroom Catalogue [see Dingley]

Cline, Edward, 'The Composer's Use of Words, the Language and Music of Gerald Finzi', *British Music*, vol. xiv (1992), pp. 8–24

Cobbe, Hugh, 'The correspondence of Gerald Finzi and Ralph Vaughan Williams', *Finzi Trust Friends Newsletter*, vol. 10, no. 1 (1992), pp. 9–14

Cobbe, Hugh, 'Howard Ferguson at 80', *Musical Times*, vol. cxxix, no. 1748 (1988), pp. 507–10

Cole, Hugo, 'Vision of Innocent England: Celebrating Gerald Finzi', *Country Life*, vol. clxx, no. 4382 (1981), p. 575

Copley, Ian, *Robin Milford* (London, 1984)

Crum, Margaret C., 'Working Papers of Twentieth-Century British Composers', *Bodleian Library Record*, vol. viii, no. 2 (1968), pp. 101–3

Culshaw, John, 'Gerald Finzi – Dies Natalis', *Hallé*, no, 7 (Oct.–Nov. 1947), pp. 19–20

Dale Roberts, Jeremy, 'Recalling Finzi', in Burn and Rees (1990), p. 19

Dale Roberts, Jeremy, 'In Years Defaced', *Finzi Trust Friends Newsletter*, vol. 18, no. 2 (2000)

Dingley, Pauline, *The Finzi Book Room at the University of Reading, a catalogue* [with introduction by Adrian Caesar], Reading University Library Publications 4 (1981)

Dressler, John C., *Gerald Finzi, a Bio-Bibliography* (Westport, CT and London, 1997) [includes worklist, discography, bibliography, list of unpublished autographs]

Eaton, Sybil, 'Letter to Joy Finzi', *Finzi Trust Friends Newsletter*, vol. 4, no. 1 (1986), pp. 13–14

Ferguson, Howard, 'Gerald Finzi (1901–1956)', *Music & Letters*, vol. xxxviii (1957), pp. 130–5

Ferguson, Howard, 'Gerald Finzi (1901–1956), *Hallé Magazine*, no. 100 (1957), pp. 8–11 [includes an account of *The Fall of the Leaf*]

Ferguson, Howard, notes to recordings of Finzi songs on Lyrita SRCS 38 (1968); 51 (1971)

Ferguson, Howard, *Music, Friends and Places* (London, 1977), pp. 29–32

Ferguson, Howard, 'People, events and influences' in Ridout (1989), pp. 7–15

Ferguson, Howard and Hurd, Michael, *Letters of Gerald Finzi and Howard Ferguson* (Woodbridge, 2001)

Finzi Trust Friends Newsletter, vol. 1, no. 1, January 1983 and onwards [includes articles and reprints of obituaries] renamed *The Finzi Journal* in 2009

Finzi, Christopher, note to recording of Dies Natalis by Finzi (World Record Club SCM 50, 1964)

Finzi, Christopher, ed., *Joy Finzi 1907–1991: tributes from her friends* (privately printed, 1992)

Finzi, Christopher, 'Memories of my Father', *Finzi Friends Newsletter*, vol. 19, no. 1 (2001)

Finzi, Joy, 'Gerald Finzi 1901–1956', speech at opening of Finzi Bookroom 1973 [unpublished typescript, Reading University Library]

Finzi, Joy, *In that Place, the Portrait Drawings of Joy Finzi* (Marlborough, 1987) [portraits, with brief memoirs, of G. Finzi and their circle]

Finzi, Kate John, *Eighteen Months in the War Zone: The Record of a Woman's Work on the Western Front* (London, 1916)

Foreman, Lewis, 'Reputations . . . bought or made?', *Musical Times*, vol. cxxi (1980), p. 27

Frankel, Benjamin, 'His music caught the meaning of words', *Music and Musicians*, vol. v (December 1956), pp. 15, 35

Gallagher, David, 'Composer of the Week', *Finzi Trust Friends Newsletter*, vol. 18, no. 1 (2000)

Harman, Claire, ed., *The Diaries of Sylvia Townsend Warner* (London, 1994), pp. 218, 248

Hold, Trevor, ' "Checkless Griff" or Thomas Hardy and the Songwriters', *Musical Times*, vol. cxxxi, no. 1768 (1990), pp. 309–10

Hold, Trevor, *Parry to Finzi: Twenty English Song-Composers* (Woodbridge, 2002)

Howes, Frank, 'A poet's musician, the works of Gerald Finzi', *The Times*, 5 October 1956, p. 3

Hull, Robin, in *British Music of our Time*, ed. A. L. Bacharach (Harmondsworth and New York, 1946), pp. 222–3

Hurd, Michael, *The Ordeal of Ivor Gurney* (Oxford 1978), pp. 181ff.

Jordan, Rolf, ed., *The Clock of the Years: a Gerald and Joy Finzi Anthology* (Lichfield, 2007)

Kavanagh, P. J., *Collected Poems of Ivor Gurney* (Oxford and New York, 1982)

Kennedy, Michael, *The Works of Ralph Vaughan Williams* (London, 1964)

Kennedy, Michael, 'Minor Men with Major Works', *Sunday Telegraph*, 3 May 1980

Lancaster, Philip, 'Lo, the Full, Final Sacrifice: an Introduction', *Finzi Friends Newsletter*, vol. 20, no. 1 (2002)

Lancaster, Philip, 'Reflections on the Rejection of Cecilia', *Finzi Friends Newsletter*, vol. 21, no. 2 (2003)

Lee, E. Markham, 'The Student Interpreter: Gerald Finzi, A Young Man's Exhortation', *Musical Opinion*, vol. lxii (November 1938), pp. 118–19

Leighton, Kenneth, 'Memories of Gerald Finzi', *Finzi Trust Friends Newsletter*, vol. vi, no. 1 (1988), pp. 5–6 [reprinted in vol. 22, no. 1, 2004]

Long, N.G., 'The Songs of Gerald Finzi', *Tempo*, no. 17 (1946), pp. 7–10

MacDonald, Calum, 'This week's composer, The English Spirit', *The Listener*, vol. civ (1980), pp. 347–8

McVeagh, Diana, 'Finzi, Gerald (Raphael), in *The New Grove Dictionary*, ed. Stanley Sadie (London, 1980 and 2001)

McVeagh, Diana, Foreword to Boosey & Hawkes catalogue of Finzi's works (London, 1980)

McVeagh, Diana, 'Composers of our Time: Gerald Finzi', *Records & Recording*, vol. xxiii, no. 4 (1980), pp. 30–3

McVeagh, Diana, 'A Finzi Discography' [with introduction], *Tempo*, no. 136 (March 1981), pp. 19–22

McVeagh, Diana, 'Gerald Finzi, 1901–1956', *World of Church Music* (1981), pp. 16–20

McVeagh, Diana, 'Gerald Finzi (1901–1956)', *Hi-Fi News* (October 1981), pp. 67–9

McVeagh, Diana, notes to recordings of Finzi on Lyrita SRCS 75 (1975) (*Intimations of Immortality*); 92 (1977) (instrumental music); 84 (1978) (short instrumental music); 93 (1979) (vocal music), 112 (1979) (cello concerto); on Chandos CHAN 8471 (1986) (Finzi and Leighton); on Nimbus NI5101 (1987); Argo ZRG 896 (1979) (*St Cecilia, Dies Natalis*, 909 (1979) (*In Terra Pax*); Hyperion A66015 (1981) (songs by Finzi and his friends), A66161–2 (1985) (Finzi's Hardy Songs)

Mellers, Wilfrid, *Vaughan Williams and the Vision of Albion* (London, 1898), pp. 245–6

Mitchell, Donald, 'The Music of Gerald Finzi', *Musical Times*, vol. xcv (1954), pp. 490–1

Mitchell, Donald and Reed, Philip, eds, *Benjamin Britten, Letters from a Life, 1939–45* (London, 1991)

Moore, Gerald, *Singer and Accompanist* (London, 1953)

Newman, Ernest, 'Words and Music', *Sunday Times*, 15, 22, 29 July 1945

Popplewell, Clare [Finzi's grand-daughter], 'Church Farm, Ashmansworth' *Finzi Trust Friends Newsletter*, vol. 12 [recte 13], no. 1 (1995), pp. 1–3

Porter, Andrew, 'Gerald Finzi', *London Musical Events* (July 1954), pp. 18–19

Powers, Alan, 'Harmonious Mansions, Two Composers' Houses of the 1930s', *Country Life*, vol. clxxviii, no. 4593 (1985), pp. 559–63 [study of the houses built for Bliss and Finzi]

Ridout, Alan, ed., *The Music of Howard Ferguson* (London, 1989)

Rubbra, Edmund [Duncan-], 'The younger English composers VI, Gerald Finzi', *Monthly Musical Record*, vol. lix (1929), pp. 193–4

Russell, John, 'Gerald Finzi, an English Composer', *Tempo*, no. 33 (1954), pp. 9–15

Russell, John, 'Gerald Finzi', *Musical Times*, vol. xcvii (1956), pp. 630–1

Rutland, William R., *Thomas Hardy* (London, 1938)

Scott, Anthony, 'Gerald Finzi as a Tutor of Composition', *Finzi Trust Friends Newsletter*, vol. 15, no. 2 (1997)

Shirley Smith, Richard, *The Paintings & Collages* (London, 2002), pp. 3 and 140

Shuttleworth, Anna, 'Memories of Gerald Finzi, his music, home, family and the Newbury String Players 1945–65', *Finzi Trust Friends Newsletter*, vol. 12 [recte 13], no. 1 (1995), pp. 9–10

Sirbaugh, Nora, 'Gerald Finzi – A guide to the vocal and orchestral recordings', *British Music Society Newsletter*, No. 75, March 1997, pp. 74–76; No. 77. Sept 1997, pp. 146–48

Stunt, Christopher, 'The too short time', *Finzi Trust Friends Newsletter*, vol. 14, no. 2 (1996)

Stunt, Christopher, 'Who is this coming with pondering pace?', *Finzi Trust Friends Newsletter*, vol. 15, no. 2 (1997)

Thomas, Philip, 'Requiem da camera', *Finzi Trust Friends Newsletter*, vol. 8, no. 2 (1990), pp. 14–15

Thomas, Philip, 'An Introduction to Finzi's Clarinet Concerto', *Finzi Trust Friends Newsletter*, vol. 15, no. 1 (1997)

Thorpe Davie, Cedric, Introduction to *Catalogue of the Finzi Collection* [18th-century English Music], St Andrews University Library (1982), pp. iii–v

Tobin, J. Raymond, 'Living British Composers, 6, Gerald Finzi', *Pictorial Education* (March 1954)

Vaughan Williams, Ralph, *Beethoven's Choral Symphony* (London, 1953)

Vaughan Williams, Ursula, *R.V.W., a Biography* (London, 1964)

Walker, Alan, 'Gerald Finzi (1901–1956)', *Tempo*, no. 52 (1959), pp. 6–10

Webb, Barry, *Edmund Blunden, a Biography* (New Haven and London, 1990)

Wykes, Alan, 'He will have a concert to himself', *Music and Musicians* (July 1954), p. 12

www.geraldfinzi.co.uk

Newbury String Players' Repertory

The Newbury String Players repertory during Finzi's life, in the order that the works were added (some programmes do not survive). First performances and revivals are in **bold**. The accompaniments of solo songs were usually arranged by Finzi. Names of notable performers appearing with NSP for the first time follow in brackets.

1940
Boyce: Symphony No. 4 in F major
Bach: Sinfonia from Cantata No. 156
Corelli: Pastorale from Christmas Concerto, No. 8 in G minor
Bach: Violin Concerto in E (Winifred Roberts in 1944, Yfrah Neaman in 1953)
Holst: St Paul's Suite

1941
Purcell: Set of Tunes
Elgar: Serenade for strings
Purcell: 'When I am laid in earth' (Sophie Wyss)
Byrd: 'Cradle Song' ('My sweet little darling') (Wyss)
Finzi: *Dies Natalis* – 'The Salutation' only (Wyss)
Vaughan Williams: Evening Hymn from Four Hymns (Wyss)
Milford, Robin: Suite in D minor for oboe and strings
Grétry: 'Rose chérie'; 'Ariette du Tableau parlant' (Wyss)
Rameau: 'Accourez, riante jeunesse' (Wyss)
Parry: 'Jerusalem' (Newbury Music Festival)
Grieg: Holberg Suite
Bach: Concerto in D minor for two violins (Antoinette Chaplin/Rubbra)
Elgar: Elegy, Op. 58
Handel: 'Let the bright seraphim'
Purcell: Evening Hymn
Warlock: Capriol Suite
Bach: Violin Concerto in A (Sybil Eaton)
Handel: Organ Concerto in B flat, Op. 7 No. 1 (Alec Wyton in 1948)
Boyce: Symphony No. 7 in B flat
Bach: 'Sighing, weeping' from Cantata No. 21 (Wyss)
Arensky: Variations on a Theme by Tchaikovsky
Haydn (attrib.): Cello Concerto (Eileen Croxford)
Bach: Giant Fugue arr. Vaughan Williams and Foster

1942
Milford, Robin: Miniature Concerto in G
Purcell: 'Fairest Isle'
Purcell: 'Mad Bess'; 'I attempt from love's sickness'
Bach: Keyboard Concerto in D minor (Denis Matthews, Ruth Dyson in 1954)

Parry: 'England'
Sibelius: Romance for strings
Vaughan Williams: 'Orpheus with his lute'
Boyce: Symphony No. 1 in B flat
Finzi: Bridges Partsongs (by Reading Madrigal Society)
Moszkowski: Prelude and Fugue
Bach, arr. Diack and Baker: Peasant Cantata BWV 212

1943
Suk: Meditation on a Bohemian Chorale
Vivaldi: Cello Concerto
Gurney: 'Under the greenwood tree', 'Sleep', 'Spring' (Wyss)
Bach: Concerto for two keyboards in C (Howard Ferguson and Denis Matthews)
Purcell: Suite from King Arthur
Mozart: Eine kleine Nachtmusik
Hutchings: Variations and Fugue on 'Puer natus'
Morris, R. O.: Canzoni ricertati No. 6

1944
Gluck: Scenes from Orpheus
Haydn: Keyboard Concerto in D major (Ferguson)
Purcell: 'Nymphs and Shepherds' from The Libertine; 'If love's a sweet passion' from The
    Fairy Queen; 'The Shepherd's Song' from King Arthur; 'Let monarchs fight' from
    Dioclesian; 'The Sailors' Song' from Dido and Aeneas (Eric Greene)
Cimarosa, arr. Benjamin: Oboe Concerto (Leon Goossens, Joy Boughton in 1946)
Vaughan Williams: 'The New Commonwealth'
Elgar: Sospiri
Vaughan Williams: Fantasia on Greensleeves
Parry: Blest Pair of Sirens (with Reading Madrigal Society)
Corelli: Christmas Concerto, complete
Boccherini: Adagio non troppo (from Cello Concerto)
Finzi: Dies Natalis, complete (Eric Greene, Wilfred Brown in 1952)
Bach: 'Sleepers, wake', Cantata No. 140 (with Reading Madrigal Society)
Vaughan Williams: Fantasia on Christmas Carols

1945
Vaughan Williams: Tallis Fantasia (Sybil Eaton, Jean Stewart, Amaryllis Fleming)
Vaughan Williams: The Hundredth Psalm
Respighi: Ancient Airs and Dances
Bach (attrib.): Three hymns from the Schemelli Hymn-book (Joan Elwes)
Bach: Brandenburg Concerto No. 5
Bach: 'Welcome Lord' from Cantata No. 61
Mozart: Divertimento K. 136
Boccherini: Cello Concerto
Purcell: Morning Hymn
Barber: Adagio
Milford, Robin: Te Deum (with Downe House Singers)
Vaughan Williams: Concerto Accademico
Boyce: Symphony No. 8

1946
Arnold, Samuel: 'Hist! hist!' from *The Maid of the Mill* (Wyss)
Arne, M.: 'The lass with the delicate air' (Wyss)
Mussorgsky: Dolly, Evening Prayer
Grainger: Mock Morris
Bach: Sinfonia from Cantata No. 75 (Bernard Brown)
Bach: 'Mighty Lord and King all glorious' (Keith Falkner)
Purcell: Sonata for trumpet and strings Z850, ms realized Finzi (Bernard Brown)
Mozart: E flat Concerto K. 449 (Kathleen Long)
Purcell: music from anthems
Purcell: Chaconne in G minor
Howells: Elegy (Jean Stewart)
Bloch: Concerto Grosso (Kathleen Long, John Russell in 1950)
Bach, arr. Havergal: Magnificat (Monica Sinclair)
Purcell: overture from *The Rival Sisters*
Holst: 'Turn back O man'
Dunhill, T: 'Venite adoremus' from Three Pieces for organ and strings
Bach: Sinfonias to Cantatas Nos. 12 and 156 (Joy Boughton)
Corelli, arr. Malipiero: Organ Concerto from the third violin sonata
Arne, T., ed. Herbage: Keyboard Concerto No. 5 (Ruth Dyson)
Leo, Leonardo: Cello Concerto (Anna Shuttleworth)
Handel: Concerto Grosso Op. 6 No. 12
Fauré: Nocturne from *Shylock*
Bach: Air from Suite in G
Vaughan Williams: Four hymns for tenor, viola and strings (Jean Stewart)
Finzi: *Farewell to Arms*
Purcell: overture to *Dido and Aeneas*
Scott, Anthony: Prelude and Fugue

1947
Vaughan Williams, arr. Foster: Prelude on Rhosymedre
Bach: Keyboard Concerto in F minor
Gluck: 'Par un père cruel' from *Iphigénie*
Lully: 'Fermez-vous, mes tristes yeux' (Mollie Sands)
Rameau: 'Fluminus Impetus'
Vivaldi: Concerto in B minor for four violins, Op. 3 No. 11
Bach, J. C.: Symphony in B flat, Op. 21 No. 3
Vivaldi: Violin Concerto in A minor Op. 3 No. 6 (Henry Holst)
Mozart: Sinfonia Concertante (H. Holst and J. Stewart)
Holst: Two Psalms
Purcell: *Dido and Aeneas* (conducted by Herbert Sumsion)
Handel: 'Where e're you walk' (Mollie Sands)
Green, M.: 'Praised be the Lord'; 'The dying Swan', ms from BM realized by Finzi
    (Sands)
Arne: 'Water parted from the sea' (Sands)
Arne, T.: 'Requiem aeternam', ms from BM realized by Finzi
Stanley: Trumpet Tune
Haydn: Andante from trumpet sonata
Vivaldi: Concerto for two violins

Milford, Robin: Elegiac Meditation for viola and strings
Boyce: Symphony No. 3
Purcell: 'Music for awhile'
Bach: 'Thy rock and shield'
Sumsion, Herbert: Watts cradle song
Bach: 'Gladly would I take upon me', from St Matthew Passion
Purcell: Suite from *The Gordian Knot*
Arne: Piano Concerto No. 4 in G

1948
Parry: English Suite (conductor Bernard Rose)
Vivaldi, ed. d'Indy: Cello Concerto No. 6
Tartini, ed. G. Jacob: Clarinet Concerto (Stephen Trier)
Farnaby, ed. Bantok: Suite
Bartók: Romanian Dances
Corelli, arr. Barbirolli: Oboe Concerto
Stanley: Concerto No. 3 in G
Seiber, arr.: Four Greek folksongs (Wyss)
Schubert: Salve regina (1819) (Wyss)
Mozart: Divertimento K. 136
Purcell: trumpet overture from *The Indian Queen* (Philip Jones)
Finzi: 'Wonder' and 'The Salutation' from *Dies Natalis*
Parry, arr. Finzi: 'When I survey'
Stanley: Concerto No. 2

1949
Gurney: 'Orpheus', 'Under the greenwood tree', 'Sleep', 'Spring' (Elsie Suddaby)
Elgar: Introduction and Allegro
Handel: Oboe Concerto No. 1
Stanley: Concerto No. 1
Ireland: Toccata from Concertino Pastorale
Mozart: Serenade notturno K. 239 in D
Purcell: duets 'Let us wander'; 'My dearest, my fairest'; 'Sound the trumpet'
Ireland: Concertino Pastorale
Bach: 'Rejoice ye souls' from Cantata No. 34; 'Praise thy God, O Zion' from Cantata
    No. 190
Leighton, Kenneth: Symphony for strings
Bach, arr. Ferguson: Fuga ricercata from The Musical Offering
Purcell: 'Hark the echoing air'

1950
Stanley: Overture from *The Fall of Egypt*
Finzi: *Let us Garlands Bring* (Robert Irwin, John Carol Case in 1953)
Holst: Fugal Concerto (Alex Murray, James Brown)
Handel: overture from *Esther* (bassoon and strings)
Farrar: Three Spiritual Studies
Hoffmeister: Viola Concerto in D (Cynthia Freeman)
Stanley: Concerto No. 5
Telemann: Concerto 2 in D major for four violins

Wirén, Dag: Serenade
Bach: Brandenburg Concerto No. 2 (James Brown, Alex Murray)
Quantz: Flute Concerto (Catherine Powell)
Telemann: Concerto for four violins
Hughes, arr.: Irish folksongs (R. Irwin)
Leigh, Walter: Concertino for piano and strings (John Constable in 1951, Edmund
    Rubbra in 1952)
Grieg: Zwei Melodien
Leighton, Kenneth: Veris gratia
Seiber, M., arr.: Four French songs (Wyss)
Haydn: Flute Concerto in D (Johannes Feltkamp)
Britten: Ceremony of Carols
Stanley: Concerto No. 4
Vaughan Williams: Let us now praise famous men

1951
Pergolesi, arr. J. Barbirolli: Oboe Concerto
Bach, arr. Whittaker from *Gottlob nun geht*: 'Thou crownest the year'
Handel: Water Music Suite
Haydn: Spring from *The Seasons*
Gluck, arr. Whittaker: 'Turn, turn, my busy wheel' chorus from *Alceste*
Purcell: five songs for tenor, chorus, and strings (Wilfred Brown)
Stanley: 'Shall strangers weep' from *Teraminta*
Walton: two pieces from *Henry V*
Milford, Robin: The Forsaken Merman
Wesley, C.: Concerto No. 4 (John Constable)
Brahms, arr. Jacques: 'A rose breaks into bloom'
Gluck: ballet music from *Orpheus*
Handel: 'Silent worship' from *Tolomeo*; 'Endless pleasure' from *Semele* (Wilfred Brown)
Bach: 'O think my soul'
Bach: 'If thou art near'
Grieg: songs
Humfrey, Pelham: Hymn to God
Vivaldi: Sinfonia from *Holy Sepulchre*
Mozart: Romance from *Seraglio*
Finch, Ronald: 'Love's Secret'
Gluck: 'Faithful friend' (*Tauris*)

1952
Jacob, G.: Bassoon Concerto with percussion (William Waterhouse)
Mozart: Sonata for Bassoon and Cello
Handel: Organ Concerto No. 4, second set (Richard Latham)
Boyce: 'Rail no more'
Smith, J. C.: 'I burn, I burn' from *The Enchanter*
Stanley: 'Welcome death'
Boyce: 'Song of Momus to Mars' from the Secular Masque
Vaughan Williams: *Toward the Unknown Region*
Garth: Cello Concerto No. 2
Britten: Simple Symphony

Finzi: Clarinet Concerto (Colin Davis)
Cannon, Philip: 'The witch's meet', female voices and strings
Cannon, P.: Pan and Echo

1953
Garth: Concerto No. 3
Mudge: Concerto No. 4
Mahler: Adagietto for strings and harp
Wesley, C.: Concerto No. 5 (Herbert Sumsion)
Vaughan Williams: Dives and Lazurus
Stanford: *The Revenge*
Mozart: Divertimento K. 247
Kohaut: Guitar Concerto (Julian Bream)
Rubbra: Soliloquy for cello, strings, horns, timpani
Shaw, Geoffrey: Ring out ye crystal spheres
Garth: Concerto No. 4 (William Pleeth)
Garth: Concerto No. 5
Dvorak: Notturno
Ferguson, Howard: Piano Concerto (Ferguson)
Boyce: overture to New Year Ode 1772
Marcello: Oboe Concerto
Stanley: Concerto No. 6
D'Indy: Concerto for piano, flute, cello
Handel: 'Art thou troubled'; 'Rejoice greatly'

1954
Boyce: 'Softly rise' from *Solomon*
Schubert: Rondo (Yfrah Neaman)
Blow: Salvator mundi
Milford, Robin: Concertino for keyboard and strings
Parry: I was glad
Handel: The King shall Rejoice
Morris: Concerto piccolo for two violins and strings
Cruft, Adrian: Interlude
Wesley, C.: Concerto No. 1
Boyce: overture to Ode for HM birthday 1769
Teed, Roy: 'Such were the Joys' (Norman Tattersall)
Delius: Two Aquarelles
Grainger: Handel in the Strand
Holst: Brook Green Prelude
Mudge, Richard: Concerto No. 5
Jacob, Gordon: Violin Concerto (Frederick Grinke)
Sumsion, Herbert: A Mountain Tune, for cello and strings
Parry: 'Away away ye men of Mars'
Garth: Concerto No. 1
Stanley: Hercules' air from *Teraminta*
Vaughan Williams: 'Sound sleep'
Finzi: In Terra Pax

1955
Bond, Capel: Bassoon Concerto No. 6 (Waterhouse)
Bond, Capel: Concerto No 5
Boyce: duet 'Here shall soft charity' from 1772 Ode (Charles O'Byrne, Bernard Rose)
Arnell, Richard: Canzona and Capriccio
Boyce: Overture to Ode for HM birthday
Wesley, C. : Organ Concerto in C (John Constable)
Schütz: duet 'O quam tu pulchra' (Bernard Rose)
Mudge, Richard: Non nobis domine
Purcell: Te Deum in D
Seiber, arr. Baillie: Three Hungarian, Four Yugoslav Songs
Grieg and Delius: songs (Isobel Baillie)
Vaughan Williams: Benedicite (Isobel Baillie)
Stanley: Pan and Syrinx
Baines, Francis: Fantasia for strings
Milford, Robin: Fishing by Moonlight
Maconchy, Elizabeth: Oboe Suite
Bond, Capel: Concerto No. 4

1956
Bach: *Jauchzet Gott*
Bizet: Adagio from *L'Arlesienne*
Bond, Capel: Concerto No. 1 for trumpet
Byrd, ed. Terry: The leaves be green
Canon, Philip: Concertino for piano and strings
Mendelssohn: Violin Concerto, 1822 (Jack Rothstein)
Mudge: Organ Concerto No. 6
Mudge: Concerto No 2
Parry: *Glories of our blood and state* (Newbury Music Festival)
Purcell: The Blessed Virgin's Expostulation
Purcell: O sing unto the Lord (complete)
Sibelius: Suite champêtre
Vaughan Williams: *In Windsor Forest*, cantata (Newbury Festival)

Joy Finzi's Memoir of Gerald

When Joy Finzi invited me to write about Gerald I asked for her memories of their meeting. She wrote this, heading it just 'For Diana McVeagh'.

It is difficult to give you a very clear outward impression of G., because at our first meeting we immediately became implicated.

Shyness and enormous vitality – a kind of zest which fed his inner urgency. This, I discovered later, never allowed him rest.

His shyness and ill at ease in a public situation, quickly melted with his unusual empathy for people and interest in them. He was not at ease with highly sophisticated superficial people, and had a liking for simple men. This often prompted him to sign himself anonymously when on his walking tours, to enable his contacts to feel at ease with him as one of themselves. He knew that he could share their problems, but that they never could his.

He experienced the isolation of the artist – the eternal onlooker. His lonely, hurt, incompatible early surroundings made his books his companions and his few deeply chosen friends. Aristocratic, acutely sensitive, he built round himself an emphatic positive reaction to life and work. His urgency gave him an unswerving self-discipline – a dedication with which to wrestle with his utterance. Despite all this strong sense of direction his capacity for anguish was acute.

He was singularly inarticulate. Felt insignificant – plain to the point of ugliness. Inhibited and aware of it. The tension which his problems built up in him produced constant insomnia and he was acutely aware of the outside world. He had to take bromide often to help build up a possibility of sleeping (sleeping tablets, so common today, were not known then in the same way). I had never met anyone as sensitive and capable of hurt yet with such boundless vitality.

The insecurity of life had made a lasting impression on him. Even our meeting, which was such an enormous impact, filled him with grave apprehension, and I think he discussed with Howard whether anyone needing such an isolated dedicated back-ground should marry. He wondered whether it was right to expect me to happily share this with him. In my home he had seen people flow in and out, and he knew he needed the specialized conditions in which to wrestle with his work, more especially as he was so ardently interested in all life and so very easily distracted.

He had fallen in love from remote distances – Sybil Eaton his first, and one of his idols, and during our honeymoon we tried to find another blue-eyed love who had sold postcards in a shop in a village in East Anglia, and we learnt, regretfully, that she had married a parson and had several children. G. felt a Hardy sigh! He wished to show me everything that had been of significance to him, he was so starved of that warmth that makes for all flowering, and the need to communicate was so strong. That was why he laid so much emphasis on environment as against heredity (the eternal argument) and knew himself to be capable of drying up in disarticulation.

Like all who have known shadows he had an immense capacity for enjoyment and a great appreciation of many things — and infinite delight and humour. The sense of precariousness made delight an ecstasy. I wondered if I could partner such a spirit. I knew when I heard his songs for the first time (at one of the OUP concerts organized by Hubert Foss at Amen House) that I could never refuse him anything. Because we shared the same values, in wonder we entered our Eden with a complete sense of freedom.

General Index

Main entries in long lists are in **bold**

Abraham, Gerald, 176–7
Abraham, Harriette (Hadasa), 3
Agricola, 51
Aldridge, John, 127, 250
Alexander, Professor Samuel, 97
Allen, Hugh, 32
Alwyn, William, 63, 67
Amis, John, 133
Anderson, Mary, 88
Apples, 1, 13, 21, **84–5**, 129, 138, **143–4**, 152, 155, 158, 185, 201, 215, 252
Aquinas, St Thomas, 148
Aran, Islands, 83–4
Arensky, Anton, 126
Arkwright, Dr Marian, 232
Armstrong, John, 62
Armstrong, Thomas, 144
Arne, Thomas, 151, 152, 155, 183, 194, 222
Arnell, Richard, 214
Arts and Crafts, 31, 100
Atkins, James, 171
Ashmansworth (Church Farm), 90, 93, 99, **100–1**, 126–7, 129–30, 153, **167–8**, 179, 184, 226, 235, 247, 252, 255; songs buried under, 92, 113; bookroom at, 152; routine at, 175; memorials at, 251, 253
Austin, Richard, 116
Atkins, Ivor, 219
Atkinson, Marianne, 246
Auden, W. H., 63, 147, 153, 159
Augustine, St, 51
Ault, Norman, 136, 144
Austin, Sumner, 26
Austin, William, 211
Avison, Charles, 183, 184, **194–5**, 205, 208, 222

Bach, Johann Sebastian, 15, 56, 110, 119, 144, 153, 209; influence of, 45–6, 57, 59–60, 105,136, 169, 221, 262; NSP performances, 118, 120, 123, 126, 128, 131, 134, 135, 138, 145, 246
Bach, J. C., 209
Bacharach, A. L., 146
Baillie, Isobel, 87, 181
Baines, Francis, 241, 243
Bairstow, Edward C., 14, **15–16**, **19–20**, 22, **25**, 26, 27, **34**, 35, 46, 59, 60, **63**, 130, 159, 210, 215
Baldwin, Stanley, 62
Balfe, Michael, 141
Banfield, Stephen, 46, 93, 252
Bantock, Granville, 203
Barber, Samuel, 144
Barbirolli, John, 45, 203, **230**, **241**, 245, 249
Baring, Maurice, 98
Barker, George, 176–7
Barnsley, Edward and Sydney, 100
Barrie, J. M., 18
Bartók, Béla, 67, 75, 90–1, 208, 248
Bateson, Thomas, 18
Bax, Arnold, 4, 25, 67, **75**, **120**, 131, 133, 203
Bax, Clifford, 4
BBC, 67, 72, 95, 120, **123**, 139, 164, **165**, **176–7**, 205, 208, **211**, 237, 250
Beaumont, Francis, 152
Bedales School, 138–9, 141, 193, 207, 208, 235
Beech Knoll (Aldbourne), 72, 73, **74**, 90, 92, 94, 175, 184
Beecham, Thomas, 82, 83
Beethoven, Ludwig van, 3, 68, 75, 95, 96, 103, **167**, 209, 212

Behrend, Mrs J. L., 90–1, 145
Bellini, Vicenzo, 146
Bendle, Peggy, 74
Benjamin, Arthur, 182, 201, 255, 256
Bennett, Arnold, 18
Berg, Alban, 72, 203, 248
Berkeley, Lennox, 58, 133, 146, **147**, 176,
     264
Berkeley, Michael, 252
Berlioz, Hector, 19, 146, 166, **236**, 248
Bernac, Pierre, 175
Bernard, Anthony, 35
Bernhardt, Sarah, 97
Betjeman, John, **196**, 244, 246
Bible, The, **8**, 34, 54, 55, 59, 121, **122**,
     125, 173, 174; and Hardy, 40, 80
Bingles, 68, 69
Black (née Whitehorn), Amy, 68, 69, 70
Black, Ernest, 68
Black, Joyce (see Finzi, Joy)
Black, (Aunt) Lily, 71, 72, 76, 102
Black, Margaret (Mags) (Neate), 68, 69,
     72, 110, **210**, 219, 251
Blake, William, 17, 28, 48, 55, 65, **99**,
     103, 152, **157**, **165**
Bliss, Arthur 25, **48–50**, 55, 56, 58, 65,
     90, 94, 114, 117, **123**, **126**, 129, 145,
     167, 201, **202**, **231**, 235, 250, 251,
     253; comments on Finzi, 62, 104, 241;
     influence on Finzi, 46, 262
Bliss, Trudy, 50, 114, **117**, 126, 209, 231
Bliss, William, 64
Bloch, Ernest, 48, 56, 89, 145, 207
Blom, Eric, 67, 85, 94
Blow, Detmar, **31–2**, 37, 71, 100, 227
Blow, John, 31
Blow, Winifred, **31–2**, 37, 53, 54, 71, 227
Blunden, Claire, 196, 213,
Blunden, Edmund, 15, 65, 78, **86–7**, 92,
     142, 152, 169, **173**, 178, **193**, **196**,
     199, 200–1, **207–8**, 209, 212–3, **218**,
     219, **223–4**, 225, 231, 234, 235–36,
     243, 247, 249, **252**, 253, 254, 256,
     260; settings of, 69, 81, 154–63, 213,
     260; poems of, 122, 162–3, 197, 232,
     235
Boas, Franz, 93
Boccherini, Luigi, 144, 151
Bond, Capel, 222, 231, 237, 241, 250

Boosey & Hawkes, 67, **76**, **101**, 108, 146,
     158, 182, 183, 205, 222, 232, 245
Boosey, Leslie, 87, 136, 150, 173
Booth, John, 32
Botticelli, 103
Boughton, Joy, 145
Boughton, Rutland, **16–17**, 20, 51, 119,
     204, **249**
Boulay de la Meurthe, 12
Boult, Adrian, 20, 25, **34**, 38, 62, 72, 83,
     120, 123, 128, **158**, 203, **247**, 253
Bowes-Lyon, Ann, 88–9, 101, 196
Boyce, William, 32, **118**, 126, 128, 144,
     151, 152, 182, 194, 195, 207, **208**,
     222, 223, 230, **237**, 251; for Musica
     Britannica, 244–5; misattribution, 183;
     research on, 205–6, 243, 247
Brace, Mrs, 21, 225
Brahms, Johannes, 35, 39, 59, 61, **67–8**,
     69, 78, 170, **189**
Bream, Julian, 216
Brent-Smith, Alexander, 25, 99
Brewer, Herbert, 33, 54
Bridge, Frank, 131, 209, 259
Bridges, Robert, **23**, 32, **38**, 92, 152, **157**,
     165, 202, 218, 236, 243, settings of,
     77–8, 211, 227–9, 249; poems of, 98,
     118, 178, 249
Bridgewater, Leslie, 205
Bright, John, 142
British Music Society, 20, 26
Britten, Benjamin, 63, 71, 90–1, **101**, 120,
     128, 129, **141**, **145–6**, 147, 149, 150,
     159, **182**, 193, **201**, 203, 221, 228,
     251, 258, **259**, 262, 263; 'Proud
     Songsters', 80
Brooke, Edith, 109, 112, 246, 250,
Brooke, Justin, 109, 112, 139, 246, 250
Brooke, Rupert, 28, 31, 109
Brown, Bernard, 144
Brown, Harold, 249
Brown, James (Jim), 184, 243, 246
Brown, Wilfred, 207, 252, 253
Bruckner, Anton, 166
Bugsworthy, hoax, 34, 167
Bullock, Ernest, 215
Bunting, Christopher, 233, 234, 241
Bunyan, John, 173
Burne-Jones, Edward, 31

Burney, Charles, 195
Burnside, Iain, 252
Burra, Edward, 129
Busch, William, 46, 88, **94–7**, 101, **106–7**, 112, 115–16, 129, **139**, 186, 230
Bush, Alan, 67, 92, 119, 129, 146
Busoni, Ferriccio, 146
Butler, Samuel, 65, 66, 119
Butterworth, George, 19, 23, 25, **28–9**, 31, **60**
Byrd, William, 25, **27**, 34, 120, 157, 182, 209, 248, 262

Campbell, Roy, 153
Cannon, Philip, 247
Capell, Richard, 58, 67, 87, 94
Carey, Clive, 17
Carnegie Trust Publications, 31, 32, 33
Carol Case, John, 221–2, 230, 243, 251, 252
Carr-Saunders, A. M., 96
Carse, Adam, 183, 205
Carvalho, Simha, 3
Casals, Pablo, 233, 246
Cats, 1, 4, 13, 37, 48, 50, 62, 168, 201, 223
Cavour, Camillo, 3
Ceddie (see Thorpe Davie)
Cellini, Benvenuto, 18,
Chamberlain, Joseph, 116
Champion, Mrs, 24, 34
Chapman, Ernest, 108,
Charpentier, Gustave, 19
Chaucer, Geoffrey, 22
Chenhalls, Alfred T., 111, 117
Chopin, Frédéric, 76
Chosen Hill, Gloucestershire, 24, 34, **36**, 38, 51, **227**, **249–50**
Church, Richard, 218
Churchill, Winston, 111,116, 142
Cimarosa, Domenico, 138, 182
Clare, John, 17, **34**, 86–7, 152, 200, 224
Clark, Leonard, 231, 252
Clifford, Julian, 9
Clinton-Baddeley, V. C., 230
Coates, Eric, 208
Coates, John, 72
Cobbett, William, 17, 152

Coghill, Nevill, 235, 244
Cohen, Harriet, 70
Coleridge, Samuel Taylor, 208
Colles, H. C., 127
Collins, William, 154
Colum, Padraic, 22
Constable, John (painter), 232
Constable, John (pianist), 194, 200
Coomes, Ron, 127, 129–130
Cooper, Martin, 191–2, 225
Copland, Aaron, 209
Corelli, Arcangelo, 118, 138, 145
Costa, Michael, 236
Coward, Noel, 61
Cowen, Frederic, 89
Crashaw, Richard, 148
Crawford, Lord, 216
Craxton, Harold, 32
Cross, Joan, 150
Cudworth, Charles, 205, 215–16
Cummings, W. H., 232, 236
Curran, John Philpot, 142
Curwen, 26, 35, 63, 67, 72, 201

D'Indy, Vincent, 151
Dale Roberts, Jeremy, 168, 252
Dale, Benjamin, 131
Dale, Kathleen, 235
Dart, R. Thurston, 151
Darwin, Charles, 4, 5
Davidson, Malcolm, 25
Davie, Ian, 243
Davies, Meredith, 249
Davies, W. H., 22
Davies, Walford, 229
Davis, Colin, 221
Davoll, Harry, 100
Day Lewis, Cecil, 224–5, 244
Day, Norah, 53
Daymond, Emily, 201
De la Mare, Walter, 22, 23, 85–6, **112**, 209, **231**, 253, **259**
Debussy, Claude, 16, 56, 212, 257
Delius, Frederick, 19, 28, 48, 216
Demuth, Norman, 67
Dent, E. J., 17
Dickens, Charles, 17
Dieren, Bernard van, 35, 97, 146
Dietz, Gisa (Cartwright), 107, 127

Disraeli, Benjamin, 121, 167
Dixon, H. P., 215
Dobell, Bertram, 27, 43, 187
Dodgson, Stephen, 194
Dolmetsch, Arnold, 38
Dowland, John, 32, 136, **157**, 236, 262
Drew, Frank, 72
Drummond, William, **39**, 56, 253
Dryden, John, 154, 157, 159
Duke Ellington, 61
Dunhill, Thomas, 145
Dyson, George, 99, 121, 128, 201
Dyson, Ruth, 151

Eaton, Sybil, 16, 33, **51**, 70, 71, 72, 123, 140, 185, 256
Edith (see Pike)
Einstein, Albert, 96, 97
Elgar, Edward, 3, 16, 17, 19, 21, 27, **30**, 32, 36, 50, 63, 74, 88, 89, 97, 120, 123, 138, 145, 151, 174, **182**, 193, 199, 218, 228, **235**, 241; Finzi's comments on, 18, 26, 67; influence of, 79, 80, 104, 159, 160, 177, 181, 210, 221, 238, 262, 263
Elgar, Carice 235
Eliot, T. S., 153, 196, 201, 209, 213
Elwes, Joan, 144
Epstein, Jacob, 129, 164
Erlebach, Rupert, 32, 152
Eurich, Richard, 253
Evans, Audrey, 74
Evans, Edwin, 94

Falkner, Keith, 55, 57, 62, 79, 87, 144
Falkner, Meade, 231
Falla, Manuel de, 67
Farrar, Ernest Bristow **9**, **14–15**, 25, 28, 33, 65, 114, 132, 144, 207, **214**, 215, 219, 225, 228–9, 236; dedications to, 31, 131
Farrar, Olive, 15, 213, 225
Fauré, Gabriel, 145, 221
Fayrfax, Robert, 166
Fellowes, Edmund, 17, 262
Feltkamp, Johannes, 194
Felton, William, 184, 194, 195, 236
Ferguson, Howard, **47–9**, 54, 55, **56**, 57, **59**, 61, **62**, 63, 68, 69, 70, 71, 72, 75,

76, **83**, 84, **85–7**, **88**, **93**, 94, 95, 100, 103, **108**, 110, 111, **112**, **114**, 117, 118, 120, **123**, 127, **128**, 129, **131**, 133, 138, 144, 146, **147**, 149, 151, 153–4, **158**, 164, 166, 172, 173, **175**, 178, 182, 186, 199, **216–17**, 218, 223, 232, **233**, 237, 243, **247**, **249**, 251, 252, **253**, 254, 255, **256**; comments on Finzi's music, 77, 99, 101, 102, 135–6, 162, 176, 221, 227, 229, 240–1; dedications, 162, 247
Ferrier, Kathleen, 181
Festing, Michael, 205
Fiedler, Herma, 184
Finch, Ronald, 186
Finzi, Christopher (son, see Kiffer)
Finzi, Daniel (uncle), 3
Finzi, Douglas Lewis (brother), 4, 6, 7
Finzi, Edgar (brother), 4, 5, 6, 7, 8, 9, 11, 12, 13, 14, 15
Finzi, Felix John (brother), 4, 6, 7, 8
Finzi, Gerald, for Finzi's opinions of other composers, see under their entries; for first performances of his works, see appendix 1.
Absalom's Place, 121–3, 165, 196–7; amateurism versus professionalism, 16, 18, 51, 144, 150, **204**, 241; anti-establishment and -conventions, 5, **64**, 103, 174, 212, 219, 232; appearance, **16**, 38, 56, 63, **65**, **68**, 71, 90, 196, **230**, 242, **246**; articles, broadcasts, lectures, letters to the press, 133, 164–5, 166, 167, **194–5**, 204, 205, 206, 208, 212, 225–6, 230, 235, **236–7**, 244; artist, value and vision of, 15, 17, 20, 27, 40, 98, **110**, 115, 116, 117, 121, **122**, 132, 191, 224, 254; Black Book, 197–8; book and music collections, 18, 99, 130, **152–3**, 223, 252; breakdown in 1943, 131–2; catalogue of compositions, 121, 154, 253; childhood, views on, 8, 10, 28, 43, **102–3**, 138–9, 178, 187; commonplace book and collections of cuttings, 19, 89, 153, 237, 255; conductor, 76, 118, 185; conscription, 204, 232; contribution to common weal, 65, 83, 132; Crees lectures, 230, 233, **236–7**, 258, 260; crucial

experiences, 6, 8, 10, 20, 36, 132; dating and chronology, 24, 43, 46–7, 102; dedication to composing, **8**, 9, 15, 17, 31, 33, 49, 64–5, **69**, 98; domestic life, 1, 12, 24, 37, 74, 90, 100, 108, 127, 143, 153, **167–8**, 184, 247; education, views on, 7, 9, 16, 17, 28, 64, 114, 123, **138–9**, 187; environment and heredity, 7, 19, 25, 38, **66**, 82, **91–3**, 96–7, 102, 112, 237, 255; facility and virtuosity, 14, 51, 60, 61, 161, 203, 238, 262; fashion and reputations, 209, 236, 248; financial circumstances 7, 9, 13, 28, 33, 37–8, 69, 152, **153–4,** 165–6, 252; folk music, 18, 21, 26, 38, 50, 65, 74–5; health, 53, 55–6, 131, **196–9**, 211, 213, 214, 219, 230, 231–2, 233, 237, 243–4, 250; Jewishness, 4, 5, 12, 17, 65, 66, 75, 89, 93, **95–7**, 107, 112, 254, 255; Joy, relationship with, 68–73, 93, 117, 185–6, 249, 256–7; life-beliefs, 254; pacifism and patriotism, 15, 66, 89, 91, 93, **94–7**, 106, 110, 115, 121, 132, 133, 142, 229, 232, 234, 235; pastoralism, Englishness, and foreign travel 7, 8, **18**, 19, 29, **33**, 34, 38, 65, 68, 75, 76, 174, 227, 255; pianist, 8, 59, 175; posterity, 27, 54, 92, 113, 116, **122,** 197, 214; recordings, 150, 252; religion and dogma, 84, 99, 102, **116–17**, **119**, 147, 148, 165, 174, 227, 234; research and scholarship, 144, 151–2, 182–4, 194–5, 205–6, 218, 221–3, 237, 244–5, 251–2; song outlasts dynasty, 107, 115, 254; St Andrews, 206, 208, 216, 225; teacher, 63, 71, 90; vegetarianism, 16, 21, 37, 74, 84; work, importance of, 49, 66, 69, 82, 100, 101, 106, 110, 112, 121, 254; working methods, 175–76; youth, old age, and time's pressure, 15, 31, 39, **43**, 54, 57, 89, 98, **102**, 120, **125–6** 129, 131–2, 139, 191, 208, 230, 254

    musical imagery, 262–3; musical style, 44–5, 60–2, 179–81, 239–40, 259–62, and passim; words and music, 87–88, 141, 187, 236–7, 258–61 and passim

Finzi, Christopher (son, Kiffer) **72**, 113, 124, **139**, 147, 158, 168, **178**, 186, 198, 200, 203, **206,** 207, 208, 213, **231**, 232, **234**, 235, **246**, 247, **248**, 250, **251**, **252**, 253, 254, **255**

Finzi, Daniel, 3

Finzi, Douglas Lewis (brother), 4, 6, 7, 197

Finzi, Edgar (brother), 4, 5, 7, **8–9**, 11, 12, 13, 14, **15**, 197

Finzi, Felix John (brother), 4, 6, 7, 8, 197

Finzi, Giuseppe, 3

Finzi, Jack (John Abraham) (father), 3, 4, 5, 6–7, 130, 197, 211

Finzi, Judah, 3

Finzi, Joy, née Black (wife) 1, 65, 73, 74, 75, 76, 78, 80, **82**, 83, 86, 89, 90, 92, **93**, 94, 96, 98, 99, 100, 101, 102, 103, 107, 108, 109, 111, 112, 123, **127**, 129–30, 137, 141, 142, 147, 149, 152, 153–4, 167, 178, 198, **199–200**, 202, 206, 207, 208, 213, 215, 218, 219, 224, 228, 230, 233, 234, 235, 240, 241, 242, 246, **247,** 251, 252–3, 255, **256–7**, 264; as artist, 68, 72, 117, 124, 164, 212, 213, 231, 249, 253; and NSP, 118, 150, 184–6, 194, 205

Finzi, Kate Gilmour (sister), 4, 5–6, 7, 9, **10–11**, 13, **14**, 28, **66**, 72, **197**

Finzi, Layman, Clark & Co, 4, 6

Finzi, Leon Moses, 4

Finzi, Leon, 4

Finzi, Lizzie (Eliza Emma) née Leverson (mother), **3**, 4, **5–6**, **7**, **8**, 9, 12, 13, 14, 15, 22, 24, **33–4**, 37, 38, 56, 72, **82**, 88–9, 93, 115, 153, 206, 225, **242**

Finzi, Mordecai ben Abraham, 3, 229

Finzi, Neville Samuel (cousin), **4**, 6, 10, 14, 37, 45, **72**, 211–12

Finzi, Nigel (son), 82, **133**, 139, 141, 147, 158, 158, 168, **178**, 186, 198, 200, 203, **206**, 207, 208, 213, 234, **246**, 250, **251**, **253**, 254

Finzi, Samuel Leon (uncle), 3

Fishburn, C., 154

Flackton, William, 222

Flaherty, Robert, 83

Flecker, James Elroy, 17, 113
Fleming, Alexander, 10
Fleming, Amaryllis, 140
Fletcher, John, 20
Forster, E. M., 107, 112
Foss, Hubert, 45, 71, 85, 91, 127
Fox Strangways, A. H. 26, 85
Fox, Adeline and Evelyn, 109, 145
Frankel, Benjamin, 166, 251
Fraser Darling, Frank and Averil, 224, 246
Freeman, John, 23
Freeman, Cynthia, 223
Freud, Sigmund, 191
Frost, Robert, 32,
Frumkin, Gregory, 7

Galton, Francis, 93
Garbo, Greta, 111
Gardiner, Balfour, 116, 144
Gardner, John, 209
Garibaldi, Guiseppe, 3, 5
Garth, John, 205, 206, 214, 215, **222**,
    226, 241
Genghis Khan, 107
German, Edward, 248
Gibbons, Orlando, 18, 60, 155, 157, 182
Gibson, W. W., 31
Gill, Harry, 215
Gilmour, Kate (sister, see Finzi)
Gimson, Ernest, 100
Gisa (see Dietz)
Gittings, Robert, 224
Gladstone, W. E., 167
Glock, William, 263, 264
Gluck, Christoph Willibald, 138
Goddard, Scott, 196
Godden, Rumer, 68
Godfrey, Dan, 9, 32, 71, 72
Godfrey, Peter, 243, 249
Goethe, Johann Wolfgang von, 12, 224
Gomperts, Barbara, 257
Goossens, Eugene, 83
Goossens, Leon, 50, 67, 76, 77, 138
Gosse, Edmund William, 34, 255
Gotwals, Vernon, 210
Graves, A. P., 236
Graves, Robert, 22
Gray, George, 16
Gray, Thomas, 204

Greene, Eric, 137, 138, 158, 186, 242
Greene, Harry Plunket, 15, 85, 87
Greene, Maurice, 152, 236, 245
Greenwood, Michael, 216–17
Grétry, André, 120
Greville, Ursula, 32
Grieg, Edvard, 19, 97, 123, 151, 166
Griller Quartet, 67, 114
Grinke, Frederick, 199, 246
Groves, Charles, 164
Gurney, Ivor, 19, 24, 25, 31, **32–3**, **35**, 36,
    95, **102**, 108, **131**, **132**, 154, 156, 158,
    197, **223–4**, 231, **235**, 251, 252, 255,
    264; songs, 20, 85–7, 111, 200;
    poems, 21, 142, 196, 199, 218
Gurney, Ronald, 224, 235–6

Hadley, Patrick, 129
Haines, Jack, 32, 86, 111, 186, 204, 231
Haldane, Richard, 96
Hamilton, Iain, 248
Handel, George Frederick, 123, **144**, 145,
    156–7, 159, 161, 166, 183, 184, 187,
    194, **195**, 206, 215, **236**, 237
Hardy, Thomas, 1, **10**, **18**, 31, 37, **54**, 56,
    62, 65, **92**, **93**, 97, 98–9, **101**, 102,
    108, **109**, 110, **115**, **116**, **122**, 146,
    152, 156, **173–5**, 201, 208, 213, 218,
    233, 236, **244**, **245**, 247–8, 252, 253,
    257, 259, 264; settings of, 23–4,
    29–30, 39–42, 78–80, 81–2, 169–72
Hargrave, Henry, 222
Harland, Peter, 90, 100
Harris, Roy, 209
Harrison, Ruth, 70
Havergal, Henry, 201
Hawkesworth, John, 200
Hawkins, John, 149, 183, 195, 218
Hawthorne, Nathaniel, 118
Haydn, Josef, 14, 39, **56**, 110, 126, 138,
    151, 193, 205, **218**, 235
Heatherly, Frank and Thomas, 4
Heine, Heinrich, 96
Helmsley, Frederick, 14
Hemingway, Ernest, 136
Henley, W. E., 23
Henschel, George, 98
Herbage, Julian, 151
Herbert, William, 199

Herrick, Robert, 22
Herrmann, Bernard, 210
Hess, Myra, 97, 108, 131, 144, 255
Heyworth, Peter, 248
Hiatt, Iva Dee, 209–10, 226
Hindemith, Paul, 35, 67, 84, 110, 264
Hinrichsen, 205, 222, 243
Hitler, Adolf, 94, 107, 116, 117, 119
Holst, Gustav, 19, 32, 33, 48, 50, **51–2**,
    62, **68**, **70**, **71**, **72**, **77**, 91, 97, 116,
    118, 119, 120, 132, 151, **167**, 211,
    212, 214, **247**, **252**, 256; influence of,
    24, 27, 39, 41, 42, 52, 104, 159
Holst, Henry, 144
Holst, Imogen, 214, 252
Homer, 113
Hope, May, 144
Hopkins, Gerard Manley, 142
Housman, A. E., 23, 92
Howard (see Ferguson, Howard)
Howard-Jones, Evelyn, 50
Howells, Herbert 16, 20, **24**, 25, 32, **33**,
    35, 50, **56**, 63, **82**, **85–6**, **87**, 90, **91**,
    102, **111**, 128, 133, **137**, 144, 176,
    187, 199, **200**, **209**, **212**, 223, **225–6**,
    234, 255,249
Howells, Ursula, 35, 176
Howes, Frank, 67, 74–5, 161, 215, 237,
    248, 251
Hudson, W. H., 18, 105
Hughes, Rosemary, 235
Hugo, Victor, 5
Hull, Percy and Mollie, 32, 92, 97
Hull, Robin, 146
Hunt, Leigh, 208
Hussey, Walter, 147–8
Hutchings, Arthur, 87–8, 138
Hutton , Graham, 64–5, 71, 98, 251
Huxley, Julian, 96
Hyman, Kate (grand-mother), 5

Iliff, Noel, 149
Ireland, John, 17, 67, 111, 131
Irwin, Robert, 129, 131, 135, 137, 140,
    156, 168, 173
Ismay, Olive, 14

Jackson of Exeter, 184, 208, 237
Jacob, Gordon, 53, 129, 146, 151, 225

Jacobson, Maurice, 63
Jacques, Reginald, 137, 243
James, Henry, 62, 88
Jenkins, Gilmour, 130
Joachim, Joseph, 97
Jones, Philip, 182
Jones, William (Sir), 81
Jonson, Ben, 93
Joy's Journal, **82–3**, 126, 142, **199–200**,
    222, 226 and passim
Juler, Pauline, 131, 178
Jung, 191

Karpeles, Maud, 74, 83
Katin, Peter, 226
Kaye, Walter, 8, 122 fn
Keats, John, 82, 90, 97, 121, 224
Keller, Hans, 146
Kelly, Bryan, 209, 226
Kiffer (see Finzi, Christopher)
King, Thea, 230, 243
Knevet, Ralph, 136
Kodály, Zoltán, 56
Kohnstamm, Dr Von, 7, 12
Korda, Alexander, 111

Lamb, Charles, 38, 193, 208
Lambert, Constant, 51, 58, 129, 133, 151,
    183
Lambert, Georgie, 64
Lambert, Herbert, 63, 64, 69, 77, 82, 255
Landor, W. S., 167
Langley, Hubert, 151
Lasker, Vally, 53, 211
Latham, Dick (Richard), 130, 200, 210,
    247
Lawrence, D. H., 130
Lawrence, T. E., 76
Leather, Ella, 26, 27
Leigh, Walter, 194, 207, 241
Leighton, Kenneth, 182, 194, 199, 203,
    215, 248, 252
Lemare, Iris, 71, 76, 87, 108, 121
Leo, Leonardo, 145
Lethaby, W. R., 208
Leverson, Ada, 5
Leverson, Louis Pianciani (uncle), 5, 7, 12,
    17, 37, 38, 207

Leverson, Montague Richard (maternal grandfather), 5
Leverson, William Ellis (uncle), 7, 12, 17, 26, 37, 38, 153, 207
Levi, Philip, 256
Levyson, Ernest, 5
Levyson, Montague (maternal great-grandfather), 5
Lewis, Anthony, 222, 251
Lewis, C. S., 212
Lewis, Richard, 226
Lily (aunt, see Black)
Linde, Mary, 137
Liszt, Franz, 13, 146
Lloyd, Marie, 203
Locke, Matthew, 17
Lockhart, James, 218
Lockspeiser, Edward, 52
Lofthouse, Charles Thornton, 166, 211, 226
Logan, Sinclair, 87
Long, Kathleen, 62, 144–5, 233, 251
Long, N. G., 146
Lucas, F. L., 113, 121
Lushington, Susan, 201

Macleod, Fiona, 22
Macnaghten, Anne, 71, 77, 234
Maconchy, Elizabeth, 129, 146, 246
Mahler, Gustav, 52, **55**, 89, 92, 97, 105, 209, 228, 264
March church, Cambridgeshire, 38, 103
Martin, Leslie, 84
Marvell, Andrew, 125
Marx, Karl, 97
Masefield, John, 18, 30, 231
Mason, Colin, 248
Matcham, Frank, 9
Matthews, Denis, 128, 129, 131
Maurois, André, 54
May Hill, Gloucestershire, 21, 26, 31, **36**, 75, 85, 225, **251**
Mazzini, Giuseppe, 3, 5
McVeagh, Diana, 248
Mead, Margaret, 93
Meldola, Raphael, 4, 7
Mendelssohn, Felix, 89, 94, 96
Menges Quartet, 76
Menotti, Gian Carlo, 201, 209, 254–5

Merbecke, John, 160
Meredith, George, 91–2
Meyerbeer, Giacomo, 201
Michelangelo, 99
Miles, Maurice, 108, 215
Miles, Napier, 32
Milford, Humphrey, 91, 110, 212
Milford, Robin **53**, 57, **91**, 92, 95, **98**, 99, 106, 107, 108, 109, 111, 114, 115, **116–17**, 118, **119**, **121**, 125, 126, 129, 130, 138, 139, 141, 145, 146, 149, 150, 152, 156, 165, 166, 182, 193, 194, **199**, **203**, 211, **216**, **219**, 221, 226, 227, 230, **231**, **243**, 248, 253, **254**, 256; NSP performances, 120, 128, 144, 199, 204
Milhaud, Darius, 89
Milner, Anthony, 248
Milnes, Monckton, 224
Milton, John, 57–8, 98, 121, 161
Mimi, 107
Moeran, E. J., 133
Moore, Gerald, 134, 140
Moore, Henry, 147
Morley, Avril (see Fraser Darling)
Morley, Thomas, 18
Morris, Jane, 61, 62, 126
Morris, R. O., 20, **34**, 35, 46, 47, 48, **50**, 51, **55**, 58, **61–2**, 67, 70, 91, **125**, **126**, 138, **167**, 215, 225, 234
Morris, William, 65
Moszkowski, Moritz, 128
Mozart, Wolfgang Amadeus, **53**, 56, 91, 138, 144, **146**, 205, 247, 262
Mudge, Richard, 205, 215, 218, **223**, 237, 241, 251
Mullen, Barbara, 83
Mullen, Pat, 83
Murray, Alex, 184
Murray, Gilbert, 236
Murrill, Herbert, 222
Music & Letters, 19, 52, **85–6**, **87**, 89, 111, 142
Musica Britannica, 222, 231
Musical Times, 26, 87, 108, 161, 225, 245
Mussolini, Benito, 95
Mussorgsky, Modest, 85
Mycenae, 168

Napoleon Bonaparte, 95, 117
Nash, Paul, 129
Navarro, José Maria de (Toty), 1, **88–9**, 90,
    92, 99, 101, 106, **108**, 109, **115**, **117**,
    123, 128, **129**, 135, 138, **139**, **141**,
    143, 144, 150, 158, **172–3**, 196, 202,
    244, **252**
Neel, Boyd, 137, 150, 203, 204
Nero, 113
Newman, Ernest, 35, 141
Nicholson, Ralph, 69
Nicolson, Harold, 107
Niemöller, Martin, 94
Novello, Vincent, 208
NSP (Newbury String players) **118**, 120,
    123, 126, 128, 130, 131, 138, 139,
    140, 144–5, 150–2, 160, 166, 175,
    178, 179, 182, **184**, 193–4, 199, 203,
    204–5, 207, **215**, 221, 222, 223, 225,
    226, 227, 241, 243, **246**, 251, 252,
    255

Offenbach, Jacques, 89
Oldridge, Diana née Awdrey, 25, 166
Oman , Sir Charles, 130
Oxford University Press, **62**, 67, 69, **71**,
    76, 77, 85, 87, 91, 101, 111, 127, 151,
    167

Pakenham, Simona, 149
Palestrina, 34, 148
Palmer, Samuel, 227, 247
Parry, Hubert, 3, 9, 16, 19, **20**, 21, **25**, 27,
    46, 110, 128, 138, 151, **157**, 160, **161**,
    164–6, 167, 169, 187, 199, 201–2,
    204, 206, 214, 235, 236, 237, 243,
    248, 251, 262
Partridge, Ralph and Frances, 235
Pasteur, Louis, 5
Patron's Fund at RCM, 91
Peake, Mervyn, 130
Pears, Peter, 128, 129, 175
Peele, George, 18, 136
Peerson, Martin, 17, 253
Pike, Edith, 37, 48, 50, 61, 72
Pirandello, Luigi, 88
Plato, 120
Pleeth, William, 222
Ponsonby, Arthur, 235

Ponsonby, Dorothea Lady, 166, 201–2,
    204, 221, 232, 235, 242, 246, 264
Pope, Alexander, 159
Pope-Henessy, James, 224
Poulenc, Francis, 111, 134
Powell, Alfred, 208
Priestley, J. B., 15
Prokofiev, 220
Prout, Ebenezer, 34
Pu (May Cunningham), 47
Puccini, Giaccomo, 19
Purcell, Henry, 18, 31, 63, 74, 105, 120,
    133, 155, 159, 160, 161, 166; NSP
    performances, 123, 128, 138, 144, 145

Quantz, J. J., 193
Quarles, Francis, 122 fn, 132, 152, 194
Quiller-Couch, Arthur, 28, 152, 207, 214
Quilter, Roger, 259

Raleigh, Walter, 22, 94
Rameau, Jean-Phillippe, 48, 120
Ranger, S. W., 26
Ravel, Maurice, 16, 56, 89, 134, 237
Rawsthorne, Alan, 146, 176, 264
Ray, Don, 196
Raybould, Clarence, 95, 135–6
Read, Herbert, 119
Reed, W. H., 99
Rembrandt, 103
Respighi, Ottorini, 144
Richardson, Alan, 127
Riesenecker, Lydia, 107, 137
Rimsky-Korsakov, Nikolay, 85
Roberts, Morley, 117
Robinson, Bernard, 248
Rockstro, W. S., 34
Rodin, Auguste, 99
Rolland, Romain, 18
Rose, Bernard, 182
Roseingrave, Thomas, 183
Rosenthal, Albi, 251
Rossetti, Christina, 19, 22, 43
Roth, Rosie, 118, 123
Rothenstein, Michael, 129
Rothenstein, William, 89, 100, 164
Rousseau, Jean-Jacques, 103
Royal Academy of Music, 63–4, **67**, 66,
    71, 90, **164**, 168, **196**, 234, 243

Royal College of Music, 47, 75, 90, 106,
   165–6, **184**, 194, 201, 215, 218, **230**,
   234, **236–7**
Royal Musical Association, 194
Rubbra, Antoinette, 109
Rubbra, Edmund, **50**, **56**, 92, 94, 97, **109**,
   120, 125, 129, 133, 145, 147, 176,
   199, 201, 207, **214**, 226, **236**, **242**,
   247, 248, 249, 251, 264; on Finzi's
   music, 41, 46, 58–9, 60, 62, 93, 221
Ruskin, John, 31
Russell, John, 175, **199**, 203, 218,
   219–20, **226**, 237, 243, 249, 250, 251,
   256, 264
Ruth (see Harrison)
Rutland, William R., 101, 173–4

Sackville-West, Vita, 204
Sadie, Stanley, 216
Samuel, Harold, 20, 35, 45, **47–8**, 59, 75,
   83, 88, 93, 97, 255
Sands, Mollie, 152, 183, 195, 200
Sargent, Malcolm, 51, 215
Sassoon, Siegfried, 207
Scarlatti, Alessandro, 48
Schlesinger, John, 178
Schubert, Franz, 17, 25, 40, 41, 78, **91**,
   95, 110, **111**, **121**, 209, 260; Who is
   Silvia, 135
Schumann, Robert, 260
Schoenberg, Arnold, 89, 97, 129, 205, 237
Scholes, Percy, 202
Schuschnigg, Kurt von, 94
Schütz, Heinrich, 55, 56, 122 fn, 166
Schwabacher, Hettie (née Leverson) (aunt),
   5, 37–8, 66
Schwabacher, Wilhelm, 66
Scofield, Paul, 150
Scott, Charles Kennedy, 45, 72
Scott, Dr Tom, 147, 198, 250, 256
Scott, Marion, 32–3, **85–7**, 111, 196, 200,
   218–19, 223–4, **235**
Scott, Ruth, 90, 101, 114, 121, 256
Scott, Tony, **90–1**, 99, **101**, 102, **114**, 118,
   121, 127, 128, 133, 139, 141, **143**,
   145, **147**, 156, 158, 164, 165, 178,
   203, 204, **208**, 251, **256**; Finzi on his
   music, 203
Scotts Nurseries, 144, 292

Sedley Taylor, 195
Selwyn, Edward, 108
Seneca, 112, 194
Shakespeare, William 18, 55, 93, 110, 146,
   152, 232, 237; Finzi's settings, 134–6,
   149–50, 216–18
Shand, Morton, 84–5, 156
Shanks, Edward, 24
Shaw, Geoffrey 120, 128
Shaw, George Bernard, 16, 17
Shelley, Percy Bysshe, 96
Shield, William, 222
Shimmin, Sydney, 32
Shiner, Michael, 184
Shirley Smith, Richard **168**, 247, 249, 250,
   253, 257
Shuttleworth, Anna, 145, **184**, 203, 206,
   226, 251
Sibelius, Jean **88**, 95, 97, 128, **239**, 248
Sickert, Walter, 129
Sidgwick, A. H., 88
Sinclair, Monica, 145
Sitwell, Edith, 231
Skeaping, John, 72
Smart, Christopher, 154
Smetana, Bedrich, 48, 110
Smith, J. C., 183
Smith, W. C., 183, 184, 195, 245
Smyth, Ethel, 54, 68
Soames, René, 158
Somerfeld, Vera (see Strawson)
Somervell, Arthur, 260
Sophocles, 103
Spencer, Gilbert, 243, 251
Spencer, Herbert, 117
Spencer, Stanley, 109, 129, 227
Spencer, Sylvia, 64
Spohr, Ludwig, 166
Squire, Barclay, 183, 245
Stafford Smith, 195
Stainer & Bell, 32
Stanford, Charles Villiers, 9, **14**, 16, 48, 85,
   216, 236, 247
Stanley, John, 144, **182–3**, **194–5**, 200,
   205, 208, 213, 218, 222, 236, 237,
   251
Stein, Kitty, 174, 255
Stevens, Denis, 205
Stevenson, Robert Louis, 22

Stewart, Jean, **131**, 140, 144, 150, **185**, **204**, 255

Stone, Reynolds and Janet, 231, 242, 251, 252

Stratton Quartet, 108

Strauss, Richard, 47, 48, 83, 107, 182

Stravinsky, Igor, 52, 56, 72, 111, 182, 208, 237

Strawson, Frank, 17, 65, 107, 127, 130

Strawson, Vera, **17–19**, 20, 21, **24**, 25, 26, **28**, 33, 34, 39, 51, **53**, **55**, 56, 60, 62, 63, **65**, 66, **107**, 127, 138, 152, 254, 255

Suddaby, Elsie, 20, 101, 108, 128, 147

Suk, Josef, 131

Sumsion, Alice, 54, 75, 92, 114, **147**, 209, 224, 244, **249**

Sumsion, John (Herbert), **54**, **75**, 88, 92, **111**, 114, 129, 144, 147, **152**, **175**, 185, **186**, 244, 251, **253**, 256

Sutherland, Graham, 147

Synge, J. M., 83

Tallis, Thomas, 133

Tanner, Robin, 144

Tartini, Giuseppe, 151

Taverner, John, 166

Taylor, Edward, 210

Taylor, Nita, 14

Teed, Roy, 226

Telemann, G. P., 195

Tennyson, Alfred, 213, 216

Terry, Richard Runciman, 60, 262

Theyer, Jack and Olive, 167–8

Thiman, Eric, 229

Thomas, Dylan, 176

Thomas, Edward, 23, 25, 31, 32, 253

Thomas, Helen, 253

Thompson, Flora, 130

Thorpe Davie, Cedric, **67–8**, **75**, 83, 101–2, 140, 145, 152, 158, 166, **175**, 182, 183, 184, 186, 199, 209, **243**, 244, 246, **248**, **250**, **251–2**, 253, **256**; on 18th-century research, 151, 195, 205, 222, 237 , 245; and St Andrews, 206–7, 208, 225–6

Thoreau, Henry David, 199

Three Choirs Festival, 25, 68, **74**, 75, **89**, 92, **106**, 111, **147**, 152, **158**, 178,

179, 185, **186–7**, 199, 209, 228, 230, **242**, 247, **249**, **256**

Thurston, Frederick, 178, 181, 230

Tichborne, Chidiock, 197 fn

Times Literary Supplement, 10, 112, 142, 152, 153, 193, **208**, **209**

Times, The, **6**, **26**, **51**, 72, **108**, 137, 153, **161**, 167, **191**, **204**, **215**, 226, **237**, **251**

Tippett, Michael, 105, 133, 145, 146, 165, 258

Tolstoy, Count, 117

Tony (see Scott, Anthony)

Toty (see Navarro, Antonio de)

Traherne, Thomas, **27**, 32, **43–7**, **102–5**, 187, 211, 253

Tremain, Thomas, 222

Trier, Stephen, 178, 184, 206

Trollope, Anthony, 56, 147

Udall, Nicholas, 149

Valen, Fartein, 166

Vaughan, Henry, 27, 122, 175, 197, 211

Vaughan Williams (Wood) Ursula, 129, **130–1**, **178–9**, **193**, 201, 207, **211**, **223**, **248**, **249–50**

Vaughan Williams, Adeline, **50**, **68**, **69**, 72, **80**, 167, **186**

Vaughan Williams, Ralph, 3, 9, 21, **32**, 33, 34–5, 45–6, 48, 50, **53**, 54, 55, 56, **57**, 62, 67, **68**, 71, **72**, 75, **82**, 85, 86, 91, 95, 97, 101, 102, 110, 111, 116, 117, **120**, 126, **128**, **129**, **130**, 132, 133, **138**, **139–42**, **144**, **145**, 147, 149, 151, **164**, 167, **168**, 179, 186, 187, **193**, 199, **201**, **203**, **209**, 211, **212**, **214–15**, 218, 220, **223**, 224, **225**, 226, **230**, 233, **234**, 235, 247, **248–9**, 251, 253, **254**, 256, 262, 264; influence on Finzi's life, **19**, 20, 63, 107, 117, 175; influence on Finzi's music, 20, 23, 25, 26–7, 28, **29**, 30, 35, 52, 60, 104, 105, 108, 148, 160, 181, 228, 238–9, 263; VW on Finzi's music, 39, 51, 52, 77, 99, 108, 181, 234; Finzi on VW's music, 127, 142, 203, 211

Ventura, William, 209

302 Index

Vera (see Strawson)
Verdi, 25, 57, 71 103
Verstegen, Richard, 96
Villiers, Jack, 32
Vinci, Leonardo da, 147
Vivaldi, Antonio, 131, 151, 152

Waddington, S. P., 212
Wagner, Richard, 102–3
Walsh, John, 182, 183
Walton, William, 54, **75**, **83**, **95**, 111, 129, 133, 134, 145, 146, 149, **161**, **189**, 201, 210, **220**, 262, 264
Ward, A. C., 147
Warlock, Peter, 58, 123, 151
Warner, Sylvia Townsend, 242, 253–4
Waterhouse, William, 184, 206, 222, 237
Watson, D. M. S. and Mrs, 123–4, 139, 153
Watson, Janet, 127, 137
Webb, Mary, 62
Weber, Carl Maria, 146, 166, 178, 187
Webster, John, 65

Weelkes, Thomas, 18, 60, 182
Wellesz, Egon, 201
Wesley, Charles, 184, 200, 205, 215, 222
Whistler, Laurence, 246, 251, 256
Wilbye, John, 18, 60
Willcocks, David, 199, 249
Williamson, Malcolm, 256
Wilson, Steuart, 17, 32, 76, 99, 226
Wirén, Dag, 256
Witts, Dr Leslie, 198, 206, 214, 230, 231, 233
Wolf, Hugo, 81, 166, 171
Wood, Henry, 45
Wood, John, 185
Wordsworth, William, 12, 28, **70**, 103, 126–7, 152, 178, **186–92**, 201, 213
Wright, Almroth, 10
Wyk, Arnold van, 129, 166, 186
Wyss, Sophie, 120, 123. 128, 131, 152
Wyton, Alec, 147, 166

Yeats, W. B., 18, 237

Index of Finzi's Compositions

Main discussion in **bold**

'All this night', 201, 202, **211**

Allegro risoluto, from toy symphony, 23

'Amabel' from *Before and After Summer*, 168, **171–2**

'As I lay in the early sun' from *Oh Fair to See*, 24

'At a lunar eclipse' from *Till Earth Outwears*, 37, **42**, 190, 263

'At Middle-Field gate' from *I Said to Love*, 244, **257**

'August, 1914, From', from *Requiem da Camera*, 30

Bagatelles, Five, see Clarinet Bagatelles

'Battle, The', 22

Before and After Summer (set of songs), 115, 156, 168, **169–72**, 173

'Before and after summer' (song), 169

'Before the paling of the stars', 19, 22

'Birthnight, The' from *To a Poet*, 259

'Boy Johnny' from *Rossetti Children's Songs*, 22–3

Bridges partsongs, 64, 69, **77–8**, 99, 128, 211

'Brightness of this Day, The', **27**, 38

'Budmouth dears' from *A Young Man's Exhortation*, 40

By *Footpath and Stile* (song cycle), **23–4**, 26, 31, 33, 35, 39, 58, 60, 72, 169, 181, 242

Carol from *Clarinet Bagatelles*, 134, 176

Cello Concerto, 199, 203, 230, 233–4, 237, **238–41**, 242, 245, 248, 249, 250, 262, 263

'Ceremonies', 22, 32

'Channel Firing' from *Before and After Summer*, 22, 115, 168, **170–1**, 172, 173, 217, 263

'Childhood among the ferns' from *Before and After Summer*, 10, 156, 168, **169**

Clarinet Bagatelles, 131, 133, **134**, 139, 178

Clarinet Concerto, 134, 178, **179–82**, 206, 221

'Clear and gentle stream' from *Bridges partsongs*, 77–8

'Clock of the Years, The' from *Earth and Air and Rain*, 79–80

'Come away, come away, death' from *Let us Garlands Bring*, 93, **134–5**

'Comet at Yell'ham, The' from *A Young Man's Exhortation*, **41**, 78

Concolinel, from *Love's Labour's Lost*, 149, 217

'Cradle song, A', 22

'Cupboard, The', 22, 26, 32

Dance from *Love's Labour's Lost*, 217

'Dance Continued, The' from *A Young Man's Exhortation*, 42

'Dancing on the hilltops' from *Rossetti Children's Songs*, 22–3

'Dead in the cold' from *Rossetti Children's Songs*, 22–3

Diabelleries, a variation, 234

Dies Natalis, 13, 28, **43–7**, 58, 77, 83, 92, 97, 99, 101, **102–5**, 106, **108**, 115, **120**, 124, 128, 135, 136, 137, **138**, **141**, 144, 146, **147**, **150**, 158, 159, 159, 160, 190, 195, 199, **207**, 209, 215, 221, 226, 229, 230, 239–41, 242, 243, 245, 251, **252**, 258, 263

'Ditty' from *A Young Man's Exhortation*, **40**, 58, 79, 99

Drummond Elegies, **39**, 76, 77, 99

Earth and Air and Rain, 76, **78–80**, 87, 131, 140, 146, 156, 168

Eclogue, 58, 134, 203, **221**, 239, 251, 253

Elegy, 114, **134**, 182, 239, 253

Elegy, see Fall of the Leaf, The

'English hills', 23

'Epeisodia' from Before and After Summer, 171

'Even such is time', 22

'Exeunt omnes' from By Footpath and Stile, 23

'Fairies, The', 22, 32

Fall of the Leaf, The (Elegy), **39**, 133, **253**

Farewell to Arms, 45, 58, 124, 135, **136–7**, 139, 140, 145, 199

'Fear no more the heat o' the sun' from Let us Garlands Bring, 23, 69, 81, **135**

'Ferry me across the water' from Rossetti Children's Songs, 22–3

Finale from Love's Labour's Lost, 217

Five Bagatelles, see Clarinet Bagatelles

'For life I had never cared greatly' from I Said to Love, 257

For St Cecilia, 120, **154–63**, 168, 179, 182, 189, 196, 210, 211, 217, 219, 226, 260

Forlana from Clarinet Bagatelles, 134

'Former beauties' from A Young Man's Exhortation, **41**, 57, 61

Fughetta from Clarinet Bagatelles, 133

'God is gone up', 200, **210**

Grace for Hilles House, 54

Grand Fantasia and Toccata, 55, **58–60**, 62, 134, 199, 219, **219–21**, 226, 241

Gurney 'Eliza' songs (scored) 131, 132, 156, 158

'Harvest' from Oh Fair to See, 42, 249, **260–1**

'Haste on, my joys!' from Bridges partsongs, 77–8

'He abjures love' from Before and After Summer, 93, **172**, 263

'Her Temple' from A Young Man's Exhortation, **40–1**, 42, 258

'His golden locks time hath to silver turned' from Farewell to Arms, 45, 57, 59, 60, 76, **136–7**, 258

'How soon hath time' from Milton Sonnets, 22, **58**

Hunt, The from Love's Labour's Lost, 217

'I have loved flowers that fade' from Bridges partsongs, 77–8

'I look into my glass' from Till Earth Outwears, **81**, 98

'I need not go' from I Said to Love, **81**, 87

'I praise the tender flower' from Bridges partsongs, 77–8

I said to Love (set of songs), 251, **253**

'I said to Love' (song) from I Said to Love, 248, **257–8**

'I say "I'll seek her"' from Oh Fair to See, 42

'If she be made of white and red' from Love's Labour's Lost, 149

'In a churchyard' from Earth and Air and Rain, 80

'In five-score summers' from I Said to Love, 244, **257**

In Terra Pax, 199, 215, **227–30**, 232, 237, 243, 247, 249–50

'In the mind's eye' from Before and After Summer, 171

'In time of "The breaking of nations"' from Requiem da Camera, 29

'In years defaced' from Till Earth Outwears, 81

Interlude, see Oboe Interlude

Intimations of Immortality, 30, 70, 88, 91, 159, 172, 178, **186–92**, 194, 199, 211, 215, 217, 219, 226, 228, 239, 241, 263

'Intrada' from To a Poet, 43, **46–7**, 258

Intrada (strings) from Dies Natalis, **43–6**, 102

Introduction from Love's Labour's Lost, 217

' The helmet now an hive for bees becomes' from Farewell to Arms, 136

Introit from Violin Concerto, **52**, 60, 71, 72, 134, 144, 221, 239

'Is it not sure a deadly pain' from Love's Labour's Lost, see Colconinel

'It never looks like summer here' from Till Earth Outwears, 244, **257**

'It was a lover and his lass' from Let us Garlands Bring, 135

Jerusalem (scored) **20**, 25

'June on Castle Hill' from To a Poet, 113

'Lament' from Requiem da Camera, 31

'Let me enjoy the earth' from Till Earth Outwears, **81**, 87

Let us Garlands Bring, 129, 137, **134–5**, 137, 221, 222
'Let us now praise famous men', 211
'Life a right shadow is' from Drummond Elegies, 39
'Life laughs onwards' from Till Earth Outwears, 233, **257**
'Lily has a smooth stalk, The' from Rossetti Children's Songs, 22–3
'Linnet in a gilded cage, A' from Rossetti Children's Songs, 22–3
'Lo, the Full, Final Sacrifice', **147–8**, 156, 158, 159, 160, 188, 211
Love's Labour's Lost, incidental music, **149–50**, 179, **216–18**
Love's Labour's Lost, suite from, 208, **217–18**
Love's Labour's Lost, see Soliloquies
'Lullaby, oh lullaby' from Rossetti Children's Songs, 23

Magnificat, 209, **210**, 216
'Margaret has a milking-pail' from Rossetti Children's Songs, 22–3
'Market-girl, The' from Till Earth Outwears, **113**, 263
'Master and the leaves, The' from By Footpath and Stile, **23–4**, 27
Milton Sonnets, 22, **57–8**, 76, **87–8**, 135, 138, 141
Moth from Love's Labour's Lost, 217
'Muses and Graces', 211
'My lovely one', 210
'My spirit sang all day' from Bridges partsongs, 78
'My Spirit will not haunt the mound', 23

New Year Music (Nocturne), **38–9**, 60, 67, 71, 76, 150, 159, 164, 227
'Nightingales' from Bridges partsongs, 72, 77
Nocturne from Love's Labour's Lost, 217
Nocturne, see New Year Music

'O dear me!', 22
Oboe Interlude, 71, 76, **77**, 108, 133, 146, 181
'Ode on the rejection of St Cecilia' from To a Poet, 176–7
Oh Fair to See (set of songs), 253

'Oh fair to see' from Oh Fair to See, **43**, 217
'O mistress mine' from Let us Garlands Bring, 129, **135**
'On parent knees' from To a Poet, 81
'Only a man harrowing clods' from The Requiem da camera, **29–31**, 115
'Only the wanderer' from Oh Fair to See, 28, **35–6**
'Overlooking the river' from Before and After Summer, 109, **169**, **260**
'Oxen, The' from By Footpath and Stile, **23**, 174

Parry 'When I survey' (scored), 166, 187
Partsongs (R. Bridges), see Bridges Partsongs
Passer-by, A, 23
'Paying calls' from By Footpath and Stile, 23, 242
'Phantom, The' from Earth and Air and Rain, 79
Prelude from Clarinet Bagatelles, 134
Prelude for strings, **39**, 253
Prelude from Requiem da Camera, 30, 35
Prelude and Fugue for string trio, 93, 126, **133**, 146
'Proud songsters' from Earth and Air and Rain, 69, **80**, 98, 124, 172

Quodlibet (Clowns) from Love's Labour's Lost, 217

'Rapture, The (danza)' from Dies Natalis, 43, 101, 102, **103–4**, 135, 160
Recovery, The, 27, 28
'Reed player, The', 22
Requiem da camera, 22, 28, **29–30**, 58, 60, 77, **115**, 131, 160
'Rhapsody (recitativo stromentato)' from Dies Natalis, **43–5**, 77, 146, 150, 259
'Riddle Song', see 'If she be made of white and red'
'Rollicum-rorum' from Earth and Air and Rain, 22, **79**, 259
Romance from Clarinet Bagatelles, 134
Romance for strings, 199, **221**
'Rondel', 22
'Rosy Maiden Winifred' from Rossetti Children's Songs, 22–3
Rossetti Children's Songs, **22**, 76, 113

'Salutation, The' from *Dies Natalis*, **43–6**, 57, 59, 60–1, **102–35**, 136, 141
'Self-unseeing, The', from *Before and After Summer*, 168, **169**
Severn Rhapsody, A, 22, **28–9**, 30, 31, 32, 33, 35, 54, 58, 77, 181
Seven Unaccompanied Partsongs, see Bridges Partsongs
Short Fug(e) in praise of G. C. C., 64
'Shortening Days' from *A Young Man's Exhortation*, 40, **41**
'Sigh, The' from *A Young Man's Exhortation*, **41**, 99
'Since we loved' from *Oh Fair to See*, **249**, 259, 260
'So I have fared' from *Earth and Air and Rain*, **79**, 125–6
Soliloquies from *Love's Labour's Lost*, **150**, **217**
'Some one', 23
Song of Hiems, see '*When daisies pied*'
Song of Ver, see '*When icicles hang*'
'Summer Schemes' from *Earth and Air and Rain*, **78**, 208

'Tall nettles', 23
Ten Children's songs, see *Rossetti Children's Songs*
'The helmet now' from *Farewell to Arms*, 136
'There's snow on the fields', from *Rossetti Children's Songs*, 22–3
'This life, which seems so fair' from *Drummond Elegies*, 39
'This world a hunting is' from *Drummond Elegies*, 39
'Thou dids't delight mine eyes', **211**, 227
Three Short Elegies, see *Drummond Elegies*
Till Earth Outwears (set of songs), 253
'Time to rise', 22
'Time was upon the wing', 22
To a Poet (set of songs), 253
'To a poet' (song), 17, 92, **113**, 264
'To Joy' from *Oh Fair to See*, 69, **81**, 154
'To Lizbie Brown' from *Earth and Air and Rain*, **79**, 171
'Too short time, The' from *Before and After Summer*, 168, **171**, 173

'Transformations' from *A Young Man's Exhortation*, 41–2
'Twilit waters, The', 22, 23
'Two lips' from *I Said to Love*, 42
Two motets, 27, 32, 33, 34, 159
Two Sonnets, see *Milton Sonnets*

'Up to those bright and gladsome hills' (Psalm 121), 27
'Upon a child', 22

Violin Concerto, **51–2**, 53, 57, 58, 59, 60, 91, 134, 161
'Voices from things growing in a churchyard' from *By Footpath and Stile*, **23–4**, 41

'Waiting both' from *Earth and Air and Rain*, **54**, **78**
Waltz in the Finzi *Weeklies*, 11
'Welcome Sweet and Sacred Feast', 175, **210**
'When daisies pied' from *Love's Labour's Lost*, 149
'When I consider' from *Milton Sonnets*, 57
'When I set out for Lyonesse' from *Earth and Air and Rain*, 76, **78**
'When icicles hang' from *Love's Labour's Lost*, 149
'Where the picnic was' from *By Footpath and Stile*, 23
'Wherefore tonight so full of care' from *Bridges partsongs*, 77
'White-flowering days', **213**, 216, 252
'Who is Sylvia?' from *Let us Garlands Bring*, 65, **135**, 136
'Winter now has bared the trees', 35, **176**
'Wonder (arioso)' from *Dies Natalis*, 43–4, 92, 97, 99

'Young man's exhortation, A' (song) from *A Young Man's Exhortation*, **40**, 172, 260
Young Man's Exhortation, A (set of songs), **39–42**, 62, 71, 72, 78, 80, 168, 189